Gre

I know the Bible says that, but I just don't see it that way.

It doesn't matter what I do, God knows my heart.

I know my church doesn't do deliverance, minister the baptism of the Holy Spirit and heal the sick, but it's a wonderful church and I love the pastor.

I know the people I listen to preach a lot of garbage, but every now and then there's a nugget.

We should all just set aside our doctrines and learn to get along.

I just don't have time for all this end-time stuff; I'm too busy walking with the Lord every day.

We'll all find out when the time comes.

Yes, the Bible *is* the Word of God, but *we* believe there's more.

God addresses those who cling to deception in Proverbs 14:12:

**There is a way which seems right to a man,
but its end is the way of death.**

The Rapture

The Tribulation

And Beyond

B.D. Hyman

The B.D. Hyman Ministry
Charlottesville, Virginia

All Scripture quotations, unless otherwise indicated, are taken from
the New King James Version. Copyright © 1982 by Thomas Nelson, Inc.
Used by permission. All rights reserved.

The Rapture, The Tribulation, And Beyond

ISBN 1-881419-15-0

Copyright © 2002 B.D. Hyman and Jeremy A. Hyman

Published by The B.D. Hyman Ministry, an arm of
King's Corner Fellowship, Inc.
P.O. Box 7107, Charlottesville, VA 22906

Printed in the United States of America.

All rights reserved. The reproduction or utilization of this work in whole or in
part in any form by any electronic, mechanical or other means, now known or
hereafter invented, including xerography, photocopying and recording, or in
any information storage or retrieval system, is forbidden without the written
permission of the publisher.

CONTENTS

Preface

1	Jesus Unveils The Last Days	7
2	A Whole Lot Of Shaking Going On	21
3	The Timing Of The Age	37
4	Headline News—Up Close And Personal	61
5	The Ministry Of Angels	93
6	The Sequence Of End-Time Events	103
7	Why Is The Church Raptured?	129
8	The Seven Raptures—Untangling The Confusion	141
9	Preparation And Qualification For The Rapture	167
10	Body Or Bride Why Does It Matter?	181
11	Can We Run Out Of Time?	195
12	Fulfillment Of Pre-Rapture Prophecy	209
13	Deceitful Prophecy	219
14	False Doctrine	227
15	Separating The Wheat From The Chaff	253

16	The Judgment Seat Of Christ	263
17	A Few Good Men	273
18	Ruling And Reigning	287
19	Preparing The Way Of The Lord—The Spirit Of Elijah	301
20	The Great Tribulation	307
21	Heaven During The Great Tribulation	337
22	Armageddon	351
23	The Millennial Reign Of Christ	359
24	The Millennial Nations	365
25	Satan's Season Of Release	377
26	The Great White Throne Judgment	385
27	The Eternal Nations	391
28	The New Heavens And The New Earth—A Return To The Garden Of Eden	399
	Epilogue	407
	Topical Index	421

The Rapture
The Tribulation
And Beyond

Preface

This book is not a mere compilation of end-time facts; it is designed to be a wake-up call to the church. Most believers are aware that time is short, but what eludes them is that we, the final generation, are responsible for all that the Spirit is revealing.

The great tribulation stands between us and the rest of eternity; it will occur during the lifetimes of most of us. We face, therefore, greater risk in addition to greater blessing than earlier generations. Unless we know exactly where we fit during the events to come, and what our obligations and benefits are, we shall become confused and fail. It is not enough to have only some of the information; we must know all the Father's plans and requirements, be willing to meet them, and dominate until He comes. There are no half measures available; it is all or nothing if we want to be part of the eternal body of Christ.

Jesus says in Revelation 3:
15 I know your works, that you are neither cold nor hot. I could wish you were cold or hot.
16 So then, because you are lukewarm, and neither cold nor hot, I will vomit you out of My mouth.

To put it in the simplest of terms, complacent, self-satisfied, lukewarm Christians make God sick.

This book is for those who desire to please God, for people, therefore, who hunger to be everything and have everything that God has provided for them. If you are one of those with ears to hear, and will settle for nothing less than God's best, read on and make certain of your place in the glorified body of Christ.

If, on the other hand, you are one of the aforesaid complacent, self-satisfied, lukewarm Christians, be advised that your future rests on quicksand and, like many others cited in the Bible, when you do awaken and take notice it will be too late. For this generation, too late is when the last trump sounds for the rapture of the church. In the chapters to come you will learn the gory details of the few options remaining for those who miss the rapture.

Yes, many of those still on the earth during the tribulation will have counted themselves part of the church; they are the ones unwilling to receive the end-time revelation that God is so abundantly pouring out. They cover their ears and say, "It's so scary. I don't want to think about it. I don't think God is like that. I'm busy enough just living for God each day. I know what I believe, and anyway, we'll all find out when the time comes." Notice how many times the word "I" appears! Such people will indeed find out when the time comes; they will find they have missed it, that those with ears to hear have flown.

We are not the great I Am; God Almighty is. He is the One Who tells us how it is; He pays no heed to how we think it ought be. The measure of our relationship with Christ Jesus is not based upon us knowing Him but upon Him knowing us (Matthew 7:21-23).

The Lord prophesied about the people in this final generation who would be unwilling to be confused with facts because their minds were made up. We know He was speaking of this generation because He said He was speaking for time to come, forever and ever.

Isaiah 30
8 Now go, write it before them on a tablet, and note it on a scroll, that it may be for time to come, forever and ever:
9 that this is a rebellious people, lying children, children who will not hear the law of the Lord;
10 Who say to the seers, "Do not see," and to the prophets, "Do not prophesy to us right things; speak to us smooth things, prophesy deceits.
11 "Get out of the way, turn aside from the path, cause the Holy One of Israel to cease from before us."
12 Therefore thus says the Holy One of Israel: "Because you despise this word, and trust in oppression and perversity, and rely on them,
13 "therefore this iniquity shall be to you like a breach ready to fall, a bulge in a high wall, whose breaking comes suddenly, in an instant.
14 "And He shall break it like the breaking of the potter's vessel, which is broken in pieces; He shall not spare. So there shall not be found among its fragments a shard to take fire from the hearth, or to take water from the cistern."

Please take seriously this sobering statement from the Lord. The **instant** refers to the last trump sounding, whereupon, in a moment, in the twinkling of an eye (1 Corinthians 15:52), the body of Christ will be caught up from the earth—raptured—and glorified to dwell with Jesus from then on. You can see from God's statement that the sudden destruction to come upon those who remain will be absolute. That is why the Lord is doing all He can to chart for us a safe and blessed course through these dangerous days. God wants us to succeed, it is His will that we succeed, but it must be our will also. People constantly run around claiming they are seeking God's will for their lives, but they also claim—because of their preconceived notions—that what God states in His Word to be His will is not relevant today or does not apply to them.

I constantly receive prayer requests and pleas for ministry from people who become angry with me when I tell them God's truth. They berate me for not telling them what they want to hear, for refusing to **speak smooth things**, for refusing to tell them lies that suit them. These are the people of whom Paul spoke to Timothy.

2 Timothy 4
**3 For the time will come when they will not endure sound doctrine, but according to their own desires, because they have itching ears, they will heap up for themselves teachers;
4 and they will turn their ears away from the truth, and be turned aside to fables.**

Fables abound and more are created daily. Your safety lies solely in lining up all of God's Words and standing on them. You must not turn aside from God's truth; it is the only security there is. All else rests on sinking sand and is destined for utter destruction. I have observed that complacency, by extension, equals lack of faith. Without faith it is impossible to please God (Hebrews 11:6). If you have been a cotton-candy Christian, requiring that God's Word be sugar-coated, be honest with yourself. You have the opportunity, right this minute, to make the necessary changes and join the front lines.

When I pray for those who fearlessly and tenaciously grab hold of the whole Word, I watch Christ Jesus transform their lives. He takes them from defeat and despair into victory and joy inexpressible. That is the Lord's will for every one of His children, but it is up to you. Everything is a choice and God has given you free will. Use that free will to choose, now, to become part of the glorious church. Learn what is required, as well as the awesome rewards that God has in store for those who choose to overcome.

Deuteronomy 30
19 I call heaven and earth as witnesses today against you, that I have set before you life and death, blessing and cursing; therefore choose life, that both you and your descendants may live;

There have been many books written on the end-time and another version of the same old information is not needed. If you have ears to hear, and love God's truth, this book will fill you with delight as you see the Father's infinite love demonstrated in His extraordinary plan for you.

This is a comprehensive, all-encompassing look at every aspect of: who we are in Christ; the signs of the times; the events going on around us; the options we have for our part in the world and in the kingdom; where everybody fits; the difference between being saved from condemnation and being saved to the glory; God's end-time order; and how it all comes out.

You would not set sail on a yacht in the Caribbean without detailed charts showing the reefs and shoals, charts that would enable you to navigate through clear channels and safely reach your destination. That is just common sense. If someone told you that you did not need such charts, that you should just figure it out as you went along, you would, unless you had a death wish, refuse to be so foolish. However, that is exactly what a great many Christians do about this final hour of the age. Their complacent, faithless attitude of, "We'll all find out when we get there," will cause them to run aground on one or another of Satan's lies or treacheries and never get there at all.

Our ability in Christ to overcome sickness, disease, poverty, lack and oppression, and anything else with which the devil tries to defeat us, rests on the exercise of our faith and is part of our qualification for glory. Our assignment from Jesus Christ, as His ambassadors, is to overcome, know the requirements, take ground for the kingdom of God, and establish His covenant on the earth, now. That is how we prepare ourselves for the rapture; that is how we prepare for our future as those who will rule and reign with Christ for eternity. We must not let Satan distract us with side trips into powerless religion or the "solutions" of the world; both those liars lead to defeat. Our inheritance depends upon our success. As God's people we need to awaken and smell the sweet winds of revelation that will carry us to glory. We need to allow the Word to develop a clear picture within us of the days we are in and God's precise place of privilege for each of us.

It is my intention, as the Holy Spirit directs my writing, to present a complete manual that will transform the reader into an expert on this final hour, no longer needing a dozen different writings to sort it all out and fit it all together. My objective is to fill in the blanks so that all those with ears to hear will find the confidence and joy that has eluded them in their search for the truth, the whole truth, and nothing but the truth, regarding the end of the age.

Once it all makes sense to you, once there are no more missing pieces and you have no more unanswered questions, I am confident that you will courageously and enthusiastically embrace this hour and be thrilled that you were born for such a time as this.

B.D. Hyman
Charlottesville, Virginia
July, 2002

Chapter 1

Jesus Unveils The Last Days

Two thousand years ago Jesus came in the flesh to redeem mankind. He walked the earth, preached the gospel, and taught and performed miracles everywhere He went. He also talked of this hour. He spoke of the pre-tribulation rapture of the church even though He knew that two thousand years would pass before it would take place. God speaks the end from the beginning.

We have only recently come to understand much of what Jesus said about the end of the age; revelation comes in layers. Even though all knowledge is contained in the Word of God, the Holy Spirit has revealed to each generation only what that generation has needed to know.

> John 16
> **12 I still have many things to say to you, but you cannot bear them now.**
> **13 However, when He, the Spirit of truth, has come, He will guide you into all truth; for He will not speak on His own authority, but whatever He hears He will speak; and He will tell you things to come.**
> **14 He will glorify Me, for He will take of what is Mine and declare it to you.**
> **15 All things that the Father has are Mine. Therefore I said that He will take of Mine and declare it to you.**

The Holy Spirit, Who was sent on the day of Pentecost to baptize with power all the followers of Jesus and adopt them into the body of Christ, can only **speak** what He hears from Jesus. Jesus, being the Word made flesh, reveals the Word. The Holy Spirit unveils the mysteries.

Matthew 10
26 ...there is nothing covered that will not be revealed, and hidden that will not be known.

1 Corinthians 2
9 But as it is written: "Eye has not seen, nor ear heard, nor have entered into the heart of man the things which God has prepared for those who love Him."
10 But God has revealed them to us through His Spirit. For the Spirit searches all things, yes, the deep things of God.

Before we are born again in Christ Jesus we are unable to really love the Lord—which means to obey His Word (1 John 2:4-6)—let alone tap into the mysteries of God. Our natural, unanointed minds are simply not capable of comprehending the supernatural. That is why scholars, theologians and philosophers make such an incomprehensible mess of the Word of God. It is why the Spirit of God has been given to us to convey the knowledge of God. Once we are born again—blood-bought and baptized in the Holy Spirit (John 3:1-7)—we are spiritually recreated and become new creatures in Christ, the anointed One in His anointing.

1 John 2
20 But you have an anointing from the Holy One, and you know all things.
27 But the anointing which you have received from Him abides in you, and you do not need that anyone teach you; but as the same anointing teaches you concerning all things, and is true, and is not a lie, and just as it has taught you, you will abide in Him.

The Holy Spirit does not just tag along when one confesses Jesus as Savior. He is the third person of the Godhead and must be invited. The

The Rapture, The Tribulation, And Beyond 9

Holy Spirit is in the earth and He draws us to Jesus, then Jesus, when we yield and ask, baptizes us into the Holy Spirit and power. The Holy Spirit, only received through His baptism, which is apart from water, is the One Who makes us part of God. Jesus, in Acts 1, spoke to His disciples just before He was taken up to heaven and, **[4]commanded them not to depart from Jerusalem, but to wait for the promise of the Father, "which," He said, "you have heard from Me; [5]for John truly baptized with water, but you shall be baptized with the Holy Spirit not many days from now. [8]...you shall receive power when the Holy Spirit has come upon you."** Acts 2:4 reports that after this baptism of fire they all spoke with other tongues as the Spirit gave them utterance.

John 4
23 But the hour is coming, and now is, when the true worshipers will worship the Father in spirit and truth; for the Father is seeking such to worship Him.
24 God is Spirit, and those who worship Him must worship in spirit and truth.

For even our worship to be acceptable to God we must worship Him both in our Holy Ghost language, tongues, and with our understanding in our earthly language. Our worship must also be based on the truth, the Word of God. The Lord will not accept anything else. Without the Holy Spirit, we are without one third of the Godhead and are thus maimed. If you were missing one third of your physical body you would certainly be considered maimed. Therefore, if you are missing one third of your spiritual being, you are spiritually maimed. The body of Christ is whole, not maimed.

Ephesians 2:12 tells us that without the Holy Spirit we are without God in this world. The Father and the Son are seated on Their thrones in the heavenlies; we can know Them, but we cannot be with Them until we are glorified in the rapture. Jesus sent the Holy Spirit at Pentecost to be God on earth, God in us. What an awesome privilege to have God in us and speaking through us. I am astonished at how many there are who say they love Jesus but resist this gift.

Believers have no excuse for being deceived by false teaching; the

Holy Spirit, the teacher of the church, dwells within them. When you learn to hear Him, He will confirm the truth of what you hear or classify it as a lie. No human being knows all things. However, the One Who does know all things dwells within us, through the baptism of the Holy Spirit, and He will reveal all knowledge to us as the Father releases it to each generation. That is what Jesus was saying in John 16:12-15. Jesus was the greatest teacher to ever walk this earth. He knew that the Word had to be proclaimed and then witnessed and confirmed in us by the Holy Spirit.

Romans 10
14 How then shall they call on Him in whom they have not believed? And how shall they believe in Him of whom they have not heard? And how shall they hear without a preacher?
15 And how shall they preach unless they are sent? As it is written: "How beautiful are the feet of those who preach the gospel of peace, who bring glad tidings of good things!"

Manna In The Wilderness

We can see, in God's provision for the children of Israel, a type for His release of just the right amount of revelation, or spiritual nourishment, for each generation.

Exodus 16
4 Then the Lord said to Moses, "Behold, I will rain bread from heaven for you. And the people shall go out and gather a certain quota every day, that I may test them, whether they will walk in My law or not.
5 "And it shall be on the sixth day that they shall prepare what they bring in, and it shall be twice as much as they gather daily."

They called this **bread** manna, and it was as sweet as honey on the day it was given, but it was only for that day. If it was not eaten on the day it was given, but gathered and stored until the next day, it became full of worms and stank.

The manna is a type for each generation receiving and walking in all the revelation that God gives it for its time, but you will notice that, on the sixth day, they gathered twice as much and it stayed sweet. The sixth day—2 Peter 3, [8]**with the Lord one day is as a thousand years, and a thousand years as one day**—is a type for the six thousand years of man's lease upon the earth (see Chapter 3). Six thousand years is the lease God gave Adam and which Adam handed over to Satan in the Garden of Eden when he committed high treason.

We are at the end of the age, in our **sixth day**, and, just as the Israelites needed a double portion on their sixth day, so do we. We are the final generation. God is giving us twice as much revelation because we need it to prevail in this hour. The double portion of manna was to carry the children of Israel into and through the Sabbath. The Sabbath was the seventh day. The thousand year reign of Christ, following the tribulation, is our seven thousandth year.

From the beginning, the Lord has built into His Word clues of the time to come. He encapsulated His wisdom and knowledge to be revealed to us at just the right time. I think of it as time-release capsules of revelation. Jesus, Himself, likened the revelation of the Spirit to each generation to the giving of manna to the children of Israel.

John 6
29 Jesus answered and said to them, "This is the work of God, that you believe in Him whom He sent."
30 Therefore they said to Him, "What sign will You perform then, that we may see it and believe You? What work will You do?
31 "Our fathers ate the manna in the desert; as it is written, 'He gave them bread from heaven to eat.'"
32 Then Jesus said to them, "Most assuredly, I say to you, Moses did not give you the bread from heaven, but My Father gives you the true bread from heaven.
33 "For the bread of God is He who comes down from heaven and gives life to the world."
34 Then they said to Him, "Lord, give us this bread always."
35 And Jesus said to them, "I am the bread of life. He who

comes to Me shall never hunger, and he who believes in Me shall never thirst."

The Word is the bread, or manna, of life. Each generation is fed just the right amount of bread, or Word, for its time. Jesus knew that as each generation passed, the Holy Spirit would increase man's knowledge and that, when the last generation came, it would receive twice as much, enough to carry it into the millennial reign of Christ. Only when we hunger and thirst after righteousness, have ears to hear, and are obedient to the Word, will we receive this manna and qualify as the body of Christ.

Watch, Therefore

The body of Christ is the glorious church for whom Jesus is coming. Jesus told us that we all had to come to Him as little children. Little children do not think they already have all the answers. Little children are teachable. Little children are totally dependant upon their parents to teach them. We need to be totally dependant upon our heavenly Father to teach us. We need to come to Him with the realization that all our worldly, religious, and scholarly ideas and opinions are foolishness before Him. We need to lay all that at the foot of the cross and open the Word of God with teachable minds and hearts.

> Mark 13
> **32 But of that day and hour no one knows, neither the angels in heaven, nor the Son, but only the Father.**
> **33 Take heed, watch and pray; for you do not know when the time is.**
> **34 It is like a man going to a far country, who left his house and gave authority to his servants, and to each his work, and commanded the doorkeeper to watch.**

Jesus, returning to the Father in heaven with His ministry completed, is the obvious parallel to the **man going to a far country**. He **left His house**—the kingdom of God on earth—and, by His blood, His Name, and the Holy Spirit, gave Christians authority on earth, each to our own assignment, and commanded us to keep watch and be ready for His return.

Mark 13
35 Watch therefore, for you do not know when the master of the house is coming, in the evening, at midnight, at the crowing of the rooster, or in the morning
36 lest, coming suddenly, he find you sleeping.
37 And what I say to you, I say to all: Watch!

In Joshua 1:8 God instructed Joshua never to allow the Word of God to depart from his mouth, but to meditate in it day and night, and to be sure to do everything that was written in it. God said that this was the only way to have good success and be prosperous. God is El Shaddai, the God of more than enough.

God's prosperity does not extend to finances alone; God's prosperity is also being prosperous in one's mental, physical and emotional health, one's family, one's social standing, and one's relationship with God. If any of these areas is poverty-stricken, one is not prospering. God's prosperity also includes one's ability to avoid the tribulation to come.

Being prepared for the rapture of the church depends no less upon meditation in the Word than does anything else. It is why Jesus talked about the end of the age. Much of what He said was veiled until this generation but, even so, He wanted His disciples to set their sights on the whole picture. He wanted them to know that their time on earth was only a preparation for the time to come. He wanted them, and all coming generations of believers, to know that leaving this world, whether by the natural sleep of death or in the rapture of the church, was not an end but a beginning.

The natural mind considers death to be an end. It is not. God created us as eternal beings. Our decisions and actions during our lifetimes determine not whether we are eternal, but where we spend eternity. We can have eternal life with Christ Jesus or eternal death with Satan. The natural, unsaved man, who instinctively fears death because he believes death to be the end—a body buried underground in darkness, rotting and coming to nothing—fears the wrong thing. He fears the unknown when, in fact, he should fear the known: eternity in the wrong place.

Earthly death, for born-again believers, is merely shedding our physical bodies and moving on to the fulfillment of our real lives in glory. Our lives in the here and now are where we prepare, where we have the opportunity to prove ourselves faithful stewards of the anointing, where we qualify as the body of Christ. Some people refer to the death of true Christians as "going on to their reward." I love that expression; it is accurate. Leaving this life, with all its battles and limitations, and moving on to eternity with Jesus, is the only true and lasting reward.

If you are a born-again believer and do not have this view of death, you do not truly believe. There are many people who call themselves Christians, and attend church regularly, who do not truly believe. They would not live the way they do, submitted to the world's ways and fearful of so much, if they did truly believe.

The life of a believer is a life of faith. Faith rests on acceptance, with no shadow of doubting, that God's Word is true. It also requires living by God's wisdom for, without God's wisdom, the believer will inevitably be led into deception and foolishness.

James 1
5 If any of you lacks wisdom, let him ask of God, who gives to all liberally and without reproach, and it will be given to him.
6 But let him ask in faith, with no doubting, for he who doubts is like a wave of the sea driven and tossed by the wind.
7 For let not that man suppose that he will receive anything from the Lord;
8 he is a double-minded man, unstable in all his ways.

God created the worlds by faith. Jesus, when He walked the earth in the flesh, lived by faith. We, also, must live by faith if we are to please God (Hebrews 11:6), and receive His promises, His blessings and our full inheritance.

Jesus said that He came to divide (Luke 12:51). We are called, even now, to be separated from the world system and unto God. That is the definition of holiness. The Lord has commanded that we be holy because we are, as the body of Christ, part of Him and He is a holy God (1 Peter 1:15-16). Living a life of true faith will separate us from the world and all who are of it. We are not of this world even though, for a time, we are in it. We are of the kingdom of God.

Luke 12
**54 Then He also said to the multitudes, "When you see a cloud rising out of the west, immediately you say, 'A shower is coming'; and so it is.
55 "And when you see the south wind blow, you say, 'There will be hot weather'; and there is.
56 "Hypocrites! You can discern the face of the sky and of the earth, but how is it you do not discern this time?"**

In order for the men of Jesus' time to know that rain came from the west and hot weather from the south, they had to have studied the surrounding air currents and weather patterns. Jesus rebuked them for failing to apply the same diligence to understanding the spiritual times and seasons. How much more do we qualify as hypocrites if we, in this most critical of times, fail to receive the revelation that the Holy Spirit is pouring out for our generation?

We, the final generation, the ones who have the opportunity to be part of the rapture of the church, have more to know than any previous generation and, therefore, the availability of twice as much manna. This certainly is not because we are any better than any past generation, let alone any smarter or more spiritual, but because we need to know how to escape the imminent and certain devastation of the tribulation.

God has always made a way of escape for His people. Noah and his family floated out in the ark, but not without extraordinary faith and preparation. We need to build our own ark of faith.

God, because of His covenant with Abraham and Abraham's faith and obedience, delivered Lot and his family out of Sodom before He destroyed it by raining down fire and brimstone. Likewise, based on our faith and obedience, God will deliver us from the coming destruction through the pre-tribulation rapture of the church.

God led the children of Israel out of the bondage of Egypt and into the promised land in whole families, in health and with the wealth of the whole nation. He parted the Red Sea, so that they passed over on dry land, then closed the waters over the heads of Pharaoh's army when it tried to pursue them. This is a type for the rapture of the church. We shall go out in whole families, in health and with the wealth of the world having been turned over to us—for our use during this time, obviously, not to take with us—and where we are going the world cannot follow.

Peter addressed the subject of these final days.

2 Peter 3

1 Beloved, I now write to you this second epistle (in both of which I stir up your pure minds by way of reminder),

2 that you may be mindful of the words which were spoken before by the holy prophets, and of the commandment of us the apostles of the Lord and Savior,

3 knowing this first: that scoffers will come in the last days, walking according to their own lusts,

4 and saying, "Where is the promise of His coming? For since the fathers fell asleep, all things continue as they were from the beginning of creation."

5 For this they willfully forget: that by the word of God the heavens were of old, and the earth standing out of water and in the water,

6 by which the world that then existed perished, being flooded with water.

7 But the heavens and the earth which now exist are kept in store by the same word, reserved for fire until the day of judgment and perdition of ungodly men.

He thus reminds us of the flood of Noah, when the people mocked Noah and scoffed at the building of the ark. The earth had been around for a while then, too. Noah tried to tell them. He reported what God had said. He explained that he was building the ark out of obedience to God, but the people continued, and even increased, in their derisive laughter, branding the ark as foolishness. Then the rain started! The time was up, the floods came, and only Noah and his family, together with all the animals, were saved.

I am certain there were many people pounding on the hull of the ark when the water was up to their ankles and rising, but the door was closed. It was too late. The scoffers had gone their own way and were now reaping their reward. They all perished, every last one of them.

Jesus told Peter, and the rest of the disciples, that the earth was in store for the same kind of judgment. Ungodliness would reap its reward in the fire of the tribulation. Peter did not mock. Peter lined up all the prophecies and saw the truth.

2 Peter 3
9 The Lord is not slack concerning His promise, as some count slackness, but is longsuffering toward us, not willing that any should perish but that all should come to repentance.

It is not God's will that any perish, although He is well aware and states in many places, among them Matthew 7, [14]**narrow is the gate and difficult is the way which leads to life, and there are few who find it**. The broad way, the easy way, Jesus says, is the way that leads to destruction and, sadly, altogether too many people choose that path. Please do not be one of them; choose the narrow way, now.

Revelation 3
3 Remember therefore how you have received and heard; hold fast and repent. Therefore if you will not watch, I will come upon you as a thief, and you will not know what hour I will come upon you.

This Scripture definitively separates the pre-tribulation rapture of the church from the second advent. Jesus has put it in one paragraph. First, He tells us that we need to **hold fast** and to **watch**. He points out the need to watch for, grab hold of, and refuse to let go of, our rapture. We must know what is coming and be in a state of expectancy, looking for the promise of the rapture of the church. If we are looking for a different rapture, or no rapture at all, we shall be left behind.

Jesus also says to maintain a repentant heart. We must keep short books with the Lord. As Psalm 24 says, [3]**Who may ascend into the hill of the Lord? Or who may stand in His holy place?** [4]**He who has clean hands and a pure heart, who has not lifted up his soul to an idol, nor sworn deceitfully**. We must learn to recognize our mistakes and immediately repent. 1 John 1:9 assures us that, when we confess our sins to the Lord and repent, He always forgives us and cleanses us from all unrighteousness. We need that cleansing of the blood of the Lamb daily as part of our preparedness.

There are many false doctrines trying to convince Christians they must go through the tribulation. That assuredly is not God's plan for them—the tribulation will be a time of inconceivable horror—but the free will God has given them will enable them to make the wrong choice, to be here when His accumulated wrath is poured out. Jesus says to those who will not watch, **I will come upon you as a thief, and you will not know what hour I will come upon you**.

As will be covered in Chapter 8, there are seven raptures, three of which have already taken place. The evidence that the rapture of the church, the fourth rapture, occurs immediately before the tribulation is overwhelming. The second advent and Armageddon, which do not take place until the end of the tribulation, are also covered in that chapter. Once you see these matters precisely lined up and accounted for in Scripture, you will no longer be confused about the difference between the rapture and the second advent, or anything else that might cause you to claim, because of false teaching or just plain lack of knowledge, "We'll all find out when the time comes."

The Command To Overcome

We are responsible for what we choose to believe. We have the Word and the Holy Spirit to lead us into all truth. There are no acceptable excuses for believing a lie. Do not forget Mark 11:23-24, in which Jesus establishes that we shall have whatsoever we say.

> Revelation 3
> **10 Because you have kept My command to persevere, I also will keep you from the hour of trial which shall come upon the whole world, to test those who dwell on the earth.**

We must fight the good fight of faith and run the race well if we are to qualify for the rapture. We, the body of Christ, are not of this world.

We may live in this world but, as citizens of heaven, we are aliens here. Those **who dwell on the earth** are the unbelievers, those without Christ. Jesus says that we must continue in the Word and in faith so that He can keep us from the tribulation that will overtake the whole world.

Revelation 3
11 Behold, I come quickly! Hold fast what you have, that no one may take your crown.

Since this was written approximately two thousand years ago, Jesus obviously did not mean immediately. I **come quickly** is a description of the moment of His coming. We shall all be changed, as we are told in 1 Corinthians 15, [52]**in a moment, in the twinkling of an eye, at the last trumpet**. We must be ready and expecting Christ's appearing or we shall miss the rapture. When Jesus comes it will be quickly, or suddenly. There will not be time for people to get out their Bibles, open their concordances, and re-examine their covenant.

The crown Jesus refers to is the one we receive at the judgment seat of Christ, immediately following the rapture of the church; this is also mentioned in 2 Timothy 4, [7]**I have fought the good fight, I have finished the race, I have kept the faith. **[8]**Finally, there is laid up for me the crown of righteousness, which the Lord, the righteous Judge, will give to me on that Day, and not to me only but also to all who have loved His appearing**.

The judgment seat of Christ is for the body of Christ, the glorious church. It is a place of reward (1 Corinthians 3:11-17). Our crown is our reward, our rank or status, in New Jerusalem for all eternity. Jesus is warning us not to let anyone or anything talk us out of it. Do not confuse the great white throne judgment—which is for the nations, and happens at the end of the millennial reign of Christ—with the judgement seat of Christ.

Revelation 3
12 He who overcomes, I will make him a pillar in the temple of My God, and he shall go out no more. And I will write on him the name of My God and the name of the city of My God, the

> New Jerusalem, which comes down out of heaven from My God. And I will write on him My new name.
> **13 He who has an ear, let him hear what the Spirit says to the churches.**

This is the establishment of the church as the body of Christ. The church is part of the bridegroom, Jesus. After the wedding of the Lamb, when Jesus, with us as His body, is married to our bride, the city of New Jerusalem, we take our new name. At a wedding, the two become one. We shall carry not only the name of our God but of our bride, New Jerusalem (Revelation 21:2 and 9-27), and become a part, **a pillar in the temple of...God** for ever and ever.

> Revelation 3
> **21 To him who overcomes I will grant to sit with Me on My throne, as I also overcame and sat down with My Father on His throne.**
> **22 He who has an ear, let him hear what the Spirit says to the churches.**

This is the overview Jesus wanted us to have, both of this final generation as it now exists, and of the time to come. It is astonishing how many times Jesus repeats the admonition, **He who has an ear, let him hear what the Spirit says**. Sadly, there are many who do not choose to hear, or receive, what He says.

Our full inheritance, our destination when we obey Jesus' command to overcome—which means running well the race of faith, passing all the tests, and overcoming every attack of the devil—is to sit with Him in His throne, as His eternal body, and rule and reign with Him. That is what one does from a throne, but first we must overcome.

Chapter 2

A Whole Lot Of Shaking Going On

Major changes are coming, changes leading up to the pre-tribulation rapture of the church. God is preparing His people to handle extraordinary responsibility as He turns over the wealth and prestige of the world to the anointed church (Isaiah 60:5-7 and 11-12). This will give the end-time revival the momentum needed to accomplish God's purpose. This is not a new idea. God's purpose for placing wealth in the hands of His people was set forth in the old covenant.

> Deuteronomy 8
> **18 And you shall remember the Lord your God, for it is He who gives you power to get wealth, that He may establish His covenant which He swore to your fathers, as it is this day.**

God demonstrates His love for us by providing for us. He provides healing, deliverance, protection and finances. These are the same things that we, as ambassadors for Christ, are to offer to the world.

> James 2
> **15 If a brother or sister is naked and destitute of daily food,**
> **16 and one of you says to them, "Depart in peace, be warmed and filled," but you do not give them the things which are needed for the body, what does it profit?**

God has established a system of sowing and reaping that has a guaranteed, hundredfold return. The result of your working correctly, obediently, within this system, and having the Father's heart and desire to give cheerfully, is that, as stated in 2 Corinthians 9, [8]**God is able to make all grace abound toward you, that you, always having all sufficiency in all things, have an abundance for every good work.**

It has always been the Father's plan that His people reflect His goodness and glory. God has never changed. It is we, through religious doctrine, who have been talked out of it.

> Deuteronomy 28
> **1 Now it shall come to pass, if you diligently obey the voice of the Lord your God, to observe carefully all His commandments which I command you today, that the Lord your God will set you high above all nations of the earth.**
> **2 And all these blessings shall come upon you and overtake you, because you obey the voice of the Lord your God:**
> **6 Blessed shall you be when you come in, and blessed shall you be when you go out.**
> **10 Then all peoples of the earth shall see that you are called by the name of the Lord, and they shall be afraid of you.**
> **12 The Lord will open to you His good treasure, the heavens, to give the rain to your land in its season, and to bless all the work of your hand. You shall lend to many nations, but you shall not borrow.**
> **13 And the Lord will make you the head and not the tail; you shall be above only, and not be beneath, if you heed the commandments of the Lord your God, which I command you today, and are careful to observe them."**

When the Lord says, **you shall lend to many nations, but you shall not borrow**, He is telling us that we shall have such abundance that we shall have no need to borrow. Think about the significance of this for a moment. It is possible that not just individuals, but whole nations, will come to the body of Christ to have their needs met.

These blessings in Deuteronomy 28 have been quoted over and over again, but few grasp the full impact of God saying He **will make you the head and not the tail; you shall be above only, and not be**

beneath, if you heed the commandments of the Lord your God, which I command you today, and are careful to observe them.

God makes it very clear, however, that He requires much of those to whom He gives much. Jesus reaffirms this.

Matthew 5
40 If anyone wants to sue you and take away your tunic, let him have your cloak also.
41 And whoever compels you to go one mile, go with him two.
42 Give to him who asks you, and from him who wants to borrow from you do not turn away.

Since the Scripture tells us in 2 Corinthians 9 that we shall always have [8]**all sufficiency in all things**, it is obvious that we shall have more than enough to fulfill this instruction and still be blessed with an abundance for ourselves and our families. Despite all this, we are reminded that we are never to seek the things, but to seek God and His ways.

Matthew 6
33 But seek first the kingdom of God and His righteousness, and all these things shall be added to you.

The church, at the moment, has little credibility in the world. Sadly, most of God's people are, and are seen by the world to be, poor, sick, afflicted, and defeated. Even sadder, they are content with this because religion has taught them the abominable lie that such pitiful conditions are indicative of holiness. At the other end of the spectrum, many high-profile ministries are seen as nothing more than a bunch of money-grubbing charlatans who are only interested in "fleecing the flock."

The church, thus, does not consistently represent God in a way that will draw the world to Jesus; sometimes, it even seems that the church's purpose is to keep the world at bay. This situation must change, and God says that it is about to. If the world is to want our wonderful Jesus, it must first want our lives, respect our witness, and trust our word. For this to be so, our lives must come to reflect the goodness, peace, joy, health, prosperity and love of Christ Jesus. The unbelieving world must see that we are not only different, but that we are extremely successful and blessed because of our covenant with almighty God. This is how the end-time revival will come to pass. The world will seek answers and come to us to get them.

Hebrews 12

26 whose voice then shook the earth; but now He has promised, saying, "Yet once more I shake not only the earth, but also heaven."

27 Now this, "Yet once more," indicates the removal of those things that are being shaken, as of things that are made, that the things which cannot be shaken may remain.

28 Therefore, since we are receiving a kingdom which cannot be shaken, let us have grace, by which we may serve God acceptably with reverence and godly fear.

29 For our God is a consuming fire.

Everything the world has built apart from God is in the process of coming unglued. The signs are apparent everywhere: we have the insanity of political correctness in the place of human decency and ethics; there is the decline of our schools; the moral disintegration and greed-motivated litigiousness of society; political corruption; the desire for "the fast buck" instead of the desire for hard work and honest gain; the list is endless.

God says that only the kingdom system will stand in this final hour. People, to succeed, will have no choice but to turn to God and His righteous ways. The world system will no longer work the way it has in the past, but God's ways will. We have seen only the barest beginnings as the world prepares, as it must, for the tribulation. But do not despair, the complete breakdown of everything will not happen until the church is removed from the earth. In the following Scriptures the **what** that is restraining is the church, and **he who now restrains** is the body of Christ.

2 Thessalonians 2

6 And now you know what is restraining, that he may be revealed in his own time.

The Rapture, The Tribulation, And Beyond 25

7 For the mystery of lawlessness is already at work; only he who now restrains will do so until he is taken out of the way.

If you belong to God, have ears to hear, and have any wisdom at all, you will not be here for the tribulation. I know that I won't. If you have rejected the world with its vain philosophies and empty deceits (Colossians 2:8), and are standing firmly on the rock of the kingdom, these evidences of the imminent coming of Jesus will thrill you. The meaning of "gospel" is "good news." We have the gospel of peace in which to be confident. Fear of the end-time is the result of ignorance of God's provision.

While God is shaking things up, and lifting His obedient people up and out of worldly limitations, the world itself will continue to groan with the weight of its own sin. All the earthquakes, floods, droughts, fires, pollution and violent crimes are a result of sin. Do not, I repeat do not, confuse this with the judgment of God. God's judgment is reserved for the tribulation and it will not be loosed until then.

Mark 13
**5 And Jesus, answering them, began to say: "Take heed that no one deceives you.
6 "For many will come in My name, saying, 'I am He,' and will deceive many.
7 "And when you hear of wars and rumors of wars, do not be troubled; for such things must happen, but the end is not yet.
8 "For nation will rise against nation, and kingdom against kingdom. And there will be earthquakes in various places, and there will be famines and troubles. These are the beginnings of sorrows."**

God Is The Deliverer

All evil and destruction until the end of the age is Satan's doing. Every sickness, disease, poverty, lack, oppression, disaster and tragedy is his work. Jesus Christ, by the blood He shed on the cross (Galatians 3:13), redeemed every believer from destruction by buying his salvation and redeeming him from the curse of the Law (Deuteronomy 28). God is the deliverer and blesser. That is why Jesus said that in the world we would have tribulation but to rejoice because, for all those in Him, He had overcome the world (John 16:33).

God says that no man, when he is tested, should say that he is tested by God. God absolutely does not test in the new covenant. In James 1:13, the Greek word *peirazo*, translated as "tempted," is as accurately translated as "tested." Bear that in mind as you read the following Scriptures.

James 1
13 Let no one say when he is tempted, "I am tempted by God"; for God cannot be tempted by evil, nor does He Himself tempt anyone.
14 But each one is tempted when he is drawn away by his own desires and enticed.
15 Then, when desire has conceived, it gives birth to sin; and sin, when it is full-grown, brings forth death.
16 Do not be deceived, my beloved brethren.
17 Every good gift and every perfect gift is from above, and comes down from the Father of lights, with whom there is no variation or shadow of turning.

God does not afflict His children, nor does He allow affliction, which is the same thing. God is not a child abuser. If you have ever accused Him of being one, apologize to the Lord, repent right now, and get your thinking straight.

God gave Adam dominion over the world. Since the day Adam fell, and thereby gave his dominion to Satan, the world has been Satan's camp. He has authority over the world, but not over a blood-bought, Spirit-filled child of God, even while that child of God is in the world. The devil is always, as we are told in 1 Peter 5, [8]**seeking whom he may devour**. "May" does not mean "can"—which is "able to"—"may" means "permitted to." You, by your own shortcomings, have to give Satan permission to devour you. Jesus was without sin, so Satan could only make Him an offer. You must resist the devil through the blood, the anointing, Word-knowledge, and obedience. God is always the answer, never the problem.

God promises, through the prophet Isaiah, that during the time of our covenant He will never again be angry with us, nor pour out His wrath upon us. He promises that His kindness and peace shall never again be removed from us. Since there is nothing kind or peaceful about the tribulation, and the Lord has declared that He will pour out all His wrath during the second three and a half years thereof—the very wrath He elected to withhold for the past two thousand years—He certainly does not plan for His people to be here when He does it.

Isaiah 54 (The Amplified Bible)
9 For this is like the days of Noah to Me; as I swore that the waters of Noah should no more go over the earth, so have I sworn that I will not be angry with you or rebuke you.
10 For though the mountains should depart and the hills be shaken or removed, yet My love and kindness shall not depart from you, nor shall My covenant of peace and completeness be removed, says the Lord, Who has compassion on you.

Every promise of the Bible will be fulfilled before Jesus comes. If you are fully familiar with the Word, you know there is much still to be accomplished in the life of every believer. Because of all God's promises that must come to pass in this generation, the Holy Spirit is equipping us. We have twice as much "manna" so that we may know what is lacking, get into faith for it, and be strong enough in Christ to receive it and walk it out in righteousness.

Ephesians 1
9 having made known to us the mystery of His will, according to is good pleasure which He purposed in Himself,
10 that in the dispensation of the fullness of the times He might gather together in one all things in Christ, both which are in heaven and which are on earth in Him,
11 in whom also we have obtained an inheritance, being predestined according to the purpose of Him who works all things according to the counsel of His will,

Our Father is not a liar. He is going to get the job done through those of us who are in Christ. That is why He is now revealing all the mysteries to us. We must know **the mystery of His will** and be of unshakable faith throughout the rest of our time in this world so that He can use us effectively. God is about to shake heaven and earth. He intends the body of Christ to walk securely in all its inheritance in Him and to occupy the earth in victory until He comes.

The Wealth Of The Wicked

As you read the following verses, consider their significance in light of the shaking that is coming. Consider the place of unshakable confidence, prosperity, and responsibility to be occupied by God's righteous children.

> Psalm 112
> **1 Praise the Lord! Blessed is the man who fears the Lord, Who delights greatly in His commandments.**
> **2 His descendants will be mighty on earth; The generation of the upright will be blessed.**
> **3 Wealth and riches will be in his house, And his righteousness endures forever.**
> **4 Unto the upright there arises light in the darkness; He is gracious, and full of compassion, and righteous.**
> **5 A good man deals graciously and lends; He will guide his affairs with discretion.**
> **6 Surely he will never be shaken; The righteous will be in everlasting remembrance.**
> **7 He will not be afraid of evil tidings; His heart is steadfast, trusting in the Lord.**
> **8 His heart is established; He will not be afraid, Until he sees his desire upon his enemies.**

What an excellent representation of who we are in Christ. What a powerful declaration of what our faith must consistently be, especially when we get a bad report.

I use this passage of Scripture frequently in my prayers. The evil tidings spoken of refer not only to personal things, but to the bad reports on the news, what we see around us, and the crumbling situations. We must learn how to react, how to view everything through the Father's eyes instead of our own. Psalm 112 also establishes why wealth and riches, beyond enough for our own needs, must be in our houses. We must have a constant surplus to enable us to give to the poor and meet the needs of the families of the earth. God's wealth in the hands of the body of Christ is a crucial method by which He will draw the world to us, and through us to Jesus.

Do not get in a fuss that many will come for the wrong reason. Wealth, that sparkling, shiny substance so coveted and pursued by the world, will draw the world to the light. People do not have to know why they are drawn. When they come to the light, we shall be there to reveal the truth of Christ Jesus to them. The body of Christ will not have to chase people to try to convince them of their need for Jesus. People will come to us because they will want lives as blessed as ours.

As God shakes heaven and earth, and things as we have known them are turned upside down, He plans to bring full restoration into the body of Christ. That means the turning over of the hundredfold harvest (Mark 10:29-30) of every seed that has been sown without a harvest being reaped since Adam fell. God also intends His people to receive repayment from Satan for six thousand years of thievery. Satan will be forced by God to take it all back from the wicked and hand it over because, as it says in Proverbs 13, [22]**the wealth of the sinner is stored up for the righteous**.

Joel 2
25 So I will restore to you the years that the swarming locust has eaten, the crawling locust, the consuming locust, and the chewing locust...
26 You shall eat in plenty and be satisfied, and praise the name of the Lord your God, who has dealt wondrously with you; and My people shall never be put to shame.

The various locusts represent the various forms of destruction that have come upon, and the various and sundry ways in which the devil has stolen from, God's people throughout the ages.

Joel 2
28 And it shall come to pass afterward that I will pour out My

Spirit on all flesh; your sons and your daughters shall prophesy, your old men shall dream dreams, your young men shall see visions;
29 And also on My menservants and on My maidservants I will pour out My Spirit in those days.

After the restoration of, and transfer of the world's wealth to, the glorious church, the Lord will pour out His Spirit on all flesh. All flesh, every human being in the world, will have the witness of the Holy Spirit before Jesus comes again.

Why will this not occur prior to the restoration of the church? Think about it. Is the church ready to handle, spiritually or financially, the huge numbers of people who will rush to it during this unprecedented tidal wave of needy souls? Are you able to leave your job and be available to do God's bidding, to minister upon demand to all who need you? Do you have the answers they will seek?

Raise your sights and embrace the greater picture. This is what every believer in this generation is called to fulfill. That is why we must be in position physically, financially, spiritually and socially. We must be strong and of good courage, strengthened with the Word and the Spirit to do our part. Everyone with ears to hear is needed to accomplish all that must be done during the last and greatest revival of all time.

Haggai 2
**6 For thus says the Lord of hosts: "Once more (it is a little while) I will shake heaven and earth, the sea and dry land;
7 "and I will shake all nations, and they shall come to the Desire of All Nations, and I will fill this temple with glory," says the Lord of hosts.
8 "The silver is Mine, and the gold is Mine," says the Lord of hosts.
9 "The glory of this latter temple shall be greater than the former," says the Lord of hosts. "And in this place I will give peace," says the Lord of hosts.**

Verse 6 is quoted, in part, in Hebrews 12:26 to remind us, in the new covenant, of what God prophesied through Haggai. We are to focus our attention upon what He purposed in His heart, so very long ago, to do during the time of this final generation.

The wealth, possessions, fame, and fortune, now possessed by the world but to be turned over to the righteous, is **the Desire of All Nations**. Verse 7 says that, in this end-time shake up, the nations—the unsaved world—having been stripped of all it desires, will have no choice but to turn to the body of Christ to which the wealth, possessions, fame, and fortune will have been transferred.

Understand the full impact of this. The nations, the unsaved world, will not come to us because we are nice, or kind, or wise, or because they like our personalities, or to hear about Jesus; they will come because of the wealth we possess, because of **the Desire of All Nations**.

As I said before, do not get in a fuss about this. God knows what He is doing. God's people cry out for revival, but then make so bold as to decry His methods. Jesus would call them hypocrites. It is not for us to say that people must seek salvation for the right reasons. Any reason is the right reason. God understands the fallen nature of man far better than we ever will. God desires that no one perish. If wealth is the only thing to draw the world to the light, to force it to value us and what we have to say, who are we to question it?

We shall never cease to understand that true wealth lies in our relationship with God, that worldly wealth is only a tool in our hands. This is the realm of the Spirit for which we are being prepared. It requires that we walk in all Spirit and virtually no flesh, that we be able to maintain God's perspective. If you are susceptible to the misuse of this wealth, it is doubtful that you will receive it.

Please grasp the fact that God is talking about giving this exceeding abundance to you, yes, you. When you are baptized in the Holy Spirit you are the latter temple (1 Corinthians 3:16-17). God is filling each believer with His glory, which includes unprecedented wealth. This is not just for those in ministry; this is for each and every Christian who has chosen to have ears to hear.

You are not to blame if you have a less than exuberant view of wealth in the hands of the church. Until now, regrettably, a display of wealth in the hands of a Christian has usually been a ministry head bragging about how much he spends on television, or his lavish modes of transportation, or the mansion he has just built, and who is behaving, for the most part, in a worldly fashion that would be unthinkable for Jesus. In the next breath, this same person begs for contributions to support his ministry. This has left a bad taste in people's mouths. It has given the enemy much to use against us and, understandably, put many of God's people off when the subject of prosperity arises.

Wealth in the hands of the body of Christ is not, despite how it may seem to many, a matter of ministries and ministers getting rich off the sweat of believers' brows. When God turns the wealth of the wicked over to the just it will be for the entire body of Christ, not just for those in the five-fold ministry. When you hear someone say "the church," you need to know that is you. Even though God's principle of sowing and reaping will continue, there will be more than enough for all and money will no longer be a dirty word. It will become just another tool to be used. All of our individual needs will be extravagantly met, the outreaches and meeting costs of ministries will be provided for, and there will be plenty left over to meet the needs of everyone else as well.

The Father intends that we enjoy living in gorgeous homes, driving good cars, dressing well, and being able to go anywhere and do anything that He instructs without a thought to cost. The Father intends that we be blessed going out and blessed coming in. What we must not do is shift our focus from the kingdom to the world. We must have the mind of Christ and see all the opulence as the bait to draw lost souls. When Jesus told Peter to leave his fishing fleet and learn to be a fisher of men, He knew that the best fishermen have the best bait.

I must remind you again, though, of the need to walk in righteousness, God's way of doing and being right. You must put yourself in position to receive all these blessings, and you do this through uncompromised obedience to the Word. Tithing is a central issue of obedience. No wealth will ever come to you from God unless you are obedient in the tithe.

Wolves In Sheep's Clothing

When God says that He will shake not only earth but heaven as well, He refers to the kingdom. Teachers who promote false doctrine will be shaken out. Those within the church who embrace false doctrine will be shaken out. Those with itching ears who heap up for themselves teachers who tell them what they want to hear, and turn aside to fables rather than the truth, will be shaken out.

Matthew 7
15 Beware of false prophets, who come to you in sheep's clothing, but inwardly they are ravenous wolves.

Jesus refers to false prophets coming in **sheep's clothing** because they are false prophets within the church. Jesus said that they would abound as we approach the final moments of the age. As I listen to what is being taught today, it is clear that this is the case; fables and lies from within the church are spreading like cancer.

Matthew 7
16 You will know them by their fruits. Do men gather grapes from thornbushes or figs from thistles?
17 Even so, every good tree bears good fruit, but a bad tree bears bad fruit.
18 A good tree cannot bear bad fruit, nor can a bad tree bear good fruit.
19 Every tree that does not bear good fruit is cut down and thrown into the fire.

God is going to clean His house and get everything in order before the end of the age. He has provided each of us the opportunity to be part of the world-wide revival and, at the last moment, the opportunity to get into the ark when that last trump sounds.

Wealth Greater Than Solomon's

God says that the glory of this latter temple, which includes wealth, will be greater than that of the former temple. That is an amazing statement. The final generation of new covenant believers, who have ears to hear, are destined to be more wealthy and more prominent than

Abraham and Lot. Abraham and Lot had so much wealth and so many possessions that God had to give them each a country to contain it all.

We are to have more wealth and prominence than King David. David's personal wealth financed the building of most of the first temple of the Lord, a temple constructed of gold, silver, jewels and all the costly and precious materials that then were known. That temple was, in fact, a type for New Jerusalem (Revelation 21).

Solomon was in the former temple. People came from all over the world just to see the extraordinary, breathtaking wealth that Solomon possessed. The Queen of Sheba fainted when she beheld Solomon's wealth. Even Solomon's servants were dressed more richly than was royalty elsewhere. Solomon had so much that silver was piled in dunes outside the palace. Solomon could not be bothered to count it or use it; anyone could just help himself. When people came to Solomon they received his words as God's wisdom. Why did they do that? His uncountable wealth.

We all know that poor people have no clout and little credibility. When a poor man tries to share a sound piece of advice with someone, it is most likely that he will be brushed off with, "If you're so smart, why aren't you rich?"

Ecclesiastes 9

16 ...Wisdom is better than strength. Nevertheless the poor man's wisdom is despised, and his words are not heard.

God plans to prove that His wisdom is in us by giving us wealth. We shall enjoy credibility. The world will finally choose to hear our words.

Isaiah 60

1 Arise, shine; For your light has come! and the glory of the Lord is risen upon you.
2 For behold, the darkness shall cover the earth, and deep darkness the people; but the Lord will arise over you, and His glory will be seen upon you.
3 The Gentiles shall come to your light, and kings to the brightness of your rising.
4 Lift up your eyes all around, and see: they all gather together,

The Rapture, The Tribulation, And Beyond 35

> **they come to you; your sons shall come from afar, and your daughters shall be nursed at your side.**
> **5 Then you shall see and become radiant, and your heart shall swell with joy; because the abundance of the sea shall be turned to you, the wealth of the Gentiles shall come to you.**
> **11 Therefore your gates shall be open continually; they shall not be shut day or night, that men may bring to you the wealth of the Gentiles, and their kings in procession.**

The **Gentiles** are the unsaved world. When we place ourselves in a position to receive, God will send people to us with money and possessions. He knows exactly how He will accomplish this. It is far beyond our ability to fathom, let alone accomplish. We must receive it by faith, just as we receive by faith healing, deliverance, the restoration of our families, and all of God's miracles.

God gave Daniel a vision and he prophesied of this time. The angel Gabriel said to Daniel in Daniel 8, [17]**Understand, son of man, that the vision refers to the time of the end**. In the rest of Daniel 8 you will see a description of the decay of the world and its system. It was so horrifying that it made Daniel faint and become physically sick for days afterward. Gabriel also told Daniel to, [26]**seal up the vision, for it refers to many days in the future**. We are privileged to be in the time in which it is being revealed, and to see it fulfilled.

Daniel 11
> **32 Those who do wickedly against the covenant he shall corrupt with flattery; but the people who know their God shall be strong, and carry out great exploits.**
> **33 And those of the people who understand shall instruct many...**
> **35 ...because it is still for the appointed time.**

The devil is the one who deceives people with flattery. Remember the **smooth words** and **prophesied deceits**—which the people demanded and which were spoken of in Isaiah 30:10—and the destruction that ensued? Satan can only corrupt the wicked. To be corrupted, a person must choose to believe Satan's lies, to believe false doctrine.

The only way to know a lie is to first know the truth. That is why

God tells us to meditate in His Word day and night, to keep it in our eyes, our ears and our mouths, and observe to do all that is written therein. If we are not diligent in loving the Word, and making it the priority in our lives, we shall be deceived by the devil's flattery.

We cannot know God without knowing His Word; He is His Word. The Bible is not about God, it is God. Knowing God is the only way to be strong and carry out His great work. Those of us who do know God are the ones He will use in the end-time revival.

> Jeremiah 33
> **3 Call to Me, and I will answer you, and show you great and mighty things, which you do not know.**
> **6 Behold, I will bring it health and healing; I will heal them and reveal to them the abundance of peace and truth.**
> **9 Then it shall be to Me a name of joy, a praise, and an honor before all nations of the earth, who shall hear all the good that I do to them; they shall fear and tremble for all the goodness and all the prosperity that I provide for it.**

These Scriptures perfectly describe the true, glorious, end-time church. This is what God has called us to walk in. Become familiar with these words; make them your own. Use them as a battle cry and a praise unto almighty God. Be one of those with an established heart who will never be shaken. Make yourself available to be used by God to win as many as possible to the body of Christ.

Chapter 3

The Timing Of The Age

When Daniel received his vision from the angel Gabriel he did not understand it; it was not for his generation. It was for **the time of the end**; it was for us.

> Daniel 12
> 8 **Although I heard, I did not understand. Then I said, "My lord, what shall be the end of these things?"**
> 9 And he said, "Go your way, Daniel, for the words are closed up and sealed till the time of the end.
> 10 "Many shall be purified, made white, and refined, but the wicked shall do wickedly; and none of the wicked shall understand, but the wise shall understand."

The **end of these things** is the end of the tribulation—for Daniel's vision included the horror of the great tribulation—however, the **time of the end** is where we are now. The many who **shall be purified, made white, and refined** are the souls who will be saved in the end-time revival. Those in the body of Christ are the **wise** who **shall understand**.

Ever since the resurrection, believers have been looking about them and saying, "Surely, it can't get any worse than this. This must be the end of time," while others, who do not think Jesus will ever come back, have been saying, as in 2 Peter 3, [4]**Where is the promise of His coming? For since the fathers fell asleep, all things continue as they were from the beginning of creation.**

Peter goes on to say that those who say such things willfully disregard the fact that God flooded the whole earth, electing to save only righteous Noah and his family. The people of Noah's time scoffed at Noah. There he was, foolishly building on dry land a thing that would float on water. The people had never seen rain—the land was watered by dew in those days (Genesis 2:6)—but then it started to rain. One can only imagine the pleading and the banging on the door of the ark as the waters rose. It is the same today with respect to the rapture of the church.

2 Peter 3
8 But, beloved, do not forget this one thing, that with the Lord one day is as a thousand years, and a thousand years as one day.

This is the key to unlocking the timing of the age. It is the key to certainty that we are the last generation before the tribulation. God says in Isaiah 46 that He speaks the end from the beginning, [10]**Declaring the end from the beginning, and from ancient times things that are not yet done, saying, "My counsel shall stand, and I will do all My pleasure."**

The Six Days Of Creation

Genesis 1 establishes that there were six days of creation followed by a day of rest, the seventh day. This is a type for man's six thousand year lease upon the earth, followed by the millennial reign of Christ, the seventh thousand years. The six thousand year time span was already established when God placed Adam and Eve in the Garden of Eden; it was built into the timing of creation, itself. God gave Adam dominion over all He had created, thus man's six thousand year lease upon the earth.

Genesis 1
26 Then God said, "Let Us make man in Our image, according to Our likeness; let them have dominion over the fish of the sea, over the birds of the air, and over the cattle, over all the earth

and over every creeping thing that creeps on the earth."
27 So God created man in His own image; in the image of God He created him; male and female He created them.
28 Then God blessed them, and God said to them, "Be fruitful and multiply; fill the earth and subdue it; have dominion over the fish of the sea, over the birds of the air, and over every living thing that moves on the earth."

God created the garden in which to have fellowship with His man. He wanted His man to be blessed, but He also wanted him to have free will. To accomplish this, God gave Adam a single injunction with a dire consequence for disobedience.

Genesis 2
16 And the Lord God commanded the man, saying, "Of every tree of the garden you may freely eat;
17 "but of the tree of the knowledge of good and evil you shall not eat, for in the day that you eat of it you shall surely die."

Adam and Eve committed high treason by choosing to ignore God's injunction. They ate of the tree that was forbidden, thus bowing their knee to Satan. They chose to be deceived and thereby forfeited to Satan their six thousand year lease of dominion over the earth and everything in it. God had given it to them, so it was theirs to forfeit. God's people do the same thing today. By ignoring the Word they forfeit their inheritance.

Because of their disobedience, Adam and Eve were thrown out of the garden and a curse came upon the earth that remains to this day. Satan usurped Adam's dominion, stole the lease, and became the god of this world for the next six thousand years.

Four thousand years later we see, in Luke 4, clear evidence of Satan still being the god of this world when he tests Jesus in the wilderness after His forty day fast, **[5]Then the devil, taking Him up on a high mountain, showed Him all the kingdoms of the world in a moment of time. [6]And the devil said to Him, "All this authority I will give You, and their glory; for this has been delivered to me, and I give it to whomever I wish."**

Satan was tempting Jesus just as he tempted Eve. Jesus rebuked him fiercely in Luke 4, **⁸And Jesus answered and said to him, "Get behind Me, Satan! For it is written, 'You shall worship the Lord your God, and Him only you shall serve.'"**

It is interesting to note that the tree of the knowledge of good and evil was the first type for the tithe. The whole garden was Adam's except for the tree. The tree belonged to God. It was God's part. The tithe, the first tenth of our income, is also God's part; it is holy unto Him (Malachi 3:8-14 and Hebrews 7). We, just like Adam, bring a curse upon ourselves when we eat of God's part.

We know from the Bible—through the accumulated years of all the "begats" as well as other evidence—that there were two thousand years from Adam to Abraham, and two thousand years from Abraham to Jesus. That leaves two thousand years until Jesus comes again and Satan is overthrown. Jesus prophesied of the termination of this lease in John 12 when He said, **³¹Now is the judgment of this world; now the ruler of this world will be cast out**.

God's Year 2,000

None of our man-made calendars agree about when the biblical year 2,000 is. The Hebrew calendar says one thing, while all the others, including our own, say something else. Despite the fact that the Father says that only He knows the precise time of the end—not even Jesus or the angels know (Mark 13:32)—there have always been misguided people who insist on predicting the day. They think they are privy to information that even the King of kings does not have. Anyone who knows Scripture avoids such people like the plague. Jesus told us to discern the season, be ready to be caught away in the rapture, to watch and pray, and to leave the specifics to Him.

John 16

12 I still have many things to say to you, but you cannot bear them now.

13 However, when He, the Spirit of truth, has come, He will guide you into all truth; for He will not speak on His own

authority, but whatever He hears He will speak; and He will tell you things to come.
14 He will glorify Me, for He will take of what is Mine and declare it to you.
15 All things that the Father has are Mine. Therefore I said that He will take of Mine and declare it to you.

The Holy Spirit will tell us at the moment of the rapture that the time has come. We must, however, have ears to hear what He is saying to the church in the meantime (Revelation 3:6). The moment will occur suddenly and we must be ready.

Matthew 25
6 And at midnight a cry was heard: "Behold, the bridegroom is coming; go out to meet him!"
7 Then all those virgins arose and trimmed their lamps.
8 And the foolish said to the wise, "Give us some of your oil, for our lamps are going out."
9 But the wise answered, saying, "No, lest there should not be enough for us and you; but go rather to those who sell, and buy for yourselves."
10 And while they went to buy, the bridegroom came, and those who were ready went in with him to the wedding; and the door was shut.

I am convinced that the profusion of different calendars producing different dates, and the consequent disagreement regarding the year 2,000, is not an accident. I believe that God deliberately confused the recording of time so that we would not have the ability to pervert His intention for these last moments of the age. At the tower of Babel (Genesis 11:1-9), God not only confused man's language but man's understanding in general.

The builders of the tower of Babel were Noah's descendants who had one language. They decided to turn from God and rule the earth their way. God went down to see the city they had built, saw that they were in perfect unity, and declared that because of that unity they would not fail. To preclude this evil—their rejection of Him—God confused their language and scattered them over the face of the earth. God makes it clear that He is the timekeeper.

> Ecclesiastes 3
> **1 To everything there is a season, a time for every purpose under heaven:**
> **10 I have seen the God-given task with which the sons of men are to be occupied.**
> **11 He has made everything beautiful in its time. Also He has put eternity in their hearts, except that no one can find out the work that God does from beginning to end.**
> **12 I know that there is nothing better for them than to rejoice, and to do good in their lives,**

Simply put, we are to fulfill God's plans and purposes for our lives in obedience and faith. It is for us to **rejoice and to do good** in our lives. It is not for us to question God's plans, and that includes His timing.

This is confirmed for us in Galatians 6, [9]**And let us not grow weary while doing good, for in due season we shall reap if we do not lose heart**. We are to keep the Word of God and establish His covenant upon the earth. We are not to fuss about the precise hour, although we are responsible for discerning the season. As Jesus said in Mark 13, [33]**Watch and pray**.

God has provided many clues to help us understand the timing of the age and, since He desires that we do indeed understand, He has made it relatively simple. We must, however, always be mindful that God's Word, old testamental as well as new, is for those with eyes to see and ears to hear. God uses numbers prophetically throughout His Word—this is not to be confused with the satanic practice of numerology—as a way of speaking in parables, a way of speaking only to those with such eyes and ears.

Solomon Builds The House Of The Lord

In order to proceed with this examination of prophecy, one must first accept that all numbers in the Bible have meaning beyond their

The Rapture, The Tribulation, And Beyond

immediate context. When one comes across a biblical account of God's completion of any individual task, the numbers contained within that account also reveal clues to the timing of the age. Additionally, one must understand that if any number, when added to, or multiplied or divided by, another number, should produce results that coincide with other significant numbers in the Bible, close examination is not only justified but strongly called for.

Genesis 6
3 And the Lord said, "My Spirit shall not strive with man forever, for he is indeed flesh; yet his days shall be one hundred and twenty years."

Leviticus 25
10 And you shall consecrate the fiftieth year, and proclaim liberty throughout all the land to all its inhabitants.

120 and 50 are numbers instrumental in unlocking the timing of the age. When God states that man's **days shall be one hundred and twenty years**, He is announcing that He will contend for a hundred and twenty years with the fallen nature of man before He judges the earth. In Leviticus He declares that every fiftieth year is a year of Jubilee, a year of restoration. After a hundred and twenty Jubilees, 120 times 50, comes restoration.

The dimensions of the house of the Lord that Solomon built are an excellent confirmation.

2 Chronicles 3
3 This is the foundation which Solomon laid for building the house of God: The length was sixty cubits (by cubits according to the former measure) and the width twenty cubits.
4 And the vestibule that was in front of the sanctuary was twenty cubits long across the width of the house, and the height was one hundred and twenty. He overlaid the inside with pure gold.
8 And he made the Most Holy Place. Its length was according to the width of the house, twenty cubits, and its width twenty

**cubits. He overlaid it with six hundred talents of fine gold.
9 The weight of the nails was fifty shekels of gold; and he overlaid the upper area with gold.**

The foundation for the house of God was 60 cubits long and 20 cubits wide. The Most Holy Place was 20 cubits, the width of the house, by 20 cubits in the other direction. Add them all together: 120.

The weight of the nails that were used equaled 50 shekels of gold. It is also interesting to note that the dimensions of the house are separated into two parts. The dimensions of the main building total 80 which, when multiplied by 50, equals four thousand, the number of years from Adam to Jesus. The dimensions of the Most Holy Place total 40 which, when multiplied by 50, equals two thousand, the years of the church age from the birth of Jesus to His return.

Since the days of a man are a hundred and twenty years, and we have seen in biblical timing that this means a hundred and twenty Jubilees, the height of the vestibule, by which one approaches the house of the Lord, indicates the six thousand years it will take to arrive at New Jerusalem.

2 Chronicles 9
**17 Moreover the king made a great throne of ivory, and overlaid it with pure gold.
18 The throne had six steps, with a footstool of gold, which were fastened to the throne;**

The six steps represent man's six thousand year lease, leading up to the time when the body of Christ will sit with Him on His throne to rule and reign during the seventh millennium (Revelation 3:21). The golden footstool attached to the throne represents the time when Jesus puts His enemies under His feet at the end of His millennial reign.

1 Corinthians 15
**22 For as in Adam all die, even so in Christ all shall be made alive.
23 But each one in his own order: Christ the firstfruits, afterward those who are Christ's at His coming.**

**24 Then comes the end, when He delivers the kingdom to God the Father, when He puts an end to all rule and all authority and power.
25 For He must reign till He has put all enemies under His feet.
26 The last enemy that will be destroyed is death.**

In verses 22 and 23 we have the resurrection and rapture of Christ, and the rapture of the church two thousand years later. **Then comes the end** refers to the seventh millennium, at the end of which, at the great white throne judgment, the last enemy, death, is cast into the lake of fire (Revelation 20:14). At that time all enemies, symbolized by the golden footstool, will be under Christ Jesus' feet.

Psalm 110
1 The Lord said to my Lord, "Sit at My right hand, Till I make Your enemies Your footstool."

This Scripture, wherein Father God speaks to His Son about making His enemies His footstool, is cited six times in the New Testament: Matthew 22:44, Mark 12:36, Luke 20:42-43, Acts 2:34-35, Hebrews 1:13, Hebrews 10:13. This confirms the significance of **The throne had six steps, with a footstool of gold, which were fastened to the throne**.

The next important numbers in understanding the end-time are 7 and 10. We are told in 2 Chronicles 7 that Solomon, [8]**kept the feast seven days** when the house of the Lord was finished. This is a type for the marriage supper of the Lamb in New Jerusalem at the end of the seven year tribulation. 2 Chronicles 9 gives us the account of the queen of Sheba—Solomon's first recorded visitor after the completion of the house of the Lord—who, hearing of Solomon's fame, comes to question him and gives him a hundred and twenty talents of gold. Sheba is Hebrew for seven.

Leviticus 25
8 And you shall count seven sabbaths of years for yourself, seven times seven years; and the time of the seven sabbaths of years shall be to you forty-nine years.

**9 Then you shall cause the trumpet of the Jubilee to sound on the tenth day of the seventh month; on the Day of Atonement shall make the trumpet to sound throughout all your land.
10 And you shall consecrate the fiftieth year, and proclaim liberty throughout all the land to all its inhabitants. It shall be a Jubilee for you; and each of you shall return to his possession, and each of you shall return to his family.**

On the tenth day of the seventh month, in the fiftieth year, the trumpet of Jubilee sounded. In the year of Jubilee all debts were cancelled and all of God's people received back everything they had lost. Jubilee is the year of the complete restoration of all things. Remember Joel 2, where God says that everything the devil has stolen, and all forms of destruction he has perpetrated, will be restored to the church at the end of the age.

Seven is, of course, the number of years of the tribulation. Also, as an additional prophetic reference, we multiply the tenth day by the seventh month and get the seventy years of Babylonian captivity.

God told His people Israel, in Exodus 31, that they, [16]**shall keep the Sabbath, to observe the Sabbath throughout their generations as a perpetual covenant**. This applied prophetically to the seventy years of Israel's captivity, after which came its freedom.

Exodus 31
17 It is a sign between Me and the children of Israel forever; for in six days the Lord made the heavens and the earth, and on the seventh day He rested and was refreshed.

This couples the **perpetual covenant** of the Sabbath with the six thousand years of earth's history, followed by the seventh millennium.

The Number Of The Beast

2 Chronicles 9
13 The weight of gold that came to Solomon yearly was six hundred and sixty-six talents of gold.

The quantity of gold received by Solomon annually is mentioned after

The Rapture, The Tribulation, And Beyond 47

the house of the Lord is completed and in the same year as the visit of the queen of Sheba.

The number 666 is the number of Antichrist. In Revelation 13 we see that during the tribulation the people left on the earth will be forced to, **¹⁶receive a mark on their right hand or on their foreheads, ¹⁷and that no one may buy or sell except one who has the mark or the name of the beast, or the number of his name. ¹⁸Here is wisdom. Let him who has understanding calculate the number of the beast, for it is the number of a man: His number is 666.**

The number of man is six, for God created man on the sixth day. 666 represents the satanic trinity: Antichrist, the false prophet, the beast. Satan corrupted man in the garden and the fallen nature of man has continued to bow its knee to him. This is at the root of today's secular humanism.

666 is also mentioned in Ezra 2, **¹³the people of Adonikam, six hundred and sixty-six.** At the end of the seventy years of Israel's Babylonian captivity, King Cyrus set Israel free, including the people of Adonikam, and they returned to Jerusalem to rebuild the city and the temple.

Adonikam means in Hebrew, "the Lord has risen," thus Adonikam and his people are a type for the body of Christ being raptured and taken up into New Jerusalem. The number of Adonikam's people being 666 is a declaration of the rule of Antichrist during the tribulation immediately following the rapture of the church.

It was the Romans who later destroyed the rebuilt temple, and the first six Roman numerals declare the number of Antichrist:

```
D     = 500
C     = 100
L     =  50
X     =  10
V     =   5
I     =   1
        ───
        666
```

Clouds Of Angels

2 Chronicles 5
12 and the Levites who were the singers, all those of Asaph and

Heman and Jeduthun, with their sons and their brethren, stood at the east end of the altar, clothed in white linen, having cymbals, stringed instruments and harps, and with them one hundred and twenty priests sounding with trumpets
13 indeed it came to pass, when the trumpeters and singers were as one, to make one sound to be heard in praising and thanking the Lord, and when they lifted up their voice with the trumpets and cymbals and instruments of music, and praised the Lord, saying: "For He is good, for His mercy endures forever," that the house, the house of the Lord, was filled with a cloud,
14 so that the priests could not continue ministering because of the cloud; for the glory of the Lord filled the house of God.

...their sons and their brethren represent the glorified church.
...clothed in white linen refers to the righteous acts of the saints (Revelation 19:8) which will adorn the bride, New Jerusalem.
...one hundred and twenty priests sounding with trumpets represents the hundred and twentieth Jubilee.
...trumpeters and singers were as one represents the unified body of Christ, praising and thanking the Lord.
...the house of the Lord was filled with a cloud represents the cloud of angels which will carry the saints to glory in the rapture.

The angels are the clouds of heaven. When Jesus was raptured, the cloud that carried Him was a cloud of angels. The two men in white apparel, in verse 10 below, are also angels.

Acts 1
9 Now when He had spoken these things, while they watched, He was taken up, and a cloud received Him out of their sight.
10 And while they looked steadfastly toward heaven as He went up, behold, two men stood by them in white apparel,
11 who also said, "Men of Galilee, why do you stand gazing up into heaven? This same Jesus, who was taken up from you into heaven, will so come in like manner as you saw Him go into heaven."

Luke 16
22 So it was that the beggar died, and was carried by the angels to Abraham's bosom...

The moment when Jesus comes with His angels to rapture the church, whereafter comes the judgment seat of Christ where we receive our crowns—our rewards and positions in New Jerusalem—is described in Matthew 16, **[27]For the Son of Man will come in the glory of His Father with His angels, and then He will reward each according to his works**.

Some Other Examples Of The Timing Of The Age

The forty years that God fed manna to the children of Israel in the wilderness (Exodus 16) symbolizes forty Jubilees totalling the two thousand years of the church age.

Isaiah 54
**9 "For this is like the waters of Noah to Me; for as I have sworn that the waters of Noah would no longer cover the earth, so have I sworn that I would not be angry with you, nor rebuke you.
10 "For the mountains shall depart and the hills be removed, but My kindness shall not depart from you, nor shall My covenant of peace be removed," says the Lord, who has mercy on you.**

The forty days and forty nights that it rained are denoted by **the waters of Noah**.

For the mountains shall depart and the hills be removed, but My kindness shall not depart from you is how God ties Noah's flood to the new covenant. Moses was on Mt. Sinai, listening to God for forty days and forty nights. It was forty days from the time of Jesus' resurrection to His rapture. The resurrection represents the new birth of each believer and is another example of the forty Jubilees before the rapture of the church.

Exodus 21:2 tells us of Hebrew servants being bound for six years and released in the seventh year.

God said to Joshua (a type for Jesus) in Joshua 6:
3 "You shall march around the city, all you men of war; you shall go all around the city once. This you shall do six days.
4 "And seven priests shall bear seven trumpets of rams' horns before the ark. But the seventh day you shall march around the city seven times, and the priests shall blow the trumpets.
5 "Then it shall come to pass, when they make a long blast with the ram's horn, and when you hear the sound of the trumpet, that all the people shall shout with a great shout; then the wall of the city will fall down flat. And the people shall go up every man straight before him."

The body of Christ, which is the army of God, is denoted by **all you men of war**. At the second advent, at the end of the tribulation, Christ and His body will ride back from New Jerusalem, after the wedding, to judge the earth.

...six days represent the six thousand years of God's warning to the world of its sin.
...seven priests shall bear seven trumpets is a type for the seven year tribulation.
...a long blast with the ram's horn is the last trump, announcing the coming of Jesus for His church just before the tribulation.
...all the people shall shout with a great shout represents the body of Christ receiving their coming Lord.
...then the wall of the city will fall down flat symbolizes the removal of all separation between God and His man.
...And the people shall go up represents the body of Christ being raptured.

Revelation 11
15 Then the seventh angel sounded: And there were loud voices in heaven, saying, "The kingdoms of this world have become the kingdoms of our Lord and of His Christ, and He shall reign forever and ever!"
16 And the twenty-four elders who sat before God on their thrones fell on their faces and worshiped God,

17 saying: "We give You thanks, O Lord God Almighty, the One who is and who was and who is to come, because You have taken Your great power and reigned.
18 "The nations were angry, and Your wrath has come, and the time of the dead, that they should be judged, and that You should reward Your servants the prophets and the saints, and those who fear Your name, small and great, and should destroy those who destroy the earth."

...the seventh angel sounded proclaims the end of the seven year tribulation and the establishment of the thousand year reign of Christ on earth.

...and Your wrath has come refers to God pouring out His wrath during the last three and a half years of the tribulation.

...and the time of the dead, that they should be judged describes the great white throne judgment (Revelation 20:11-12) at the end of the millennial reign of Christ.

...and that You should reward Your servants the prophets and the saints describes the judgment seat of Christ (1 Corinthians 3:13-17).

...and should destroy those who destroy the earth refers to the destruction of the armies of Antichrist (Revelation 19:11-21).

Jesus Tempted In The Wilderness

Following His baptism in the Holy Spirit in the river Jordan, Jesus became the "container" of the Holy Spirit on earth. The Spirit "came upon" people from time to time, but no one other than Jesus "contained" the anointing. When Jesus sent the Holy Spirit at Pentecost, each of us was given the privilege of receiving the baptism of the Holy Spirit and becoming another "container" of the anointing. Jesus in the flesh was the body of Christ; we, as anointed ones through the baptism of the Holy Spirit, become part of His body.

In the fourth chapters of Matthew and Luke, Jesus goes into the wilderness for forty days and Satan tests Him. Jesus overcomes Satan with the Word and Satan departs, whereafter the angels come to minister to Jesus. Romans 8 says: **[14]For as many as are led by the Spirit** of God, these are sons of God**. Jesus is the Son of God and we, as the body of Christ, become **sons of God**.

Matthew 4
**1 Then Jesus was led up by the Spirit into the wilderness to be tempted by the devil.
2 And when He had fasted forty days and forty nights, afterward He was hungry.
3 Now when the tempter came to Him, he said, "If You are the Son of God, command that these stones become bread."**

...**the wilderness** represents the world, of which Satan is god.
...**forty days and forty nights** represent forty Jubilees, the two thousand year church age.
...**the tempter came to Him** represents the testing of the church.

Matthew 4
**4 But He answered and said, "It is written, 'Man shall not live by bread alone, but by every word that proceeds from the mouth of God.'"
5 Then the devil took Him up into the holy city, set Him on the pinnacle of the temple,
6 and said to Him, "If You are the Son of God, throw Yourself down. For it is written: 'He shall give His angels charge concerning you,' and, 'In their hands they shall bear you up, lest you dash your foot against a stone.'"
7 Jesus said to him, "It is written again, 'You shall not tempt the Lord your God.'"
8 Again, the devil took Him up on an exceedingly high mountain, and showed Him all the kingdoms of the world and their glory.
9 And he said to Him, "All these things I will give You if You will fall down and worship me."
10 Then Jesus said to him, "Away with you, Satan! For it is written, 'You shall worship the Lord your God, and Him only you shall serve.'"
11 Then the devil left Him, and behold, angels came and ministered to Him.**

In verses 4, 7 and 10 we learn how to fight the good fight of faith, defeat the devil, and escape the coming destruction. Since Satan is the god of this world, and we must live in the enemy's camp, we, too, are required to overcome the devil. Our foremost offensive weapon, after qualification by the blood and the Spirit, is declaring the Word, **Man shall not live by bread alone, but by every word that proceeds from the mouth of God**. No matter what the devil uses against us, we are able to defeat him with the Word. James 4 tells us, [7]**Therefore submit to God. Resist the devil and he will flee from you**. You resist him with the Word. Jesus set the example.

God spoke through the prophet in Isaiah 54:9-10, and declared that during the new covenant His kindness and peace would never depart nor be removed from us, and that He would never again be angry with us, nor rebuke us, nor pour out His wrath upon us.

When the Lord talks of peace, it comes from the Hebrew root word *shalem*, whence the Jewish greeting of *shalom*. *Shalem* means much more than lack of war, it means "wholeness," which in turn is defined as: nothing broken, nothing missing, and nothing ignored. When you see the word "peace" in Scripture, connect it to this kind of "wholeness."

You shall not tempt the Lord your God relates to obedience. Jesus tells us in John 14:23-24 that if we love Him we will obey Him, and if we do not obey Him we do not love Him. Do not play games with God; do not see how much sin you can get away with. God is a holy God and we are called to holiness. He says that we should be holy because He is holy (1 Peter 1:13-19).

When Jesus says to the devil, **You shall worship the Lord your God, and Him only you shall serve**, He declares His love, service and worship of God, and God alone. God says that He is God and there is no other (Isaiah 45:18 and 46:8-11).

When **angels came and ministered to** Jesus it was a type for the bearing up by the angels of the church, the body of Christ, in the rapture.

1 John 3
8 ...For this purpose the Son of God was manifested, that He might destroy the works of the devil.

Believers must never compromise the Word. When we are in Christ, our purpose is to **destroy the works of the devil**. If we try to mix a life of faith with the world's thinking and methods, we are doomed to failure. If Jesus had agreed to any of the devil's temptations, God's plan of redemption would have failed. If we believe and act on any of the devil's lies, our own deliverance, blessings and inheritance are put at risk.

Jesus successfully resisted the devil. He did not fall for any of his trickery. He completed the test and overcame. We shall do the same if we know the Word and walk it out.

Daniel's Seventieth Week

God elected to insert the seven years of the tribulation between the end of man's six thousand year lease and the beginning of Christ's millennial reign. This is foretold in Daniel's seventieth week, a week of years. God set aside seventy weeks to discipline disobedient Israel, however, He stopped short at sixty-nine weeks. He reserved the last week to pour out His judgment.

> Daniel 9
> **24 Seventy weeks are determined for your people and for your holy city, to finish the transgression, to make an end of sins, to make reconciliation for iniquity, to bring in everlasting righteousness, to seal up vision and prophecy, and to anoint the Most Holy.**
> **25 Know therefore and understand, that from the going forth of the command to restore and build Jerusalem until Messiah the Prince, there shall be seven weeks and sixty-two weeks; the street shall be built again, and the wall, even in troublesome times.**

The reference to **seven weeks and sixty-two weeks**, rather than a simple reference to sixty-nine weeks, has complex underpinnings.

> **...the going forth of the command to restore and build Jerusalem** occurred in 454 B.C. The restoration was completed

seven weeks—forty-nine years—later, in 405 B.C.
...sixty-two weeks, or 434 years—counting from the restoration of Jerusalem—is the time between that restoration and the cutting off of Messiah by the Jews when they crucified Him. Although the math would thus seem to produce a date of 29 A.D. for the death of Jesus, the count is so close to accurate that the already discussed inaccuracy of our calendars is quite sufficient to cover the discrepancy.

The Mount Of Transfiguration

The sixteenth and seventeenth chapters of Matthew give us a wonderful and detailed picture of the rapture of the church and the timing of the age.

> Matthew 16
> **28 Assuredly, I say to you, there are some standing here who shall not taste death till they see the Son of Man coming in His kingdom.**

Jesus said this two thousand years ago, and we know that all of the disciples to whom He was speaking have long since physically died. We also know that Jesus has not yet come again. So, since He was not lying, what did He mean?

> Matthew 17
> **1 Now after six days Jesus took Peter, James, and John his brother, and brought them up on a high mountain by themselves,**

The six days signify six thousand years and the three disciples are those **standing here who shall not taste death till they see the Son of Man coming in His kingdom**.

When God takes someone up to a mountain, in connection with a vision, the mountain is the kingdom of heaven. The high mountain in this case, would seem to indicate the very throne room of God.

Matthew 17
2 and was transfigured before them. His face shone like the sun, and His clothes became as white as the light.

When Jesus comes for the church, He will come in all His glory. That is when He will shine **like the sun** and radiate pure light. Jesus will not be seen like this until the rapture. Revelation 21 says, [23]**And the city had no need of the sun or of the moon to shine in it, for the glory of God illuminated it, and the Lamb is its light**.

The body of Christ, after glorification in the rapture and as one with the Lord, will also be this light. Jesus says in Matthew 13, [43]**Then the righteous will shine forth as the sun in the kingdom of their Father. He who has ears to hear, let him hear!**

Matthew 17
3 And behold, Moses and Elijah appeared to them, talking with Him.

When Jesus appeared as pure light to Peter, James and John they also saw Moses and Elijah talking to Him. Since Moses had died and Elijah had been raptured, they were both in heaven. Peter, James and John, therefore, had also to be in heaven since God forbids communication with the dead by the living (Deuteronomy 18:11-12). Why Moses and Elijah? Jesus was painting a picture of the rapture.

Moses lived exactly a hundred and twenty years (Deuteronomy 34:7) and died a natural death, in health and strength, at the time of God's choosing. He represents the righteous dead.

Elijah was caught up into heaven by a whirlwind in a chariot of fire (2 Kings 2:11). Jeremiah 4 says, [13]**Behold he shall come up as clouds, and His chariots shall be as a whirlwind: his horses are swifter than eagles**. Psalm 68 (KJV) tells us, [17]**The chariots of God are twenty thousand, even thousands of angels: the Lord is among them**. The rapture of Elijah is a type for the rapture of those who are alive and remain.

1 Thessalonians 4
16 For the Lord Himself will descend from heaven with a shout,

**with the voice of an archangel, and with the trumpet of God. And the dead in Christ will rise first.
17 Then we who are alive and remain shall be caught up together with them in the clouds to meet the Lord in the air. And thus we shall always be with the Lord.**

The body of Moses was buried in the land of Moab—across the Jordan in the same location from which Elijah was taken up—but was never found.

Deuteronomy 34
**5 So Moses the servant of the Lord died there in the land of Moab, according to the word of the Lord.
6 And He buried him in a valley in the land of Moab, opposite Beth Peor; but no one knows his grave to this day.**

In Jude 9, the archangel Michael, who will oversee the resurrection of the righteous dead and be in charge of the rapture of the church, disputes with the devil over the body of Moses.

Daniel 12
**1 At that time Michael shall stand up, the great prince who stands watch over the sons of your people; And there shall be a time of trouble, such as never was since there was a nation, even to that time. And at that time your people shall be delivered, every one who is found written in the book.
2 And many of those who sleep in the dust of the earth shall awake, some to everlasting life, some to shame and everlasting contempt.**

The matter that has been ignored by teachers of the Word throughout time is: Why did Michael dispute with the devil over Moses' body? Preachers get all involved with Michael asking God to rebuke Satan, instead of doing it himself, and totally fail to address his reason for doing so.

Moses is a singular phenomenon. He died and the location of his grave was recorded. Then it vanished. **And He buried him in a valley**

in the land of Moab, opposite Beth Peor; but no one knows his grave to this day. Why is this even reported unless significance attaches?

It was not yet time for the righteous dead to rise, however, God required the body of Moses to be in heaven—to be witnessed for all generations—as part of a vision of the three constituent parts of the rapture of the church:

1. Moses representing the dead in Christ
2. Elijah representing those who are alive and remain
3. Jesus, shining as the sun, when He appears

The body of Moses had to have been resurrected for Peter, James and John to be able to see him in a vision in heaven, standing and talking with Jesus and Elijah. That is why Michael had to contend with Satan for his body. As the type for the righteous dead, Moses had to be present in heaven in a resurrected body. If he were not resurrected, he could only be there in spirit.

Michael contended with Satan for Moses' body at the same time that Elijah was raptured. Moses and Elijah had to be taken up together in order to be an accurate type for the rapture of the church. This is why Moses was buried in the same place as that from which Elijah, as we are told in 2 Kings 2, [11]**went up by a whirlwind into heaven**. The hosts of angels with Michael at their head—the chariot of fire—who came to collect Elijah, also collected the resurrected body of Moses.

Matthew 17
4 Then Peter answered and said to Jesus, "Lord, it is good for us to be here; if You wish, let us make here three tabernacles: one for You, one for Moses, and one for Elijah."

God gave Peter, James and John a vision of the rapture of the church. It is obvious from Peter's reaction that they, just as Daniel before them, failed to understand the vision. Why was this? It was meant for our generation.

Matthew 17
5 While he was still speaking, behold, a bright cloud

overshadowed them; and suddenly a voice came out of the cloud, saying, "This is My beloved Son, in whom I am well pleased. Hear Him!"
6 And when the disciples heard it, they fell on their faces and were greatly afraid.
7 But Jesus came and touched them and said, "Arise, and do not be afraid."
8 And when they had lifted up their eyes, they saw no one but Jesus only.
9 Now as they came down from the mountain, Jesus commanded them, saying, "Tell the vision to no one until the Son of Man is risen from the dead."

The **bright cloud** that **overshadowed them** was a cloud of angels that carried Peter, James and John down from heaven. After Jesus touched them and told them to arise, they were back on earth. The vision had ended, they had come **down from the mountain**, and now they beheld only Jesus in His earthly state.

Watch And Pray

Although we are not to know the precise time of the rapture and all that follows, only the season, we must not think that the timing of the age is an issue apart from the rest of our walk with the Lord. Understanding the season is of the essence of being prepared for the rapture. God went to extraordinary lengths to place in His Word every morsel of information needed by those of the last generation to qualify for the rapture; provided, that is, they have ears to hear.

Chapter 4

Headline News—Up Close And Personal

Saints of God are not ostriches. When trouble comes, ostriches become afraid and confused; they bury their heads in the sand and think that by doing so they are invisible and safe. Ostriches only fool themselves. They not only look ridiculous but they remain susceptible to whatever danger exists. By refusing to face responsibility they make themselves vulnerable, whereas, if they were to keep their heads up they would see how to deal with whatever it was that confronted them.

God never intended us to bury our heads in the sand. In fact, Jesus instructs us in Matthew 16:3, Matthew 26:41, and Luke 12:56, to **watch and pray** and to **discern** the times we are in. Christians who deliberately remain ignorant of world events are ostriches. Ignorance will not keep them safe. Safety lies in keeping our heads up with our eyes open and focussed. Only thus can we be equipped to walk the precise path that Jesus prepared for us in these final moments of the age.

We need to be alert to what is taking place around us if we are not to be among those destroyed for lack of knowledge. We must line it up with Scripture and follow God's plan. We have nothing to fear if we remember that "gospel" means "good news." We have nothing to fear if we are reborn of the Spirit—the definition Jesus gives of "born again" in John 3:5—if we know who we are in Christ, the body and not the bride, and if we eagerly expect the pre-tribulation rapture of the church.

We must hold clearly in mind that the incessant bad news is for the unbelieving world. We must never forget this. We must understand our place, as opposed to the world's place, in all that is going on and never confuse the two. The world, whether it likes it or not, is preparing for the tribulation, and there is much taking shape that will not come to fruition until the reign of Antichrist begins. Everything necessary for Antichrist's one-world-order, and his total reign of terror beginning with the mark of the beast, must be prepared before he ever steps onto the world stage. All this is coming together now, but we must neither fear nor despair. We, the body of Christ, are the restraining force, keeping it all in check until we are taken out of the world.

2 Thessalonians 2
6 And now you know what is restraining, that he may be revealed in his own time.
7 For the mystery of lawlessness is already at work; only he who now restrains will do so until he is taken out of the way.

The anointed church is **he who now restrains**. The Lord tells us in 2 Timothy 1 that He, [7]**has not given us a spirit of fear, but of power and of love and of a sound mind**. We have the mind of Christ, a mind anointed and available to receive all the wisdom of God. We must understand the Father's plan, cast out fear, and submit to the Holy Spirit that He may show us the way. Fear about the days we are in, and what is happening in the world around us, is the result of ignorance. That ignorance is the product either of ostrich mentality or of false teaching that is blindly received without ever putting it to the Word test.

Luke 21
24 And they will fall by the edge of the sword, and be led away captive into all nations. And Jerusalem will be trampled by Gentiles until the times of the Gentiles are fulfilled.
25 And there will be signs in the sun, in the moon, and in the stars; and on the earth distress of nations, with perplexity, the sea and the waves roaring;
26 men's hearts failing them from fear and the expectation of those things which are coming on the earth, for the powers of heaven will be shaken.

The Rapture, The Tribulation, And Beyond 63

**27 Then they will see the Son of Man coming in a cloud with power and great glory.
28 Now when these things begin to happen, look up and lift up your heads, because your redemption draws near.**

As previously mentioned, God says in Hebrews 12 that He will shake heaven and earth and only the things of the kingdom will stand. Here it is again in Luke. The **distress of nations**—not the millennial nations but the now existing nations—is happening now, and will continue and increase until the body of Christ is taken out. Once the tribulation begins, all hell will break loose in the world, but this will not happen while we, the restraining force, still occupy the earth. That is why Jesus says, **look up and lift up your heads**. Our greatest journey will soon begin and we must be ready. Ostriches, determined to keep their heads in the sand, are firmly dug into the path of destruction. We must not be ostriches; we must look up, embrace the truth, and choose to embrace the awesome future God has prepared for us.

The people of this world have, and will continue to have until the last moment, the opportunity to turn from evil and receive Christ Jesus. But, if they continue to reject Him, they have every reason to be desperate about what they see around them, and terrified of what is coming. Only God's kingdom will stand. Men's hearts will fail them **from fear and the expectation of those things which are coming on the earth**. It is interesting to note that heart disease has only recently been proclaimed by the secular world to be the number one killer. Fear produces stress, and stress is the root of heart disease. We, as children of God, have to realize that fear must be cast out of every corner of our being. To qualify to sit with Jesus in His throne and rule and reign with Him (Revelation 3:21), we are required to fulfill His command to overcome. We must march through this time and into the next millennium with our heads held high, proclaiming our victory in Christ.

The time of the **distress of nations**, with fear running riot in the unbelieving world, will immediately be followed by **the Son of Man coming in a cloud with power and great glory**, which is the rapture of the church. Every time I read these, and similar Scriptures, I feel a thrill of anticipation run through me. We are a privileged people. We should be excited. If we really trust and believe God we shall be.

So, how do we view the threatening situations around us? What is our response to reports of the latest incurable disease, the destruction of our ecology, the Godless liberal agenda taking over, violence in our schools, witchcraft as a common and open practice, and homosexuality becoming acceptable?

Knowledge of the Word, knowledge of the Word, and more knowledge of the Word. Romans 10 tells us, [17]**faith comes by hearing, and hearing by the word of God**. We must operate by faith and walk in all godly wisdom. When we know and understand God's divine plan for us we shall be able to stand, fearless and victorious, even in the midst of the world preparing for the tribulation.

> James 1
> **5 If any of you lacks wisdom, let him ask of God, who gives to all liberally and without reproach, and it will be given to him.**
> **6 But let him ask in faith, with no doubting, for he who doubts is like a wave of the sea driven and tossed by the wind.**
> **7 For let not that man suppose that he will receive anything from the Lord;**

We must do nothing based upon emotion or intellect, but only upon the truth of the Word. That includes our perception of, and reaction to, the daily unfolding of events around us.

An Invasion Of Witchcraft

Witchcraft is everywhere we look and increasing daily. The print media write about it, television produces documentaries about it and makes sitcoms that trivialize its import and give it the appearance of benevolence. Witchcraft, and all other practices of the occult, are forms of Satanism. They are works of the god of this world who will, as soon as the body of Christ is out of the way, rise up and rule for seven years. The attributes of Antichrist, witchcraft among them, are taking an ever firmer hold in our society as the coming of Jesus draws closer. Not only are they out in the open, they are aggressively permeating every area of society.

We should view them in the same way we would a king cobra, hood extended, coiled to strike, and staring us right in the eye. If we had any sense at all we would give it a wide berth. Not only that but, knowing of its existence, we would keep watch for it in order to avoid any contact. The cobra cannot harm us by its existence, but it can kill us if we get too close.

John 3
19 And this is the condemnation, that the light has come into the world, and men loved darkness rather than light, because their deeds were evil.
20 For everyone practicing evil hates the light and does not come to the light, lest his deeds should be exposed.
21 But he who does the truth comes to the light, that his deeds may be clearly seen, that they have been done in God.

The rules for avoiding the ploys and snares of the enemy are no different than those for avoiding the cobra. Satan constantly sets alluring traps to draw believers, and especially their children, into demonic territory. Satan cannot overpower us—he does not have the authority—so, to draw us into his influence, he has to lure, tempt, and intimidate.

It is our responsibility to resist such temptations and intimidations. It is our responsibility to recognize the seemingly harmless when it is not harmless at all. It is our responsibility to remember 1 Corinthians 5, **[6]a little leaven leavens the whole lump**. Complacency and scriptural ignorance are the primary shortcomings enabling the devil to lead Christians and their children into harm's way, even to total disaster. There is no satanic power that can stand against the blood of Jesus, but ours is the responsibility to invoke the blood and stand invincible.

Revelation 12
11 And they overcame him by the blood of the Lamb and by the word of their testimony, and they did not love their lives to the death.

Even if there are two dozen high priests of Satan chanting incantations and performing black magic in front of our houses, trying to put all manner of curses upon us and our families, they are doomed to failure unless we receive their evil. Why? They will run smack dab into the blood of Jesus. But, to fear them on any level is to receive their evil. When we know and walk in our authority in Christ we can laugh at the devil, as God does, and make him our footstool. Curses will bounce off us and return to the devil where they belong.

Dealing with witchcraft in the world around us is not the same as overcoming generational curses. Generational curses are in a different category. They must be directly broken and cut off by the power of the blood and the anointing. They are curses that have come down, for any number of reasons, through the generations. Some ancestor may have practiced divination. A relative may have accepted a curse that has travelled down through the generations unchecked. This can take any form: heart disease, cancer, diabetes, arthritis, depression, nervous disorders, insanity, divorce, early death, suicide, or any other destructive agenda that may run in a family.

It is good to have generational curses broken off infants while they are still in the womb, so that they are born free of any rights-of-way that the devil may hold. I believe that all children born with birth defects are a result of generational curses. Everyone coming to Christ later in life needs this same cleansing. It is part of putting the past to death.

Strength comes from knowledge. We learn in Matthew 4 that Jesus defeated the devil three times in the wilderness with, **It is written**. He did not get all disturbed and scared and start wringing His hands and cry out, "Oh, Father, what am I going to do?" He did not search frantically for His copy of the Scriptures and thrash through them for a verse that applied to the situation.

"Of course not!" you think. "That's absurd!" you say. "He would never behave in such a manner!" you proclaim. "He was Christ Jesus, the King of kings and the Lord of lords!"

Ah-ha! Are you, yourself, not in Christ? 1 John 2 says, [6]**He who says he abides in Him ought himself also to walk just as He walked**.

Confronted by Satan, the Word of God flowed out of Jesus' mouth. He responded with the Word, in total authority, and contemptuously dismissed the devil who, thereupon, had no choice but to mutter inanities and leave. Contempt is the only correct response to the devil. Jesus went into hell, after His death on the cross, and took back all the authority and dominion that Adam had given away in the garden. You must realize that the devil is, after all, a stupid fool who has already been defeated. Jesus made a public mockery of him and his demons, triumphing over them for all to see.

> Colossians 2
> **6 As you have therefore received Christ Jesus the Lord, so walk in Him,**
> **7 rooted and built up in Him and established in the faith, as you have been taught, abounding in it with thanksgiving.**
> **8 Beware lest anyone cheat you through philosophy and empty deceit, according to the tradition of men, according to the basic principles of the world, and not according to Christ.**
> **9 For in Him dwells all the fullness of the Godhead bodily;**
> **10 and you are complete in Him, who is the head of all principality and power.**
> **15 Having disarmed principalities and powers, He made a public spectacle of them, triumphing over them in it.**

Satan cannot overpower a blood-bought, Spirit-filled believer unless given permission by the believer. Satan gets permission to afflict or curse whenever someone accepts what he is trying to do. He gets permission when someone fears his alleged power. The way to deny the devil is to proclaim God's Word and act on it.

> 1 Peter 5
> **8 Be sober, be vigilant; because your adversary the devil walks about like a roaring lion, seeking whom he may devour.**
> **9 Resist him, steadfast in the faith, knowing that the same sufferings are experienced by your brotherhood in the world.**
> **10 But may the God of all grace, who called us to His eternal glory by Christ Jesus, after you have suffered a while, perfect, establish, strengthen, and settle you.**
> **11 To Him be the glory and the dominion forever and ever. Amen.**

People's lack of comprehension of Scripture stems, in good measure, from their lack of understanding, not of Hebrew or Greek, but of the

English language itself. **The devil walks about like a roaring lion, seeking whom he may devour.** "May" means "permitted" or "allowed" to; it does not mean "able" to. It is our obligation to resist the devil and all his forms of destruction, including sickness, disease, poverty, lack, and oppression of every kind. He cannot prevail against us when we deny him our permission.

To have **suffered a while** means to have resisted. Resisting is much tougher than giving in, even when giving in leads to pain. Resist sin, resist affliction, resist weakness, resist all that Jesus bore for you on the cross (Deuteronomy 28:15-68). Suffering does not mean bearing the curse of the Law. That is a big, fat, hairy religious lie! Jesus has already done that on our behalf. God created us to be the head and not the tail, above and not beneath.

John 16
33 These things I have spoken to you, that in Me you may have peace. In the world you will have tribulation; but be of good cheer, I have overcome the world.

In the world you will have tribulation does not refer to the great tribulation that will follow the rapture of the church; it refers to the tribulation that we all experience in our every-day lives. It does not, however, constitute an instruction to meekly accept tribulation. Jesus gave us His Holy Spirit to remove every burden and destroy every yoke. 1 Peter 2 calls us, [9]**a chosen generation, a royal priesthood, a holy nation, His own special people.** We are in the world, but we are not to be of it. We are called to be separate, separated unto God.

I do not know which is more dangerous, the fear of witchcraft or playing with it. The former grants it power; the latter is referred to in 1 Corinthians 15, [33]**Do not be deceived: Evil company corrupts good habits.** Certain destruction is the fruit of either one. The correct posture is to recognize witchcraft and know that it has no authority over us unless we grant it, however, we must avoid it to the best of our ability just because it is evil. So, to repeat the principle: bending every effort to stay away from witchcraft is wisdom, but fearing it grants it power. We must refuse to let divination, in any form, have any part in our lives. Romans 12 tells us to, [9]**Abhor what is evil. Cling to what is good.** Make this your yardstick.

Isaiah 54
17 "no weapon formed against you shall prosper, and every tongue which rises against you in judgment you shall condemn. This is the heritage of the servants of the Lord, and their righteousness is from Me," says the Lord.

This is a powerful and comforting promise. We should have confidence in it. We also, however, need to take seriously our part in overcoming those things which threaten us. We must actively condemn everything that rises up against us.

People tend to be intrigued with witchcraft. They are conditioned to it from childhood. Think about the Disney movies, both old and new: *The Sorcerer's Apprentice, Snow White, Cinderella, The Wizard of Oz, Beauty and the Beast, Aladdin,* and all the rest. Yes, I agree that these movies, until we knew better, were funny, cute, and drew us into a world of delightful fantasy. Or were they?

"What could be so wrong?" we ask. "No one takes that stuff seriously," we defend. "After all, it's just fantasy, and good always overcomes evil," we aver.

That may be true but, and this is the crux of the matter, witchcraft, spells, divination and incantations were thus presented to us, and are now presented to our children, in an intriguing way, a way that renders witchcraft acceptable. The very fact that we did not take it seriously allowed it to enter in. The hard truth is that there are foul spirits attached to all such things, and they enter through our eyes and ears when we are unaware. They are now entering the children of all those who permit these "harmless fantasies" into their households.

When we see through the eyes of the Spirit, in the wisdom of God, we recoil in the face of any occult practice, no matter how adorable its packaging. The church must take off its blinders and see the devil's tactics for what they really are. I know that I loved, yes loved, the animated Disney movies. I not only adored them in my youth, but enjoyed them just as much when I watched them with my own children. I was completely drawn in to the whole atmosphere. One of the most difficult things for me to do was reject them. I did not want to, but when the Lord stripped off the veneer and showed me the devil's agenda and the raw evil contained in these so-called harmless fantasies, the truth was undeniable. Even though I did not want to accept the truth, I finally opened my eyes and repented. Witchcraft in all its forms is pure evil, an abomination in God's sight.

> Deuteronomy 18
> **9 When you come into the land which the Lord your God is giving you, you shall not learn to follow the abominations of those nations.**
> **10 There shall not be found among you anyone who makes his son or his daughter pass through the fire, or one who practices witchcraft, or a soothsayer, or one who interprets omens, or a sorcerer,**
> **11 or one who conjures spells, or a medium, or a spiritist, or one who calls up the dead.**
> **12 For all who do these things are an abomination to the Lord, and because of these abominations the Lord your God drives them out from before you.**
> **13 You shall be blameless before the Lord your God.**
> **14 For these nations which you will dispossess listened to soothsayers and diviners; but as for you, the Lord your God has not appointed such for you.**

My older son was fourteen and my younger son six when I was born again. Quite a few years passed before I realized how thoroughly the children and I had become desensitized to witchcraft by seemingly innocent movies. When I accepted the truth I started noticing that pastors, even in charismatic churches, used Disney movies in their children's ministries, movies laden with witchcraft. When I made so bold as to question the use of such movies as part of church agenda, one would think, from leadership reaction, that I had just challenged the existence of God. I was rebuked for being out of line, and my objections were brushed aside without consideration.

One of these pastors recommended to me a C.S Lewis series of books for children, *The Tales of Narnia*. I scanned the pages, expressed astonishment, and asked why the pastor was condoning the witchcraft contained in these books.

"Oh, don't worry," he said soothingly, "After all, they were written by a very famous Christian. Surely you don't think he would have done anything wrong? Don't tell me you have a problem with him, too?"

"Wake up," I wanted to scream. "What about the *Magician's Nephew*, or *The Lion, the Witch and the Wardrobe*, don't you understand? What about the concept of witches is so elusive?" I held my tongue but, perhaps, I should just have let fly. What was there to lose?

Leadership is flesh and, regrettably, frequently wrong; wrong about the Word, wrong about things of the world, and wrong in its counseling. We must never forget that we are responsible for searching out the truth for ourselves. It will avail us no more to blame Satan's little victories in our lives on the pastor than to blame them on ignorance. They are both the same thing, our own failure to put everything we hear, see, and read to the Word test.

Children's fare such as *The Wizard of Oz, Bedknobs and Broomsticks*, and a couple of movies my mother, Bette Davis, made for Disney called *Watcher in the Woods* and *Return to Witch Mountain*, were tremendously popular. They, and many like them, are still shown on television. As time has passed, Satan's agenda to indoctrinate children has intensified. This has caused almost no ripples in the church which has been lulled into a false sense of security where entertainment is concerned. Christians are prone to say, "No one takes it seriously, so what's the big deal?" The big deal is that foul spirits come through any representation of witchcraft, and those spirits can and will attach to anyone participating in it.

There is a reason that children are so rebellious these days. Rebellion is a foul spirit. Parents, teachers, and even pastors, battle rebellion in their children while, through ignorance, they open the door by which that very same spirit of rebellion gains entry.

I Samuel 15
**22 ...Behold, to obey is better than sacrifice, and to heed than the fat of rams.
23 For rebellion is as the sin of witchcraft, and stubbornness is as iniquity and idolatry. Because you have rejected the word of the Lord, He also has rejected you from being king.**

Even Spirit-filled people, who cannot be possessed, can be oppressed. Demons can attach to the flesh and be just as destructive as if they were indwelling. They are aggressive and do not need much of an opening to do their dirty work. Do not be deceived by the popular myth that you have to agree with evil to have it overtake. That is wrong. All you have to do is give it a tiny opening. The spirits of divination, witchcraft, wizardry, idolatry, and all familiar spirits are a work of the flesh and can attach to the flesh. Remember that Satan is merely a fallen angel. He can only work through the realm of the flesh.

> Galatians 5
> **19 Now the works of the flesh are evident, which are: adultery, fornication, uncleanness, licentiousness,**
> **20 idolatry, sorcery, hatred, contentions, jealousies, outbursts of wrath, selfish ambitions, dissensions, heresies,**
> **21 envy, murders, drunkenness, revelries, and the like; of which I tell you beforehand, just as I also told you in time past, that those who practice such things will not inherit the kingdom of God.**

Many years ago *Bewitched* was a successful television series starring my long-ago friend Elizabeth Montgomery. She played Samantha the witch and the show presented her as sweet, funny, and thoroughly lovable. It thus presented witchcraft as harmless and amusing. The devil's purpose is to spoon-feed the world his evil with a sugar coating. This show is still effecting people today in reruns.

Another highly successful television series, which more closely targets young people, is *Sabrina the Teenage Witch*. It features a clever, funny, teenage witch as the title character and, no big surprise, it first appeared on the network owned by Disney.

There is an ever-increasing section on New Age and the occult in every bookstore and, not only that, but such things as *The Teen Witch Kit* that claim to teach the reader how to cast spells, shape change, and transport, are readily available. The theme of witchcraft has found its way into an increasingly high percentage of our television programs, movies and books.

This conditioning, brainwashing if you will, has numbed a startling number of Christians to the point where they vehemently defend their right to do as their flesh pleases and completely ignore the Word of

The Rapture, The Tribulation, And Beyond

God. **Now the works of the flesh are evident, which are...idolatry, sorcery**.

1 Thessalonians 5
**21 Test all things; hold fast what is good.
22 Abstain from every form of evil.**

Parents trying to open their spiritual eyes ask me how to judge the books, programs, and movies available for their children to watch. They ask how to know whether or not something is satanic. I suggest a simple test: is anything or anyone being portrayed as having supernatural powers who does not directly and openly attribute those powers to Jesus Christ? If there is any such, it is satanic. That pretty well sweeps the decks clean, doesn't it?

The merchandising of youth-oriented entertainment has become a well-oiled machine. Long before a new movie is shown, whether animated or with live actors, the toys and games that accompany it are available in the stores and, as premiums, in *McDonald's*, *Burger King*, and elsewhere. This puts witchcraft physically into the hands of our children. Figures, cards, stickers, clothes, jewelry, board games, and video games that allow children to participate actively in the occult are available in abundance. Staggering numbers of children begin to identify with the evil characters and satanic plots, even mimicking the incantations they see and hear.

We see these products saturate the marketplace with lightning speed. Things like *Pokemon* and *Harry Potter* suddenly appear everywhere "as if by magic." Every store one enters and every check-out counter at which one stands has them prominently on display. *Pokemon* actually means "pocket monster." It promotes a world of "friendly" demons and, just like *Dungeons and Dragons* before it, is preparing and indoctrinating children to accept monsters and evil people as friends. Satan's purpose is to condition the world to accept the beast and his mark when the tribulation begins. Once people are indoctrinated into the occult, or simply numbed to the existence of it, they will not even struggle against taking the mark of the beast.

Harry Potter is a series of books in which the title character is an apprentice warlock, or wizard. The reader learns spells and curses as these tales unfold. Each book takes Harry higher in ability and rank in the occult. As this happens, the reader climbs with him and becomes more and more obsessed with spells, incantations, transportation, and shape changing.

So many Christians have such an alarming determination to remain ignorant ostriches that witchcraft is running rampant among our younger generation. Because *Harry Potter* is classified as fiction it is dismissed as mere fantasy. Even though Harry may be a fictional character in fictional situations, I assure you that the witchcraft is real.

Matthew 18
2 And Jesus called a little child to Him, set him in the midst of them,
3 and said, "Assuredly, I say to you, unless you are converted and become as little children, you will by no means enter the kingdom of heaven.
4 "Therefore whoever humbles himself as this little child is the greatest in the kingdom of heaven.
5 "And whoever receives one little child like this in My name receives Me.
6 "But whoever causes one of these little ones who believe in Me to sin, it would be better for him if a millstone were hung around his neck, and he were drowned in the depth of the sea.
7 "Woe to the world because of offenses! For offenses must come, but woe to that man by whom the offense comes!"

Witchcraft is evil. It is bad enough that people are sufficiently deluded to think there is benign, or "white," witchcraft, but to be so blind as to indoctrinate, or permit the indoctrination of, their children into witchcraft, divination and wizardry is despicable. All those parents who are buying *Harry Potter* and its paraphernalia, enabling their children to learn the black arts and to be led into darkness, will bear the wrath of God. **For offenses must come, but woe to the man by whom the offense comes!**

Every parent, grandparent, aunt, uncle, sister, brother or friend who pulls a child away from Jesus by making this satanic filth available to him is doomed. Christian parents are responsible for keeping *Harry*

Potter and all such abomination out of the hands of their children.

I have had born-again, Word-loving Christian parents say to me that they just cannot bring themselves to forcibly remove *Harry Potter* from their children. They say their children see nothing wrong, that they think it is harmless fantasy. They want me to pray that their children will see the evil and choose to get rid of it. That irresponsible policy will lead to the children becoming fully indoctrinated and unable to turn away. It does not matter what the child, whether five or fifteen, thinks, the parent's house is God's dwelling place and it is up to the parent to keep it holy.

If your child were playing with a loaded gun in his room, would you reason with him or forcibly remove it, leaving the reasoning until later? If your child suffered from anorexia and then developed a taste for rat bait, would you say? "Well, at least she's eating." If your child were lazy in science class, but developed a sudden interest in building bombs, would you say? "Well, at least he's studying."

Of course you wouldn't!

Well, many poor, misguided souls who have permitted *Harry Potter* books into the house say of their children, "Well, at least they're reading." May God forgive you if you are one such!

We are all watchmen in the kingdom of God. We are required to warn those around us of evil, particularly when they are children. If we do not, and they perish in their ignorance, we, the watchmen, are responsible (Ezekiel 33:6).

Christians who permit *Pokemon* and *Harry Potter* into their homes are playing right into the devil's hands. They are likely to be the same parents who refuse to take satanic rock music away from their children. Satan uses groups like *Marilyn Manson* to overtake young people. Marilyn Manson openly declared himself to be a high priest of Satan. The disgusting things typical of him and his group do not even bear mentioning. Lucifer was trained in the creation of music by God, Himself, before he was cast down and became Satan (Ezekiel 28:16). The devil knows how to use music to corrupt and destroy. God's people must be sober, vigilant, and knowledgeable, and refuse to back down from the fight of faith. It is a fight to the end and we have the weapons to win.

The satanic agenda in entertainment is not a new idea on the devil's part. Such things as *Grimm's Fairy Tales*, magicians, sorcerers,

Frankenstein, Dracula, werewolves, and divers other monsters, have been around for a very long time. The appeal of all of them is based on fear. Fear opens the door to the demonic. Fear and faith are directly opposed to each other. They cannot coexist. No Christian has any business watching a horror movie or anything else that begets fear. God has no part in fear. Receiving fear is receiving the devil. When fear raises its ugly head, a believer must immediately cast it out. He certainly should not seek it out for a cheap thrill.

2 Timothy 1
7 For God has not given us a spirit of fear, but of power and of love and of a sound mind.

In many cities Wicca, a witchcraft cult, is openly advertised in newspapers and on local television and is promoted as a benevolent religion. It draws many into the lie that there is white, or good, witchcraft. Wrong! Witchcraft is black and evil. Do not entertain any other view.

The psychic networks and people who offer Tarot card readings are also poison. Do not even watch their commercials. There are deceiving spirits waiting there to draw you into their web. The moment you give place to it you are open to witchcraft. Do not think you can watch and be amused by it and remain unaffected by its evil. Some people even call the psychic hot-lines in the mistaken belief they can witness to the people on the other end of the phone. There is no good fruit there. Playing in a toxic waste dump can kill you.

Likewise, astrology is a form of witchcraft. Do not even read the horoscopes in newspapers and magazines. When someone says to you, "What's your sign?" tell them you are under the sign of the cross. Do not be categorized by an astrological sign and, thereby, participate in divination. Magicians and astrologers are placed in the same category as wizards, soothsayers, and all other occult practices (Daniel 1:20, 2:2,10,27, 4:7, 5:7-15 and Isaiah 47:12-15). These things are not a game. They are evil.

Magic, even if referred to as illusion, has its roots in, and therefore carries the spirits of, witchcraft. To start with, the whole purpose of magic is to induce one to believe a lie. Ignorant parents sometimes encourage their children to participate in various forms of magic/witchcraft in games and events. Ouija boards are a prime example.

I have heard from some, who were high level witches and warlocks before they were delivered and born again, that their journey with Satan began with a Ouija board someone gave them as a child. As they played with it, the forces of darkness moved into them and they were "hooked." Be sure that there is nothing of this sort in your house. Do not be intimidated by your children into allowing such evil in their lives. It is your house, sanctified to the Lord, and you must not permit evil to inhabit your dwelling. If your children bring such things in, you are responsible to throw them out.

Halloween is another abomination. Every element of it is rooted in ancient paganism. Halloween is the high holy day of the church of Satan. Human infants are sacrificed on Satan's altars on that night. Teenage virgin girls are drugged and raped by every male in the coven and then slaughtered as an offering to Satan. The whole coven then drinks their blood and dances naked around their mutilated bodies. Some even eat their flesh. If you want to verify any of this, go to a library or a chain bookstore and read the satanic bible or a book on Satanism. Do not bring these books into your home, but look at them in the library or the bookstore and leave them there.

Most of the Halloween images and symbols with which we are familiar are based in the practice of witchcraft. Even the popular scene of witches' cauldrons bubbling and foaming as the witches toss in all sorts of disgusting things, while chanting curses and spells, are not to be taken lightly. Art imitates life. Shakespeare wrote these cackling creatures of darkness into his work. Witchcraft in any form is evil and, therefore, an abomination to God. Those who practice it in any form, or aid and abet it in any way, make themselves an equal abomination.

There is no excuse for a Christian to partake of Halloween. Even if you dress your child as an angel, a ballerina, or a biblical character, and then go to a Halloween party or door to door "trick-or-treating," you are partaking of evil. I post a sign in front of my house on October 31st which says, "Halloween is a satanic celebration. We are Christians and do not partake of evil."

Seances, which purport to call up the dead, are divination. They open doors to demonic realms. Ghosts, voices, table-knocking, etc., no matter their appearance, are not manifestations relating to real people who have died. They are demons mimicking people who have died for the purpose of finding a home, which is to say, joining with the flesh of those stupid enough to indulge in this form of witchcraft. If you belong to Jesus you are part of the light and must walk in the light. There are no half-measures. There is no slack. This is all or nothing.

In this day and time we cannot assume that anything or anybody is benign. All must be tested against the Word. Satan is the master deceiver and works his evil through men. Men run churches and thus, regrettably, Satan is fully capable of working his evil through churches.

> 2 Corinthians 11
> **13 For such are false apostles, deceitful workers, transforming themselves into apostles of Christ.**
> **14 And no wonder! For Satan himself transforms himself into an angel of light.**
> **15 Therefore it is no great thing if his ministers also transform themselves into ministers of righteousness, whose end will be according to their works.**

There is no communication with the dead as many, principally half a billion or so members of a large denomination, believe. The spirits whom such people believe to be those of their relatives are demons, the disembodied spirits of the pre-Adamic race. These spirits either indwell the people with whom the living are trying to communicate, or are just imitating them. Either way, the living are not communicating with dead people but with demons.

> Leviticus 20
> **6 And the person who turns after mediums and familiar spirits, to prostitute himself with them, I will set My face against that person and cut him off from his people.**
> **7 Sanctify yourselves therefore, and be holy, for I am the Lord your God.**

Believing that one has been reincarnated is also the result of communication with demons. People have vivid, accurate memories of past lives and, quite naturally, believe their own minds. All that is happening, actually, is that a demon within them is feeding their minds with the memories of its own previous hosts. There is no such thing as reincarnation. God creates each person, only once, as a unique being with an eternal spirit. We do not come and go in different forms. When people get caught up in past lives they have fellowship with demons. They will be overcome by evil, giving new host bodies to the same foul spirits that dwelt in those they think they are.

The pre-Adamic race is the race God created before He created Adam. We are the Adamic race. Genesis 1 says, [1]**In the beginning God created the heavens and the earth.** [2]**The earth was without form, and void;**—"tohu and bohu" in the Hebrew, meaning utter chaos—**and darkness was on the face of the deep**. What God created in verse 1 was perfect. He did not have to create chaos and then create order out of it. When Lucifer rebelled, and took his people, the pre-Adamic race, to eternal damnation, God destroyed His creation and rendered it "tohu and bohu." Isaiah 14:20 tells us that Lucifer's people shall ever remain nameless for their transgression, thus our need to refer to them as "Lucifer's people," or the "pre-Adamic race." God next created order, all over again, for us, His second creation, the race beginning with Adam. Lucifer's people were not created, as we were, in God's image.

The pre-Adamic race is described in Isaiah 14 and Ezekiel 26-28, and there are clues elsewhere. One such is God telling Adam and Eve to depart the garden, in Genesis 1 (KJV), and [28]**replenish the earth**. There had to have been people there before if they were to *re*plenish the earth.

It is important to understand this for two reasons. The first is to understand the nature of fallen angels, as opposed to demons. Fallen angels do not need our bodies as hosts; demons do. The second is that we are not to be disturbed by scientific discoveries that date things as having occurred millions, or hundreds of millions, of years ago. Such discoveries do not contradict the Bible; they merely relate to events that are part of pre-Adamic history. Dinosaurs, cave paintings, and prehistoric man are all part of the first creation. We have no idea how many millions or billions of years lie between Genesis 1:1 and Genesis 1:2, and it does not matter.

God put the cities of the pre-Adamic race under the sea forever (chapters 26-28 of Ezekiel). If archaeologists ever find the submerged city they call Atlantis, it will be one of these cities. God intends us to know these things in order that we remain confident in the unshakable reality of His Word.

Know Your Enemy

A Christian must never participate in an activity or organization unless he knows its roots. There are many seemingly benign organizations that have their roots in the occult and/or eastern mysticism. They are often disguised by good works.

Freemasonry and the Shriners are involved in Satan worship. The Mormon church, the Jehovah's Witnesses, the Church of Scientology, and many denominations, are actually cults. Many other denominations, by their professed tenets, openly and brazenly deny the baptism of the Holy Spirit and tongues and, thus, are guilty of the unpardonable sin, blaspheming the Holy Spirit. The list goes on.

Civil War reenactment and organizations that focus on the Confederacy are merely guises to promote racism. They are much the same as the Aryan Nation, the John Birch Society, and the Ku Klux Klan. Anyone who even thinks along the lines of racial purity is dangerously deceived. God recognizes only two races of people: covenant people, who are all of the seed of Abraham; and non-covenant people, who are not.

> Matthew 5
> **33 Again you have heard that it was said to those of old, "You shall not swear falsely, but shall perform your oaths to the Lord."**
> **34 But I say to you, do not swear at all: neither by heaven, for it is God's throne;**
> **35 nor by the earth, for it is His footstool; nor by Jerusalem, for it is the city of the great King.**
> **36 Nor shall you swear by your head, because you cannot make one hair white or black.**
> **37 But let your "Yes" be "Yes," and your "No," "No." For whatever is more than these is from the evil one.**

Jesus classifies the swearing of oaths to be of the devil. He also promises to make every secret thing come to light. Everything associated with Christ Jesus is done in the light, out in the open for all to see. There is nothing hidden, nothing in the dark. When something is a secret society, and involves oaths, it should cause alarm bells to ring in your spirit and you should run for your life.

New Age has become popular, particularly on college campuses. There are foolish people who think their beliefs are sanctified because Jesus is mentioned and Scriptures are sprinkled through the same text as a mass of spiritual garbage. New Age is just another form of the occult.

Leviticus 19
31 Give no regard to mediums and familiar spirits; do not seek after them, to be defiled by them: I am the Lord your God.

Tattooing and otherwise defacing the body are ungodly practices. Even though the following Scriptures are from the Old Testament they represent principles important to God. Simply put, God created us in His image. Defacing that image is wrong.

Leviticus 19
28 You shall not make any cuttings in your flesh for the dead, nor tattoo any marks on you: I am the Lord.

Anyone tattooed or defaced prior to his or her new birth should renounce the significance of the tattoos or defacements, cut off the spirits, receive sanctification, and let the blood cover them if they are not removable.

We have the account of Elijah and his confrontation with the four hundred and fifty prophets of Baal and four hundred prophets of Asherah. They strived in vain all day to get their god to demonstrate his power by burning up an offering. Elijah, in 1 Kings 18, showed his contempt for, and mocked, these prophets who, [28]**cried aloud, and cut themselves, as was their custom, with knives and lances, until the blood gushed out on them**. All such marring of the flesh was designed in advance by the devil to mock the pierced hands, feet, and side of Jesus on the cross.

Then it was Elijah's turn. He built his altar and called upon the Lord

God almighty Who immediately burned up the sacrifice, even after Elijah had poured water on it. Elijah should be our example in this hour. Far from being drawn into evil practices, we should stand firm and mock the devil, knowing that our God is the only One and there is no other.

Another pastime in which Christians unwisely get involved is martial arts. Some churches even allow the use of their facilities for classes in them and encourage their youth to participate. Many, through ignorance, think this is a healthy and useful pursuit for young people. The trouble is, the roots of all forms of martial arts lie in eastern mysticism. I have spoken to serious Christians who used to practice martial arts and they tell me that all the words, sounds, and even the breathing, involve the names of demons upon whom they were calling for power and strength.

The yin-yang is featured as a symbol in virtually all martial arts clubs and has become common elsewhere. I am sure you have seen it. It is a circle divided in half by a curving line. One side is white and the other black, a contrasting dot in the center of each side. The yin-yang has become extremely popular among young people and I have heard it defended as representing balance. Wrong! It actually represents the divided mind, divided between light and dark. It is a sign of great evil and will have an effect on all who wear it, or have it, because the antichrist spirit is attached to it. Get rid of it wherever you find it. You should look for it on stickers, jewelry, video games and your child's school materials.

Stay away from any unknown symbols. Things such as the yin-yang, crystals, and the pentagram are to be avoided like the plague. Make sure your children do not have any of them. The cross is all we need as a symbol, although the Christian fish is also fine and I have one on my car. Both signify only Jesus.

Never assume that something with which you are unfamiliar is acceptable. This is serious business. The ankh, an Egyptian symbol of worship which is sort of a cross with a loop at the top, and all pyramids and other Egyptian symbols, are anathema. Much of this is incorporated in jewelry design, wallpaper, and fabric patterns, even furniture, carpets, and architecture.

Isaiah 19

3 "The spirit of Egypt will fail in its midst; I will destroy their counsel, and they will consult the idols and the charmers, the mediums and the sorcerers.
4 "And the Egyptians I will give into the hand of a cruel master, and a fierce king will rule over them," says the Lord, the Lord of hosts.

The **fierce king** is Satan. All Egyptian symbolism has sorcery attached to it, and that sorcery will attach to anyone who embraces it.

The Spirit Of The Antichrist

The antichrist spirit is set in opposition to the Holy Spirit. Antichrist himself will not be revealed until the beginning of the great tribulation, however, the antichrist spirit has long been at work in the world and Christians must be able to identify it. It exists in religion, as well as the world, and is becoming more aggressive as we approach the end of the age. Anything that opposes the baptism of the Holy Spirit and the evidence of tongues, or even limits it, is an antichrist spirit.

1 John 4

2 By this you know the Spirit of God: Every spirit that confesses that Jesus Christ has come in the flesh is of God,
3 and every spirit that does not confess that Jesus Christ has come in the flesh is not of God. And this is the spirit of the Antichrist, which you have heard was coming, and is now already in the world.

Confessing that Jesus Christ walked upon the earth in human flesh is not a criterion for anything. Even Satan admits that, along with atheists, demons, Buddhists, Muslims, Hari Krishnas, and all the rest. **Every spirit that confesses that Jesus Christ has come in the flesh** refers to the acknowledgement that Jesus Christ, by the baptism of the Holy Spirit, has come into, and dwells in, the flesh of all true believers. That is where the battle lines are drawn.

There are whole denominations that proclaim tongues to be from the devil and reject out of hand the Holy Spirit baptism. Do not be deceived by their using the Name of the Holy Spirit in prayer; it is not the same thing. Reverencing the Holy Spirit, and receiving His power in our flesh, is so important that Jesus declared the attribution of the Holy Spirit's work to Satan to be the one unforgivable sin.

Mark 3
22 And the scribes who came down from Jerusalem said, "He has Beelzebub," and, "By the ruler of the demons He casts out demons."
23 So He called them to Him and said to them in parables...
28 "Assuredly, I say to you, all sins will be forgiven the sons of men, and whatever blasphemies they may utter;
29 "but he who blasphemes against the Holy Spirit never has forgiveness, but is subject to eternal condemnation"
30 because they said, "He has an unclean spirit."

There are only two forces at work in the world, God and Satan, so let us get something absolutely clear: there is no difference between, a) attributing the work of the Holy Spirit to Satan, and, b) declaring that a sign, wonder or miracle was not the work of the Holy Spirit. I am going to say that again: there is no difference between saying the Holy Spirit did not do it, and saying Satan did do it. When someone denies that the Holy Spirit is responsible for a miracle, he attributes that miracle to the devil. It is one or the other because there is no third alternative. The Holy Spirit is God on earth and must be reverenced and loved. To do otherwise is to commit the unforgivable sin and be **subject to eternal condemnation**.

Mark 16
16 "He who believes and is baptized will be saved; but he who does not believe will be condemned.
17 "And these signs will follow those who believe: In My name they will cast out demons; they will speak with new tongues;
18 "they will take up serpents; and if they drink anything deadly, it will by no means hurt them; they will lay hands on the sick, and they will recover."

**19 So then, after the Lord had spoken to them, He was received up into heaven, and sat down at the right hand of God.
20 And they went out and preached everywhere, the Lord working with them and confirming the word through the accompanying signs. Amen.**

The baptism referred to by Jesus in verse 16 is the Holy Spirit baptism, as verses 17 and 18 reveal. Water baptism, though wonderful and scriptural, is not a salvation requirement. Water baptism is merely an outward sign of an inward work. One can be submerged all day long but, without the Holy Spirit, one does not become a new creature in Christ. Christ is not Jesus' last name. It means "the anointed One in His anointing." The term "Christ Jesus" lets us know that we are talking about the anointed Jesus. Jesus did no miracles until God baptized Him with the Holy Spirit—anointed Him—at the river Jordan.

In order to **cast out demons...speak with new tongues...lay hands on the sick, and they will recover**, one must be baptized in the Holy Spirit and, thus, be one **who believes**. Those very things are what identify one as a believer. If you want to know whether a person is a believer, or an organization or church is made up of believers, all you have to do is find out whether they cast out demons, speak with other tongues, and lay hands on the sick that they recover. If they do not do it—and I don't mean they just talk about it or say they believe in it, I mean they do it—they are not believers. Don't blame me; Jesus said it.

Acts 10
38 how God anointed Jesus of Nazareth with the Holy Spirit and with power, who went about doing good and healing all who were oppressed by the devil, for God was with Him.

This is the anointing, received through the baptism of the Holy Spirit, that on the day of Pentecost Jesus commanded His disciples—therefore us as well—to receive (Acts 1:4-8). Ephesians 2 tells us that if we do not have the Holy Spirit we are, [12]**without God in the world.** God the Father is on His throne in heaven and God the Son is on His throne at the Father's side. We are here and They are there. We may know Them but They are not present with us on earth. God the Holy Spirit is with us and in us. 1 John 4 tells us this is the only way we can overcome the spirit of Antichrist, **⁴because He who is in you is greater than he who is in the world.**

Ephesians 2
12 that at that time you were without Christ, being aliens from the commonwealth of Israel and strangers from the covenants of promise, having no hope and without God in the world.

Romans 8
9 But you are not in the flesh but in the Spirit, if indeed the Spirit of God dwells in you. Now if anyone does not have the Spirit of Christ, he is not His.

The Holy Spirit is, we are told in Romans 8, **¹⁵the Spirit of adoption by whom we cry out, "Abba, Father."** The antichrist spirit is working overtime in this final generation because it is Satan's last-ditch, desperate attempt to head off his own demise. He believes that if he succeeds in eliminating the glorious church for which Jesus will return, Jesus will not return; then he, Satan, will never go to the lake of fire. You cannot blame Satan for trying, but make sure you are not guilty of aiding and abetting him.

2 John
7 For many deceivers have gone out into the world who do not confess Jesus Christ as coming in the flesh. This is a deceiver and an antichrist.
8 Look to yourselves, that we do not lose those things we worked for, but that we may receive a full reward.
9 Whoever transgresses and does not abide in the doctrine of Christ does not have God. He who abides in the doctrine of Christ has both the Father and the Son.
10 If anyone comes to you and does not bring this doctrine, do not receive him into your house nor greet him;
11 for he who greets him shares in his evil deeds.

Abiding in the **doctrine of Christ**, or failing to do so, determines whether or not we are of God. To be the body of Christ, we need to have the fullness of the Godhead bodily. If we are not baptized in the Holy Ghost, we are not the body of Christ. Jesus has a perfect body, not a maimed one, and, without the Holy Ghost indwelling us, we would be maimed. We would have but two thirds of God. That is why God made it all or nothing. If we have fellowship with people who deny this doctrine, we give place to the antichrist spirit. That is why we are told to flee from anyone who embraces it, lest we share **in his evil deeds**.

I do not know how the Lord could have made it clearer. It amazes me that people who have received Jesus, and claim to love Him, continue to deny His baptism. How can they have missed this glaring truth? Born-again means born of water and the Spirit (John 3:3-7), born of the amniotic fluid of our natural birth, followed by the baptism of the Holy Spirit.

Antichrist Is A Homosexual

Revelation 11
**7 Now when they finish their testimony, the beast that ascends out of the bottomless pit will make war against them, overcome them, and kill them.
8 And their dead bodies will lie in the street of the great city which spiritually is called Sodom and Egypt, where also our Lord was crucified.**

The antichrist spirit is inherent in the homosexual agenda. Make no mistake, it is not only an agenda but a very aggressive one. There is a reason that gay rights are a major political issue, and that homosexuality has been introduced into so many television shows and movies: Antichrist is a sodomite, a homosexual.

Although the above Scriptures talk about the two end-time witnesses, notice that Jerusalem is referred to spiritually as Sodom. Excepting this one instance, Jerusalem is always referred to as the "great city," "the holy city," "the city of David," or just plain Jerusalem. It is never referred to in a negative way until Revelation 11:8, and then it is likened spiritually to Sodom. Sodomites committed vile acts, foremost among them homosexuality. Their very name came to mean homosexuality.

Genesis 19
**4 Now before they lay down, the men of the city, the men of Sodom, both old and young, all the people from every quarter, surrounded the house.
5 And they called to Lot and said to him, "Where are the men who came to you tonight? Bring them out to us that we may know them carnally."**

How will the holy city suddenly become Sodom? Antichrist will make his throne there during the tribulation and sit in the temple of God (2 Thessalonians 2:4). His vile nature will pollute the city and it will take on his character for seven years.

Antichrist is, even now, gathering his people together, brazenly, out in the open, to be ready for his rule. The world is being forced not only to accept but to approve his agenda. Even the public school system has fallen into line and is conditioning our children to accept homosexuality as an alternative lifestyle rather than a perversion. It has become a punishable offence to say that homosexuality is wrong.

God makes His position clear. The practice of homosexuality, male or female, is an abomination in His sight. Anyone who practices homosexuality, or condones it, does not belong to God. Homosexuals can repent and be born again if they choose to. They can be delivered from the homosexual spirit and be cleansed, whereafter they can live a life of holiness unto God but, so long as they continue in their perversion, they remain a stench in God's nostrils.

Romans 1
**24 Therefore God also gave them up to uncleanness, in the lusts of their hearts, to dishonor their bodies among themselves,
25 who exchanged the truth of God for the lie, and worshiped and served the creature rather than the Creator, who is blessed forever. Amen.
26 For this reason God gave them up to vile passions. For even their women exchanged the natural use for what is against nature.**

27 Likewise also the men, leaving the natural use of the woman, burned in their lust for one another, men with men committing what is shameful, and receiving in themselves the penalty of their error which was due.
28 And even as they did not like to retain God in their knowledge, God gave them over to a debased mind, to do those things which are not fitting;
29 being filled with all unrighteousness, sexual immorality, wickedness, covetousness, maliciousness; full of envy, murder, strife, deceit, evil-mindedness; they are whisperers,
30 backbiters, haters of God, violent, proud, boasters, inventors of evil things, disobedient to parents,
31 undiscerning, untrustworthy, unloving, unforgiving, unmerciful;
32 who, knowing the righteous judgment of God, that those who practice such things are worthy of death, not only do the same but also approve of those who practice them.

1 Corinthians 6
9 Do you not know that the unrighteous will not inherit the kingdom of God? Do not be deceived. Neither fornicators, nor idolaters, nor adulterers, nor homosexuals, nor sodomites,
10 nor thieves, nor covetous, nor drunkards, nor revilers, nor extortioners will inherit the kingdom of God.

Anyone who continues to have doubts regarding God's view of homosexuality is beyond my help.

Leprechauns, Fairies, And All That

The "little people" of Ireland, so beloved in Irish folklore and usually made to appear benevolent, are actually fierce, dark, vicious demons. Ireland, including the Roman Catholic Church, is famous for its superstitions and witchcraft. To hear the press tell it, the countryside is fairly seething with fairies and leprechauns. It is a pity the press does not know enough to mention that fairies and leprechauns are demons.

Do not be deceived by this dark spirit-world that is frequently depicted as light and sweet and fun. That is the alluring veneer with which Satan coats his evil. Fairies may look whimsical and adorable, and be so depicted in the arts, but they are another of Satan's evil concoctions.

Santa Claus and the Easter Bunny should also be categorized as demons. The facts must be faced. Do you love Jesus or do you love the world and, therefore, the god of this world? Santa sits on a big throne, calling all children to come unto him so that he can love them and give them gifts. Santa takes the place of God in children's lives. Magic is attached to him, and the way to get gifts from him is by good behavior (good works). Songs like *Santa Claus is Coming to Town* are even included in Christian Christmas albums. He sure is coming to town; it is called the rise of Antichrist in the tribulation. If you think I am being obsessive, I suggest you spend more time in the Word. There is nothing wrong with the celebration of the birth of Christ, the time we call Christmas, but let's keep demons out of it.

What can possibly be wrong with the cute, fuzzy, generous Easter bunny? you may ask. He is a demon. Easter is the name of a pagan holiday celebrating Eostre, the Teutonic goddess of spring for whom an annual festival was held. Easter was and is a pagan springtime fertility ritual. The rabbit was used as a symbol because of its famous rate of reproduction. The eggs also represent fertility. This fertility rite is still practiced among heathen tribes in Africa, Asia and South America. It includes sexual orgies and occult rituals. The custom of exchanging eggs was practiced in ancient times when Egyptians and Persians dyed eggs and gave them as gifts. The Persians believed that the earth had hatched from a giant egg. The Catholic Church, somewhere back in history, attached Easter to the Lord's resurrection. It has since been proclaimed as a Christian celebration. Rabbits are God-created animals, and eggs are perfectly good food, but they are not religious symbols to be accepted by God's people.

Christians should rejoice over and celebrate Resurrection Sunday. It is an awesome time for the body of Christ, a time to focus on the power of the resurrection. It is not a time for egg-laying rabbits and other pagan rituals.

Romans 8
10 And if Christ is in you, the body is dead because of sin, but

**the Spirit is life because of righteousness.
11 But if the Spirit of Him who raised Jesus from the dead dwells in you, He who raised Christ from the dead will also give life to your mortal bodies through His Spirit who dwells in you.**

We must be ready and willing to judge everything by the Word of God. If Satan cannot draw us into actual fellowship with his demons, he will try to divert us from the truth of Jesus Christ through distractions like weeping or bleeding statues, special waters that are supposed to heal, or stigmata. These are all designed by the devil to lead people into idol worship. Those who believe in these things worship not Christ Jesus but the statue, the rock, the pool of water, the wounds, the holes, the blood or whatever. All these things are lying signs and wonders, as are the priests and nuns who spontaneously bleed on specific holy days.

The Political Arena

A great deal is said about politics and world events during discussions of the final moments of the age. I am not going to get into specifics in this area because they are daily subject to change. Christians who major in geopolitics must constantly make adjustments to accommodate unexpected swings on the world scene. My aim is to give readers a practical view of the events around us. My focus is the events and situations that directly impact our lives. We need to understand why mothers are casually murdering their children, why teenage girls are dropping their newborns in dumpsters, why children are regularly shooting other children in schools, why rebellion is running riot among our youth, and why there is a general and marked deterioration in the quality of life as we knew it.

It is undeniable that biblical prophecy is being fulfilled daily. Everything that happens is significant, further evidence of the soon coming of Christ Jesus. The fact that abortion has become a political issue is evidence of the condition of the world. Candidates are either pro-life or pro-abortion. It is a litmus test. I do not recognize the label of pro-choice because we all have freedom of choice in all things. God said in Deuteronomy 30, [19]**I have set before you life and death, blessing**

and cursing; therefore choose life, that both you and your descendants may live. Women have the choice to be celibate until marriage. They have the choice, after marriage, not to conceive unwanted children. Birth control is available and effective. God has no problem with that.

It is no wonder that violence is increasing rapidly; there is no sanctity of human life any more. People get hysterical if a litter of kittens is drowned, or someone wears a fur coat, or an obscure fish in a river in Brazil becomes extinct, but they will proudly apply bumper stickers to their cars proclaiming the desirability of murdering unborn babies.

One sees prophecy fulfilled daily, particularly in the Middle East and Europe. Events in Israel are significant, and their unfolding gives believers an excellent handle on the world's progression toward the tribulation.

The unification of Europe, and the eurodollar, are indications of the move toward the one-world-order of Antichrist. We have no need, as members of the body of Christ, to be distressed by these things; we shall not be here for the tribulation. However, everything must be in place for Antichrist to take over immediately upon our removal from the earth.

Do not be an ostrich. Take your rightful place. Be a responsible Christian who is part of all that God is accomplishing in this time. Keep your eyes and ears open and, most importantly, weigh everything against the Word. Make the Word the priority in your life, fasten your seat belt, and occupy until He comes.

Chapter 5

The Ministry Of Angels

Psalm 91
11 For He shall give His angels charge over you, To keep you in all your ways.

Angels are our messengers and our body guards. God has provided them to encamp about us, do our bidding, and battle for us in the Spirit. People in dangerous and threatening circumstances frequently hire bodyguards for protection. God's angels are better protection than any human security force could possibly be. We need them now more than ever. To use them effectively we must understand who they are and how they function.

The world has a woefully inaccurate view of angels, as do many believers. God's angels are neither harp-bearing ladies with flowing blonde hair, nor are they fat little babies. Angels are a magnificent race of male beings, and every scriptural reference to them is as males.

Even though angels are supernatural warrior beings, we are never to make them objects of worship. Paul warns in Colossians 2, [18]**Let no one defraud you of your reward, taking delight in false humility and worship of angels.** Angel worship is abomination and can cost you your birthright. Worship is reserved only unto the Lord our God.

Revelation 22
8 Now I, John, saw and heard these things. And when I heard

and saw, I fell down to worship before the feet of the angel who showed me these things.
9 Then he said to me, "See that you do not do that. For I am your fellow servant, and of your brethren the prophets, and of those who keep the words of this book. Worship God."

We are asked in 1 Corinthians 6, **[3]Do you not know that we shall judge angels?**, to which I add the question, "Why would we worship beings whom God has subjected to our authority?"

Many are deceived into worshipping angels; some even pray to them. There is a reason that this is so appealing: angels require neither faith nor commitment. Angels are not controversial. They are perceived as benign, non-threatening beings who help people without question, no matter what those people believe, and expect nothing in return.

2 Corinthians 11
14 And no wonder! For Satan himself transforms himself into an angel of light.

Anyone who prays to an angel, and has a supernatural encounter, has an encounter with **an angel of light**, a demon. Demons are the only supernatural beings who can respond to false worship or unscriptural prayer. Many people are deceived and pulled into darkness this way.

When God created man, He placed him above the angels and just under Himself. Confusion attends anyone who is not aware of the mistranslation—in many but not all versions—of Psalm 8, **[5]For You have made him** (man) **a little lower than the angels**. The word translated "angels" in this instance is the Hebrew word "Elohim," which means Father, Son and Holy Spirit, the triune God, not angels.

When we are born-again, we are in Christ and He is in us. We are now seated with Him in heavenly places (Ephesians 2:6). The angels are not seated. When they are in the presence of God, they stand around and before the throne in worship. Hebrews 1 says, **[13]But to which of the angels has He ever said: "Sit at My right hand, till I make Your enemies Your footstool"?** There is no position between us and Him. The angels know this. They served God from the beginning and now they also serve those who are in Christ.

Angels are a separate race whom God created for specific purposes. He needed fellowship beyond His angels and created Adam. Adam and we, his descendants, are created in God's image and likeness (Genesis 1:26); the angels are not. Angels are not people who die, go to heaven, earn their wings, and get promoted to angel status. This is a concept born and fostered in the arts and is pure nonsense.

John 17
20 I do not pray for these alone, but also for those who will believe in Me through their word;
21 that they all may be one, as You, Father, are in Me, and I in You; that they also may be one in Us, that the world may believe that You sent Me.
22 And the glory which You gave Me I have given them, that they may be one just as We are one:
23 I in them, and You in Me; that they may be made perfect in one, and that the world may know that You have sent Me, and have loved them as You have loved Me.
24 Father, I desire that they also whom You gave Me may be with Me where I am, that they may behold My glory which You have given Me; for You loved Me before the foundation of the world.

As you can see from these Scriptures, dying and becoming an angel would not be a promotion but a demotion. We are part of God, we are in Christ. The angels, a separate creation, were with the Father long before Adam came on the scene. After God created Adam He expanded the responsibilities of the angels by assigning them to man as servants.

Psalm 103
Bless the Lord, you His angels, who excel in strength, who do His word, heeding the voice of His word.

God's angels, **who excel in strength**, are a mighty resource not to be overlooked. They are huge, powerful and faithful. They do not answer to just anyone. They answer to God and they answer to His Word when uttered by a born-again believer. Not even a believer can cause an angel to do other than God's Word. God's angels are loyal and absolutely trustworthy, and they work for us.

Hebrews 1
14 Are they not all ministering spirits sent forth to minister for those who will inherit salvation?

God has assigned legions of powerful angels to each believer (Matthew 18:10). We should not overlook this tremendous asset that has been put at our disposal. I constantly charge my angels to go forth on my behalf. I send them before us, when we travel by car, to clear the roads of all possible obstructions and harm, not the least of which are storms. I tell them to surround our car and keep us from all harm every time we go anywhere. I command them to uphold all airplanes on which I fly, and to oversee the maintenance of the ones I shall be travelling on. I ask the angels to make sure that my flights are on time, and I send one angel with each suitcase to guarantee its safe delivery. If you are laughing, please realize that my flights are always on schedule and always arrive safely, as does my luggage.

I send my angels to guard and protect my children everywhere they go. I post them at the edges of our property to keep it safe. I send them forth to bring in our financial harvest according to God's promises. I charge them to speak of me to those with whom I need favor. I station an angel to stand at my bedside at night to guard me and do battle for me against any demonic force that would try to disturb my rest. I also pray this for those troubled with nightmares. There is no end to the applications to which these mighty servants can be put.

I could fill an entire book with testimonies of the times I have seen or felt my angels remove me, my husband or my sons from harm. Every day we live takes us closer to the rapture of the church, thus Satan daily becomes more desperate to corrupt the glorious church and put off his demise. We must use every resource, keep ourselves saturated with the Word, and stop the devil at every turn.

There are several angelic categories and they have differing authorities and assignments. I shall begin with the seraphim.

Isaiah 6
1 In the year that King Uzziah died, I saw the Lord sitting on a

throne, high and lifted up, and the train of His robe filled the temple.
2 Above it stood seraphim; each one had six wings: with two he covered his face, with two he covered his feet, and with two he flew.
3 And one cried to another and said: "Holy, holy, holy is the Lord of hosts; the whole earth is full of His glory!"
4 And the posts of the door were shaken by the voice of him who cried out, and the house was filled with smoke.
5 Then I said: "Woe is me, for I am undone! Because I am a man of unclean lips, and I dwell in the midst of a people of unclean lips; for my eyes have seen the King, the Lord of hosts."
6 Then one of the seraphim flew to me, having in his hand a live coal which he had taken with the tongs from the altar.
7 And he touched my mouth with it, and said: "Behold, this has touched your lips; your iniquity is taken away, and your sin purged."

Angels will be those sent by God to preach the gospel during the second half of the tribulation.

Revelation 14
6 Then I saw another angel flying in the midst of heaven, having the everlasting gospel to preach to those who dwell on the earth to every nation, tribe, tongue, and people
7 saying with a loud voice, "Fear God and give glory to Him, for the hour of His judgment has come; and worship Him who made heaven and earth, the sea and springs of water."
8 And another angel followed, saying, "Babylon is fallen, is fallen, that great city, because she has made all nations drink of the wine of the wrath of her fornication."
9 Then a third angel followed them, saying with a loud voice, "If anyone worships the beast and his image, and receives his mark on his forehead or on his hand,
10 "he himself shall also drink of the wine of the wrath of God, which is poured out full strength into the cup of His indignation. And he shall be tormented with fire and brimstone in the

presence of the holy angels and in the presence of the Lamb.
11 "And the smoke of their torment ascends forever and ever; and they have no rest day or night, who worship the beast and his image, and whoever receives the mark of his name."

Revelation 5 tells us that this angelic host will number, [11]**ten thousand times ten thousand and thousands of thousands**, a number well in excess of 100,000,000. They are the only ones capable of finding and witnessing to every soul on earth. They will fulfill Matthew 24, [14]**And this gospel of the kingdom will be preached in all the world as a witness to all the nations, and then the end will come.**

Many preach that **the end** is the end of the age before the rapture. This is not so. Daniel 8, [19]**for at the appointed time the end shall be**, establishes **the end** as the end of the tribulation and declares it to be for **the appointed time**. That is when the **witness to all the nations** will be fulfilled. It is not the duty of this last generation to fulfill this Scripture. God has no intention of holding up time while He waits for mere mortals to accomplish a superhuman task. Matthew 24:14 will be fulfilled by angels.

The next angelic category is the Cherubim, who bear no resemblance to the chubby, baby-like beings presented to us by the arts. The cherubim, like the seraphim, are huge, powerful, winged creatures. They are not to be trifled with. Even though similar to the seraphim, the cherubim are different in their countenance and have four wings instead of six.

Ezekiel 10
1 And I looked, and there in the firmament that was above the head of the cherubim, there appeared something like a sapphire stone, having the appearance of the likeness of a throne.
2 And He spoke to the man clothed with linen, and said, "Go in among the wheels, under the cherub, fill your hands with coals of fire from among the cherubim, and scatter them over the city." And he went in as I watched.
3 Now the cherubim were standing on the south side of the temple when the man went in, and the cloud filled the inner court.

4 Then the glory of the Lord went up from the cherub, and paused over the threshold of the temple; and the house was filled with the cloud, and the court was full of the brightness of the Lord's glory.
5 And the sound of the wings of the cherubim was heard even in the outer court, like the voice of Almighty God when He speaks.
14 Each one had four faces: the first face was the face of a cherub, the second face the face of a man, the third the face of a lion, and the fourth the face of an eagle.
19 And the cherubim lifted their wings and mounted up from the earth in my sight. When they went out, the wheels were beside them; and they stood at the door of the east gate of the Lord's house, and the glory of the God of Israel was above them.
20 This is the living creature I saw under the God of Israel by the River Chebar, and I knew they were cherubim.
21 Each one had four faces and each one four wings, and the likeness of the hands of a man was under their wings.

Originally there were three archangels, Lucifer, mentioned in Isaiah 14, [12]**How you are fallen from heaven, O Lucifer, son of the morning!**; Gabriel, whose first mention in the New Testament is in Luke 1, [19]**And the angel answered and said to him, "I am Gabriel, who stands in the presence of God."**; and Michael, whose first mention in the New Testament is in Jude, [9]**Yet Michael the archangel, in contending with the devil...**

We know that Lucifer rebelled and was cast down from heaven, taking one third of the angels with him (Revelation 12:3-4 and 7-9). He is thereafter referred to as Satan. Jesus said in Luke 10, [18]**I saw Satan fall like lightning from heaven**. God has chained in hell (Jude 6) the angels whom Lucifer took with him. There they will remain until the great white throne judgment, when the body of Christ will judge them (1 Corinthians 6:3).

The hierarchy of the satanic force is laid out in Ephesians 6, [12]**principalities...powers...rulers of the darkness of this age... spiritual hosts of wickedness in the heavenly places**. There certainly is no wickedness in God's heaven. God is a holy God. The **heavenly places** full of **wickedness** refers to hell, which was created when God set apart a lower portion of His heaven and made it a prison for Satan and his angels. That is where the satanic angels are incarcerated until they are judged, their final destination being the lake of fire.

The archangels Gabriel and Michael serve God upon the earth. Gabriel told Mary of Elizabeth's conception of John in Luke 1:36, prophesied to Zacharias about his son John in Luke 1:11-20, and told Mary of the Holy Ghost coming upon her to place Jesus in her womb in Luke 1:26-35.

The clouds of heaven that will accompany the saints to glory at the rapture of the church are clouds of angels led by Michael. Michael has charge over the resurrection of the righteous dead and the catching away of the body of Christ.

Daniel 12
1 At that time Michael shall stand up, the great prince who stands watch over the sons of your people; And there shall be a time of trouble, such as never was since there was a nation, even to that time. and at that time your people shall be delivered, every one who is found written in the book.
2 And many of those who sleep in the dust of the earth shall awake, some to everlasting life, some to shame and everlasting contempt.
3 Those who are wise shall shine like the brightness of the firmament, and those who turn many to righteousness like the stars forever and ever.

Even though Michael is not specifically named in the following Scriptures, we know from Daniel 12 that **the voice of an archangel** refers to him.

1 Thessalonians 4
16 For the Lord Himself will descend from heaven with a shout, with the voice of an archangel, and with the trumpet of God. And the dead in Christ will rise first.

The Rapture, The Tribulation, And Beyond

17 Then we who are alive and remain shall be caught up together with them in the clouds to meet the Lord in the air. And thus we shall always be with the Lord.

The angels usually seen during every-day life, who frequently take on human appearance, would seem to be wingless. Whenever I have been privileged to see one of these angels, recognizing him only by the Spirit, I have looked for wings and seen none.

Hebrews 13
2 Do not forget to entertain strangers, for by so doing some have unwittingly entertained angels.

God's angels, throughout history, have been sent to speak to people. There are many records in the Old Testament of God dispatching His angels to speak on His behalf, to instruct, direct, and encourage individuals, or even the whole nation of Israel (Exodus 23:20-23).

We see the ministry of angels throughout the book of Acts. An angel opened the prison doors, released the imprisoned apostles, and gave them God's instructions (Acts 5:18-20). An angel spoke to Philip, in Acts 8:26, and directed him to go to Gaza. Cornelius saw an angel in a vision who told him that his prayers had been answered, and directed him to send for Peter that he might minister to him and his household (Acts 10:3-7).

When Peter was chained in prison, in Acts 12:5-11, it was an angel who went in, loosed Peter's chains, and guided him out of the prison. When Peter, thereafter, went to Mary's house, his friends, believing him still to be in prison, did not believe it was Peter at the door. They said it was his angel and did not want to bother to let him in. Seeing angels was such a common thing that no one thought it notable. Finally, as Peter kept knocking, they did open the door (Acts 12:12-16).

God sent an angel to speak to Paul in the middle of a fierce and prolonged storm at sea (Acts 27:21-26) to tell him that, even though the ship would run aground on an island and be lost, his life and the lives of all others aboard would be spared.

In these times of challenge and opportunity, our angels, whom God has put at our beck and call, are a much needed resource. The Lord has instructed us to occupy the earth until He comes (Luke 19:13). We must never forget that our angels are ready, willing, and more than able to carry out God's Word on our behalf.

Chapter 6

The Sequence Of End-Time Events

God has arranged the last moments of the age in a specific order. He has provided recognizable stepping stones leading up to the great tribulation and the millennial reign of Christ that follows. Ignorance of what is to come and where we fit into it is dangerous. Ignorance leads to confusion. Those who live in confusion are susceptible to lies and false prophecy, either of which can cheat them of their inheritance.

There are times when we are positive that something we believe to be true is in the Word, only to find, when we search diligently through the concordance and endlessly turn pages in the Bible, that it is not there. This is usually the result of hearing something preached so many times that we come to accept it as fact even when it is not. When we are seekers after truth we must put everything to the Word test. We must be willing to examine the concepts with which we are familiar to ensure that they are not just religious thinking but stand up in the light of the whole gospel.

Do you remember a puzzle called *Rubik's Cube*? It was all the rage some years back. It was a frustrating plastic cube made up of smaller cubes of various colors. The purpose was to twist and turn the cubes in all directions in order to unscramble the colors. When we first try to untangle Matthew, Revelation, Daniel, Ezekiel, and Isaiah, it can seem like the ultimate *Rubik's Cube*. We look at this tangle of seemingly disconnected and frequently foreign concepts and see a blur of horns, toes, scrolls, lampstands, beasts, kings, fire, smoke, thundering, and all manner of terror and destruction. We turn the statements this way and that, just like the colors in *Rubik's Cube*, and get more and more frustrated as we try to make them fit. When our every attempt fails, we throw it down and walk away. That is not a problem when we are dealing with a toy, but it most assuredly is a problem when we are dealing with the Word. Ignorance of the Word can kill us. Never forget Hosea 4, **[6]My people are destroyed for lack of knowledge**.

Deuteronomy 30
19 I call heaven and earth as witnesses today against you, that I have set before you life and death, blessing and cursing; therefore choose life, that both you and your descendants may live;
20 that you may love the Lord your God, that you may obey His voice, and that you may cling to Him, for He is your life and the length of your days; and that you may dwell in the land which the Lord swore to your fathers, to Abraham, Isaac, and Jacob, to give them.

Somewhere in the midst of all the fire, smoke, and dragon's breath, we need to find the path of God's kindness. We need to find the peace which He promises and has established for us. After all, only a fool sails in uncharted waters, and God did not raise His children to be fools.

Isaiah 54
9 "For this is like the waters of Noah to Me; for as I have sworn that the waters of Noah would no longer cover the earth, so have I sworn that I would not be angry with you, nor rebuke you.
10 "For the mountains shall depart and the hills be removed, but My kindness shall not depart from you, nor shall My covenant of peace be removed," says the Lord, who has mercy on you.

God is not a liar. If we wish to stay in His rest on this fabulous journey to our place in eternity, we must let Him show us the way.

The Jews, The Greeks, The Church

The first step in sorting out our eschatology is the separation of the three categories of people whom God has established. The Word always speaks to or about one of them. The three groups encompass all the people who dwell on the earth.

1 Corinthians 10
32 Give no offense, either to the Jews or to the Greeks or to the church of God,

There are portions of the Word that speak specifically and only to the Jews. There are other portions that speak specifically and only to or about what is variously referred to as the "unbelieving world," the "Greek," or the "Gentile." The third group, to or about which the Word speaks specifically, is the church. Many preachers misapply the Word by taking Scriptures that are only for the Jews or the Gentiles and applying them to the church, or vice-versa. No believer can afford to be in a position wherein he can be confused. Everything to which he holds fast must be supported by all of Scripture; it cannot rest on man's opinion apart from Scripture.

When we know to which of these three groups—the Jews, the Greeks (Gentiles, unbelieving world) or the church—the Word is speaking, we shall keep our end-time doctrine straight. I have heard others preach this but then go straight ahead and break their own rule, thus making an unholy mess of the truth.

In the old covenant all living people were either Jews or Gentiles, or, in other words, covenant people or non-covenant people. In the new covenant there is also the church, the body of Christ, which is made up of former Jews and former Gentiles. Do not become confused by thinking that Messianic Jews, Jews who have received Christ, are a fourth category. They are not, they are part of the church. Once a Jew receives Christ as Messiah he, just like a non-Jew, becomes a new creature in Christ, part of a brand new race of born-again people. When the Word speaks to the Jews it is not speaking to born-again people. Even when someone was a Jew before he was born again, the Word no longer refers to him as a Jew but as the church. Being a Christian means being in Christ.

2 Corinthians 5
17 Therefore, if anyone is in Christ, he is a new creation; old things have passed away; behold, all things have become new.

1 Peter 2
9 But you are a chosen generation, a royal priesthood, a holy nation, His own special people, that you may proclaim the praises of Him who called you out of darkness into His marvelous light;
10 who once were not a people but are now the people of God, who had not obtained mercy but now have obtained mercy.

The End Of The Age

In Chapter 3 we established the 6,000 year lease that God gave man. If you are not yet fully established in this, go back and read it again before continuing. The 6,000 year lease was usurped by Satan when Adam committed high treason. We know that there were 2,000 years from Adam to Abraham, 2,000 years from Abraham to Jesus, and a further 2,000 years until Jesus' return. Since only Father God knows the exact year 2,000, we must never attempt to predict the day and hour. However, we do know the season. Jesus told us to be aware of it and we can see by the signs that the time is short. That is why our generation cannot afford to remain ignorant.

The world is preparing for the tribulation while we, the body of Christ, are preparing to be raptured. This is a vast separation of purpose and, if we are to find and walk in God's peace, we need always, in all circumstances, to make this clear distinction. To qualify for the pre-tribulation rapture of the church we must be blood-bought, baptized in the Holy Spirit, know who we are in Christ, and expect the glorious appearing.

Being blood-bought, baptized in the Holy Spirit, and knowing who we are in Christ, constitutes the foundation of our relationship with Christ Jesus and, thus, our position in the rapture of the church. Once this foundation is laid we must walk in righteousness, being hearers and doers of the Word. Jesus commands that we be overcomers. He requires that we overcome the world by faith, now, that we may become glorified in due season.

Revelation 3
10 Because you have kept My command to persevere, I also will keep you from the hour of trial which shall come upon the whole world, to test those who dwell on the earth.
11 Behold, I come quickly! Hold fast what you have, that no one may take your crown.
12 He who overcomes, I will make him a pillar in the temple of My God, and he shall go out no more. And I will write on him the name of My God and the name of the city of My God, the New Jerusalem, which comes down out of heaven from My God. And I will write on him My new name.
13 He who has an ear, let him hear what the Spirit says to the churches.
21 To him who overcomes I will grant to sit with Me on My throne, as I also overcame and sat down with My Father on His throne.

1 John 5
4 For whatever is born of God overcomes the world. And this is the victory that has overcome the world our faith.

There is no such thing as faith apart from the Word of God, for nothing else is absolute and unchangeable. It would not be possible to have faith in something that was not carved in the rock of ages, forever and ever, Amen.

Psalm 119
89 Forever, O Lord, Your word is settled in heaven.
90 Your faithfulness endures to all generations; You established the earth, and it abides.

Psalm 138
2 I will worship toward Your holy temple, and praise Your

name for Your lovingkindness and Your truth; for You have magnified Your word above all Your name.

Hebrews 1
3 ...and upholding all things by the word of His power...

Living, as it is instructed in Matthew 4, **⁴by every word that proceeds out of the mouth of God**, is what sanctifies and keeps the church pure enough to be raptured and glorified. The Scriptures declare that this is the only way for the body of Christ to be made holy.

Ephesians 5
26 that He might sanctify and cleanse it with the washing of water by the word,
27 that He might present it to Himself a glorious church, not having spot or wrinkle or any such thing, but that it should be holy and without blemish.

The Last Trump

The event for which we are all preparing and waiting is the sounding of the last trump—at God's preordained moment at the end of this age—when Jesus will come to gather His body and take us out of the world to escape the tribulation.

1 Thessalonians 1
10 and to wait for His Son from heaven, whom He raised from the dead, even Jesus who delivers us from the wrath to come.

It is not God's plan that His born-again children come under the rule of Antichrist, let alone the abundance of His wrath (Revelation 6:17) that will be poured out during the tribulation.

1 Thessalonians 4
16 For the Lord Himself will descend from heaven with a shout, with the voice of an archangel, and with the trumpet of God. And the dead in Christ will rise first.

17 Then we who are alive and remain shall be caught up together with them in the clouds to meet the Lord in the air. And thus we shall always be with the Lord.

1 Thessalonians 5
4 But you, brethren, are not in darkness, so that this Day should overtake you as a thief.
5 You are all sons of light and sons of the day. We are not of the night nor of darkness.
6 Therefore let us not sleep, as others do, but let us watch and be sober.
7 For those who sleep, sleep at night, and those who get drunk are drunk at night.
8 But let us who are of the day be sober, putting on the breastplate of faith and love, and as a helmet the hope of salvation.
9 For God did not appoint us to wrath, but to obtain salvation through our Lord Jesus Christ,
10 who died for us, that whether we wake or sleep, we should live together with Him.

The Saints Glorified

At the pre-tribulation rapture of the church we, the body of Christ, will be taken out of the world and glorified—made to be like Christ in the form in which He appeared after His resurrection—to dwell with Him in New Jerusalem forever. Do not confuse the terms referring to the rapture of the church with those referring to the second advent, when Christ returns from heaven with His army after the wedding of the Lamb. This is a separate event, seven years later at the end of the tribulation, with different terms used to describe it.

Terms referring to the rapture of the church in Scripture are: **the blessed hope and glorious appearing** (Titus 2:13); **His coming** (1 Corinthians 15:23); **coming in the clouds** (Mark 13:26); **taken up** (Acts 1:9); **taken out** (2 Thessalonians 2:7).

Terms referring to the second advent are: **return** (Acts 15:16); **the day of the Lord** (Zephaniah 1:7); **thief** (Revelation 3:3); **thief in the night** (2 Peter 3:10).

Once one becomes familiar with the terminology used for these two events one will immediately recognize to which event a particular passage of Scripture refers. When the Lord catches up His body to meet Him in the air at the rapture, only the body will see Him. When He returns from heaven at the end of the tribulation—the second advent—with us following Him in military order, the whole world will see Him.

The Judgment Seat Of Christ

As soon as we are glorified we shall stand before the judgment seat of Christ. This is not something by which to be intimidated. There will be no knee-knocking or hand-wringing or other such foolishness that many preach. This is a moment of triumph and privilege. We are about to receive, as we stand joyously face to face with Jesus, the crowns of glory we shall wear with our robes of righteousness. Get rid of all the religious lies you have heard; this is a glorious moment, the beginning of our real lives in Christ.

> Hebrews 9
> **27 And as it is appointed for men to die once, but after this the judgment,**
> **28 so Christ was offered once to bear the sins of many. To those who eagerly wait for Him He will appear a second time, apart from sin, for salvation.**

This is not judgment in the way most people view it. This judgment is **apart from sin**. Only the glorified body of Christ will be there. Sin will not be an issue because, by the blood of the Lamb, it will have been done away with. We shall have been glorified. Corruption will have put on incorruption. The flesh will be no more. The **salvation** mentioned is not salvation from condemnation, obviously, but salvation from the tribulation from which we have just been delivered.

1 Corinthians 15
51 Behold, I tell you a mystery: We shall not all sleep, but we shall all be changed
52 in a moment, in the twinkling of an eye, at the last trumpet. For the trumpet will sound, and the dead will be raised incorruptible, and we shall be changed.
53 For this corruptible must put on incorruption, and this mortal must put on immortality.
54 So when this corruptible has put on incorruption, and this mortal has put on immortality, then shall be brought to pass the saying that is written: "Death is swallowed up in victory."

Each member of the body of Christ was judged righteous by the blood of Jesus the moment he was born again. We have already been transformed into the righteousness of God in Christ Jesus (Isaiah 54:17). Therefore, clearly, the judgment seat of Christ is not a question of salvation, but of reward. It is the establishing of our eternal position, or rank, in New Jerusalem.

1 Corinthians 3 (KJV)
11 For other foundation can no man lay than that is laid, which is Jesus Christ.
12 Now if any man build upon this foundation gold, silver, precious stones, wood, hay, stubble;
13 Every man's work shall be made manifest: for the day shall declare it, because it shall be revealed by fire; and the fire shall try every man's work of what sort it is.
14 If any man's work abide which he hath built thereupon, he shall receive a reward.
15 If any man's work shall be burned, he shall suffer loss: but he himself shall be saved; yet so as by fire.
16 Know ye not that ye are the temple of God, and that the Spirit of God dwelleth in you?

That which **shall be burned** is all the useless, worldly things we have done. This includes all our so-called good works that have nothing to do with the exercise of faith. Lest you be confused by **but he himself**

shall be saved, this refers to the fact that the individual here is no longer in danger of damnation for, as we see, he is **the temple of God**. This statement reaffirms that at the judgment seat of Christ salvation is not an issue. Verses 13 and 14 talk about how well we have kept the covenant, how many acts of faith will be accounted to us as righteousness. James 2 tells us, [20]**faith without works is dead**, which does not refer to good works in the sense that religion defines them.

> Romans 4
> **20 He did not waver at the promise of God through unbelief, but was strengthened in faith, giving glory to God,**
> **21 and being fully convinced that what He had promised He was also able to perform.**
> **22 And therefore "it was accounted to him for righteousness."**
> **23 Now it was not written for his sake alone that it was imputed to him,**
> **24 but also for us. It shall be imputed to us who believe in Him who raised up Jesus our Lord from the dead,**
> **25 who was delivered up because of our offenses, and was raised because of our justification.**

Abraham's faith, we learn in Galatians 3, [6]**was accounted to him for righteousness**, and because we are the seed of Abraham in Christ Jesus, so it will be with us.

Every time we receive healing by faith, every time we look to the Lord and not to flesh for our finances, every time we receive restoration for our family and trust God to do it without our help, every time we put the past to death, forgive without resentment, and count everything joy, we have performed a work of faith.

Walking by faith and not by sight is the basis of our reward at the judgment seat of Christ. If we want jewels in our crowns we must be obedient; we must practice faith at every opportunity; we must be quick to repent; we must be quick to pray effectively; we must believe the promises God has given us, no matter what it looks like, feels like, smells like, sounds like, or what anyone else says about it; we must speak words of victory only and overcome the devil at every turn. These are the works of faith that become the jewels in our crowns.

If you think your crown is going to lack sparkle and be puny, get to work. Start doing the works of faith. Then start doing neck exercises so that you will have the strength to wear your jewel-laden crown with aplomb. Anticipate the judgment seat of Christ with the joy and excitement it deserves.

Preparing To Rule And Reign

The body of Christ will not be on earth during the seven years of the tribulation. It will have been raptured, glorified, and decked out in its magnificent robes of righteousness and dazzling jeweled crowns. It will spend those seven years in heaven with Christ Jesus, learning how to sit with Him in His throne when His millennial reign begins.

> Revelation 2
> **25 But hold fast what you have till I come.**
> **26 And he who overcomes, and keeps My works until the end, to him I will give power over the nations**
> **27 "He shall rule them with a rod of iron; as the potter's vessels shall be broken to pieces" as I also have received from My Father;**

> Revelation 3
> **21 To him who overcomes I will grant to sit with Me on My throne, as I also overcame and sat down with My Father on His throne.**

At the end of the tribulation the wedding of the Lamb takes place. The bridegroom—Jesus united with His body, the church—and the bride—the holy city, New Jerusalem—become one, and the body of Christ is sealed forever. Immediately following the wedding, we ride back with Jesus at our head to watch Him purify the earth and set up His thousand year reign.

The Great Tribulation

A time of unspeakable horror will begin as soon as the church, **he who now restrains** in verse 7 below, has been removed.

> 2 Thessalonians 2
> **6 And now you know what is restraining, that he may be revealed in his own time.**
> **7 For the mystery of lawlessness is already at work; only he who now restrains will do so until he is taken out of the way.**
> **8 And then the lawless one will be revealed, whom the Lord will consume with the breath of His mouth and destroy with the brightness of His coming.**
> **9 The coming of the lawless one is according to the working of Satan, with all power, signs, and lying wonders,**
> **10 and with all unrighteous deception among those who perish, because they did not receive the love of the truth, that they might be saved.**
> **11 And for this reason God will send them strong delusion, that they should believe the lie,**
> **12 that they all may be condemned who did not believe the truth but had pleasure in unrighteousness.**

It will be a time of hail and fire mingled with blood. A third of the trees and all the green grass will be burned up, a third of the sea will become blood, a third of all the creatures in the sea will die, a third of all ships will be destroyed, a third of the waters will be bitterly poisoned unto death for those who drink it, and darkness will increase. There will be locusts in the shape of horses, with faces like men, hair like women, teeth like lions, breastplates of iron, huge thunderous wings, having a sting like a scorpion in their tails, who will have the power to hurt and torment all the inhabitants of the earth, stopping just short of killing them. People will pray for death but not die. There will be abomination, depravity, terror, agony, plagues, tyranny and totalitarianism (Revelation 8:5-13 and 9:1-21).

The First Three And A Half Years

During the first half of the tribulation Antichrist will be hailed as the great peacemaker (Daniel 9:27). He will actually bring peace to the earth, including Israel, for a time, and establish his one-world order. All currency, laws and governments will be dissolved. All power and authority will rest in the hands of the satanic trinity: Antichrist, the false prophet, and the beast. The mark of the beast will be instituted.

> Revelation 13
> **15 He was granted power to give breath to the image of the beast, that the image of the beast should both speak and cause as many as would not worship the image of the beast to be killed.**
> **16 And he causes all, both small and great, rich and poor, free and slave, to receive a mark on their right hand or on their foreheads,**
> **17 and that no one may buy or sell except one who has the mark or the name of the beast, or the number of his name.**
> **18 Here is wisdom. Let him who has understanding calculate the number of the beast, for it is the number of a man: His number is 666.**

There is no repentance for those who receive the mark of the beast. Eternal condemnation and torment in the lake of fire will, without exception, be their end.

> Revelation 14
> **9 Then a third angel followed them, saying with a loud voice, "If anyone worships the beast and his image, and receives his mark on his forehead or on his hand,**
> **10 "he himself shall also drink of the wine of the wrath of God, which is poured out full strength into the cup of His indignation. And he shall be tormented with fire and brimstone in the presence of the holy angels and in the presence of the Lamb.**
> **11 "And the smoke of their torment ascends forever and ever; and they have no rest day or night, who worship the beast and his image, and whoever receives the mark of his name."**

God, in His infinite mercy, has still provided a way of escape for those who find themselves on earth when the tribulation begins. Those who considered themselves Christians, but failed to qualify for the rapture, will have two ways to escape eternal damnation.

The first and best alternative is to be caught during the first three and a half years by the "beast police," as I call them, refuse the mark, and be executed for their faith. As grizzly as this will be, those with the fortitude and courage to go through with it will be resurrected at midtribulation—the fifth rapture—and join the body of Christ in heaven.

Revelation 6
9 When He opened the fifth seal, I saw under the altar the souls of those who had been slain for the word of God and for the testimony which they held.
10 And they cried with a loud voice, saying, "How long, O Lord, holy and true, until You judge and avenge our blood on those who dwell on the earth?"
11 And a white robe was given to each of them; and it was said to them that they should rest a little while longer, until both the number of their fellow servants and their brethren, who would be killed as they were, was completed.

Revelation 7
13 Then one of the elders answered, saying to me, "Who are these arrayed in white robes, and where did they come from?"
14 And I said to him, "Sir, you know." So he said to me, "These are the ones who come out of the great tribulation, and washed their robes and made them white in the blood of the Lamb.
15 "Therefore they are before the throne of God, and serve Him day and night in His temple. And He who sits on the throne will dwell among them."

Revelation 20
4 And I saw thrones, and they sat on them, and judgment was committed to them. And I saw the souls of those who had been beheaded for their witness to Jesus and for the word of God, who had not worshiped the beast or his image, and had not

received his mark on their foreheads or on their hands. And they lived and reigned with Christ for a thousand years.
5 But the rest of the dead did not live again until the thousand years were finished. This is the first resurrection.
6 Blessed and holy is he who has part in the first resurrection. Over such the second death has no power, but they shall be priests of God and of Christ, and shall reign with Him a thousand years.

The only other way of escape when the tribulation begins is, according to Revelation 6, to run and hide [15]**themselves in the caves and in the rocks of the mountains** to avoid taking the mark of the beast. Those who succeed in this will be gathered by Jesus at the end of the tribulation, just before the battle of Armageddon (Matthew 24:13). The Jewish remnant, who will have hidden in the desert, will also be gathered at the end of the tribulation (Revelation 12:13-17). God will do this in order to honor His first covenant with the Jews. Each of these groups will be part of the nations who will dwell upon the purified earth during the millennial reign of Christ.

During the first half of the tribulation there will be 144,000 Jewish evangelists whom God will raise up as soon as the tribulation begins. They are male virgins who will be born again and protected by God from the mark of the beast by the seal of God on their foreheads. These men will preach the gospel during the first three and a half years and will bring many to salvation. The 144,000 are entirely different people than the Jewish remnant (Revelation 7:3-8).

The ministry of the 144,000 will end at mid-tribulation and they will be raptured to join the body of Christ in heaven, which is the sixth rapture.

Revelation 14
1 Then I looked, and behold, a Lamb standing on Mount Zion, and with Him one hundred and forty-four thousand, having His Father's name written on their foreheads.
3 And they sang as it were a new song before the throne, before the four living creatures, and the elders; and no one could learn that song except the hundred and forty-four thousand who were redeemed from the earth.

4 These are the ones who were not defiled with women, for they are virgins. These are the ones who follow the Lamb wherever He goes. These were redeemed from among men, being firstfruits to God and to the Lamb.
5 And in their mouth was found no guile, for they are without fault before the throne of God.

The Second Three And A Half Years

As if things were not bad enough during the first half of the tribulation, things really get nasty during the second half. Antichrist does an about-face, breaks all his peace accords, declares himself to be God, and ascends the throne of the Lamb (2 Thessalonians 2:4) in the temple in Jerusalem. God then pours out His wrath as His judgment upon the earth. The battle of Armageddon follows (Revelation 16:16) and that is the end.

Revelation 16
1 Then I heard a loud voice from the temple saying to the seven angels, "Go and pour out the bowls of the wrath of God on the earth."
2 So the first went and poured out his bowl upon the earth, and a foul and loathsome sore came upon the men who had the mark of the beast and those who worshiped his image.
3 Then the second angel poured out his bowl on the sea, and it became blood as of a dead man; and every living creature in the sea died.
4 Then the third angel poured out his bowl on the rivers and springs of water, and they became blood.
8 Then the fourth angel poured out his bowl on the sun, and power was given to him to scorch men with fire.
9 And men were scorched with great heat, and they blasphemed the name of God who has power over these plagues; and they did not repent and give Him glory.
10 Then the fifth angel poured out his bowl on the throne of the beast, and his kingdom became full of darkness; and they gnawed their tongues because of the pain.

The Rapture, The Tribulation, And Beyond

11 And they blasphemed the God of heaven because of their pains and their sores, and did not repent of their deeds.
12 Then the sixth angel poured out his bowl on the great river Euphrates, and its water was dried up, so that the way of the kings from the east might be prepared.
17 Then the seventh angel poured out his bowl into the air, and a loud voice came out of the temple of heaven, from the throne, saying, "It is done!"
18 And there were noises and thunderings and lightnings; and there was a great earthquake, such a mighty and great earthquake as had not occurred since men were on the earth.
19 Now the great city was divided into three parts, and the cities of the nations fell. And great Babylon was remembered before God, to give her the cup of the wine of the fierceness of His wrath.
20 Then every island fled away, and the mountains were not found.
21 And great hail from heaven fell upon men, every hailstone about the weight of a talent. And men blasphemed God because of the plague of the hail, since that plague was exceedingly great.

Immediately following the rapture of the 144,000 at mid-tribulation, and during the outpouring of His wrath, God releases the angels to preach the gospel to the earth.

Revelation 14
6 Then I saw another angel flying in the midst of heaven, having the everlasting gospel to preach to those who dwell on the earth to every nation, tribe, tongue, and people.

This is when Matthew 24 is fulfilled, [14]**And this gospel of the kingdom will be preached in all the world as a witness to all the nations, and then the end will come.** The angels will reach every mountain top, deep into every jungle and every obscure island, and into every nook and cranny upon the whole earth.

Finally, God sends His two end-time witnesses, Enoch and Elijah, to represent Him upon the earth. We know it is Enoch and Elijah because they are the only two men since the beginning of time who did not die but were raptured (Hebrews 11:5 and 2 Kings 2:11). Hebrews 9 says, **[27]it is appointed for men to die once, but after this the judgment**.

Revelation 11
**3 And I will give power to my two witnesses, and they will prophesy one thousand two hundred and sixty days, clothed in sackcloth.
4 These are the two olive trees and the two lampstands standing before the God of the earth.
5 And if anyone wants to harm them, fire proceeds from their mouth and devours their enemies. And if anyone wants to harm them, he must be killed in this manner.
6 These have power to shut heaven, so that no rain falls in the days of their prophecy; and they have power over waters to turn them to blood, and to strike the earth with all plagues, as often as they desire.**

These two, Enoch and Elijah, will harass Antichrist and his government without mercy until the final three days of the tribulation. Satan will not be able to kill them until they have completed their assignment.

Revelation 11
**7 Now when they finish their testimony, the beast that ascends out of the bottomless pit will make war against them, overcome them, and kill them.
8 And their dead bodies will lie in the street of the great city which spiritually is called Sodom and Egypt, where also our Lord was crucified.
9 Then those from the peoples, tribes, tongues, and nations will see their dead bodies three and a half days, and not allow their dead bodies to be put into graves.
10 And those who dwell on the earth will rejoice over them, make merry, and send gifts to one another, because these two prophets tormented those who dwell on the earth.
11 Now after the three and a half days the breath of life from**

**God entered them, and they stood on their feet, and great fear fell on those who saw them.
12 And they heard a loud voice from heaven saying to them, "Come up here." And they ascended to heaven in a cloud, and their enemies saw them.**

This is the seventh rapture and marks the end of the tribulation. All is complete and the wedding of the Lamb takes place in New Jerusalem in the heavenlies (Revelation 19:7-9).

Within this same hour (Revelation 11:13) Jesus and His body, the army of God, ride back from heaven for the battle of Armageddon. There is no need for a honeymoon. All has been made ready. We shall have been trained to ride with our Lord. Jesus will get right down to the business of gathering the nations (Matthew 24:31), crushing the remaining evidence of evil civilization on the earth (Revelation 19:19-21), destroying the two hundred million (Revelation 9:16) man army of Antichrist, putting Satan into the pit for 1,000 years (Revelation 20:1-2), casting the false prophet and the beast into the lake of fire (Revelation 19:20), purifying and restoring the earth, rebuilding His temple (Zechariah 6:12-15), and setting up His millennial reign.

The Millennial Reign of Christ

There will be a thousand years of peace after the battle of Armageddon.

Revelation 20
**1 Then I saw an angel coming down from heaven, having the key to the bottomless pit and a great chain in his hand.
2 He laid hold of the dragon, that serpent of old, who is the Devil and Satan, and bound him for a thousand years;
3 and he cast him into the bottomless pit, and shut him up, and set a seal on him, so that he should deceive the nations no more till the thousand years were finished. But after these things he must be released for a little while.**

Christ Jesus, the prince of peace, will be in absolute control during His millennial reign. Satan will be sealed in the bottomless pit, completely shut off from any influence upon man. No evil will exist in any form. God will bring New Jerusalem down to rest right above earthly Jerusalem, centered over the brand new temple of the Lamb. We, the glorified body of Christ, will dwell in New Jerusalem because we are part of her. We shall be kingdom government and will travel back and forth to earth.

The Millennial Nations

The nations will have escaped destruction but will not be part of the body of Christ. The wedding will have taken place and the body of Christ will have been sealed forever.

> **Matthew 25**
> **10 And while they went to buy, the bridegroom came, and those who were ready went in with him to the wedding; and the door was shut.**

The nations live on a perfected earth, free from all evil. However, they do have to fulfill God's requirements in order to be blessed. Evil has been removed, but the result of disobedience, for the nations, will be God's instant punishment.

> Zechariah 14
> **16 And it shall come to pass that everyone who is left of all the nations which came against Jerusalem shall go up from year to year to worship the King, the Lord of hosts, and to keep the Feast of Tabernacles.**
> **17 And it shall be that whichever of the families of the earth do not come up to Jerusalem to worship the King, the Lord of hosts, on them there will be no rain.**
> **18 If the family of Egypt will not come up and enter in, they shall have no rain; they shall receive the plague with which the Lord strikes the nations who do not come up to keep the Feast of Tabernacles.**

19 This shall be the punishment of Egypt and the punishment of all the nations that do not come up to keep the Feast of Tabernacles.

Make no mistake, the status of the nations is far below the place of privilege held by the body of Christ.

Satan Released For A Season

At the end of the millennial reign of Christ the bottomless pit will be opened and Satan will be loosed upon the nations. The length of Satan's season of release is not specified.

> Revelation 20
> **7 Now when the thousand years have expired, Satan will be released from his prison**
> **8 and will go out to deceive the nations which are in the four corners of the earth, Gog and Magog, to gather them together to battle, whose number is as the sand of the sea.**
> **9 They went up on the breadth of the earth and surrounded the camp of the saints and the beloved city. And fire came down from God out of heaven and devoured them.**
> **10 And the devil, who deceived them, was cast into the lake of fire and brimstone where the beast and the false prophet are. And they will be tormented day and night forever and ever.**

It is truly amazing that, after one thousand years of peace and God's love, there will still be as many **as the sand of the sea** who will choose Satan over God. The fallen nature of man is truly an abomination. I shudder every time I hear a humanist reject Jesus and say that he prefers to believe in the inherent goodness of man. There is no goodness in man apart from Christ.

Understand clearly that it is the nations who are being tested, not the body. The glorified body of Christ is now incorruptible (1 Corinthians 15:52-54), and will have been ruling and reigning with Christ for a thousand years. The nations still have the fallen nature of man to deal with. They will continue to marry and have children during the thousand years and those children will never have had to make the choice between good and evil. It is necessary, therefore, that they be tested with evil, and that is why Satan is released.

The Great White Throne Judgment

Immediately after those who attack the holy city have been burned up and cast, with Satan, into the lake of fire, the great white throne judgement takes place.

> Revelation 20
> **11 Then I saw a great white throne and Him who sat on it, from whose face the earth and the heaven fled away. And there was found no place for them.**
> **12 And I saw the dead, small and great, standing before God, and books were opened. And another book was opened, which is the Book of Life. And the dead were judged according to their works, by the things which were written in the books.**
> **13 The sea gave up the dead who were in it, and Death and Hades delivered up the dead who were in them. And they were judged, each one according to his works.**
> **14 Then Death and Hades were cast into the lake of fire. This is the second death.**
> **15 And anyone not found written in the Book of Life was cast into the lake of fire.**

God's mercy is astounding. Even those in hell can join the eternal nations if their works stand and they bow their knee to Jesus. I point out again that those standing before the great white throne cannot become part of the body of Christ; they can only join the nations.

Standing for judgment at the great white throne will be those of the millennial nations who resist Satan's test and remain loyal to the Lord, plus all those who will have come up out of hell. These are all **the dead**, the spiritually dead, who stand to be evaluated according to their works. They are not born-again; they have forever missed the chance to be judged righteous by the blood of the Lamb, even when they bow their knee to Jesus.

This is when the sheep and the goats are separated.

Matthew 25
31 When the Son of Man comes in His glory, and all the holy angels with Him, then He will sit on the throne of His glory.
32 All the nations will be gathered before Him, and He will separate them one from another, as a shepherd divides his sheep from the goats.
33 And He will set the sheep on His right hand, but the goats on the left.
34 Then the King will say to those on His right hand, "Come, you blessed of My Father, inherit the kingdom prepared for you from the foundation of the world:
35 "for I was hungry and you gave Me food; I was thirsty and you gave Me drink; I was a stranger and you took Me in;
36 "I was naked and you clothed Me; I was sick and you visited Me; I was in prison and you came to Me."
37 Then the righteous will answer Him, saying, "Lord, when did we see You hungry and feed You, or thirsty and give You drink?
38 "When did we see You a stranger and take You in, or naked and clothe You?
39 "Or when did we see You sick, or in prison, and come to You?"
40 And the King will answer and say to them, "Assuredly, I say to you, inasmuch as you did it to one of the least of these My brethren, you did it to Me."
41 Then He will also say to those on the left hand, "Depart from Me, you cursed, into the everlasting fire prepared for the devil and his angels:
42 "for I was hungry and you gave Me no food; I was thirsty and you gave Me no drink;
43 "I was a stranger and you did not take Me in, naked and you did not clothe Me, sick and in prison and you did not visit Me."
44 Then they also will answer Him, saying, "Lord, when did we see You hungry or thirsty or a stranger or naked or sick or in prison, and did not minister to You?"

45 Then He will answer them, saying, "Assuredly, I say to you, inasmuch as you did not do it to one of the least of these, you did not do it to Me."
46 And these will go away into everlasting punishment, but the righteous into eternal life.

The sheep are the eternal nations who inherit the perfected earth. The goats are those whose works do not meet the test at the great white throne, who, along with the devil and his angels, are sent to the lake of fire. The sheep and the goats come only from the nations, not from the body of Christ.

After the great white throne judgment the following Scripture is fulfilled:

Romans 14
9 For to this end Christ died and rose and lived again, that He might be Lord of both the dead and the living.
11 For it is written: "As I live, says the Lord, every knee shall bow to Me, and every tongue shall confess to God."

At this point only New Jerusalem and the lake of fire remain. God has removed everyone from the earth and destroyed the empty planet, a planet devastated by the tribulation. He has emptied hell of all its inhabitants and cast hell and death into the lake of fire.

The New Heaven and the New Earth

God now creates a new heaven and a new earth in perfection, just as the Garden of Eden was before the serpent entered. Those whose works have stood at the great white throne judgment are set down as the eternal nations upon the new earth. The body of Christ now rules and reigns with Christ Jesus over the universe. All others, who did not pass judgment, are in the lake of fire. New Jerusalem, heaven, is part of the earth, and the two forever become one in God's recreated perfection.

Revelation 21
1 And I saw a new heaven and a new earth, for the first heaven and the first earth had passed away. Also there was no more sea.

2 Peter 3
13 Nevertheless we, according to His promise, look for new heavens and a new earth in which righteousness dwells.

The Eternal Nations

Despite the fact that the eternal nations will have escaped the lake of fire, they will still have to toe the line.

Isaiah 66
22 "For as the new heavens and the new earth which I will make shall remain before Me," says the Lord, "So shall your descendants and your name remain.
23 "And it shall come to pass that from one New Moon to another, and from one Sabbath to another, all flesh shall come to worship before Me," says the Lord.

God's perfect creation is now in order and will remain so for ever and ever, Amen.

Chapter 7

Why Is The Church Raptured?

God knows the end from the beginning and has always provided a way of escape for His people. The rapture of the church is God's way for the body of Christ to escape the outpouring of His judgment during the tribulation. When Noah was the only righteous man left on earth, God planned a way of escape for him and his whole family. God had become unwilling to bear any longer the corruption and abominations of the world, so He took Noah aside and gave him instructions for building the ark. He chose to preserve Noah and his family because, as we are told in Genesis 6, He saw that, **[9]Noah was a just man, perfect in his generations. Noah walked with God.**

Genesis 6
**12 So God looked upon the earth, and indeed it was corrupt; for all flesh had corrupted their way on the earth.
13 And God said to Noah, "The end of all flesh has come before Me, for the earth is filled with violence through them; and behold, I will destroy them with the earth.
14 "Make yourself an ark of gopherwood; make rooms in the ark, and cover it inside and outside with pitch.
15 "And this is how you shall make it: The length of the ark shall be three hundred cubits, its width fifty cubits, and its height thirty cubits.
16 "You shall make a window for the ark, and you shall finish**

it to a cubit from above; and set the door of the ark in its side. You shall make it with lower, second, and third decks.

17 "And behold, I Myself am bringing floodwaters on the earth, to destroy from under heaven all flesh in which is the breath of life; everything that is on the earth shall die.

18 "But I will establish My covenant with you; and you shall go into the ark you, your sons, your wife, and your sons' wives with you."

God's instructions to Noah were specific and extensive. God had a plan, not only for Noah but for his whole family, to escape the coming destruction. Had Noah, however, not listened to God he would have perished with the rest of the corrupt world. God made the provision, but there is no doubt that Noah had to bear the scorn of the world as he followed God's instructions.

Genesis 6

22 Thus Noah did; according to all that God commanded him, so he did.

Genesis 7

1 Then the Lord said to Noah, "Come into the ark, you and all your household, because I have seen that you are righteous before Me in this generation."

Noah is a type for this last generation. We are in the same place that he was. God has laid out in His Word every detail of the coming tribulation. Our ark is the rapture of the church. Just as He did with Noah, God has instructed us in how to qualify for the rapture, how to build our ark in the Spirit

It is not now, nor was it ever, God's will that the righteous perish. That is why He has provided the church with a means of escape. Just as with Noah's time, however, there are those foolish enough to ignore God's warnings, foolish enough to scoff and go on with business as usual. They will, despite God's wishes and provision, perish. This will happen through either their unbelief or their lack of knowledge; either way, it will be nobody's fault but their own.

It is significant that God took not only Noah into the ark but all his **household** as well. Our merciful Lord has made the same provision for us.

Isaiah 49
25 But thus says the Lord: "Even the captives of the mighty shall be taken away, and the prey of the terrible be delivered; for I will contend with him who contends with you, and I will save your children."

Acts 16
31 So they said, "Believe on the Lord Jesus Christ, and you will be saved, you and your household."

If we are willing to be separated from the world and walk with God in righteousness, we shall have the same results as Noah. Walking with God means believing and living by His Word to the exclusion of all else. Just as there is no doubt that the sinful world mocked Noah while he was building the ark, it will mock and/or argue with us until the moment of destruction comes. Our time does differ from Noah's in that everyone has the opportunity to board the latter-day ark, however, note that the operative word here is opportunity. God took only Noah and his family into the ark, and the door was shut. Jesus will catch away only those who have qualified as the body of Christ; the rest will be left behind.

To qualify we must:

a. Be blood bought, which makes us the righteousness of God in Christ Jesus; and,
b. Be baptized in the Holy Spirit with the evidence of tongues, which is our adoption into the family of God; and,
c. Know who we are in Christ as His body, choosing to walk in righteousness as part of the bridegroom and not the bride; and,
d. Be eagerly expecting the pre-tribulation rapture of the church.

Get "Whatever! We'll all find out when the time comes" out of your thinking. If Noah had felt that way, he and his whole family would have been swept away in the flood. Even his righteousness would not have saved him. His righteousness qualified him to be saved, but he had to build the ark and get into it.

Noah qualified on two counts. First, he was a **just man**, meaning he walked by faith in God. We, like Noah, are justified by our faith, ours being in Christ Jesus. Second, Noah qualified as a man **perfect in his generations**. That meant that his seed was not corrupted by the Nephilim, the giants on the earth who were the fallen angels. This was one of many attempts by Satan to stop Jesus from coming to redeem mankind.

Genesis 6
**1 Now it came to pass, when men began to multiply on the face of the earth, and daughters were born to them,
2 that the sons of God saw the daughters of men, that they were beautiful; and they took wives for themselves of all whom they chose.
3 And the Lord said, "My Spirit shall not strive with man forever, for he is indeed flesh; yet his days shall be one hundred and twenty years."
4 There were giants on the earth in those days, and also afterward, when the sons of God came in to the daughters of men and they bore children to them. Those were the mighty men who were of old, men of renown.
5 Then the Lord saw that the wickedness of man was great in the earth, and that every intent of the thoughts of his heart was only evil continually.**

Adam—until he sinned and became a son of the devil—was a son of God because God had created him. As a consequence of his treason, however, Adam's descendants were not sons of God. Adam chose to become a son of the serpent and, thereafter in the Old Testament, the sons of God were always, and only, angels. It was not until the new birth in Christ Jesus that we again became sons of God, and are thus referred to in the New Testament.

When **the sons of God came in to the daughters of men and they**

bore children to them their offspring were a corrupted, perverted line. The Nephilim, who appeared as flesh, mated with the daughters of men for the sole purpose of corrupting the Adamic line. If Satan could have corrupted all the families of the earth with his seed, Jesus would not have been able to be born of woman, and God's plan of redemption would have failed. We know from Genesis 6:8-9 that the generations of Noah escaped this corruption and thus qualified to be saved.

We, as the body of Christ, are in the same position. Through Christ we are made perfect in our generations.

Galatians 3
13 Christ has redeemed us from the curse of the law, having become a curse for us (for it is written, "Cursed is everyone who hangs on a tree"),
14 that the blessing of Abraham might come upon the Gentiles in Christ Jesus, that we might receive the promise of the Spirit through faith.
16 Now to Abraham and his Seed were the promises made. He does not say, "And to seeds," as of many, but as of one, "And to your Seed," who is Christ.

Even though, through the fall of Adam, we were born into a sinful line —and categorized thus as sons and daughters of the devil—we become part of the seed of Abraham through the new birth. By becoming new creatures in Christ, a new race of beings reborn in the purity of the blood of the Lamb, we are again sons and daughters of God.

1 Corinthians 15
22 For as in Adam all die, even so in Christ all shall be made alive.
23 But each one in his own order: Christ the firstfruits, afterward those who are Christ's at His coming.

We must, however, just like Noah, walk in the ways of righteousness, obeying the Word of God. Noah and his family were only eight in number, an insignificant percentage of the population at the time. I do not believe that those qualifying for the rapture will be a significant percentage either. Matthew 7 (KJV) tells us that, [14]**strait is the gate, and narrow is the way, which leadeth unto life, and few there be that find it**.

The **few there be** that find life will be those who go the whole way and qualify for the rapture. That is why you must not run with the crowd, believe every wind of doctrine you hear, and wind up destroyed with the majority. You must think for yourself and put everything to the Word test, including this writing.

Jesus Came to Divide

> Luke 12
>
> **49** "I came to send fire on the earth, and how I wish it were already kindled!
>
> **50** "But I have a baptism to be baptized with, and how distressed I am till it is accomplished!
>
> **51** "Do you suppose that I came to give peace on earth? I tell you, not at all, but rather division.
>
> **52** "For from now on five in one house will be divided: three against two, and two against three.
>
> **53** "Father will be divided against son and son against father, mother against daughter and daughter against mother, mother-in-law against her daughter-in-law and daughter-in-law against her mother-in-law."
>
> **54** Then He also said to the multitudes, "When you see a cloud rising out of the west, immediately you say, 'A shower is coming'; and so it is.
>
> **55** "And when you see the south wind blow, you say, 'There will be hot weather'; and there is.
>
> **56** "Hypocrites! You can discern the face of the sky and of the earth, but how is it you do not discern this time?"

The Father sent Jesus to judge, or divide, the earth. It was hard for Him to see how few had ears to hear. He hated the sin and rebellion He was forced to witness. He longed for the end to come and the fires of purification to be over. He grieved with the Father over the condition of man. In Luke 12 He was in agony on behalf of those who were missing the point so completely. He called those who were ignorant of the signs of the times **hypocrites.**

The same applies to the church today.

We are called to be separated from those who do not believe because unbelief is evil (Hebrews 3:12). We are not only to be separated from the unsaved world, but also from faithless Christians, because evil company corrupts (1 Corinthians 15:33). Faithless Christians tend to be far more of a destructive influence upon the unwary than anyone else; the guard of the unwary is down when they regard those about them as brethren. A little leaven leavens the whole batch and a little unbelief spreads like cancer.

The most glaring example of this is found right in churches. Mark 16 tells us, **[17]these signs will follow those who believe: In My name they will cast out demons; they will speak with new tongues; [18]they will take up serpents; and if they drink anything deadly, it will by no means hurt them; they will lay hands on the sick, and they will recover.** Any church, even if it calls itself charismatic, that does not do all of the above on a regular basis is a place of unbelief, a dead church. Dead churches produce dead saints.

I hasten to add that taking up serpents has nothing to do with dancing or playing with snakes, notwithstanding the fact that there are cults who have made this part of their so-called worship. Jesus is talking about false doctrine.

Psalm 58
3 The wicked are estranged from the womb; they go astray as soon as they are born, speaking lies.
4 Their poison is like the poison of a serpent;

Serpents are venomous snakes, and believers are charged by Jesus to take hold of the venom of false doctrine and evict it from the church.

2 Timothy 2
15 Be diligent to present yourself approved to God, a worker who does not need to be ashamed, rightly dividing the word of truth.

**16 But shun profane and vain babblings, for they will increase to more ungodliness.
17 And their message will spread like cancer. Hymenaeus and Philetus are of this sort,**

The Greek word for **cancer** is *gangraina*, which means gangrene. The only way to get rid of gangrene is to cut it out. The dictionary definition of gangrene is, "The rotting of tissue in the body, caused by a failure in the circulation of the blood, as from infection." The spiritual application of this secular definition is that, when the body of Christ is contaminated with false doctrine, the blood of Jesus is rendered ineffective. False doctrine can cause the whole body to die of decay unless it is cut out.

Likewise, drinking anything deadly does not mean deliberately swallowing poison. It relates to sanctifying our food with the Word of God, so that pesticides, hormones and harmful bacteria that could otherwise harm us are nullified.

2 Corinthians 6
**17 Therefore "Come out from among them and be separate," says the Lord. "Do not touch what is unclean, and I will receive you.
18 "I will be a Father to you, and you shall be My sons and daughters," says the Lord Almighty.**

It is time for us to get our house in order so that we qualify to be rescued. The rapture is our final division from the world. We must have confidence in the Word, confidence in ourselves, confidence in our righteousness. We must not be ashamed of anything when Jesus comes.

1 John 2
**28 And now, little children, abide in Him, that when He appears, we may have confidence and not be ashamed before Him at His coming.
29 If you know that He is righteous, you know that everyone who practices righteousness is born of Him.**

We must be willing to let Jesus divide us from all unrighteousness—which includes unbelief—if we are to be His body. If we are upset by this, and unwilling to accept it, we shall not overcome. We must walk by faith. We must regard the scorn of unbelievers as a badge of honor.

John 15
18 If the world hates you, you know that it hated Me before it hated you.
19 If you were of the world, the world would love its own. Yet because you are not of the world, but I chose you out of the world, therefore the world hates you.

People who are not on the same spiritual page with us will, sooner or later, hate us; about this there is no doubt. The antichrist spirit in them hates the Holy Spirit in us. The most frequent lament I hear from Christians who have finally chosen the narrow path is that they are lonely. People call me and say they are miserable because they no longer have the fellowship of all the faithless friends and family they enjoyed and were used to.

People blessed enough to find a believing church occasionally tell me that they have become outcasts in the Christian community. If they are looking for sympathy or a pat on the back from me, they are sorely disappointed. I point out to them that going to a believing church puts them in position to be healed, delivered, made whole, and to learn how to overcome every weapon formed against them. I tell them that none of us can have it both ways. If being surrounded with whining, faithless friends and family is important to you, if having people say nice things about your church and your pastor is what you seek, if winning the Christian congeniality award is your measure of happiness, you are lost.

God made a way of escape for Abraham and Lot. He separated them from Sodom and Gomorrah before He rained fire and brimstone down upon those abominable places and destroyed them. He did this to rescue them and preserve His perpetual covenant with Abraham. This covenant of promise continues for those who are Abraham's descendants in Christ Jesus.

Lot's wife, even though she had escaped destruction, could not let go; she looked back and perished. She was not willing to be divided;

her heart was back there in Sodom. Maybe she was thinking of those friends who were about to perish and how much she would miss them. Maybe she was thinking of her home there. Whatever it was that held that place in her heart, it was her downfall.

For people today who are not willing to be divided from a dying world, and who choose to stay part of it, the result will be the same.

Luke 9
62 But Jesus said to him, "No one, having put his hand to the plow, and looking back, is fit for the kingdom of God."

If You Do Not Obey Him, You Do Not Love Him

John 14
23 Jesus answered and said to him, "If anyone loves Me, he will keep My word; and My Father will love him, and We shall come to him and make Our home with him.
24 "He who does not love Me does not keep My words; and the word which you hear is not Mine but the Father's who sent Me."

If we do not obey the Lord, we do not love the Lord; if we do not love the Lord, we cannot be separated unto Him. Think of love as a beautiful cutting-horse. The horse (Love) goes into the herd, with the rider (Jesus) sitting above him, and divides those who love Him from those who do not. The loving ones are herded into the Lord's barn; the others are left behind. The focus of our love is the determining factor in whether we are gathered into the Lord's barn or left behind.

John 14
15 If you love Me, keep My commandments.
16 And I will pray the Father, and He will give you another Helper, that He may abide with you forever,
17 even the Spirit of truth, whom the world cannot receive, because it neither sees Him nor knows Him; but you know Him, for He dwells with you and will be in you.
18 I will not leave you orphans; I will come to you.

Jesus requires that we allow ourselves to be divided from all unrighteousness and come into full obedience to Him and His Word. When the last trump sounds we, the body of Christ, will be gathered into His barn. The rest will be left and the vast majority of them will take the mark of the beast and burn in the lake of fire forever.

> Matthew 13
> **30 Let both grow together until the harvest, and at the time of harvest I will say to the reapers, "First gather together the tares and bind them in bundles to burn them, but gather the wheat into my barn.**
> **43 "Then the righteous will shine forth as the sun in the kingdom of their Father. He who has ears to hear, let him hear!"**

God created Adam for fellowship and His objective has not changed. He has spent six thousand years providing His man—now the faithful, believing body of Christ—with the opportunity to get back into right-standing with Him. He must remove us from the earth while He judges the wicked world and purifies it once again, just as Noah floated in his ark above the earth until the waters that flooded and purified it were dried up. That judgment was by water, the next will be by fire, but the principle is the same. Were it not for the coming rapture of the church, all of God's efforts would have been in vain.

Chapter 8

The Seven Raptures—Untangling The Confusion

Much of the confusion surrounding the rapture of the church derives from the fact that there is not just one rapture but seven. Once this is recognized in Scripture, difficulty about whether and when the church is raptured is greatly diminished.

Accepting the concept of a rapture is not a matter of faith; three of the seven raptures have already taken place. Faith is required for things we cannot see, things that have not yet happened, things that do not yet exist. The three raptures that have already taken place are clearly recorded in the Word. So are the four yet to come.

The catching up of the church to meet the Lord in the air (1 Thessalonians 4:17) came to be called a "rapture" in 1830 when two ladies in Scotland had a vision and prophesied about the end-time. The words of the prophecy referred to the removal of the church from the world as the "rapture." I have no doubt that it came by revelation from the Spirit because in 1997, one hundred and sixty-seven years later, the Bible codes revealed the word *Ha'Natzal* within the first two chapters of Genesis. *Ha'Natzal* means: the rapture; snatching up (*His Name Is Jesus, The Mysterious Yeshua Codes,* pages 76,77; Yacov Rambsel, 1997, Frontier Research Publications, Inc.).

The Bible codes were what God was referring to when He said that much of what He had told Daniel in the vision was for a time in the future. God said in Daniel 12, ⁴"**But you, Daniel, shut up the words,** and seal the book until the time of the end: many shall run to and fro, and knowledge shall increase." ⁹And He said, "Go your way, Daniel, for the words are closed up and sealed until the time of the end." This is now **the time of the end** and the words that were **closed up and sealed** were not in a separate document, but in a book within a book—the Bible—opened by the discovery of the codes.

The *Bible Code* (Michael Drosnin, 1997, Simon & Schuster), which reveals the sealed **book**, was written by a man who, by his own words, did not even believe in God. This was obviously part of God's plan, a clever way to get the world's attention. If a believer had first published this discovery the world would have dismissed it out of hand. As it was, however, *The Bible Code* quickly achieved the *New York Times* best seller list. The world became fully intrigued with this scientific, technological discovery, and it received huge attention. It was even discussed on television news programs.

Drosnin's book focussed exclusively on the accounts of past historical events revealed in the text of the codes. Details of wars, leaders, assassinations, etc., were so specific that everyone was astounded. The church already knew that the Bible was the Word of God; this was a sign for the world. The codes established that the Bible was indeed a supernatural book. Drosnin's book was followed by others written by believers who used the codes to unveil the astounding fact that Jesus and the essentials of the New Testament are revealed in Genesis.

The First Rapture

Enoch was the first to be raptured. Enoch did not die; he was simply taken up by God, just as we shall be. We know that Enoch was a man of faith and walked with God for three hundred years.

> Genesis 5
> **21 Enoch lived sixty-five years, and begot Methuselah.**
> **22 After he begot Methuselah, Enoch walked with God three hundred years, and begot sons and daughters.**
> **23 So all the days of Enoch were three hundred and sixty-five years.**

The Rapture, The Tribulation, And Beyond

24 And Enoch walked with God; and he was not, for God took him.

The Hebrew word for **took** is *laqah*, which means: to be led away; taken away; sent for; taken out; taken up.

Lest we miss the significance of Enoch, his rapture is also recorded in the New Testament.

> Hebrews 11
> **5 By faith Enoch was translated so that he did not see death, "and was not found because God had translated him"; for before his translation he had this testimony, that he pleased God.**
> **6 But without faith it is impossible to please Him, for he who comes to God must believe that He is, and that He is a rewarder of those who diligently seek Him.**

The word **translated** appears twice, and **translation** once, in one Scripture. The Greek word for **translated** is *metatithami*, meaning: change from one place or position to another; take away; carry over; remove.

Enoch walked with God and pleased God through faith, which was his testimony and qualification to be the first to be raptured.

The Second Rapture

Elijah was the second to be raptured and we know much more about him than we do Enoch. His life was one of faith and power with signs and wonders following his ministry (1 Kings 17,18,19; 2 Kings 1, 2).

> 2 Kings 2
> **11 Then it happened, as they continued on and talked, that suddenly a chariot of fire appeared with horses of fire, and separated the two of them; and Elijah went up by a whirlwind into heaven.**

Elijah was very much alive when God took him up **into heaven**, and this time there was a witness: Elisha.

2 Kings 2
12 Now Elisha saw it, and he cried out, "My father, my father, the chariot of Israel and its horsemen!" So he saw him no more. And he took hold of his own clothes and tore them into two.

Note that the moment of the rapture came **suddenly**. Elijah and Elisha were **separated** the moment the chariot of fire **appeared**, and Elijah **went up...into heaven**. The rapture of the church will occur in the same way. The body of Christ will be separated from the earth and go up in the twinkling of an eye when Jesus appears in the air at the last trumpet. We shall be glorified without physical death.

The Third Rapture

The third rapture was Jesus. Yes, Jesus was raptured, even though He was God in the flesh. When He finished His earthly ministry, at the end of the forty days following His resurrection, He was taken up into heaven by a cloud of angels. Jesus' rapture followed the issuance of His final instructions to His disciples and was witnessed by a whole crowd of people.

Acts 1
**9 Now when He had spoken these things, while they watched, He was taken up, and a cloud received Him out of their sight.
10 And while they looked steadfastly toward heaven as He went up, behold, two men stood by them in white apparel,
11 who also said, "Men of Galilee, why do you stand gazing up into heaven? This same Jesus, who was taken up from you into heaven, will so come in like manner as you saw Him go into heaven."**

Another account of the rapture of Jesus is at the end of the Gospel of Mark.

Mark 16
19 So then, after the Lord had spoken to them, He was received up into heaven, and sat down at the right hand of God.

Yet another account of Jesus' rapture comes at the end of the Gospel of Luke.

> Luke 24
> **51 Now it came to pass, while He blessed them, that He was parted from them and carried up into heaven.**

Interestingly enough, the rapture of Jesus is acknowledged by most denominations, though, of course, they have another name for it: The Ascension. Many famous paintings of The Ascension were commissioned by the Catholic Church.

The Fourth Rapture

Now we come to the rapture of the church, which occurs just before the great tribulation.

> Revelation 4
> **1 After these things I looked, and behold, a door standing open in heaven. And the first voice which I heard was like a trumpet speaking with me, saying, "Come up here, and I will show you things which must take place after this."**
> **2 Immediately I was in the Spirit; and behold, a throne set in heaven, and One sat on the throne.**

John, to whom God spoke the book of Revelation, is, in these Scriptures, a type for the body of Christ, and this is the last mention of the body of Christ being on earth. The **door standing open in heaven** signifies the entrance made available to us. The voice **like a trumpet** is, of course, the last trumpet. The words, **Come up here**, are Jesus calling us to Himself at His appearing. After Revelation 4:1, all references to the body of Christ place it in heaven, never again on earth.

The rest of Revelation 4 describes the throne room of God in New Jerusalem, where the church then is, and in Revelation 5 Jesus begins the tribulation by opening the scroll and loosing its seven seals.

God spoke through the prophet Isaiah and established that the body of Christ would not be on earth during the tribulation. The prophecy of John, placing the church in New Jerusalem before God's judgment is loosed, is confirmation of Isaiah's earlier prophecy.

Isaiah 54

9 "For this is like the waters of Noah to Me; for as I have sworn that the waters of Noah would no longer cover the earth, so have I sworn that I would not be angry with you, nor rebuke you.
10 "For the mountains shall depart and the hills be removed, but My kindness shall not depart from you, nor shall My covenant of peace be removed," says the Lord, who has mercy on you.

The reference to **the waters of Noah**, when God destroyed all wickedness on the face of the earth, is a type for the rapture of the church. God will deliver us from the tribulation just as He delivered Noah and his family from the destruction of the flood.

When God says, **My kindness shall not depart from you, nor shall My covenant of peace be removed**, He gives us assurance that there is nothing from which He will not deliver us, and that includes the tribulation. God never intended that His children be subject to the rule of Antichrist.

That the rapture of the church is pre-tribulation is evidenced in many other places in Scripture. In 1 Thessalonians 1 we are told, [10]**to wait for His Son from heaven, whom He raised from the dead, even Jesus who delivers us from the wrath to come**. How could it be clearer than this? Jesus is coming back from heaven to deliver us from the horror of Antichrist and the outpouring of God's wrath.

And then, of course, there is:

Revelation 3

10 Because you have kept My command to persevere, I also will keep you from the hour of trial which shall come upon the whole world, to test those who dwell on the earth.

There are some who believe that the rapture of the church occurs at mid-tribulation because God does not pour out His wrath (Revelation

16:1-21) until the second three and a half years. God does not, however, intend that we escape only half the horror, but all of it. The **covenant of peace** in Isaiah 54:10 means wholeness, not half-ness. The Hebrew word for **peace** in the context is *shalom,* defined as: safety, security, prosperity, wholeness, well being, intactness.

The fifth and sixth raptures do, indeed, occur at mid-tribulation, but they are not for the church; they are for two entirely different groups, as will be explained in a moment.

Another proof that the rapture of the church cannot be other than pre-tribulation is that we, the anointed church, by our presence on earth, are the ones who are restraining the take-over of Antichrist. Satan cannot overtake the world system, hard as he may try, while the church continues to occupy the earth.

2 Thessalonians 2
6 And now you know what is restraining, that he may be revealed in his own time.
7 For the mystery of lawlessness is already at work; only he who now restrains will do so until he is taken out of the way.
8 And then the lawless one will be revealed, whom the Lord will consume with the breath of His mouth and destroy with the brightness of His coming.

The reason the world is in such abysmal condition and such horrible things are happening is that Satan, who can only work through those available to him, has a majority of the population through whom to work. The moment the church is raptured, the last resistance to Satan is eliminated and he will be able to rise to power.

2 Thessalonians 2
1 Now, brethren, concerning the coming of our Lord Jesus Christ and our gathering together to Him, we ask you,
2 not to be soon shaken in mind or troubled, either by spirit or by word or by letter, as if from us, as though the day of Christ had come.
3 Let no one deceive you by any means; for that Day will not come unless the falling away comes first, and the man of sin is revealed, the son of perdition,

4 who opposes and exalts himself above all that is called God or that is worshiped, so that he sits as God in the temple of God, showing himself that he is God.
5 Do you not remember that when I was still with you I told you these things?

The first two verses focus on **the coming of our Lord Jesus Christ and our gathering together to Him**, and that we are **not to be soon shaken in mind or troubled**. This is the glorious appearing of Christ Jesus, Who comes in the air to gather us up to Him. We are admonished not to be deceived.

Verse 3 tells us that deception about the end-time comes in many guises, many **means**, and must be avoided. To fully understand this verse we must understand that **that Day** refers to the second advent, and we must come to grips with **the falling away**. 2 Thessalonians 2:3 is the only place where a falling away is mentioned in connection with the end-time so, to make sure we have this right, we shall go back to the Greek.

The Greek word translated as **falling away** is *apostasia*. For four hundred years it has been accepted as meaning a wholesale backsliding of the church, a falling away from faith. Not only is this not confirmed by any other Scripture, but it makes no sense in the context. How can there simultaneously be a falling away from the church and the greatest revival of all time?

Literally, *apostasia* means: separate from the state; divorce. The footnotes in *The Amplified Bible* state that another definition of *apostasia* is: departure (of the church). *The New Scofield Study Bible* gives *apostasia* as the word for **falling away** in the study notes and defines it as: the departure. Weymouth, greatly noted for his foreign language and linguistic skills, realized that **falling away** made no sense within the context and left the word *apostasia* in his translation (*The New Testament in Modern Speech*).

With the exception of Weymouth, it apparently did not occur to translators in general that it made absolutely no sense that there would be an unprecedented backsliding during the greatest revival of all time, when God would be pouring out His Spirit on all flesh (Joel 2:28). The only reasonable explanation for translators missing this it that they had no revelation of the rapture of the church. This is a perfectly reasonable assumption; the Holy Spirit did not start to reveal it in full measure until the nineteenth century.

Given all of this, the only reasonable and acceptable translation of *apostasia,* within the context of 2 Thessalonians 2:3, is the separation, or divorce, of the glorious church from the state, the world system, to wit: the rapture, or departure, of the church from the world. Any reasonable seeker after truth must realize that **falling away** cannot stand close scrutiny when the whole context is considered, particularly in view of verses 1 and 7.

So, verse three, accurately paraphrased should be, "Do not be deceived, it will not be possible for Jesus to return at the end of the tribulation, at the second advent, unless the departure of the church from the earth occurs first and Antichrist is revealed."

2 Thessalonians 2
6 And now you know what is restraining, that he may be revealed in his own time.
7 For the mystery of lawlessness is already at work; only He who now restrains will do so until He is taken out of the way.

We now understand that **what is restraining** and **he who now restrains** both refer to the body of Christ during our occupation of the earth, and **will do so until he is taken out of the way** perfectly describes the departure of the church, the rapture, just before the start of the tribulation.

1 Thessalonians 5
1 But concerning the times and the seasons, brethren, you have no need that I should write to you.
2 For you yourselves know perfectly that the day of the Lord so comes as a thief in the night.
3 For when they say, "Peace and safety!" then sudden destruction comes upon them, as labor pains upon a pregnant woman. And they shall not escape.

Paul says to the **brethren,** the body of Christ, that we must **know**

perfectly that when Jesus returns as the **thief in the night**, which is at the end of the tribulation, **sudden destruction comes upon them**, the unbelieving world, **and they shall not escape**.

> 1 Thessalonians 5
> **4 But you, brethren, are not in darkness, so that this Day should overtake you as a thief.**
> **5 You are all sons of light and sons of the day. We are not of the night nor of darkness.**
> **6 Therefore let us not sleep, as others do, but let us watch and be sober.**
> **7 For those who sleep, sleep at night, and those who get drunk are drunk at night.**
> **8 But let us who are of the day be sober, putting on the breastplate of faith and love, and as a helmet the hope of salvation.**

We, the **brethren, are not in darkness, so that this Day should overtake** us **as a thief**. How much clearer could it be? The additional description of the body of Christ as the **sons of light and sons of the day**, while the unbelieving world is **those who...sleep at night, and those who...are drunk at night**, surely puts to rest any possible failure to comprehend.

> 1 Thessalonians 5
> **9 For God did not appoint us to wrath, but to obtain salvation through our Lord Jesus Christ,**
> **10 who died for us, that whether we wake or sleep, we should live together with Him.**
> **11 Therefore comfort each other and edify one another, just as you also are doing.**

We are reminded that **God did not appoint us to wrath, but to obtain salvation through our Lord Jesus Christ**. The word **salvation** is the Greek word *soteria,* which means: rescue; deliverance. It usually refers to the state of believers as being safe from righteous wrath through proper relationship with God.

We are instructed to **comfort** and **edify one another** with this knowledge of God's plan. Anyone who chooses to have eyes to read and ears to hear cannot deny this truth. You can also see how vital it is to comprehend the terms that relate to the rapture of the church, as opposed to those that relate to the second advent. Once one grasps the terminology, understanding immediately follows.

Knowing and accepting the timing of the rapture of the church is of the essence of qualifying for it. It is not good enough to simply believe in any old rapture at any old time. Our rapture, like all else in our covenant, is for whomsoever will.

Revelation 22
17...And whoever desires, let him take the water of life freely.

The Lord has given us free will and will never, even if it is for our own good, force anything upon us. Everything, every good and perfect gift from above (James 1:17), is available to whomsoever will. We must choose life.

Deuteronomy 30
19 I call heaven and earth as witnesses today against you, that I have set before you life and death, blessing and cursing; therefore choose life, that both you and your descendants may live;

Think about it: every provision of God requires that we choose to receive it; God has left it up to us. If this were not so, every single person in the world would have been saved when Jesus came two thousand years ago to bring salvation (John 3:16).

We must choose to receive Jesus as Savior.

Even when we choose salvation from condemnation, we can miss being born again if we do not choose to be baptized in the Holy Spirit.

We can be born again but stay sick if we do not choose the healing Jesus has provided.

We can choose healing but reject deliverance and stay oppressed.

We can be born again, be healed and delivered, but live in lack if we do not choose financial prosperity.

Jesus has paid the price and all these results of the cross are ours, but not unless we choose to be a whosoever will. The pre-tribulation rapture of the church is no different. We must choose it for ourselves and refuse to be bullied out of it.

All three of the raptures that have already taken place, Enoch, Elijah and Jesus, were received by the choice of faith. Look again at those Scriptures and you will see it for yourself.

Every Scripture relating to the pre-tribulation rapture of the church requires that we love His appearing (2 Timothy 4:8), are looking (Titus 2:13), are eagerly waiting (Hebrews 9:28), are watching (Revelation 3:3), or, as we are told in 1 Thessalonians 4, expect His coming, **[14]For if we believe... [17]Then we who are alive and remain shall be caught up together with them in the clouds to meet the Lord in the air.**

Titus 2
11 For the grace of God that brings salvation has appeared to all men,
12 teaching us that, denying ungodliness and worldly lusts, we should live soberly, righteously, and godly in the present age,
13 looking for the blessed hope and glorious appearing of our great God and Savior Jesus Christ,
14 who gave Himself for us, that He might redeem us from every lawless deed and purify for Himself His own special people, zealous for good works.
15 Speak these things, exhort, and rebuke with all authority. Let no one despise you.

This is one of the most powerful exhortations in Scripture regarding our attitude and behavior concerning the rapture of the church.

The **salvation** of verse 11 is the Greek word *soterion*, which means: method or means to salvation. It differs from *soteria*, which describes the state of salvation. In other words, the way, through the blood of Jesus, has been provided, and it is up to us to choose it.

We are told to walk in righteousness and be **looking for the blessed hope and glorious appearing of our great God and Savior Jesus Christ**. The blessed hope and the glorious appearing are both expressions referring to the rapture of the church.

We are not to keep quiet about our blessed hope. We are told to speak about it and refuse to be hushed up and intimidated. We are to exhort others to be excited about it and spread the good news. We are also told to be ready to defend our blessed hope, and deal with anyone who comes against the awesome promise of the rapture by being ready to **rebuke with all authority**.

Authority is only in Christ through the Word, so we must be armed with the Word and prepared and eager to cite it at any and every opportunity. We are not to be influenced by men despising us because of our confidence in the rapture of the church. We must be like blind Bartimaeus who, when told by the crowd to be quiet, called out even more loudly for the mercy of Jesus, and received it.

Eagerly **looking for the blessed hope and glorious appearing of our great God and Savior Jesus Christ** is not, in any way, a conflict with walking in our authority in Christ now. We have been commanded to occupy the earth until Jesus returns for us (Luke 19:13). The dominion God gave to Adam, which Satan stole in the garden, was taken back by Jesus when He went to hell between His death on the cross and His resurrection. We have that authority now, and are required to walk in the victory of it, but it is not without the devil's resistance. That is why we must fight the good fight of faith and bind the strong man.

1 John 3
**2 Beloved, now we are children of God; and it has not yet been revealed what we shall be, but we know that when He is revealed, we shall be like Him, for we shall see Him as He is.
3 And everyone who has this hope in Him purifies himself, just as He is pure.**

Colossians 3
4 When Christ who is our life appears, then you also will appear with Him in glory.

The anti-rapture teachers, who are leading people into the tribulation by the tens of thousands and will stand accountable for it, are actually promoting the doctrine of Antichrist. These sadly and dangerously deceived people, some of them important figures in the Christian world, promote the lie that the sudden disappearance of a whole lot of people will not be the rapture of the church but the removal of the wicked at the end of the age, whereafter the righteous who remain will invite Jesus to set up His kingdom on earth. This foul, false doctrine is how the devil himself will explain the rapture of the church at the beginning of the tribulation, and bring the world to accept him as God.

Jesus Himself separates the rapture of the church from the second advent.

Revelation 3
3 Remember therefore how you have received and heard; hold fast and repent. Therefore if you will not watch, I will come upon you as a thief, and you will not know what hour I will come upon you.

He says that if we **shall not watch** we shall miss the rapture, be stuck in the tribulation, and have no choice but to wait for the **thief in the night**, which is the second advent.

The terrible truth is that those who proclaim that the church is going through the tribulation will do so. Jesus tells us in Mark 11:23 that we shall have whatsoever we say. Our words determine our future in every way, including whether we are part of the rapture. Proverbs 18:21 tells us that life and death are in the power of the tongue. That is why Paul told Titus to speak aloud to others and proclaim our blessed hope, and to **rebuke with all authority** those who deny it. The preachers of the doctrine of Antichrist cannot keep you or me here, bless God, but they are dooming themselves, and all who "hear" them, to the tribulation.

Another significant factor is Jesus saying that they **will not know what hour I will come upon** them. It is yet another evidence that the church is raptured. We are exhorted to recognize the signs and the seasons attending our going, whereas, at the end of the tribulation they will be totally unaware.

I am fully cognizant that Jesus said that not even He knows the day and hour of His coming, but only the Father knows. I agree that it is abomination to try to predict the moment of the rapture and that those who do are deceived unto utter foolishness. However, that is not all Jesus said on the subject.

The Rapture, The Tribulation, And Beyond

Matthew 24
36 But of that day and hour no one knows, no, not even the angels of heaven, but My Father only.
37 But as the days of Noah were, so also will the coming of the Son of Man be.
38 For as in the days before the flood, they were eating and drinking, marrying and giving in marriage, until the day that Noah entered the ark,

During the years the ark was being built, no one knew when the rain would come **until the day that Noah entered the ark**. But on that last day, when Noah and his family entered the ark, they knew. The world only knew when the rain started; Noah knew before it started. Noah was prepared; Noah was not standing out in the rain with everyone else, then slipping and sliding his way through the mud to barely make it into the ark when God told him to get aboard and close the door. Noah and his family did not even get wet.

There is no partiality with God (Romans 2:11). What He does for one He will do for all. Therefore, I am happy to tell you that there will not be the wholesale destruction that most of us used to assume would attend the disappearance of the church. On the day of our departure we shall not be caught unaware. We may not know on the day before the rapture, but on the day itself we shall. Pilots will not fly, air traffic controllers will stay home, drivers will not drive, train engineers will not show up, mothers will not send their children to school, and businessmen will not go to work. We shall know. We shall all be looking up into the eastern sky, jumping up and down for joy in the knowledge that the glorious appearing is finally come.

Noah is not the only type for this. Let's look at the account of Elijah's rapture.

2 Kings 2
1 And it came to pass, when the Lord was about to take up Elijah into heaven by a whirlwind, that Elijah went with Elisha from Gilgal.
2 Then Elijah said to Elisha, "Stay here, please, for the Lord has sent me on to Bethel." And Elisha said, "As the Lord lives, and

as your soul lives, I will not leave you!" So they went down to Bethel.
3 And the sons of the prophets who were at Bethel came out to Elisha, and said to him, "Do you know that the Lord will take away your master from over you today?" And he said, "Yes, I know; keep silent!"
4 Then Elijah said to him, "Elisha, stay here, please, for the Lord has sent me on to Jericho." And he said, "As the Lord lives, and as your soul lives, I will not leave you!" So they came to Jericho.
5 And the sons of the prophets who were at Jericho came to Elisha and said to him, "Do you know that the Lord will take away your master from over you today?" So he answered, "Yes, I know; keep silent!"
6 Then Elijah said to him, "Stay here, please, for the Lord has sent me on to the Jordan." And he said, "As the Lord lives, and as your soul lives, I will not leave you!" So the two of them went on.

On that last day, before Elijah was **taken up into heaven by a whirlwind**, Elijah and Elisha entered three cities: Bethel, Jericho, and Jordan. In each of these cities the **sons of the prophets** approached Elisha and told him that **the Lord will take away your master from over you today**. Elisha responded, **Yes, I know; keep silent!** This did not happen once, but three times. The prophets—those sensitive to the Spirit, as will be all of us who have qualified for the rapture—were fully aware of what would happen that day.

2 Kings 2
9 And so it was, when they had crossed over, that Elijah said to Elisha, "Ask! What may I do for you, before I am taken away from you?" And Elisha said, "Please let a double portion of your spirit be upon me."
10 So he said, "You have asked a hard thing. Nevertheless, if you see me when I am taken from you, it shall be so for you; but if not, it shall not be so."
11 Then it happened, as they continued on and talked, that

suddenly a chariot of fire appeared with horses of fire, and separated the two of them; and Elijah went up by a whirlwind into heaven.

As time was running out at the end of the day, Elijah turned to Elisha and said, **Ask! What may I do for you, before I am taken away from you?** It was not long after that, on that day, that **Elijah went up by a whirlwind into heaven.**

By the Holy Spirit, speaking to each of us who is ready and waiting and eagerly expecting, we shall know on the day of departure. Jesus instructed us to recognize the time and the season of His coming, which is not the same as predicting the day. This knowledge is not for unbelievers, which is why Elisha told the prophets to keep silent.

We have no account of Enoch on the day of his rapture, but we know he went by faith; to go by faith he had to be expecting. Elijah knew and Jesus knew and so, likewise, shall we know. I believe that at midnight (Matthew 25:6) the Holy Spirit will awaken all who are qualified and say, "This is the day of your departure; prepare." We shall cancel all plans that we had and begin to shout and praise the Lord. I believe that we shall all be outside, perhaps gathered together in small groups, in the greatest worldwide celebration of faith ever known. We shall be looking up, laughing, dancing, praising, singing, straining our ears, and ready to fly.

1 Thessalonians 4
16 For the Lord Himself will descend from heaven with a shout, with the voice of an archangel, and with the trumpet of God. And the dead in Christ will rise first.
17 Then we who are alive and remain shall be caught up together with them in the clouds to meet the Lord in the air. And thus we shall always be with the Lord.
18 Therefore comfort one another with these words.

It does not matter whether the body of a Christian has been burned, beheaded, drawn and quartered, boiled in oil, buried at sea, eaten by the fishes, rotted in the ground, or been embalmed and preserved in a sealed bronze coffin. God knows where every atom is, and all will be restored. This applies to everyone, past, present, and future.

We shall be changed in the **twinkling of an eye** into glorified saints and receive our crowns of glory just before the tribulation begins.

The Fifth Rapture

This is one of two raptures that take place at mid-tribulation. It is for the saints here on earth who:

a. Fail to qualify for the rapture of the church; and, therefore,
b. Are on earth for the tribulation; and,
c. Are executed for their faith because they refuse to take the mark of the beast.

Revelation 6
9 When He opened the fifth seal, I saw under the altar the souls of those who had been slain for the word of God and for the testimony which they held.
10 And they cried with a loud voice, saying, "How long, O Lord, holy and true, until You judge and avenge our blood on those who dwell on the earth?"
11 And a white robe was given to each of them; and it was said to them that they should rest a little while longer, until both the number of their fellow servants and their brethren, who would be killed as they were, was completed.

When these martyrs exalt the Lord and cry out for justice they are told that they must wait **a little while longer** until the time is **completed** for all the others **who would be killed as they were** to join them. God is going to deal with them as a group.

In the next verse, Revelation 6:12, the sixth seal is opened and God prepares to pour out His wrath. This marks the end of the first three and a half years of the tribulation and establishes the time of the rapture of the mid-tribulation saints. They are taken up before God's wrath is released.

Revelation 6
17 For the great day of His wrath has come, and who is able to stand?

We next see these **ones who come out of the great tribulation** in the throne room of God.

Revelation 7
**9 After these things I looked, and behold, a great multitude which no one could number, of all nations, tribes, peoples, and tongues, standing before the throne and before the Lamb, clothed with white robes, with palm branches in their hands,
10 and crying out with a loud voice, saying, "Salvation belongs to our God who sits on the throne, and to the Lamb!"
13 Then one of the elders answered, saying to me, "Who are these arrayed in white robes, and where did they come from?"
14 And I said to him, "Sir, you know." So he said to me, "These are the ones who come out of the great tribulation, and washed their robes and made them white in the blood of the Lamb.
15 "Therefore they are before the throne of God, and serve Him day and night in His temple. And He who sits on the throne will dwell among them."**

They have been raptured and will join the body of Christ in New Jerusalem. As grisly as the journey is for those who find themselves still in the world after the rapture of the church, being killed for their faith is the best available alternative.

It is important to remember that the wedding of the Lamb takes place at the end of the tribulation but before the return of Jesus at the head of the armies of heaven. Of those on earth during the tribulation, only those killed for their faith (fifth rapture), the 144,000 Jewish evangelists (sixth rapture), and the two end-time witnesses (seventh rapture) will join the body of Christ in heaven. Those who are not killed for their faith, but who, until the end of the tribulation, successfully hide in the rocks and the caves without taking the mark of the beast, will join the nations; they will not join the body of Christ.

Those killed for their faith are mentioned again. They are in the throne room of God with the body of Christ when Jesus sets up His millennial reign.

> Revelation 20
> **4 And I saw thrones, and they sat on them, and judgment was committed to them. And I saw the souls of those who had been beheaded for their witness to Jesus and for the word of God, who had not worshiped the beast or his image, and had not received his mark on their foreheads or on their hands. And they lived and reigned with Christ for a thousand years.**
> **5 But the rest of the dead did not live again until the thousand years were finished. This is the first resurrection.**
> **6 Blessed and holy is he who has part in the first resurrection. Over such the second death has no power, but they shall be priests of God and of Christ, and shall reign with Him a thousand years.**

The Sixth Rapture

The sixth rapture also occurs at mid-tribulation and is for the 144,000 Jewish, male, virgin (Revelation 14:4) evangelists, 12,000 from each of the twelve tribes of Israel (Revelation 7:5-8). They will be born again and protected from the beast by the mark of God on their foreheads. They will be raised up to preach the gospel during the first three and a half years of the tribulation.

> Revelation 7
> **2 Then I saw another angel ascending from the east, having the seal of the living God. And he cried with a loud voice to the four angels to whom it was granted to harm the earth and the sea,**
> **3 saying, "Do not harm the earth, the sea, or the trees till we have sealed the servants of our God on their foreheads."**
> **4 And I heard the number of those who were sealed. One hundred and forty-four thousand of all the tribes of the children of Israel were sealed:**

Revelation 13 tells us, **[5]And he was given a mouth speaking great things and blasphemies, and he was given authority to continue for forty-two months.** Although this refers to the beast, we must infer, because in the next reference to the 144,000 they are in the throne room of heaven, that they were raptured at this point.

>Revelation 14
>**1 Then I looked, and behold, a Lamb standing on Mount Zion, and with Him one hundred and forty-four thousand, having His Father's name written on their foreheads.**
>**2 And I heard a voice from heaven, like the voice of many waters, and like the voice of loud thunder. And I heard the sound of harpists playing their harps.**
>**3 And they sang as it were a new song before the throne, before the four living creatures, and the elders; and no one could learn that song except the hundred and forty-four thousand who were redeemed from the earth.**
>**4 These are the ones who were not defiled with women, for they are virgins. These are the ones who follow the Lamb wherever He goes. These were redeemed from among men, being firstfruits to God and to the Lamb.**
>**5 And in their mouth was found no guile, for they are without fault before the throne of God.**

The 144,000 are an entirely different group from the remnant of the Jews, whom God has reserved unto Himself to honor His covenant. The remnant will be hidden in the desert during the tribulation (Revelation 12:13-17) and will be gathered at the end (Matthew 24:29-31), with those from the rocks and hills, to move on to the nations.

Immediately after the rapture of the 144,000 Jewish evangelists God releases the angels to preach the gospel for the second half of the tribulation (Revelation 14:6).

The Seventh Rapture

The seventh and final rapture is for the two end-time witnesses. They are, without question, Enoch and Elijah. Yes, they are raptured twice, but that is the way God established it. The two end-time witnesses, whom God sends from heaven (Revelation 11:4), will be killed and resurrected at the end of the tribulation. Enoch and Elijah are the only two in heaven who have not died, and God says that we can only die once.

Hebrews 9
27 And as it is appointed for men to die once, but after this the judgment,

The two end-time witnesses are publicly killed, lie in the streets of Jerusalem for three and a half days, and are then resurrected and raptured to re-join the body of Christ.

Some insist that the two end-time witnesses are Moses and Elijah because they appeared with Jesus in the vision on the Mount of Transfiguration. Not so. That event had nothing to do with the identity of the witnesses. Moses, who died at a hundred and twenty years old, was there to represent the righteous dead; Elijah, who was caught up very much alive in a whirlwind, was there to represent those who would be alive and remain to be caught up in the fourth rapture, the rapture of the church.

"Wait a minute," you say. "If we're all to die once, what about all of us who stay alive all the way to the judgment seat of Christ? Explain that one!" Thank you for asking, I shall be happy to. In Christ, the old man dies and we rise to new life in Him. Therefore, we are already dead and have been judged righteous by the blood of Jesus.

Romans 6
8 Now if we died with Christ, we believe that we shall also live with Him,

Colossians 3
2 Set your mind on things above, not on things on the earth.
3 For you died, and your life is hidden with Christ in God.
4 When Christ who is our life appears, then you also will appear with Him in glory.

The Rapture, The Tribulation, And Beyond 163

2 Timothy 2
11 This is a faithful saying: For if we died with Him, we shall also live with Him.
12 If we endure, we shall also reign with Him. If we deny Him, He also will deny us.

Now we can get back to the two end-time witnesses. God sends them back to the earth during the second half of the tribulation, with unlimited supernatural power, to harass and torment Antichrist and his people and witness on the Lord's behalf.

Revelation 11
2 But leave out the court which is outside the temple, and do not measure it, for it has been given to the Gentiles. And they will tread the holy city under foot for forty-two months.
3 And I will give power to my two witnesses, and they will prophesy one thousand two hundred and sixty days, clothed in sackcloth.
4 These are the two olive trees and the two lampstands standing before the God of the earth.
5 And if anyone wants to harm them, fire proceeds from their mouth and devours their enemies. And if anyone wants to harm them, he must be killed in this manner.
6 These have power to shut heaven, so that no rain falls in the days of their prophecy; and they have power over waters to turn them to blood, and to strike the earth with all plagues, as often as they desire.

Desperate to be rid of these two tormentors, Antichrist pulls out all the stops. He releases his most ferocious beast from the bottomless pit to make war on Enoch and Elijah, and finally manages to kill them.

Revelation 11
7 Now when they finish their testimony, the beast that ascends out of the bottomless pit will make war against them, overcome them, and kill them.
8 And their dead bodies will lie in the street of the great city

which spiritually is called Sodom and Egypt, where also our Lord was crucified.
9 Then those from the peoples, tribes, tongues, and nations will see their dead bodies three and a half days, and not allow their dead bodies to be put into graves.
10 And those who dwell on the earth will rejoice over them, make merry, and send gifts to one another, because these two prophets tormented those who dwell on the earth.

Antichrist, who has an unending capacity for stupidity, is ecstatic and again thinks he has beaten God. God allows the two witnesses to remain in death for three and a half days, then resurrects and raptures them. To add insult to injury, their departure is followed in the same hour by a huge, devastating earthquake that causes the people who survive it to give glory to God.

Revelation 11
11 Now after the three and a half days the breath of life from God entered them, and they stood on their feet, and great fear fell on those who saw them.
12 And they heard a loud voice from heaven saying to them, "Come up here." And they ascended to heaven in a cloud, and their enemies saw them.
13 In the same hour there was a great earthquake, and a tenth of the city fell. In the earthquake seven thousand men were killed, and the rest were afraid and gave glory to the God of heaven.

It is interesting to note that the words spoken to the two witnesses, **Come up here,** are the very same ones used to describe the rapture of the church in Revelation 4:1. The two witnesses then **ascend to heaven in a cloud**. Once these last two members of the body of Christ arrive back in heaven, the bridegroom is complete and the wedding of the Lamb takes place.

Revelation 19
1 After these things I heard a loud voice of a great multitude in

The Rapture, The Tribulation, And Beyond

heaven, saying, "Alleluia! Salvation and glory and honor and power to the Lord our God!

2 "For true and righteous are His judgments, because He has judged the great harlot who corrupted the earth with her fornication; and He has avenged on her the blood of His servants shed by her."

3 Again they said, "Alleluia! And her smoke rises up forever and ever!"

4 And the twenty-four elders and the four living creatures fell down and worshiped God who sat on the throne, saying, "Amen! Alleluia!"

5 Then a voice came from the throne, saying, "Praise our God, all you His servants and those who fear Him, both small and great!"

6 And I heard, as it were, the voice of a great multitude, as the sound of many waters and as the sound of mighty thunderings, saying, "Alleluia! For the Lord God Omnipotent reigns!

7 "Let us be glad and rejoice and give Him glory, for the marriage of the Lamb has come, and His wife has made herself ready."

8 And to her it was granted to be arrayed in fine linen, clean and bright, for the fine linen is the righteous acts of the saints.

9 Then he said to me, "Write: 'Blessed are those who are called to the marriage supper of the Lamb!'" And he said to me, "These are the true sayings of God."

The triumphant strains of the seventh trumpet fill the earth. The final moment of God's judgment has arrived. When the people look up they see the armies of heaven, astride their white horses, filling the sky in military ranks as Jesus returns to reclaim the earth.

Revelation 11

15 Then the seventh angel sounded: And there were loud voices in heaven, saying, "The kingdoms of this world have become the kingdoms of our Lord and of His Christ, and He shall reign forever and ever!"

Chapter 9

Preparation And Qualification For The Rapture

Who among us, when about to take a long journey, does not prepare? We pack suitcases with clothes and everything else we shall require and make sure that everything that needs to be done before we leave is done. My husband and I make a check list of everything we need to remember. That way, when we walk out the door and lock it behind us, we are confident that all is in order and nothing has been forgotten. We have peace of mind and can enjoy the trip.

The departure of the body of Christ from the earth will be the longest and most exciting journey any of us has ever taken. What we need to take with us on this trip, however, will not be physical things but spiritual things. God has provided us a check-list of what we need; it is in His Word. Once we know that we are qualified for the rapture—blood-bought, baptized in the Holy Spirit, know who we are in Christ, and expect the pre-tribulation rapture of the church—we move on to the preparations.

Since there have already been three raptures, we can study what marked the lives of those selected and use them as examples. Our lives should be marked by the same qualities. It is obvious why Jesus was raptured, but if we had to describe the lives of Enoch and Elijah, in just a few words, how would we do it?

Righteousness. Faith. Power. They walked with God and cared not for the opinion of men.

In 1 John 2 the Word says, **⁶He who says he abides in Him ought himself also to walk just as He walked.** Enoch and Elijah did just that. God does not instruct us to do anything of which we are not capable. In Christ, through the power of the anointing, we can do all things. Our lives, as we prepare for our blessed hope, should also be ones of righteousness, faith, and power as we walk with God, our top priority being to please Him.

<u>Enoch</u>

There is not much said about Enoch but, in the brief accounts of his life before he was raptured, God tells us that he possessed these qualities: that he walked with God in righteousness and was a man of faith.

> Genesis 5
> **24 And Enoch walked with God; and he was not, for God took him.**

> Hebrews 11
> **5 By faith Enoch was translated so that he did not see death, "and was not found because God had translated him"; for before his translation he had this testimony, that he pleased God.**
> **6 But without faith it is impossible to please Him, for he who comes to God must believe that He is, and that He is a rewarder of those who diligently seek Him.**

Also evident in Enoch's life was the power. The Spirit of the Lord must have been upon him; he prophesied of the return of Christ Jesus with the armies of heaven to finalize God's judgment upon the earth.

> Jude
> **14 Now Enoch, the seventh from Adam, prophesied about these men also, saying, "Behold, the Lord comes with ten thousands of His saints,**
> **15 "to execute judgment on all, to convict all who are ungodly among them of all their ungodly deeds which they have**

committed in an ungodly way, and of all the harsh things which ungodly sinners have spoken against Him."

Enoch was a blessing to God.

Elijah

Elijah, who served God during the reign of Ahab, led a life of faith that was a constant demonstration of the manifestation of God's power. He cared nothing for the opinion of men, but only for the holiness and glory of God.

> 1 Kings 16
> **30 Now Ahab the son of Omri did evil in the sight of the Lord, more than all who were before him.**
> **31 And it came to pass, as though it had been a trivial thing for him to walk in the sins of Jeroboam the son of Nebat, that he took as wife Jezebel the daughter of Ethbaal, king of the Sidonians; and he went and served Baal and worshiped him.**
> **32 Then he set up an altar for Baal in the temple of Baal, which he had built in Samaria.**
> **33 And Ahab made a wooden image. Ahab did more to provoke the Lord God of Israel to anger than all the kings of Israel who were before him.**

Elijah, outraged over this evil in the land, was moved by God to prophesy to Ahab that there would be no rain in the land, nor even dew, unless he, Elijah, said so (1 Kings 17:1). As we continue to read 1 Kings we learn that Elijah was not dependant upon the provision of Ahab, the earthly king, but upon his heavenly King. We are promised the very same thing in Philippians 4, [19]**And my God shall supply all your need according to His riches in glory by Christ Jesus**.

God provided supernaturally for Elijah by the Brook Cherith. The ravens brought him bread and meat each morning and evening and he drank the waters of the brook. When the waters of the brook dried up because of the drought, Elijah did not panic. God told him to go to

Zarephath, to a widow whom, God said, He had commanded to provide for him. Elijah did not question and was quick to obey.

Obedience is the essence of righteousness. God always has a plan for the obedient. Elijah took God at His Word, even though many would be harsh critics of what he did next: he asked a poor widow—who was about to share with her son the last morsel of food she had and then die—to bring him some food before eating herself.

God gives us here a type for the tithe, the principle of firstfruits. Elijah knew that God had commanded this woman to provide for him and he told her God's plan of provision for her if she obeyed. The widow had heard from God; she had opportunity to overcome her lack through obedience.

1 Kings 17

13 And Elijah said to her, "Do not fear; go and do as you have said, but make me a small cake from it first, and bring it to me; and afterward make some for yourself and your son.

14 "For thus says the Lord God of Israel: 'The bin of flour shall not be used up, nor shall the jar of oil run dry, until the day the Lord sends rain on the earth.'"

15 So she went away and did according to the word of Elijah; and she and he and her household ate for many days.

16 The bin of flour was not used up, nor did the jar of oil run dry, according to the word of the Lord which He spoke by Elijah.

We have, today, the same opportunity to be faithful to do all that God commands us in His Word and, no matter the condition of the world, to receive God's provision, His hundredfold return, as promised by Jesus in Mark 10:29-30. Just like Elijah, we are required to depend upon our covenant with the Lord, not the world system. This is powerfully revealed in the account of Elijah and the widow. Elijah's obedience blessed the widow because she was obedient. Not only did she prosper financially, but later, when her son was ill unto death, she had a call upon the man of God and, because of her obedience and faithful partnership, Elijah was able to go to God on her behalf, raising the son from death.

There is an important thing to note in this account of the boy's resurrection. When we operate in faithful obedience we are in position to call upon the Lord and He will deliver us no matter how dire the circumstances. Unless we believe every word that proceeds out of the mouth of God, however, and are quick to act on it, how can we call ourselves people of faith?

Romans 10
**14 How then shall they call on Him in whom they have not believed? And how shall they believe in Him of whom they have not heard? And how shall they hear without a preacher?
15 And how shall they preach unless they are sent? As it is written: "How beautiful are the feet of those who preach the gospel of peace, who bring glad tidings of good things!"
16 But they have not all obeyed the gospel. For Isaiah says, "Lord, who has believed our report?"
17 So then faith comes by hearing, and hearing by the word of God.**

The widow was willing to be God's instrument in providing for Elijah, and Elijah took her welfare and that of her son as a personal matter. The Spirit of the Lord upon Elijah was available to be poured out upon the boy. God heard Elijah and the boy lived. We learn from this that, as God is faithful to answer, so was Elijah faithful to pray in the power God had given him to bless those who blessed him.

Another demonstration of the righteousness, faith, and power that marked Elijah's life occurred on Mt. Carmel. The people then wanted, just as people today want, God's results while doing things their own way, the world's way, the devil's way. Elijah rose up against this hypocrisy.

1 Kings 18
21 And Elijah came to all the people, and said, "How long will you falter between two opinions? If the Lord is God, follow Him; but if Baal, then follow him." But the people answered him not a word.

Elijah demonstrated the power of God and exposed the pathetic, useless, powerless, so-called god they chose to serve. He declared that, even though he was only a single prophet of the true God against four hundred and fifty prophets of Baal, his God would prove His power and authority to all of them. 1 Kings 18:22-35 tells us that they agreed to take a bull, cut it up, and lay it on dry wood without lighting a fire. Elijah told the prophets of Baal to call upon their gods and he would call upon the Name of the Lord. Whichever answered by fire was truly God. Elijah told the others to go first and all four hundred and fifty of them leaped about the altar they had made and called upon the name of Baal from morning until noon.

Elijah mocked them and told them to cry louder so that their god might awaken and hear them. He suggested that their god might have gone on a long journey or be meditating. His taunts spurred on the prophets of Baal and they not only shouted louder but cut themselves with knives so that they bled excessively, which was their custom. When evening came, however, nothing had changed. The meat remained raw and cold upon the dry wood of their altar.

Elijah then told the people to come and see Who his God was. He built his altar, dug a deep trench around it, placed the wood, put the bull on top, and then had four waterpots poured over the bull and the wood three times, until everything was soaked and the trench was full of water. Elijah was overflowing with confidence because he knew his God. He was without fear because he knew God could not fail.

1 Kings 18
36 And it came to pass, at the time of the offering of the evening sacrifice, that Elijah the prophet came near and said, "Lord God of Abraham, Isaac, and Israel, let it be known this day that You are God in Israel, and that I am Your servant, and that I have done all these things at Your word.
37 "Hear me, O Lord, hear me, that this people may know that You are the Lord God, and that You have turned their hearts back to You again."
38 Then the fire of the Lord fell and consumed the burnt sacrifice, and the wood and the stones and the dust, and it licked up the water that was in the trench.
39 Now when all the people saw it, they fell on their faces; and they said, "The Lord, He is God! The Lord, He is God!"

We do not, today, demonstrate to others the supernatural power of God by building altars and sacrificing bulls. The time for that passed when Jesus came and established the new covenant in His divine blood. The fire with which the Lord answers us today is the same fire that sat upon the heads of those at Pentecost. We have daily opportunities to demonstrate the yoke-destroying, burden-removing power of the Holy Spirit. We can, and must, show the world that Jesus is the only true healer, deliverer, provider, restorer and source of prosperity that exists, and demonstrate our faith in Him.

> Matthew 7
> **24 Therefore whoever hears these sayings of Mine, and does them, I will liken him to a wise man who built his house on the rock:**
> **25 and the rain descended, the floods came, and the winds blew and beat on that house; and it did not fall, for it was founded on the rock.**
> **26 Now everyone who hears these sayings of Mine, and does not do them, will be like a foolish man who built his house on the sand:**
> **27 and the rain descended, the floods came, and the winds blew and beat on that house; and it fell. And great was its fall.**

Elijah despaired over the hypocrisy and faithlessness of the people of his day, much as many of God's servants today are tempted to do. There is, however, a world of difference between God's dispensation for those of His first covenant, under the Law, and for us of the new covenant, under grace.

We, having the blood of Jesus and the Holy Spirit, are without excuse (Romans 1:20). It is not good enough for us simply not to become Satanists; we must choose Jesus, and walk in righteousness, in order to be the body of Christ and qualify for the rapture of the church.

Christ Jesus

The life of Jesus, which we are supposed to reflect, was defined in Matthew 26 by His statement to the Father the night before His crucifixion, [39]**nevertheless, not as I will, but as You will**. We must have the same heart.

Matthew 7
21 Not everyone who says to Me, "Lord, Lord," shall enter the kingdom of heaven, but he who does the will of My Father in heaven.

We can only know the will of the Father by meditating in His Word day and night; we must take it literally and act on it by faith. We must also have face-to-face encounters with Him in times of prayer and worship. We must not neglect our prayer language; it is essential to hearing God's voice. We are told to worship in Spirit and in truth, which means in tongues as well as in our natural language.

Jesus demonstrated the power of the anointing (Acts 10:38) everywhere He went. He healed and delivered all those in the villages and synagogues wherever He travelled. When He sent the Holy Spirit at Pentecost this power was given to all who chose to receive it. Jesus was speaking of the Holy Ghost baptism, not water baptism, in His final address to His disciples at the end of the book of Mark.

Mark 16
**16 "He who believes and is baptized will be saved; but he who does not believe will be condemned.
17 "And these signs will follow those who believe: In My name they will cast out demons; they will speak with new tongues;
18 "they will take up serpents; and if they drink anything deadly, it will by no means hurt them; they will lay hands on the sick, and they will recover."
19 So then, after the Lord had spoken to them, He was received up into heaven, and sat down at the right hand of God.
20 And they went out and preached everywhere, the Lord working with them and confirming the word through the accompanying signs. Amen.**

We should be surrounded by miracles in this day more than ever. In John 14:12 Jesus said that not only would we do the same miracles that

He did but even greater ones because, when He returned to the Father's side, He would send the Holy Spirit to dwell in us and empower us.

Jesus was the begotten Son of the Father and now we, through the new birth in Christ, are also sons and daughters of the Father. The most extraordinary thing is that, despite our many weaknesses and failures, Father God's love for us equals His love for Jesus.

John 17
22 And the glory which You gave Me I have given them, that they may be one just as We are one:
23 I in them, and You in Me; that they may be made perfect in one, and that the world may know that You have sent Me, and have loved them as You have loved Me.

We must accept and return that awesome love through obedience, just as Jesus always did.

The Parable Of The Wedding Feast

We are about to be invited to the wedding of the Lamb. We are now being prepared; we must pay attention to the instructions spelled out for us in a parable by Jesus.

Matthew 22
2 The kingdom of heaven is like a certain king who arranged a marriage for his son,

The **king** is Father God and the **son** is Jesus.

Matthew 22
3 and sent out his servants to call those who were invited to the wedding; and they were not willing to come.
4 Again, he sent out other servants, saying, "Tell those who are invited, 'See, I have prepared my dinner; my oxen and fatted cattle are killed, and all things are ready. Come to the wedding.'"

**5 But they made light of it and went their ways, one to his own farm, another to his business.
6 And the rest seized his servants, treated them spitefully, and killed them.**

Those **not willing to come**, of course, are those in the old covenant, the Jews, who were the first to be invited. Never overlook that Jesus preached only to the Jews. He was born a Jew of the tribe of Judah, the **Lion of the tribe of Judah** (Revelation 5:5). Even the first apostles were sent to preach to the Jews and, only later, to the Gentiles. The invitation to become the body of Christ, and the invitation to the wedding of the Lamb, was sent first to the Jews, but they spurned it. They **went their ways, one to his own farm, another to his business**, and **seized** the king's **servants, treated them spitefully, and killed them**.

Matthew 22
7 But when the king heard about it, he was furious. And he sent out his armies, destroyed those murderers, and burned up their city.

Hebrews 8 tells us that God burned up the old covenant, [9]**because they did not continue in My covenant, and I disregarded them, says the Lord**. Hebrews 8 goes on to say that God made a new covenant in the blood of His Son, which was available to all, [13]**In that He says, "A new covenant," He has made the first obsolete**.

Matthew 22
**8 Then he said to his servants, "The wedding is ready, but those who were invited were not worthy.
9 "Therefore go into the highways, and as many as you find, invite to the wedding."
10 So those servants went out into the highways and gathered together all whom they found, both bad and good. And the wedding hall was filled with guests.**

In the new covenant all people, Jew and Gentile, male and female, slave and free (Galatians 3:27-28), have been invited to come. We are all equal in God's sight, no matter where we came from or how we got here. We all have the same opportunity to do all the will of the Father. We all have the same opportunity to receive salvation, be baptized in the Holy Ghost, know who we are in Christ, and expect the pre-tribulation rapture of the church. We all, therefore, have the same opportunity to qualify for the wedding of the Lamb. The question that too many people ignore, however, is postulated in Matthew 7:23: You may know Jesus, but does Jesus know you?

Is everyone who thinks he is qualified for the wedding actually qualified?

Many so-called believers reject the baptism of the Holy Ghost; they are disqualified.

Many have been baptized in the Holy Ghost but turn from faith and deny the power—draw back to perdition (Hebrews 10:39)—and they are disqualified.

Many have been baptized in the Holy Ghost but think they are the bride; they are disqualified.

Many persist in a lifestyle of willful sin; they are disqualified.

All these and more are disqualified, but none, including those stupid enough to blaspheme the Holy Ghost, are specifically condemned in Scripture to the lake of fire, which brings us to:

Matthew 22
11 But when the king came in to see the guests, he saw a man there who did not have on a wedding garment.
12 So he said to him, "Friend, how did you come in here without a wedding garment?" And he was speechless.
13 Then the king said to the servants, "Bind him hand and foot, take him away, and cast him into outer darkness; there will be weeping and gnashing of teeth."

The words **when the king came** represent the appearing of Jesus when He comes to gather unto Himself, rapture, those who are blood-bought, baptized in the Holy Spirit, know who they are in Christ, and who are expecting the pre-tribulation rapture of the church, to wit, those clothed in robes of righteousness.

The king **saw a man there who did not have on a wedding garment**, a man not clad in robes of righteousness. Who is this man?

He is someone who is, because of his lack of **a wedding garment**, cast **into outer darkness** where **there will be weeping and gnashing of teeth**. Only the lake of fire is described as **outer darkness** and the place where there is **weeping and gnashing of teeth**.

So what did this man do that none of the other disqualified people did?

Hebrews 6
4 For it is impossible for those who were once enlightened, and have tasted the heavenly gift, and have become partakers of the Holy Spirit,
5 and have tasted the good word of God and the powers of the age to come,
6 if they fall away, to renew them again to repentance, since they crucify again for themselves the Son of God, and put Him to an open shame.
7 For the earth which drinks in the rain that often comes upon it, and bears herbs useful for those by whom it is cultivated, receives blessing from God;
8 but if it bears thorns and briars, it is rejected and near to being cursed, whose end is to be burned.

The man without the wedding garment is one of those who are **partakers of the Holy Spirit**, and who **tasted the good word of God and the powers of the age to come**, but who **fall away** and **crucify again for themselves the Son of God, and put Him to an open shame**. The man without the wedding garment is, therefore, someone who received the fullness of the Godhead bodily, and then turned away.

The Lord shows us the path but it is up to us to stay on it.

Matthew 22
14 For many are called, but few are chosen.

Many make the initial choice to receive Jesus as Savior, but few make the choice to complete the journey, which is to say, do the will of the

Father and live by every word that proceeds out of His mouth (Matthew 4:4). The choosing is up to us; when we make a choice we become chosen of that choice. When we are obedient, legitimate sons and daughters of God, we are His **chosen**. We are reminded in Matthew 22:14 that the chosen are few, the few who have chosen the narrow way.

Revelation 3
4 You have a few names even in Sardis who have not defiled their garments; and they shall walk with Me in white, for they are worthy.
5 He who overcomes shall be clothed in white garments, and I will not blot out his name from the Book of Life; but I will confess his name before My Father and before His angels.

If we are to walk with God—as did those who qualified for the first three raptures—we must put on the whole armor of God (Ephesians 6:11) and be able to stand in the evil day. We must show forth the light and glory of Christ as His successful ambassadors. Righteousness and power must mark our lives, as it did the lives of Enoch, Elijah and Jesus. Complacency and unbelief are the enemy.

Chapter 10

Body Or Bride—Why Does It Matter?

Accepting that we are the body of Christ and not the bride is an issue of birthright. Anyone clinging to the false image of himself as the bride of Christ can forfeit his place in eternity with Christ Jesus. Church-as-bride doctrine, though promoted from most pulpits, is not supported by a single Scripture. The declaration of something to be true, no matter how many times or by how many people, does not make it true.

Only the Word of God can declare the truth of this matter, and it declares that we are the body of Christ. It declares that, at the wedding of the Lamb, we shall be part of the bridegroom, His body.

Colossians 1
18 And He is the head of the body, the church, who is the beginning, the firstborn from the dead, that in all things He may have the preeminence.

1 Corinthians 12
12 For as the body is one and has many members, but all the members of that one body, being many, are one body, so also is Christ.
13 For by one Spirit we were all baptized into one body whether Jews or Greeks, whether slaves or free and have all been made to drink into one Spirit.
14 For in fact the body is not one member but many.

20 But now indeed there are many members, yet one body.
27 Now you are the body of Christ, and members individually.

God The Father

God is either your Father or your Father-in-law-to-be. You cannot have it both ways.

Stop and consider some basic facts. If the church were the bride we would be waiting to marry Jesus at the end of the tribulation. God, during our lifetimes, would not be our Father but our Father-in-law-to-be. Does anyone pray, "Our Father-in-law-to-be, Who art in heaven...?" Of course not; that would be absurd. But, if we were the bride-to-be, that would be the only accurate way to pray.

If God were our Father-in-law-to-be we would no longer be His children, His heirs in Christ Jesus. Even after the wedding He would not be our Father but our Father-in-law. Our birthright is based upon our being heirs according to the promises of Abraham and his seed (Galatians 3:16). It is based upon our being the sons and daughters of God, not his sons- and daughters-in-law. Our birthright would be null and void.

1 John 3
1 Behold what manner of love the Father has bestowed on us, that we should be called children of God! Therefore the world does not know us, because it did not know Him.
2 Beloved, now we are children of God; and it has not yet been revealed what we shall be, but we know that when He is revealed, we shall be like Him, for we shall see Him as He is.
3 And everyone who has this hope in Him purifies himself, just as He is pure.

Our Authority In The Name Of Jesus

We have been given authority to use the Name of Jesus. If we were the bride-to-be we would not, now, have any such authority. A woman does not have the legal right to use her future husband's name until after the wedding. It would be illegal for us to use the name of our husband-to-be, yet Jesus tells us to use His Name. That is our authority and He gave it to us because we are not His bride-to-be, but His body. We are one with Christ now and have authority in Him.

John 16
23 And in that day you will ask Me nothing. Most assuredly, I say to you, whatever you ask the Father in My name He will give you.
24 Until now you have asked nothing in My name. Ask, and you will receive, that your joy may be full.

John 14
13 And whatever you ask in My name, that I will do, that the Father may be glorified in the Son.
14 If you ask anything in My name, I will do it.

Colossians 3
17 And whatever you do in word or deed, do all in the name of the Lord Jesus, giving thanks to God the Father through Him.

Purity Or Perversion

Holiness is a requirement of our relationship with the Lord. Holiness means to be set apart in Him.

1 Peter 1
15 but as He who called you is holy, you also be holy in all your conduct,
16 because it is written, "Be holy, for I am holy."

Being in Christ, and one with Christ, is the essence of our identity. Those who find their identity in being the bride have, by so doing, declared themselves to be outside the covenant. Whenever we see the words "in Him"—which occur constantly in the New Testament—our intimacy as one with Christ, and through Him with the Father, is defined.

> John 17
> **20 I do not pray for these alone, but also for those who will believe in Me through their word;**
> **21 that they all may be one, as You, Father, are in Me, and I in You; that they also may be one in Us, that the world may believe that You sent Me.**
> **22 And the glory which You gave Me I have given them, that they may be one just as We are one:**
> **23 I in them, and You in Me; that they may be made perfect in one, and that the world may know that You have sent Me, and have loved them as You have loved Me.**
> **24 Father, I desire that they also whom You gave Me may be with Me where I am, that they may behold My glory which You have given Me; for You loved Me before the foundation of the world.**
> **25 O righteous Father! The world has not known You, but I have known You; and these have known that You sent Me.**
> **26 And I have declared to them Your name, and will declare it, that the love with which You loved Me may be in them, and I in them.**

An intimate relationship between a man and a woman prior to marriage is fornication. Fornication is sin, an offence to God, and defiles the perpetrator. If the bride of Christ were intimate with Him before the wedding it would be spiritual fornication.

Would God promote such an unholy union? Never.

Is it possible to cause Jesus to sin? No.

We have intimacy with Jesus and the Father through the Holy Spirit because we are the body of Christ, part of Him, now.

It is not possible to corrupt Jesus, however, one can corrupt one's own soul by embracing this complete oneness in Christ while, at the same time, proclaiming oneself His bride-to-be. Anyone who does this commits spiritual fornication, and no fornicator shall have an inheritance in the kingdom of God.

Ephesians 5
**5 For this you know, that no fornicator, unclean person, nor covetous man, who is an idolater, has any inheritance in the kingdom of Christ and God.
6 Let no one deceive you with empty words, for because of these things the wrath of God comes upon the sons of disobedience.
7 Therefore do not be partakers with them.**

2 Corinthians 13
5 Examine yourselves as to whether you are in the faith. Prove yourselves. Do you not know yourselves, that Jesus Christ is in you? unless indeed you are disqualified.

God has already qualified us, by the blood of Jesus and the anointing of the Holy Spirit, to be accepted in the beloved. Even so, we have the ability to disqualify ourselves by embracing the abomination of church-as-bride doctrine.

"Esau Have I Hated" (Malachi 1:3)

Why did God say that He hated Esau? What did Esau do that was such an abomination in God's sight that God actually hated him? Esau defiled himself and, thereby, cost himself his birthright.

I asked the Lord many years ago why Esau, of all people, was mentioned in the New Testament. I received my answer when God revealed to me that church-as-bride doctrine was a birthright issue. He showed me that a born-again believer who declared himself to be the bride of Christ defiled himself by spiritual fornication and, thus, became a profane person.

Hebrews 12
**12 Therefore strengthen the hands which hang down, and the feeble knees,
13 and make straight paths for your feet, so that what is lame may not be dislocated, but rather be healed.**

**14 Pursue peace with all men, and holiness, without which no one will see the Lord:
15 looking diligently lest anyone fall short of the grace of God; lest any root of bitterness springing up cause trouble, and by this many become defiled;
16 lest there be any fornicator or profane person like Esau, who for one morsel of food sold his birthright.
17 For you know that afterward, when he wanted to inherit the blessing, he was rejected, for he found no place for repentance, though he sought it diligently with tears.**

Wrong thinking can be corrected by seeing the truth and acting on it. Jesus said in Mark 7, [13]**making the word of God of no effect through your tradition which you have handed down.** Do not allow your traditions to cheat you of your birthright. Without holiness, and one must renounce church-as-bride doctrine to be holy, **no one will see the Lord**. You cannot get more serious than that. Many refuse to let go of old, false concepts even though those very misconceptions cause them to become defiled, just like Esau; and leave us not forget, God hated Esau.

One is warned not to be a **fornicator** or **profane person like Esau**. This does not refer to natural fornication, but spiritual. If you have made the bride an idol in your life, you are selling your birthright, just as Esau did, for a bowl of soup. That is profanity.

Esau never got his birthright back, even after realizing what a horrible thing he had done. **He sought it diligently with tears**, but there was **no place for repentance**.

"Hold on a minute!" you say, "Esau did not have the blood of Jesus, and I do. The blood always has room for repentance and restoration." Yes, absolutely, until the last trump sounds. You still have time, now, to correct your thinking, however, when the last trump sounds and the body of Christ is raptured, time is up. Bawling, squalling, panic, and howls of anguish will not change the fact that people clinging to church-as-bride doctrine will be left behind for the tribulation. Even if they are killed for their faith, and are raptured at mid-tribulation, they will still need to come to terms with this truth to be at the wedding. There is only one bride at a wedding.

The Bride Unveiled

> Revelation 21
> **2 Then I, John, saw the holy city, New Jerusalem, coming down out of heaven from God, prepared as a bride adorned for her husband.**
> **9 Then one of the seven angels who had the seven bowls filled with the seven last plagues came to me and talked with me, saying, "Come, I will show you the bride, the Lamb's wife."**
> **10 And he carried me away in the Spirit to a great and high mountain, and showed me the great city, the holy Jerusalem, descending out of heaven from God,**
> **11 having the glory of God. And her light was like a most precious stone, like a jasper stone, clear as crystal.**

We need help to misunderstand this. Jesus has a bride and, therefore, we have a bride. She is New Jerusalem. Do not fly off the handle and declare that a city cannot be a bride. You must think in the supernatural, not the natural. God says that she is **the bride, the Lamb's wife**. The more deeply you get into this revelation, the more affection and love you will develop for New Jerusalem. You will be able to see her as your precious bride. She is glorious and beautiful and God has prepared her just for us. New Jerusalem is a real city and her buildings are constructed of fine gemstones set upon streets of pure, transparent gold (Revelation 21:12-21).

> Revelation 21
> **23 And the city had no need of the sun or of the moon to shine in it, for the glory of God illuminated it, and the Lamb is its light.**

As the light of Jesus, multiplied and shining through every member of His body, provides the light for the city, we become one. Our light streams through the emeralds, rubies, sapphires, topaz, amethysts and diamonds. Their vivid colors radiate and envelop us in a kaleidoscope that penetrates the transparent streets of gold. Our light enters and gives life to the city. The city surrounds us with her jewelled buildings, and her colors reflect upon us. We and our bride become one.

That is why all the building materials of New Jerusalem are transparent. Words cannot even come close to describing this glorious and holy union. As you yield, the Holy Spirit will cause this knowledge to become so real to you that you will have no trouble with the concept of having a city for your bride.

We, the saints, are the living stones of New Jerusalem.

1 Peter 2
5 you also, as living stones, are being built up a spiritual house, a holy priesthood, to offer up spiritual sacrifices acceptable to God through Jesus Christ.

The city, our beautiful bride, is adorned with the righteous acts of the saints.

Revelation 19
**7 Let us be glad and rejoice and give Him glory, for the marriage of the Lamb has come, and His wife has made herself ready.
8 And to her it was granted to be arrayed in fine linen, clean and bright, for the fine linen is the righteous acts of the saints.
9 Then he said to me, "Write: 'Blessed are those who are called to the marriage supper of the Lamb!'" And he said to me, "These are the true sayings of God."**

There is always a great deal of preparation for a wedding. We, even now, have our part in this endeavor. It is our job, as part of the bridegroom, to prepare our bride. We prepare her with our acts of righteousness, which are faith, love, joy, peace, gentleness, self-control, kindness, long suffering and goodness, the fruits of the Spirit (Galatians 5:22-23). Every time we choose faith, and eschew doubt and unbelief, every time we walk in covenant ways, not worldly ways, and every time we praise and give glory to God, we are preparing and adorning our bride.

Isaiah 62
1 For Zion's sake I will not hold My peace, and for Jerusalem's sake I will not rest, until her righteousness goes forth as brightness, and her salvation as a lamp that burns.
2 The Gentiles shall see your righteousness, and all kings your glory. You shall be called by a new name, which the mouth of the Lord will name.
3 You shall also be a crown of glory in the hand of the Lord, and a royal diadem in the hand of your God.
4 You shall no longer be termed Forsaken, nor shall your land any more be termed Desolate; But you shall be called Hephzibah, and your land Beulah; for the Lord delights in you, and your land shall be married.
5 For as a young man marries a virgin, so shall your sons marry you; and as the bridegroom rejoices over the bride, so shall your God rejoice over you.

The land of New Jerusalem will marry the sons of God in the greatest, most spectacular wedding there has ever been.

Nothing That Defiles Shall Enter

Revelation 21
27 But there shall by no means enter it anything that defiles, or causes an abomination or a lie, but only those who are written in the Lamb's Book of Life.

New Jerusalem is a virgin and will only receive her bridegroom. As part of the bridegroom, we shall join with her in holiness. Those who have defiled themselves with church-as-bride doctrine will be barred from entry.

Revelation 22
17 And the Spirit and the bride say, "Come!" And let him who hears say, "Come!" And let him who thirsts come. And whoever desires, let him take the water of life freely.

The Holy Spirit and the holy city, our bride, are, even now, beckoning us to get ready to come up. We are he **who hears** the invitation issued by the Holy Spirit and the holy city and we, in turn, say **Come!** to the Lord Jesus, meaning we express our eagerness for His glorious appearing.

> Revelation 22
> **18 For I testify to everyone who hears the words of the prophecy of this book: If anyone adds to these things, God will add to him the plagues that are written in this book;**
> **19 and if anyone takes away from the words of the book of this prophecy, God shall take away his part from the Book of Life, from the holy city, and from the things which are written in this book.**

A Twisted Tale

Many areas of Scripture have been twisted and reshaped to promote church-as-bride doctrine. In the parable of the ten virgins it has been taught that the virgins are the bride. Wrong. The virgins are not the bride. The five wise virgins who receive Jesus (the light), and whose lamps are full of oil (the Holy Spirit), are the children of the bridechamber, the friends of the bridegroom, the brethren, the body of Christ.

> Matthew 25
> **1 Then the kingdom of heaven shall be likened to ten virgins who took their lamps and went out to meet the bridegroom.**
> **2 Now five of them were wise, and five were foolish.**
> **3 Those who were foolish took their lamps and took no oil with them,**
> **4 but the wise took oil in their vessels with their lamps.**
> **5 But while the bridegroom was delayed, they all slumbered and slept.**
> **6 And at midnight a cry was heard: "Behold, the bridegroom is coming; go out to meet him!"**

> **7** Then all those virgins arose and trimmed their lamps.
> **8** And the foolish said to the wise, "Give us some of your oil, for our lamps are going out."
> **9** But the wise answered, saying, "No, lest there should not be enough for us and you; but go rather to those who sell, and buy for yourselves."
> **10** And while they went to buy, the bridegroom came, and those who were ready went in with him to the wedding; and the door was shut.
> **11** Afterward the other virgins came also, saying, "Lord, Lord, open to us!"
> **12** But he answered and said, "Assuredly, I say to you, I do not know you."
> **13** Watch therefore, for you know neither the day nor the hour in which the Son of Man is coming.

This parable is a type for the rapture. At midnight, on the day of the coming of the bridegroom, the church is awakened, alerted to the imminent appearing of the bridegroom. The five wise virgins are ready and expecting. They have kept their lamps full of oil and their lights burning brightly. With the lead time they have been given they have **trimmed their lamps**, put their affairs in order. When the bridegroom comes they go **out to meet him**.

After the bridegroom has gathered to himself his brethren, the children of the bridechamber, he takes them **with him to the wedding** where the bride is waiting. After they go in, the door is shut. Despite the pleas of those who were not ready, the door remains shut; and so shall it be when Jesus comes to rapture us, His brethren, the children of the bridechamber, the church.

Ephesians 5:22-32 are Scriptures used erroneously to promote church-as-bride doctrine. They actually confirm that the church is the body of Christ. The comparison of the love that Christ has for His church with the love that a husband should have for his wife is no more and no less than a teaching for husbands regarding the depth of affection and protective attitude they should have for their wives. It is an emotional comparison only.

> Ephesians 5
> **23 For the husband is head of the wife, as also Christ is head of the church; and He is the Savior of the body.**
> **28 So husbands ought to love their own wives as their own bodies; he who loves his wife loves himself.**
> **29 For no one ever hated his own flesh, but nourishes and cherishes it, just as the Lord does the church.**
> **30 For we are members of His body, of His flesh and of His bones.**
> **32 This is a great mystery, but I speak concerning Christ and the church.**

Notice the statements, **He is the Savior of the body**, and, **we are members of His body**. Jesus is not the Savior of the bride. This is the doctrine of Christ, not the doctrine of the bride.

I Never Knew You

The determining factor in whether or not you will sit with Jesus in His throne—ruling and reigning with Him for eternity (Revelation 3:21)—is not whether you know Jesus, but whether Jesus knows you.

> Matthew 7
> **21 Not everyone who says to Me, "Lord, Lord," shall enter the kingdom of heaven, but he who does the will of My Father in heaven.**
> **22 Many will say to Me in that day, "Lord, Lord, have we not prophesied in Your name, cast out demons in Your name, and done many wonders in Your name?"**
> **23 And then I will declare to them, "I never knew you; depart from Me, you who practice lawlessness!"**

Those crying, **Lord, Lord** are from the charismatic church. Only they could say to Jesus, **have we not prophesied in Your name, cast out demons in Your name, and done many wonders in Your name?** Those are all things accomplished by the anointing of the Holy Spirit.

So, why would Jesus say to them? **I never knew you; depart from Me, you who practice lawlessness!**

Jesus did not know them because they had declared themselves to be the bride and, therefore, not part of His body. He only knows the members of His own body. Even though these people were born again, and had ministered in the power of the Holy Spirit, they were outside the will of the Father. He who **shall enter the kingdom of heaven** is only **he who does the will of My Father in heaven**.

When someone declares himself to be the bride he declares God to be his Father-in-law-to-be. He sets himself outside the body of Christ. He becomes a spiritual fornicator, profane, an idolater, someone defiling himself and forfeiting his birthright. This is most emphatically not the will of the Father.

Chapter 11

Can We Run Out Of Time?

The Word repeatedly warns us that time is short. Jesus gives many illustrations to impress upon those with ears to hear that indeed they can run out of time. One such illustration is the parable of the ten virgins. Remember, the virgins are not the bride but the children of the bridechamber, the body of Christ.

> Matthew 25
> **1 Then the kingdom of heaven shall be likened to ten virgins who took their lamps and went out to meet the bridegroom.**

The ten virgins represent the kingdom of heaven.

> Matthew 25
> **2 Now five of them were wise, and five were foolish.**
> **3 Those who were foolish took their lamps and took no oil with them,**
> **4 but the wise took oil in their vessels with their lamps.**
> **5 But while the bridegroom was delayed, they all slumbered and slept.**

All ten are part of the kingdom of God, however, the old covenant was fulfilled when Jesus went to the cross (Hebrews 8:13) and precious few Jews, during 2000 years, have accepted Jesus as Messiah. Likewise, during that same period, precious few in the new covenant have accepted the baptism of the Holy Spirit. These are the five foolish virgins with empty lamps. They do absolutely nothing to change their situation; they do not have ears to hear; they remain complacent, satisfied with the status-quo. They **all slumbered and slept**.

Such people have a form of godliness but deny the power. Paul told us to turn away from them (2 Timothy 3:5) because they have an antichrist spirit; they are against the power of the Holy Spirit. Even those who are baptized in the Holy Spirit, but come against healing, deliverance, tongues, or any other manifestation of the power of the Holy Spirit, have an antichrist spirit. One does not need to deny the Spirit to be an antichrist. To limit Him is to oppose Him. Even when someone has the Spirit indwelling, his flesh can be opposed to Him. This is a dangerous condition.

Matthew 25
6 And at midnight a cry was heard: "Behold, the bridegroom is coming; go out to meet him!"
7 Then all those virgins arose and trimmed their lamps.
8 And the foolish said to the wise, "Give us some of your oil, for our lamps are going out."

When **at midnight a cry was heard,** and they knew the final hour had come, the virgins, both foolish and wise, expected to be part of God's kingdom, convinced they were qualified for the wedding. Even though the foolish had ignored the words of Jesus, they were satisfied that they were in good standing with God. They based this conclusion on their traditions, both past and present, totally ignoring the Word. Jesus said in Mark 7:13 that the traditions of men make the Word of God of none effect.

When time grew short the foolish awoke to the fact that more was required of them. Continuing in their foolishness, they decided they could get whatever they lacked from the wise without doing anything for themselves. They thought they could get a free ride with those who had received the baptism of the Holy Spirit, who had done all to be ready, and whose counsel they had undoubtedly ignored.

Matthew 25
**9 But the wise answered, saying, "No, lest there should not be enough for us and you; but go rather to those who sell, and buy for yourselves."
10 And while they went to buy, the bridegroom came, and those who were ready went in with him to the wedding; and the door was shut.**

When the time of the rapture comes, time is up. The time of ministry is finished for those of us who have done the will of the Father, know that we are the body and not the bride, embrace the power of the Holy Spirit, and expect the pre-tribulation rapture of the church. We, at that moment, cease being responsible for teaching the truth. It is time for our departure and we need to be filled to overflowing with the anointing. We cannot permit ourselves to be distracted by those who have consistently refused to heed our godly counsel, who have endlessly disputed with us against the Word. They are now on their own.

We know that when we minister to others the anointing flows out of us into them. The woman with the issue of blood, who came and touched the garment of Jesus, caused power to flow out of Him by her faith (Luke 8:46). To be refilled after ministering to others, we need to spend time with the Father and pray in the Spirit.

The wise virgins, therefore, told the foolish ones to go **to those who sell, and buy for** themselves what they lacked or, in other words, to go wherever they had been going—probably the dead church they had so stubbornly defended and into which they had sown their seed for so long—and try to refill their lamps there.

The reference to buying and selling is not to be taken literally. We cannot buy Jesus or His anointing. There is, however, a price to be paid for qualification for the rapture: knowledge of the Word and diligence to act on it, holiness, righteousness, faith, and walking in the manifested, demonstrated power of the Holy Spirit.

While the five foolish virgins were frantically rushing about trying to get their spiritual ducks lined up, the bridegroom came and only **those who were ready went in with him to the wedding; and the door was shut**. The time to get ready is now. Jesus will come at any moment; everything is set for His appearing. Notice that the wise virgins, the anointed church, went with the bridegroom, Jesus, to the wedding. In Jewish weddings the bride was always waiting in the wedding hall and the groom and his family went to her. It will be the same when Jesus comes and takes us, who are ready and expecting, up with Him to the bride, New Jerusalem. Time will have run out.

Matthew 25
11 Afterward the other virgins came also, saying, "Lord, Lord, open to us!"
12 But he answered and said, "Assuredly, I say to you, I do not know you."
13 Watch therefore, for you know neither the day nor the hour in which the Son of Man is coming.

The foolish ones left behind will be desperate and cry out to Jesus, but it will be too late. They will have had a lifetime to make the right decisions, a lifetime to submit to the anointed One and His anointing, a lifetime to receive the truth. That time will be over.

Jesus declares to them, **Assuredly, I say to you, I do not know you**. They, by their complacent, foolish choices, have placed themselves apart from the body of Christ; they have had a form of godliness but denied the power. Some will have defiled themselves with church-as-bride doctrine; some will have stubbornly held on to an antichrist spirit by denying the baptism of the Holy Ghost or the manifestation of Holy Ghost power; some will have denied the pre-tribulation rapture of the church; some will think their man-made dogma, the dead Law, or their traditions, will save them; some will have eschewed the walk of faith, refused to fulfill the command to overcome, and chosen the bondage and failure of the world system. There will be many ways to be disqualified, but only one way to qualify.

Matthew 7
21 Not everyone who says to Me, "Lord, Lord," shall enter the kingdom of heaven, but he who does the will of My Father in heaven.
22 Many will say to Me in that day, "Lord, Lord, have we not

> prophesied in Your name, cast out demons in Your name, and done many wonders in Your name?"
> **23** And then I will declare to them, "I never knew you; depart from Me, you who practice lawlessness!"

The people calling **Lord, Lord** believe they know Jesus—they are baptized in the Holy Ghost, for otherwise they could not have **prophesied in** His **name, cast out demons in** His **name, and done many wonders in** His **name**—but Jesus says to them, **I never knew you; depart from Me, you who practice lawlessness!** What a horrible, unthinkable thing to hear from our Lord and Savior. That chilling statement will, however, be made to all those who choose not to do all the will of the Father.

He has given us His instruction manual, the Bible, and expects us to love Him enough to obey His Word. Jesus tells us that if we love Him we will obey His Word, and if we do not obey His Word, no matter what we may think or feel, we do not love Him (John 14:23-24). That means God is not able to receive our love without obedience; in fact, He does not even recognize it as love. Our relationship with Christ Jesus is not based on whether or not we know Him, but on whether or not He knows us.

Do Not Harden Your Heart

> Hebrews 3
> **7 Therefore, as the Holy Spirit says: "Today, if you will hear His voice,**
> **8 "do not harden your hearts as in the rebellion, in the day of trial in the wilderness,**
> **9 "where your fathers tested Me, proved Me, and saw My works forty years.**
> **10 "Therefore I was angry with that generation, and said, 'They always go astray in their heart, and they have not known My ways.'**
> **11 "So I swore in My wrath, 'They shall not enter My rest.'"**
> **12 Beware, brethren, lest there be in any of you an evil heart of unbelief in departing from the living God;**

13 but exhort one another daily, while it is called "Today," lest any of you be hardened through the deceitfulness of sin.
14 For we have become partakers of Christ if we hold the beginning of our confidence steadfast to the end,
15 while it is said: "Today, if you will hear His voice, do not harden your hearts as in the rebellion."

Today is the operative word. **Today** is the day of salvation. None of us knows whether there is a tomorrow, but we do have today. Every time we choose to ignore God's Word, and go our own way, our hearts become a little more hardened. It becomes easier the next time to ignore faith and go the world's way, the way of our flesh, the way we are comfortable. The more we do that, the more hardened our hearts become, until we choose to not even hear God. Our own thoughts become our god and rebellion rules our lives. When we ignore God's Word we are guilty of the sin of rebellion.

What was God's indictment of these people, about whom He declared? **they shall not enter My rest**. Their hearts were not with Him and they were without faith and obedience. They could not claim to be ignorant of the truth, for the gospel had been preached to them. They chose to know their own ways, not God's ways, and be influenced by their flesh and the flesh of others. They cared nothing for God, but only their own concept of how things should be.

We are warned not to be like them, not to embrace evil. They had an **evil heart of unbelief in departing from the living God**. God did not move away from them; they chose to move away from Him. God never moves; in Him is no shadow of changing. We have the choice to be with Him or against Him. Those are the only options. Jesus said in Matthew 12, [30]**He who is not with Me is against Me**.

Hebrews 3
18 And to whom did He swear that they would not enter His rest, but to those who did not obey?
19 So we see that they could not enter in because of unbelief.

Those **who did not obey**, those who had hardened their hearts toward God, could not enter into the promised land **because of unbelief**.

Anyone in the final generation who is guilty of the same sin of rebellion and unbelief will fail to qualify for the rapture and will not rule and reign with Jesus.

No Excuses

> John 16
> **12 I still have many things to say to you, but you cannot bear them now.**
> **13 However, when He, the Spirit of truth, has come, He will guide you into all truth; for He will not speak on His own authority, but whatever He hears He will speak; and He will tell you things to come.**
> **14 He will glorify Me, for He will take of what is Mine and declare it to you.**
> **15 All things that the Father has are Mine. Therefore I said that He will take of Mine and declare it to you.**

Jesus was not bent on keeping secrets from His new covenant children. He said to them, when He sent the Holy Spirit at Pentecost, that the Holy Spirit would reveal all things and tell them **things to come**.

> 1 John 2
> **20 But you have an anointing from the Holy One, and you know all things.**
> **27 But the anointing which you have received from Him abides in you, and you do not need that anyone teach you; but as the same anointing teaches you concerning all things, and is true, and is not a lie, and just as it has taught you, you will abide in Him.**

> 1 Corinthians 2
> **10 But God has revealed them to us through His Spirit. For the Spirit searches all things, yes, the deep things of God.**

God planned that we would know all things. He would not have given us His Holy Spirit if we were supposed to remain ignorant. Jesus told us to be aware of the times, and taught us how to recognize the seasons, in order that we be prepared for, and in expectation of, His glorious appearing.

> Luke 21
> **25 And there will be signs in the sun, in the moon, and in the stars; and on the earth distress of nations, with perplexity, the sea and the waves roaring;**
> **26 men's hearts failing them from fear and the expectation of those things which are coming on the earth, for the powers of heaven will be shaken.**
> **27 Then they will see the Son of Man coming in a cloud with power and great glory.**
> **28 Now when these things begin to happen, look up and lift up your heads, because your redemption draws near.**
> **36 Watch therefore, and pray always that you may be counted worthy to escape all these things that will come to pass, and to stand before the Son of Man.**

Jesus expected us to pay attention to His teaching, particularly in this final generation. Much of what He said during His time on earth would not be revealed until now. Revelation comes in layers, manna for each generation. The manna we now receive is not natural food but spiritual food. We are in the sixth day, the end of the 6,000 year lease. Twice as much manna is being poured out now so that we shall be prepared for the millennial reign of Christ.

> Luke 12
> **54 Then He also said to the multitudes, "When you see a cloud rising out of the west, immediately you say, 'A shower is coming'; and so it is.**
> **55 "And when you see the south wind blow, you say, 'There will be hot weather'; and there is.**
> **56 "Hypocrites! You can discern the face of the sky and of the earth, but how is it you do not discern this time?"**

Jesus was extremely displeased with those who refused to **discern this** time. We have been given the Holy Spirit to reveal and interpret all knowledge. We are without excuse if we fail to discern our own time.

> Romans 1
> **18 For the wrath of God is revealed from heaven against all ungodliness and unrighteousness of men, who suppress the truth in unrighteousness,**
> **19 because what may be known of God is manifest in them, for God has shown it to them.**
> **20 For since the creation of the world His invisible attributes are clearly seen, being understood by the things that are made, even His eternal power and Godhead, so that they are without excuse.**

We cannot say that we were not told. Only those who choose to ignore the Word will be uninformed and caught unaware; **they are without excuse**.

Possess The Land

> Joshua 1
> **3 Every place that the sole of your foot will tread upon I have given you, as I said to Moses.**
> **5 No man shall be able to stand before you all the days of your life; as I was with Moses, so I will be with you. I will not leave you nor forsake you.**
> **6 Be strong and of good courage, for to this people you shall divide as an inheritance the land which I swore to their fathers to give them.**
> **11 Pass through the camp and command the people, saying, "Prepare provisions for yourselves, for within three days you will cross over this Jordan, to go in to possess the land which the Lord your God is giving you to possess."**

In these last moments of the age we are to rise up and **possess the land which the Lord** our **God is giving** us **to possess**. This means we are to take dominion over circumstances and destroy the works of the devil, the very purpose for which Jesus was born (1 John 3:8).

Colossians 2
9 For in Him dwells all the fullness of the Godhead bodily;
10 and you are complete in Him, who is the head of all principality and power.

We have the ability in Christ to keep Satan and all His weapons and tactics under our feet; that is where Jesus placed him and that is where he belongs. If we are to fulfill the command to overcome, we cannot give an inch. Faith takes ground, it never cedes it. Faith aggressively lays hold of divine health, abundant finances, restoration of families, peace, joy and wholeness. And never forget, wholeness is nothing missing, nothing broken and nothing ignored.

James 4
7 Therefore submit to God. Resist the devil and he will flee from you.

This is a time, as never before, to be the head and not the tail, above and not beneath (Deuteronomy 28:13).

Deuteronomy 28
7 The Lord will cause your enemies who rise against you to be defeated before your face; they shall come out against you one way and flee before you seven ways.
8 The Lord will command the blessing on you in your storehouses and in all to which you set your hand, and He will bless you in the land which the Lord your God is giving you.

We must possess the land. We are to be blessed going out and blessed coming in, blessed in the country, blessed in the city, blessed sleeping, and blessed waking.

Deuteronomy 28
1 Now it shall come to pass, if you diligently obey the voice of

> the Lord your God, to observe carefully all His commandments which I command you today, that the Lord your God will set you high above all nations of the earth.
> 2 And all these blessings shall come upon you and overtake you, because you obey the voice of the Lord your God.

Now is the time, while there is still time, to open our eyes and set our lives in order. Today, not tomorrow, is the day of salvation.

The Beginning Of Sorrows

> Matthew 24
> 3 Now as He sat on the Mount of Olives, the disciples came to Him privately, saying, "Tell us, when will these things be? And what will be the sign of Your coming, and of the end of the age?"
> 4 And Jesus answered and said to them: "Take heed that no one deceives you.
> 5 "For many will come in My name, saying, 'I am the Christ,' and will deceive many.
> 6 "And you will hear of wars and rumors of wars. See that you are not troubled; for all these things must come to pass, but the end is not yet.
> 7 "For nation will rise against nation, and kingdom against kingdom. And there will be famines, pestilences, and earthquakes in various places.
> 8 "All these are the beginning of sorrows."

As we get closer to the glorious appearing of Christ Jesus, the world becomes ever more dangerous. The earth is crumbling as the result of its sin. Not only are diseases, storms, earthquakes and volcanic eruptions increasing, but terrorist attacks threaten people's lives, even in the United States. The destruction, on September 11, 2001, of the World Trade Center in New York City, and a portion of the Pentagon in Washington D.C., was grim proof of this.

Luke 21
**25 And there will be signs in the sun, in the moon, and in the stars; and on the earth distress of nations, with perplexity, the sea and the waves roaring;
26 men's hearts failing them from fear and the expectation of those things which are coming on the earth, for the powers of heaven will be shaken.
27 Then they will see the Son of Man coming in a cloud with power and great glory.
28 Now when these things begin to happen, look up and lift up your heads, because your redemption draws near.**

The world is in a perpetual state of fear, and for good reason: apart from Jesus there is no hope. Christ Jesus is the only place of safety now, and the only way of escaping the tribulation to come.

For several years I have been teaching about the need to take Psalm 91 seriously. I made a shield-shaped sign, which I placed outside my front door, saying, "Protected by Psalm 91," with the whole Psalm printed on the reverse. I gave one to everyone in my church for Christmas.

Psalm 91
**1 He who dwells in the secret place of the Most High Shall abide under the shadow of the Almighty.
2 I will say of the Lord, "He is my refuge and my fortress; My God, in Him I will trust."**

It is our choice whether or not to **abide** with the Lord. It is our choice whether or not to have established hearts and make Him our **fortress**, to **trust** completely in Him.

Psalm 91
**3 Surely He shall deliver you from the snare of the fowler And from the perilous pestilence.
4 He shall cover you with His feathers, And under His wings you shall take refuge; His truth shall be your shield and buckler.
5 You shall not be afraid of the terror by night, Nor of the arrow that flies by day,**

6 Nor of the pestilence that walks in darkness, Nor of the destruction that lays waste at noonday.
7 A thousand may fall at your side, And ten thousand at your right hand; But it shall not come near you.
8 Only with your eyes shall you look, And see the reward of the wicked.

The **reward of the wicked** is not just for those who commit acts of war or perpetrate atrocities, but for all those who are not in Christ. Jesus said that if we were not for Him, we were against Him. We either belong to the Lord or to the devil. There is no gray area; that is a man-made myth. Anyone who is not in Christ cannot expect the Lord to protect him. God only recognizes two categories of people: covenant, the just, those who are justified by blood, Spirit and faith; and non-covenant, the wicked, those whom Jesus does not know. Being outside the covenant is being in a place of extreme risk. Being inside the covenant is being in a place of safety.

Those outside the covenant can run out of time even before the rapture because, when they die, their destination is hell. Those inside the covenant, who are not acting on every Word that proceeds out of the mouth of God (Matthew 4:4), are also at risk of running out of time because they lack the Lord's protection in these treacherous and violent days.

Psalm 91
9 Because you have made the Lord, who is my refuge, Even the Most High, your habitation,
10 No evil shall befall you, Nor shall any plague come near your dwelling;
11 For He shall give His angels charge over you, To keep you in all your ways.
12 They shall bear you up in their hands, Lest you dash your foot against a stone.
13 You shall tread upon the lion and the cobra, The young lion and the serpent you shall trample under foot.

A believer has nothing to fear. Fear is the product of unbelief. Believers are even protected against chemical warfare. During the tribulation, however, there will be no protection against anything.

Psalm 91
**14 Because he has set his love upon Me, therefore I will deliver him; I will set him on high, because he has known My name.
15 He shall call upon Me, and I will answer him; I will be with him in trouble; I will deliver him and honor him.
16 With long life I will satisfy him, And show him My salvation.**

The Lord promises to deliver His people only when they have set their love upon Him. To love Him we must obey Him (John 14:23-24).

Psalm 118
**5 I called on the Lord in distress; The Lord answered me and set me in a broad place.
6 The Lord is on my side; I will not fear. What can man do to me?
8 It is better to trust in the Lord Than to put confidence in man.
9 It is better to trust in the Lord Than to put confidence in princes.**

We must all make the right decisions now. Time is not on our side. Only God is forever on our side. These days are too treacherous to take any chances. Complacency is unbelief. None of us can afford to be without the Lord's protection.

Chapter 12

Fulfillment Of Pre-Rapture Prophecy

Do your eyeballs spin every time someone starts talking about end-time prophecy? Have you thrown up your hands and ceased trying to make sense of it? If so, this is your moment. I am not going to give you a chart filled with trumpets and dragons and bowls and horsemen to illustrate this subject. I never could make heads or tails out of those things. They look pretty and are frequently artistic, but that does not change the fact that they are mostly incomprehensible and usually inaccurate. I agree with those who postulate that the smoke rising from the pit, in the book of Revelation, will come from the burning of all those charts.

It has become a challenge to keep prophecy in perspective because of its abuse. Prophecy conferences and other such nonsense have become commonplace. There seems to be a prophet or prophetess under every rock. Year after year, churches have prophets and prophetesses come to speak, even though nothing they speak is ever fulfilled. These are false prophets and they aver such things as, "By this time next year there won't be an empty seat in this church," and, "Within a few months everyone in this fellowship will be blessed financially," and, "Your children will preach to the nations and millions will be saved," and, "The end-time revival will begin right here because of the faithfulness God sees in this place."

Although these false prophecies are greeted with shouting and waving and running around, they are obviously quickly forgotten because the same prophets and prophetesses are invited back the next year to "prophesy" more or less the same things with the same lack of result. The tragedy is that, because they speak what people want to hear, these charlatans continue to get away with it.

Never forget: That which is truly spoken by God comes to pass.

When a "prophet" consistently—and usually for personal financial gain—predicts things like a Y2K calamity, or all that nonsense I mentioned above, and no such thing comes to pass, he is a false prophet. To falsely proclaim things in the Name of the Lord on a regular basis is surely evil. Unfortunately, though, too few people judge these empty, fleshly prophecies for what they are. They have become inured to them.

A tragic result of all this empty prophecy is that many have begun to despise prophecy. This suits the devil perfectly. Nothing could make him happier than to see minimized and sidelined this important gift of the Spirit. We must take the prophetic seriously, while continuing to test all things.

1 Thessalonians 5
19 Do not quench the Spirit.
20 Do not despise prophecies.
21 Test all things; hold fast what is good.
22 Abstain from every form of evil.

There is, now, at least one "prophet's club" shamelessly declaring that God changes His Word every day, that whatever one of its adherents "hears" supersedes the Bible. I cannot think of words to describe such arrogance and ignorance of the Word.

We who hear the voice of the Holy Spirit do not claim to hear accurately every time. That is why God instructs us to **test all things** and goes on to say in 2 Corinthians 13, [1]**By the mouth of two or three witnesses every word shall be established**. We are not testing God, we are testing the accuracy of our reception. God knew from the beginning what charlatans would do with false prophecy and warned us against them.

There are, as mentioned earlier, only two yardsticks by which to **test all things**: the Bible is the first; events themselves are the second. Putting non-predictive prophecy to the Word test is simple—one only

The Rapture, The Tribulation, And Beyond 211

has to check the Bible for confirmation of the Word that was spoken—however, where predictive prophecy is concerned, only the fulfillment of the prophecy can confirm it. Much Biblical predictive prophecy, which did not claim time certain, remained unfulfilled during the life of the prophet, but that is not too likely to happen during this, the last, generation. When someone claiming to be a prophet says, "There is going to be a calamity such as mankind has never known on December 31, 1999 and we're calling it Y2K," there needs to be accountability.

It seems that Christians have been conditioned to accept with gladness anything that is told them in the name of prophecy, and then to forget the whole thing when it turns out to be nonsense, even when they have squandered their substance by attending seminars and buying books on the subject. They even continue to support the "prophet" and listen to his "prophecies." This would not matter—excepting the success of a false prophet and the deception of those who listen to him—were it not for the fact that there is end-time prophecy yet to be fulfilled. Although everything that must be fulfilled prior to the rapture of the church has been fulfilled—and any remaining end-time prophecies are of events occurring after the rapture—understanding the timing is important because it effects our ability to live in expectation of the rapture.

The Apostasia

We established in Chapter 8 that there is no wholesale backsliding of the church prior to the rapture. Do not wait for it; it is a myth. The "falling away" of 2 Thessalonians 2:3 is, as previously mentioned, the Greek word *apostasia,* meaning the departure of the church from the world via the rapture. The last moments of the age will be marked by the greatest outpouring of the Holy Spirit we have ever seen, the greatest revival of all time. It has already begun and will increase until the final trump sounds.

> Joel 2
> **28 And it shall come to pass afterward that I will pour out My Spirit on all flesh; your sons and your daughters shall prophesy,**

your old men shall dream dreams, your young men shall see visions;
29 And also on My menservants and on My maidservants I will pour out My Spirit in those days.

Every Nation, Tribe, Tongue And People

Daniel 8
19 And he said, "Look, I am making known to you what shall happen in the latter time of the indignation; for at the appointed time the end shall be."

The **latter time of the indignation** refers to the outpouring of God's wrath during the tribulation. Daniel became physically sick for days following his reception of this vision (Daniel 8:27) because the horror of it was more than he could bear. The **end** is the same one referred to by Jesus in Matthew 24, **¹⁴And this gospel of the kingdom will be preached in all the world as a witness to all the nations, and then the end will come.**

This particular **end** is the end of the tribulation, not the end of the age prior to the rapture. One must match the words of Jesus in the book of Matthew with all the other books of prophecy; it is easy to confuse the rapture and the second advent if one does not include other reference points. Jesus, obviously, knew what He was talking about, but it is our responsibility to draw the correct conclusions from what He said.

Revelation 14
6 Then I saw another angel flying in the midst of heaven, having the everlasting gospel to preach to those who dwell on the earth to every nation, tribe, tongue, and people
7 saying with a loud voice, "Fear God and give glory to Him, for the hour of His judgment has come; and worship Him who made heaven and earth, the sea and springs of water."
8 And another angel followed, saying, "Babylon is fallen, is fallen, that great city, because she has made all nations drink of

> the wine of the wrath of her fornication."
> **9 Then a third angel followed them, saying with a loud voice, "If anyone worships the beast and his image, and receives his mark on his forehead or on his hand,"**

Angels of God will preach the gospel **to every nation, tribe, tongue and people** during the second half of the tribulation. It must be the second half because their ministry follows that of the 144,000 Jewish evangelists whom God raises up to preach the gospel during the first half and who are raptured at mid-tribulation (Revelation 14:1-5).

Angels are the only ones who can reach the remotest mountaintops, the tiniest most obscure islands, and tribes in the deepest, darkest jungles in every corner of the earth. This task cannot, will not, be fulfilled by human beings and it will not be accomplished ahead of the rapture. The timing of the rapture and the end of the tribulation have been established from the beginning. They will be **at the appointed time**.

Do not be foolish enough to believe that God almighty would base His timing of the final moments of the age on whether or not mankind managed to fulfill prophecy. Yes, it is important for us to complete our assignments before Jesus comes, but this is for our own sakes; it effects our rewards at the judgment seat of Christ. Our obedience, or lack thereof, our effectiveness in carrying out our assignments, will not change the appointed time by a single second. The timing has been carved in God's eternal stone. Thinking that the actions of men can alter God's sovereign timing is as foolish as the religious belief that Jesus founded His church on the man, Peter, rather than on Peter's revelation that Jesus was the Christ, the Son of the living God (Matthew 16:16).

Rebuilding The Temple

The rebuilding of God's temple, and the throne of the Lamb within it—on the temple mount in Jerusalem where the Dome of the Rock now stands—is another area of confusion. Remember to keep the Jews, the Gentiles, and the church separated in your mind. God deals with each group differently.

The Jews will not be the builders of the millennial temple of the Lamb. Whatever the Jews do or do not do regarding the Dome of the Rock is of no significance, let alone consequence, to the church. Nor is anything the Jews believe according to their traditions. We are told to watch Israel because events there are an indication of the times and the seasons in which we live. For instance, the reestablishment of Israel as a nation in 1948 was highly significant because it was prophesied (Ezekiel 11:16-17). We, the church, however, while praying for the peace of Jerusalem (Psalm 122:6), must maintain our focus.

The rebuilding of the temple will be accomplished at the end of the tribulation when Jesus returns with His body—immediately after the wedding—sets His foot on the Mount of Olives, gathers the nations behind Him, splits the earth, destroys the two hundred million man army of Antichrist at the battle of Armageddon, casts Satan into the bottomless pit, purifies the earth, and sets up His millennial reign. After all that, Jesus Himself will build His own temple on the precise spot where it belongs.

Zechariah 6
12 Then speak to him, saying, "Thus says the Lord of hosts, saying: 'Behold, the Man whose name is the BRANCH! From His place He shall branch out, and He shall build the temple of the Lord;
13 'yes, He shall build the temple of the Lord. He shall bear the glory, and shall sit and rule on His throne; so He shall be a priest on His throne, and the counsel of peace shall be between them both.'"

Christ, when He returns to earth at the end of the tribulation, the second advent, will not just sprinkle some holy oil around and sit upon the throne where Antichrist—who is described in Matthew 24 as [15]**the abomination of desolation**—ensconced himself and declared himself to be God. Think about it. How can anyone imagine such a thing? Almighty God, come in the flesh, sitting where His bitterest enemy had previously sat? And, as if that were not enough, when Jesus' foot touches the Mount of Olives the whole region will be demolished in an earthquake. Nothing will remain standing, let alone Antichrist's previous temple.

The Rapture, The Tribulation, And Beyond

Zechariah 14

3 Then the Lord will go forth and fight against those nations, as He fights in the day of battle.
4 And in that day His feet will stand on the Mount of Olives, which faces Jerusalem on the east. And the Mount of Olives shall be split in two, from east to west, making a very large valley; half of the mountain shall move toward the north and half of it toward the south.
8 And in that day it shall be that living waters shall flow from Jerusalem, half of them toward the eastern sea and half of them toward the western sea; in both summer and winter it shall occur.
9 And the Lord shall be King over all the earth. In that day it shall be "the Lord is one," and His name one.

The battle of Armageddon is **the day of battle** (Revelation 16:16). When Jesus splits the earth and moves physical mountains **toward the north** and **toward the south**, there is no way that anything can survive. Jesus never intended that it should. That is why, from the beginning, He has planned to build His own temple at the inception of His millennial reign.

And the Lord shall be King over all the earth leaves no doubt that we are talking about the beginning of the millennial reign of Christ. Satan is the god of this world until then (2 Corinthians 4:4). This is reported in two other places.

Revelation 11

11 Now after the three and a half days the breath of life from God entered them, and they stood on their feet, and great fear fell on those who saw them.
12 And they heard a loud voice from heaven saying to them, "Come up here." And they ascended to heaven in a cloud, and their enemies saw them.
13 In the same hour there was a great earthquake, and a tenth of the city fell. In the earthquake seven thousand men were killed, and the rest were afraid and gave glory to the God of heaven.

> **15** Then the seventh angel sounded: And there were loud voices in heaven, saying, "The kingdoms of this world have become the kingdoms of our Lord and of His Christ, and He shall reign forever and ever!"

Revelation 16
> **17** Then the seventh angel poured out his bowl into the air, and a loud voice came out of the temple of heaven, from the throne, saying, "It is done!"
> **18** And there were noises and thunderings and lightnings; and there was a great earthquake, such a mighty and great earthquake as had not occurred since men were on the earth.
> **19** Now the great city was divided into three parts, and the cities of the nations fell. And great Babylon was remembered before God, to give her the cup of the wine of the fierceness of His wrath.
> **20** Then every island fled away, and the mountains were not found.

The destruction of earthly Jerusalem will be to the uttermost. **It is done!** refers to the end of the seven years of the tribulation. You can read of the fall and judgment of the place God names **great Babylon** in chapters 17 and 18 of Revelation.

Acts 15
> **15** And with this the words of the prophets agree, just as it is written:
> **16** "After this I will return and will rebuild the tabernacle of David which has fallen down. I will rebuild its ruins, and I will set it up,
> **17** "so that the rest of mankind may seek the Lord, even all the Gentiles who are called by My name," Says the Lord who does all these things.
> **18** Known to God from eternity are all His works.

These Scriptures quote Amos 9:11-12 and affirm that Jesus, when He returns at the end of the tribulation, will rebuild His temple. Do not concern yourself with whatever structure currently exists on the temple mount. Nothing that is now built or later destroyed will effect the millennial temple of the Lamb. Jesus has it all in His hands.

Every time I read the extraordinary and terrible account of the events of the second advent, and the way in which the Lord will remove sin and purify the earth, I am inexpressibly grateful that I am part of the body of Christ.

All Has Been Fulfilled

There is no unfulfilled prophetic event standing between us and the glorious appearing of our Lord and Savior Jesus Christ. All that needs to be accomplished has been accomplished. Only Father God's sovereign timing separates us from the sounding of the last trump.

Do not be deceived about the importance of this; do not be one of those who tries to avoid responsibility with, "We'll all find out when the time comes." We must understand that Jesus can come at any moment. We must be in a state of readiness and eager expectation. Our ears should be straining to hear the sweet and glorious sound of the last trump.

Chapter 13

Deceitful Prophecy

Inaccurate and misleading prophecy is the leaven of the Pharisees. It deceives and leads God's people away from His truth. It abounds in this hour and will increase as we get closer to the end. We must be alert and ready to reject any word that does not line up with Scripture. The antichrist spirit is a deceiver (2 John 7), and the fallen nature of man will readily accept a lie while resisting the truth. Whoever is subject to the world, its ways and systems, is also subject to the god of this world, who is the father of lies. Jesus told the Pharisees, and those who were biologically descended from Abraham but would not receive His Word, that their father was the devil and that they did the works of their father (John 8:37-44).

> Matthew 16
> **6 Then Jesus said to them, "Take heed and beware of the leaven of the Pharisees and the Sadducees."**
> **11 "How is it you do not understand that I did not speak to you concerning bread? but you should beware of the leaven of the Pharisees and Sadducees."**
> **12 Then they understood that He did not tell them to beware of the leaven of bread, but of the doctrine of the Pharisees and Sadducees.**

The Pharisees were the religious leaders of their time and, thus, were the principle source of deceitful prophecy. They promoted lies that served their purposes, just as, today, leadership tells people what they want to hear in order to fill churches. Nothing has changed. Even though Jesus warned against being deceived, most people tend to accept without question what is stated from the pulpit. They are supposed to put everything they hear to the Word test, but they take the easy and comfortable course, the broad way, because it is easier on the flesh. The Lord said, long ago through the prophet Isaiah, that this would pervade the church.

> Isaiah 30
> **8 Now go, write it before them on a tablet, and note it on a scroll, that it may be for time to come, forever and ever:**
> **9 that this is a rebellious people, lying children, children who will not hear the law of the Lord;**
> **10 Who say to the seers, "Do not see," and to the prophets, "Do not prophesy to us right things; speak to us smooth things, prophesy deceits.**
> **11 "Get out of the way, turn aside from the path, cause the Holy One of Israel to cease from before us."**

God saying **that it may be for time to come, forever and ever** tells us that He was not only talking about the people of that day but of our day too. The people being discussed have such contempt for the truth that they actually tell God, in the vernacular, to get out of their face. An amazing number of people today are content with lies, turning from the truth and then slandering those who defend it. I cannot count the number of people who have asked me for God's Word regarding something critically important to them who, when the truth I have given them—citing chapter and verse—has not suited them, have become angry and resentful and stormed off. Many such, who have come to my church, have never set foot in it again.

God explains what will happen to those who want lies rather than the truth.

> Isaiah 30
> **12 Therefore thus says the Holy One of Israel: "Because you**

despise this word, and trust in oppression and perversity, and rely on them,
13 "therefore this iniquity shall be to you like a breach ready to fall, a bulge in a high wall, whose breaking comes suddenly, in an instant.
14 "And He shall break it like the breaking of the potter's vessel, which is broken in pieces; He shall not spare. So there shall not be found among its fragments a shard to take fire from the hearth, or to take water from the cistern."

Sudden and utter destruction is the end for all who gladly receive false prophecy, let alone promote it. Prophecy, for the most part, is the teaching or explanation of God's Word; sometimes it is predictive, though usually it is not. To prophesy deceit—whether by false teaching or by falsely predicting such things as Y2K—is to misrepresent the Word of God. Those who declare such deceits as "Healing is passed away," "God chooses whom He will heal," "There is no need for deliverance," "Tongues are not of God," "God afflicts us in order to teach us," "We are still subject to the Law," "Homosexuality is acceptable to God," are abomination.

Such lies receive acceptance because they appease the flesh. Some condone sin, some imply that ignorance of the Word is acceptable so long as one's heart is right, but most find acceptance because they pass responsibility from the hearer to God. They release the hearer from the need to exercise faith.

2 Timothy 2
15 Be diligent to present yourself approved to God, a worker who does not need to be ashamed, rightly dividing the word of truth.
16 But shun profane and vain babblings, for they will increase to more ungodliness.
17 And their message will spread like cancer. Hymenaeus and Philetus are of this sort,
18 who have strayed concerning the truth, saying that the resurrection is already past; and they overthrow the faith of some.

19 Nevertheless the solid foundation of God stands, having this seal: "The Lord knows those who are His," and, "Let everyone who names the name of Christ depart from iniquity."

We are responsible to **shun profane and idle babblings** which **will increase** and **spread like cancer**. How can we overlook such strong statements? How can we go our own way and believe any lie that sounds appealing? It is up to us to be vessels of honor in the Lord's house. It is up to us not to dishonor ourselves with deception (2 Timothy 2:20-21). We must recognize that the deceivers are convincing because they, themselves, are fully deceived.

2 Timothy 3
13 But evil men and impostors will grow worse and worse, deceiving and being deceived.

Romans 16
18 For those who are such do not serve our Lord Jesus Christ, but their own belly, and by smooth words and flattering speech deceive the hearts of the simple.

Only those who lack knowledge of the Word, **the simple**, can be deceived. That is why God said in Hosea 4:6 that His people are destroyed for lack of knowledge. It is not that they have not heard the truth; it is that they reject it. That is what makes them **simple**.

Psalm 1
**1 Blessed is the man Who walks not in the counsel of the ungodly, Nor stands in the path of sinners, Nor sits in the seat of the scornful;
2 But his delight is in the law of the Lord, And in His law he meditates day and night.
3 He shall be like a tree Planted by the rivers of water, That brings forth its fruit in its season, Whose leaf also shall not wither; And whatever he does shall prosper.
4 The ungodly are not so, But are like the chaff which the wind drives away.**

**5 Therefore the ungodly shall not stand in the judgment, Nor sinners in the congregation of the righteous.
6 For the Lord knows the way of the righteous, But the way of the ungodly shall perish.**

We shall be **blessed**, even in these last treacherous days, if our **delight is in the law of the Lord**, which is God's Word. God said to Joshua (Joshua 1:8) that if he would meditate in His Word day and night, and seek to do all that was written in it, he would make his way successful and prosperous. It is our responsibility to know and live the truth and reject all deceitful prophecy.

Jeremiah 17
**7 "Blessed is the man who trusts in the Lord, and whose hope is the Lord.
8 "For he shall be like a tree planted by the waters, which spreads out its roots by the river, and will not fear when heat comes; but her leaf will be green, and will not be anxious in the year of drought, nor will cease from yielding fruit.
9 "The heart is deceitful above all things, and desperately wicked; Who can know it?
10 "I, the Lord, search the heart, I test the mind, even to give every man according to his ways, and according to the fruit of his doings."**

We must bear good fruit. If we bear bad fruit we shall be cut down and thrown into the fire (Matthew 3:10). Truth is good fruit; deceit is bad fruit. Things are not always as they appear. Deceit is a cancer because it eats away at, and eventually destroys, one's righteousness. When the absolute truth is not being spoken there is the risk of listening to the devil himself.

2 Corinthians 11
**12 But what I do, I will also continue to do, that I may cut off the opportunity from those who desire an opportunity to be regarded just as we are in the things of which they boast.
13 For such are false apostles, deceitful workers, transforming**

themselves into apostles of Christ.
14 And no wonder! For Satan himself transforms himself into an angel of light.
15 Therefore it is no great thing if his ministers also transform themselves into ministers of righteousness, whose end will be according to their works.

We must constantly be washed with the water of the Word (Ephesians 5:26-27) in order to be the glorious church. It is amazing how many things people believe just because they grew up with them. They got them from parents, Sunday school teachers, pastors and elsewhere. It does not matter where they got them; what matters is, if such things are contrary to God's Word they must be put to death.

That is why the Lord said we must come to Him as little children. Little children do not yet think they know it all. They are teachable. Jesus did not say children, He said little children.

Ephesians 4
20 But you have not so learned Christ,
21 if indeed you have heard Him and have been taught by Him, as the truth is in Jesus:
22 that you put off, concerning your former conduct, the old man which grows corrupt according to the deceitful lusts,
23 and be renewed in the spirit of your mind,
24 and that you put on the new man which was created according to God, in righteousness and true holiness.

By the Spirit we have the ability to do all things. We lie if we say that we cannot walk in God's whole truth. Anyone who says that is actually saying that he is not willing to change his thinking or behavior in order to please God. We cannot continue in the world and its ways, not to mention its antichrist spirit, and belong to God.

James 4
4 Adulterers and adulteresses! Do you not know that friendship with the world is enmity with God? Whoever therefore wants to be a friend of the world makes himself an enemy of God.

5 Or do you think that the Scripture says in vain, "The Spirit who dwells in us yearns jealously?"

We have a clear choice: God or the world. The world opposes God in every way, so, if we embrace its thinking we set ourselves against God. Those who cannot bring themselves to let go of the world have never developed a love of God's truth. Without love of the truth, they are open to deception.

2 Thessalonians 2
9 The coming of the lawless one is according to the working of Satan, with all power, signs, and lying wonders,
10 and with all unrighteous deception among those who perish, because they did not receive the love of the truth, that they might be saved.
11 And for this reason God will send them strong delusion, that they should believe the lie,
12 that they all may be condemned who did not believe the truth but had pleasure in unrighteousness.

Jesus called us to be separated from unbelief and unbelievers and unto Him, separated unto a place of holiness as we prepare for glorification.

Psalm 24
3 Who may ascend into the hill of the Lord? Or who may stand in His holy place?
4 He who has clean hands and a pure heart, Who has not lifted up his soul to an idol, Nor sworn deceitfully.
5 He shall receive blessing from the Lord, And righteousness from the God of his salvation.

We are all getting ready to **ascend into the hill of the Lord** and **stand in His holy place** at the rapture of the church. Therefore, we must take God's truth seriously. We must not water down, adjust, or pervert the gospel in any way. We must handle prophecy with the respect it deserves without being swayed for or against it by the size of the platform whence it comes.

The false prophecy pouring forth today from pulpits and television sets produces in Word people the tendency to discount the lot of it. We cannot do that. We must listen to sound teaching, but discriminate in the prophetic utterances we receive. To have **clean hands and a pure heart** we must wash away the filthiness of deceit and idolatry without despising prophecy.

1 Thessalonians 5
19 Do not quench the Spirit.
20 Do not despise prophecies.
21 Test all things; hold fast what is good.

Never quench the Spirit but always hold the prophet to a high standard. **Test all things** and hang on to what is of God. All God's gifts are for our benefit, and prophecy is no exception.

2 Peter 1
19 We also have the prophetic word made more sure, which you do well to heed as a light that shines in a dark place, until the day dawns and the morning star rises in your hearts;
20 knowing this first, that no prophecy of Scripture is of any private interpretation,
21 for prophecy never came by the will of man, but holy men of God spoke as they were moved by the Holy Spirit.

2 Peter 2
1 But there were also false prophets among the people, even as there will be false teachers among you, who will secretly bring in destructive heresies, even denying the Lord who bought them, and bring on themselves swift destruction.
2 And many will follow their destructive ways, because of whom the way of truth will be blasphemed.
3 By covetousness they will exploit you with deceptive words; for a long time their judgment has not been idle, and their destruction does not slumber.

Chapter 14

False Doctrine

2 Timothy 4
**2 Preach the word! Be ready in season and out of season. Convince, rebuke, exhort, with all longsuffering and teaching.
3 For the time will come when they will not endure sound doctrine, but according to their own desires, because they have itching ears, they will heap up for themselves teachers;
4 and they will turn their ears away from the truth, and be turned aside to fables.
5 But you be watchful in all things, endure afflictions, do the work of an evangelist, fulfill your ministry.**

Sadly, **itching ears** have become an epidemic. Many who deem themselves Christians do not want to hear the truth; they consider it too harsh. In fact, they find any and every excuse to reject true doctrine and **turn their ears away from the truth,** being **turned aside to fables**. Notice that this Scripture says that their opinion of what is truth is **according to their own desires**, the flesh.

It is easy today for people to **heap up for themselves teachers** who will feed them watered down or false teaching, agreeable **fables**. These **fables** appeal to the flesh and, consequently, keep the money coming in and the church full. Christian television does not lack for large ministries and well known preachers who are guilty of this. Frequently, they seem to make it up as they go along, paying no heed whatsoever to the Word.

A favorite tactic seems to be the lie designed for the moment. It is calculated to stir tens of thousands into a frenzy of emotional response. The fact that the crowd loves it, and the next convention is even more heavily attended, does not change the fact that a lie was preached and ecstatically accepted without question. Most of the people who attend such meetings, it seems, are looking for just this. When they go home they talk about the anointing, when they really mean is that everyone got hysterical and did a lot of shouting.

The clear, uncompromised truth has been dismissed in favor of performance. Show-biz reigns. That is why we are instructed in the Word to be aggressive in our stand for the true gospel, no matter what others think of us. We cannot be both God pleasers and man pleasers; it is one or the other. Those of us who love the unmitigated truth are admonished to **convince, rebuke, exhort with all longsufferring and teaching**. If we do not do this, lies will creep into our lives. This is not the well-travelled road, but it is the only road to glory.

2 Timothy 2
15 Be diligent to present yourself approved to God, a worker who does not need to be ashamed, rightly dividing the word of truth.
16 But shun profane and vain babblings, for they will increase to more ungodliness.
17 And their message will spread like cancer. Hymenaeus and Philetus are of this sort,

False doctrine has **spread like cancer**. Cancer kills. False doctrine, fables and lies will destroy our relationship with Christ. If we are not **rightly dividing**, or understanding, **the word of truth**, we shall be ashamed before God. **Profane and vain babblings** produce **ungodliness**, destruction both for those who promote it and those who blithely accept it. Receiving and agreeing with false doctrine is no different than using the Name of the Lord as a profanity. False doctrine is blasphemy, a profane act. Most believers are horrified at the thought of blaspheming the Lord, but give no thought to speaking lies against the Word.

> 2 Peter 2
> **18 For when they speak great swelling words of emptiness, they allure through the lusts of the flesh, through licentiousness, the ones who have actually escaped from those who live in error.**
> **19 While they promise them liberty, they themselves are slaves of corruption; for by whom a person is overcome, by him also he is brought into bondage.**
> **20 For if, after they have escaped the pollutions of the world through the knowledge of the Lord and Savior Jesus Christ, they are again entangled in them and overcome, the latter end is worse for them than the beginning.**

Man-made religious doctrine, of the sort found in denominations, has always opposed God's truth. Lies against healing, prosperity, the baptism of the Holy Spirit and the gift of tongues, to mention but a few, have been accepted by generations of people happy to shirk the responsibility of obeying God. That is why Jesus said in Mark 7:13 that the traditions of men make the Word of God of no effect. The religions that have led God's people into superstition, witchcraft and idolatry —such as the worship of dead relatives, Jesus' mother and even grandmother, instead of Jesus Himself—have promoted, and continue to promote, false doctrine. They hold people in bondage to their profane and idle babblings, babblings that produce ungodliness and spiritual death.

In this final hour there is an epidemic of false doctrine, seemingly added daily, to the waist-deep spiritual garbage through which we already must wade. We have identified the work of the spirit of Antichrist, but we must also identify the work of the spirit of the false prophet. I shall address several glaring examples which I believe to be extremely damaging to the faith.

> Matthew 24
> **11 Then many false prophets will rise up and deceive many.**

The Trinity

Until I heard heads of large, successful, Christ-based ministries declare that there is no Trinity, I did not think anything so fundamental to our beliefs as God the Father, God the Son, and God the Holy Spirit, working separately and as One, could ever be in dispute. However, that now seems to be the case.

There are those who say that God the Father is God all by Himself and that Jesus was merely a prophet, not in the God class at all. In that perverted doctrine, the Holy Spirit is just the personality of Jesus, His aura, so to speak.

Others proclaim Jesus to be all-in-all and that there are no other members of the Godhead. They say that Father God is merely the authority of Jesus, and the Holy Spirit is His omnipresence.

Although the word "Trinity" is not in the Bible, there is more than ample evidence of this truth.

1 John 5
6 This is He who came by water and blood Jesus Christ; not only by water, but by water and blood. And it is the Spirit who bears witness, because the Spirit is truth.
7 For there are three who bear witness in heaven: the Father, the Word, and the Holy Spirit; and these three are one.
8 And there are three that bear witness on earth: the Spirit, the water, and the blood; and these three agree as one.
9 If we receive the witness of men, the witness of God is greater; for this is the witness of God which He has testified of His Son.
10 He who believes in the Son of God has the witness in himself; he who does not believe God has made Him a liar, because he has not believed the testimony that God has given of His Son.

How can one misunderstand **these three are one**?

Matthew 3
16 Then Jesus, when He had been baptized, came up immediately from the water; and behold, the heavens were opened to Him, and He saw the Spirit of God descending like a dove and alighting upon Him.
17 And suddenly a voice came from heaven, saying, "This is My beloved Son, in whom I am well pleased."

Here again we see the three Persons of the Godhead appearing and working separately and together: God the Father speaking from heaven; the Holy Spirit being sent; and Jesus upon Whom the Holy Spirit alights.

John 4
23 But the hour is coming, and now is, when the true worshipers will worship the Father in spirit and truth; for the Father is seeking such to worship Him.
24 God is Spirit, and those who worship Him must worship in spirit and truth.
25 The woman said to Him, "I know that Messiah is coming" (who is called Christ). "When He comes, He will tell us all things."
26 Jesus said to her, "I who speak to you am He."

In order to worship Father God, we are required to do so in **spirit** (the Holy Spirit in us), and **truth** (the Word, Jesus). Unless we perceive and accept the triune Godhead, we are not even qualified to worship the Lord.

John 17
20 I do not pray for these alone, but also for those who will believe in Me through their word;
21 that they all may be one, as You, Father, are in Me, and I in You; that they also may be one in Us, that the world may believe that You sent Me.
22 And the glory which You gave Me I have given them, that they may be one just as We are one:
23 I in them, and You in Me; that they may be made perfect in one, and that the world may know that You have sent Me, and have loved them as You have loved Me.
24 Father, I desire that they also whom You gave Me may be with Me where I am, that they may behold My glory which You have given Me; for You loved Me before the foundation of the world.
25 O righteous Father! The world has not known You, but I

have known You; and these have known that You sent Me.
26 And I have declared to them Your name, and will declare it, that the love with which You loved Me may be in them, and I in them.

Our position in Christ depends upon our comprehension of the separate Persons of the Godhead.

Acts 10
38 how God anointed Jesus of Nazareth with the Holy Spirit and with power, who went about doing good and healing all who were oppressed by the devil, for God was with Him.

The operation of God the Father, God the Son and God the Holy Spirit is the foundation of our authority in Christ.

Colossians 2
2 that their hearts may be encouraged, being knit together in love, and attaining to all riches of the full assurance of understanding, to the knowledge of the mystery of God, both of the Father and of Christ,
3 in whom are hidden all the treasures of wisdom and knowledge.
4 Now this I say lest anyone should deceive you with persuasive words.

The mysteries of God will remain hidden until we have the knowledge **both of the Father and of Christ** (the anointed One and His anointing). All three Persons of the Godhead are essential to revelation knowledge.

Romans 8
15 For you did not receive the spirit of bondage again to fear, but you received the Spirit of adoption by whom we cry out, "Abba, Father."
16 The Spirit Himself bears witness with our spirit that we are children of God,

17 and if children, then heirs—heirs of God and joint heirs with Christ, if indeed we suffer with Him, that we may also be glorified together.

I point out that to **suffer** with Christ does not mean to be weak, sick, and poor. It means to resist all those conditions, just as Jesus did when He was in the flesh. Fighting the good fight of faith requires that we win. It is harder on the flesh to resist sickness than to give in to it. It is harder on the flesh to reject fear than to be overwhelmed by it. It is harder on the flesh to forgive someone who has wronged and hurt us than to hate him and want to get even. It is harder on the flesh to walk in righteousness than to give in to the ways of the world. All these things require the flesh to **suffer**. We must, through the power of the Holy Spirit, dominate the flesh if we are to have the victorious life that Jesus bought and paid for on the cross.

2 Peter 1
16 For we did not follow cunningly devised fables when we made known to you the power and coming of our Lord Jesus Christ, but were eyewitnesses of His majesty.
17 For He received from God the Father honor and glory when such a voice came to Him from the Excellent Glory: "This is My beloved Son, in whom I am well pleased."
18 And we heard this voice which came from heaven when we were with Him on the holy mountain.

Ephesians 2
18 For through Him we both have access by one Spirit to the Father.

The clear and unmistakable proof of the triune Godhead is throughout Scripture. Never be deceived into perceiving the Godhead as other than three Persons Who are One, and the One Who are Three. We, the body of Christ, are complete in the Godhead bodily (Colossians 2:9-10).

2 John
8 Look to yourselves, that we do not lose those things we worked

for, but that we may receive a full reward.
9 Whoever transgresses and does not abide in the doctrine of Christ does not have God. He who abides in the doctrine of Christ has both the Father and the Son.
10 If anyone comes to you and does not bring this doctrine, do not receive him into your house nor greet him;
11 for he who greets him shares in his evil deeds.

The Law

Several years ago—when I found myself among a group of Christians who exalted the Law while claiming to be born-again and fully in the new covenant—God took me aside and said, "The single most destructive false doctrine of the final days, more pervasive than any other, will be that which draws the body of Christ back under the Law. The ones who are thus deceived will loose their inheritance."

This is an insidious doctrine, an abomination to the Lord, and widely accepted because it uses God's Word out of context to cloak destruction. Yes, we are grafted into God's covenant with Abraham—we are grafted-in Jews—but we are not, repeat not, Old Testament Jews and subject to the Law.

One might think this to be an isolated problem but, sadly, it is being embraced by large, credible, Christian platforms, thereby spreading rapidly and leading to the deception of many.

1 Corinthians 5
6 Your glorying is not good. Do you not know that a little leaven leavens the whole lump?
7 Therefore purge out the old leaven, that you may be a new lump, since you truly are unleavened. For indeed Christ, our Passover, was sacrificed for us.

Jesus said in Matthew 16, [6]**Take heed and beware of the leaven of the Pharisees and the Sadducees.** The **leaven of the Pharisees and the Sadducees** is the Law of the old covenant and, everywhere one looks today, Christians are being told by other Christians to wear

Jewish prayer shawls, keep the sabbath, and eat according to Old Testament dietary laws. The listener is told that he is still under grace but has the privilege of keeping the Law as well. You may ask, "What's wrong with that if someone wants to do it? What's the harm?"

Condemnation and curse! That is the harm. No one was redeemed by the Law, no not one.

Galatians 3

10 For as many as are of the works of the law are under the curse; for it is written, "Cursed is everyone who does not continue in all things which are written in the book of the law, to do them."

11 But that no one is justified by the law in the sight of God is evident, for "The just shall live by faith."

12 Yet the law is not of faith, but "The man who does them shall live by them."

13 Christ has redeemed us from the curse of the law, having become a curse for us (for it is written, "Cursed is everyone who hangs on a tree")

14 that the blessing of Abraham might come upon the Gentiles in Christ Jesus, that we might receive the promise of the Spirit through faith.

Cursed is everyone who does not continue in all things which are written in the book of the law, to do them. Hello! Is anybody listening out there? When a Christian, who has been **redeemed...from the curse of the law** by the blood of Jesus, makes the choice to turn back to the Law—which was made dead to him by Jesus—he has walked out from under grace and the blood and must keep all 613 laws in order to try to be justified. No one has the luxury to select a few laws that he finds appealing and add them to the new covenant. Once one takes any law unto himself, he is obliged to keep all 613 or be cursed. Christ Jesus came to redeem us from that very thing, and we must regard the leaven of the Pharisees as spiritual poison.

Even if someone tries to be justified by the Law, he must fail for **no one is justified by the law in the sight of God**. The horrifying truth is that people who accept and participate in this false doctrine, this pack of lies, are led to think they can just choose a few laws that appeal to them and all is well. They are told that this practice enriches their walk with the Lord. Nothing could be farther from the truth.

Galatians 3
19 What purpose then does the law serve? It was added because of transgressions, till the Seed should come to whom the promise was made; and it was appointed through angels by the hand of a mediator.
20 Now a mediator does not mediate for one only, but God is one.
21 Is the law then against the promises of God? Certainly not! For if there had been a law given which could have given life, truly righteousness would have been by the law.
22 But the Scripture has confined all under sin, that the promise by faith in Jesus Christ might be given to those who believe.
23 But before faith came, we were kept under guard by the law, kept for the faith which would afterward be revealed.
24 Therefore the law was our tutor to bring us to Christ, that we might be justified by faith.
25 But after faith has come, we are no longer under a tutor.

The Law was never more than a stop-gap measure until Jesus came. God was going to kill all the people when Moses came down from the mountain and found them worshipping the golden calf in the midst of a pagan orgy. Moses interceded and God relented (Exodus 32). That was when God gave the Law, in which He took no pleasure (Hebrews 10:5-10), to preserve His people until the coming of **the Seed**, Jesus, through **whom the promise was made**.

This is where many fail to understand the Old Testament: they do not separate the promise from the Law. God put the Law to death at the birth of Jesus, but the promise is eternal. God gave the inheritance to Abraham by promise (Galatians 3:18). We are Abraham's seed, in Christ, and heirs according to that promise (Galatians 3:16). We are not heirs according to the Law.

Galatians 3
1 O foolish Galatians! Who has bewitched you that you should

The Rapture, The Tribulation, And Beyond

not obey the truth, before whose eyes Jesus Christ was clearly portrayed among you as crucified?
2 This only I want to learn from you: Did you receive the Spirit by the works of the law, or by the hearing of faith?

Paul was railing in desperation against the perversity of the Galatians. He wanted to know who had **bewitched** them. Paul likened their embracing **the works of the law** to entering into witchcraft. God put an end to the Law, made it obsolete (Hebrews 8:13), when Christ established the new covenant. The Law was fulfilled and rendered dead from the moment Jesus was born into the world. Satan is the one who has dug up this dead, stinking carcass, presented it to God's people as holy and, through deception, led many to defile themselves.

2 Corinthians 6
17 "Therefore come out from among them and be separate," says the Lord. "Do not touch what is unclean, and I will receive you.
18 "I will be a Father to you, and you shall be My sons and daughters," says the Lord Almighty.

2 Corinthians 7
1 Therefore, having these promises, beloved, let us cleanse ourselves from all filthiness of the flesh and spirit, perfecting holiness in the fear of God.

The dead Law is **what is unclean**. It is what we must leave untouched so that God **will receive** us. If we touch this unclean, dead thing, God cannot receive us.

2 Corinthians 3
6 who also made us sufficient as ministers of the new covenant, not of the letter but of the Spirit; for the letter kills, but the Spirit gives life.

The **letter** which **kills** is the letter of the Law.

Colossians 2
20 Therefore, if you died with Christ from the basic principles

of the world, why, as though living in the world, do you subject yourselves to regulations
**21 "Do not touch, do not taste, do not handle,"
22 which all concern things which perish with the using according to the commandments and doctrines of men?
23 These things indeed have an appearance of wisdom in self-imposed religion, false humility, and neglect of the body, but are of no value against the indulgence of the flesh.**

Paul's struggle in this area was great because so many of those who came to Christ in the first establishing of the church were Jews. They had difficulty letting go of their traditions. Jesus said in Mark 7, [13]**making the Word of God of no effect through your tradition which you have handed down**. It amazes me that there seem to be just as many today who are willing to put themselves back under the curse of the Law, with nary a thought to the dire consequences, as there were then. The only reasonable explanation lies with God's words in Hosea 4, [6]**My people are destroyed for lack of knowledge**.

Galatians 2
**18 For if I build again those things which I destroyed, I make myself a transgressor.
19 For I through the law died to the law that I might live to God.
20 I have been crucified with Christ; it is no longer I who live, but Christ lives in me; and the life which I now live in the flesh I live by faith in the Son of God, who loved me and gave Himself for me.
21 I do not set aside the grace of God; for if righteousness comes through the law, then Christ died in vain.**

Why would anyone want to leave the grace of God and make himself a **transgressor**?

Galatians 4
21 Tell me, you who desire to be under the law, do you not hear the law?

> 22 For it is written that Abraham had two sons: the one by a bondwoman, the other by a freewoman.
> 23 But he who was of the bondwoman was born according to the flesh, and he of the freewoman through promise,
> 24 which things are symbolic. For these are the two covenants: the one from Mount Sinai which gives birth to bondage, which is Hagar
> 25 for this Hagar is Mount Sinai in Arabia, and corresponds to Jerusalem which now is, and is in bondage with her children
> 26 but the Jerusalem above is free, which is the mother of us all.
> 30 Nevertheless what does the Scripture say? "Cast out the bondwoman and her son, for the son of the bondwoman shall not be heir with the son of the freewoman."
> 31 So then, brethren, we are not children of the bondwoman but of the free.

Those under the Law shall **not be heir** with those who are in the liberty of Christ. Even those members of the body of Christ, born again in the blood of Jesus and by His Spirit, put themselves under bondage and make the blood of no effect if they turn back to the Law.

Galatians 5
> **1 Stand fast therefore in the liberty by which Christ has made us free, and do not be entangled again with a yoke of bondage.**

The anointing has destroyed all the yokes and removed all the burdens (Isaiah 10:27) and that includes the Law. We, however, have free will and must choose to **stand fast therefore in the liberty by which Christ has made us free**, free from the Law of sin and death which condemns the flesh (Romans 8:1-2).

Deuteronomy 30
> **19 I call heaven and earth as witnesses today against you, that I have set before you life and death, blessing and cursing; therefore choose life, that both you and your descendants may live;
> 20 that you may love the Lord your God, that you may obey His**

voice, and that you may cling to Him, for He is your life and the length of your days; and that you may dwell in the land which the Lord swore to your fathers, to Abraham, Isaac, and Jacob, to give them.

Choose life! Choose blessing! The **land which the Lord swore to** give to **your fathers** in the faith, **Abraham, Isaac and Jacob**, is the land of promise, not the Law. The promise was given to Abraham and his descendants eternally. This does not refer to Abraham's biological descendants, but his descendants in the faith. Those in Christ have become the seed of Abraham by faith (Galatians 3:13-16).

John 8
**31 Then Jesus said to those Jews who believed Him, "If you abide in My word, you are My disciples indeed.
32 "And you shall know the truth, and the truth shall make you free."
33 They answered Him, "We are Abraham's descendants, and have never been in bondage to anyone. How can you say, 'You will be made free?'"
34 Jesus answered them, "Most assuredly, I say to you, whoever commits sin is a slave of sin.
35 "And a slave does not abide in the house forever, but a son abides forever.
36 "Therefore if the Son makes you free, you shall be free indeed."**

Keeping the Law is sin. Sin separates us from God. Only life in Christ Jesus, and Him alone, makes us free from the Law, which is of sin and death.

Hebrews 8
**6 But now He has obtained a more excellent ministry, inasmuch as He is also Mediator of a better covenant, which was established on better promises.
7 For if that first covenant had been faultless, then no place would have been sought for a second.**

8 Because finding fault with them, He says: "Behold, the days are coming, says the Lord, when I will make a new covenant with the house of Israel and with the house of Judah—"
13 In that He says, "A new covenant," He has made the first obsolete. Now what is becoming obsolete and growing old is ready to vanish away.

What about **obsolete** don't you understand, if you are one of those trying to be under the Law and grace at the same time? And don't try to hang your defense on **becoming obsolete and growing old is ready to vanish away**. All that means is that the Jews of that time who clung to the Law would have to die before the Law was truly ended, just as the generation that left Egypt had to die before Joshua could enter the promised land.

Hebrews 9
8 the Holy Spirit indicating this, that the way into the Holiest of All was not yet made manifest while the first tabernacle was still standing.
9 It was symbolic for the present time in which both gifts and sacrifices are offered which cannot make him who performed the service perfect in regard to the conscience
10 concerned only with foods and drinks, various washings, and fleshly ordinances imposed until the time of reformation.

Hebrews 10
5 Therefore, when He came into the world, He said: "Sacrifice and offering You did not desire, but a body You have prepared for Me.
6 "In burnt offerings and sacrifices for sin you had no pleasure.
7 "Then I said, 'Behold, I have come in the volume of the book it is written of Me to do Your will, O God.'"
8 Previously saying, "Sacrifice and offering, burnt offerings, and offerings for sin You did not desire, nor had pleasure in them" (which are offered according to the law),
9 then He said, "Behold, I have come to do Your will, O God." He takes away the first that He may establish the second.

10 By that will we have been sanctified through the offering of the body of Jesus Christ once for all.

God neither desired nor liked the Law. That alone should give us a clue. God was relieved and unburdened when He could do away with it. The Law never did, and certainly cannot now, please God. Faith is what pleases God. Without faith it is impossible to please Him (Hebrews 11:6). There is no faith in the Law, only ordinance.

Hebrews 10
29 Of how much worse punishment, do you suppose, will he be thought worthy who has trampled the Son of God underfoot, counted the blood of the covenant by which he was sanctified a common thing, and insulted the Spirit of grace?
30 For we know Him who said, "Vengeance is Mine; I will repay, says the Lord." And again, "The Lord will judge His people."
31 It is a fearful thing to fall into the hands of the living God.

There is a great deal more new covenant Scripture, volumes in fact, that denounces the Law. One is either under grace, justified by faith in the blood and anointing of Jesus, or under the condemnation of the Law. It is one or the other.

An example of a little leaven, in this context, can be something as seemingly harmless as buying a prayer shawl and then becoming intrigued with the symbolism of the threads, tassels and knots. One thing leads to the next and suddenly the entire lump is leavened; the Law is being embraced. One is compelled to liken this to Jesus saying in Matthew 5, [28]**But I say to you that whoever looks at a woman to lust for her has already committed adultery with her in his heart.** Meditating on the traditions of the prayer shawl produces a lust for the trappings of the Law.

If you are one of those who has picked up any of the Law, drop it like a hot potato, repent, be cleansed from all unrighteousness, and embrace with all your heart the new, and only the new, covenant.

Titus 1
13 This testimony is true. Therefore rebuke them sharply, that

they may be sound in the faith,
14 not giving heed to Jewish fables and commandments of men who turn from the truth.
15 To the pure all things are pure, but to those who are defiled and unbelieving nothing is pure; but even their mind and conscience are defiled.
16 They profess to know God, but in works they deny Him, being abominable, disobedient, and disqualified for every good work.

When you meditate in the Word, separate forever the promise from the Law.

Deceiving Spirits And Doctrines Of Demons

1 Timothy 4
1 Now the Spirit expressly says that in latter times some will depart from the faith, giving heed to deceiving spirits and doctrines of demons,
2 speaking lies in hypocrisy, having their own conscience seared with a hot iron,
3 forbidding to marry, and commanding to abstain from foods which God created to be received with thanksgiving by those who believe and know the truth.
4 For every creature of God is good, and nothing is to be refused if it is received with thanksgiving;
5 for it is sanctified by the word of God and prayer.
6 If you instruct the brethren in these things, you will be a good minister of Jesus Christ, nourished in the words of faith and of the good doctrine which you have carefully followed.
7 But reject profane and old wives' fables, and exercise yourself rather to godliness.
8 For bodily exercise profits a little, but godliness is profitable for all things, having promise of the life that now is and of that which is to come.
9 This is a faithful saying and worthy of all acceptance.

Old Testament dietary laws and restrictive eating programs are suddenly being promoted everywhere one looks. They, and the **deceiving spirits** that promote them, are destroying people. These regimens cause people to **depart from the faith**. They become idols. They replace Jesus as healer and deliverer. The stripes of Jesus are pushed aside and the eating program is exalted. I have watched dear Christians die from "health cures," that proclaim all animal flesh and products to be poison to the body, and put them on a regimen of vegetables, vegetable juices, fruit, fruit juices, and some grains. Any such is a **doctrine of demons**.

Satan came to kill, steal and destroy. The devil's purpose is to devour us if we are foolish enough to let him (1 Peter 5:8). A **doctrine of demons** is a doctrine that will destroy all who accept it. Read again the preceding verses in Timothy. God said that, in the new covenant, all animals were clean and for our benefit and **nothing is to be refused**. To declare anything God has made to be unclean is a **doctrine of demons**. Why would anyone in Christ want to participate in such an abomination? The Lord went out of His way to make a huge point of this.

> Acts 10
>
> **9 The next day, as they went on their journey and drew near the city, Peter went up on the housetop to pray, about the sixth hour.**
> **10 Then he became very hungry and wanted to eat; but while they made ready, he fell into a trance**
> **11 and saw heaven opened and an object like a great sheet bound at the four corners, descending to him and let down to the earth.**
> **12 In it were all kinds of four-footed animals of the earth, wild beasts, creeping things, and birds of the air.**
> **13 And a voice came to him, "Rise, Peter; kill and eat."**
> **14 But Peter said, "Not so, Lord! For I have never eaten anything common or unclean."**
> **15 And a voice spoke to him again the second time, "What God has cleansed you must not call common."**

Rise, Peter; kill and eat. Seems simple enough to me. Nothing was, or is, unclean under the new covenant. The Law was, and is, dead. God did use this vision to reassure Peter about going to the house of Cornelius, a Gentile, to witness to him, but that in no way expunges God's instruction to Peter to receive all foods as clean and good.

Colossians 2
8 Beware lest anyone cheat you through philosophy and empty deceit, according to the tradition of men, according to the basic principles of the world, and not according to Christ.
9 For in Him dwells all the fullness of the Godhead bodily;
10 and you are complete in Him, who is the head of all principality and power.
13 And you, being dead in your trespasses and the uncircumcision of your flesh, He has made alive together with Him, having forgiven you all trespasses,
14 having wiped out the handwriting of requirements that was against us, which was contrary to us. And He has taken it out of the way, having nailed it to the cross.

The Law is **the handwriting of requirements that was against us**. Since God removed it from us, and **nailed it to the cross**, it stopped at the cross. The only way the Law, and such things as eating restrictions, can be part of our lives, is if we remove the nails with which God fastened them to, and bring them to our side of, the cross. The Law and all its restrictions are actually contraband in the land of promise. If one takes a forbidden item across a national border into a new country, and is discovered to be in possession of it, one is at risk of imprisonment and death. This is how we must look at the things of the Law. The Law has been forbidden in the land of promise. It carries a severe penalty for those who insist on smuggling it in.

Colossians 2
16 Therefore let no one judge you in food or in drink, or regarding a festival or a new moon or sabbaths,
17 which are a shadow of things to come, but the substance is of Christ.

> **20** Therefore, if you died with Christ from the basic principles of the world, why, as though living in the world, do you subject yourselves to regulations
> **21** "Do not touch, do not taste, do not handle,"
> **22** which all concern things which perish with the using according to the commandments and doctrines of men?
> **23** These things indeed have an appearance of wisdom in self-imposed religion, false humility, and neglect of the body, but are of no value against the indulgence of the flesh.

All these deceptions are of **no value**. They do not work and can cause grievous harm. Anything that diverts our faith and trust in Christ is dangerous.

Into His Marvelous Light

> 1 Peter 2
> **9** But you are a chosen generation, a royal priesthood, a holy nation, His own special people, that you may proclaim the praises of Him who called you out of darkness into His marvelous light;

> 1 John 1
> **5** This is the message which we have heard from Him and declare to you, that God is light and in Him is no darkness at all.
> **6** If we say that we have fellowship with Him, and walk in darkness, we lie and do not practice the truth.
> **7** But if we walk in the light as He is in the light, we have fellowship with one another, and the blood of Jesus Christ His Son cleanses us from all sin.

There is no darkness in God. He has **called you out of darkness into His marvelous light**. Once we move into the kingdom of the Son of God, darkness has been eradicated. It is not part of God and, therefore, is no longer part of our lives once we are one with God in Christ.

The Rapture, The Tribulation, And Beyond 247

James 1
16 Do not be deceived, my beloved brethren.
17 Every good gift and every perfect gift is from above, and comes down from the Father of lights, with whom there is no variation or shadow of turning.

God is light and He is unchanging. This irrefutable fact has been established repeatedly in Scripture. The kingdom of darkness is Satan's realm. The kingdom of light is God's realm. The one has no part in the other.

James 1
13 Let no one say when he is tempted, "I am tempted by God"; for God cannot be tempted by evil, nor does He Himself tempt anyone.

Let no one say that tempting, testing, thus evil of any kind, comes from God. One would think that to be pretty straightforward. The Word says God is light, Satan darkness. Pretty straightforward. The **beloved brethren** are warned, **do not be deceived** in this matter. Attributing tribulation to God is false doctrine. Attributing darkness to God is false doctrine.

Why, therefore, have I watched on television an anointed man of God declare? "God puts people in dark rooms of tragedy and despair so that He can bring them out in triumph."

Why have I watched God's people in their tens of thousands go wild in agreement with this false, loathsome doctrine? Why did they cheer, cry, run around and jump up and down? Why did they shake their Bibles in the air and fall on their faces to celebrate this lie, making it their own?

These hysterical, deluded people were told, "Miscarriage--dark room. Your daughter becomes a lesbian--dark room. Your husband commits adultery--dark room. You become addicted to drugs--dark room. Cancer attacks your body--dark room. Your child dies in a car accident--dark room." With each lie the audience of this man of God was whipped into an even greater frenzy of blaming God, not the devil, for evil. It is a shameful, despicable thing to accuse God of being a child abuser.

Even an anointed preacher can promote fleshly, false doctrine. These performances, for that is what they are, produce reaction in the flesh because flesh responds to flesh. People would rather hear that God is oppressing them—and that it is neither their fault nor their responsibility to overcome the oppression—than the truth. The preachers who do this, I believe, become addicted to the hysteria such babblings produce and deceive themselves into thinking it is the anointing. Nothing could be farther from the truth.

Jesus commanded us to be overcomers. We are to overcome the enemy and all his darkness in every area of our lives. Jesus led us into the light, and only the light. Where would God even find darkness, since there is none in Him? He would have to get it from the devil.

The God Of Abraham

Since the September 11, 2001, attacks upon the World Trade Center in New York and the Pentagon in Washington, D.C., there has been a horrifying tendency of certain Christian ministries to promote some misguided and perverted spirit of unity between the Muslim and Christian worlds. I have heard it emphatically proclaimed that Muslims, Jews, and Christians all worship the same God. Those preaching this lie say that we all come to God in different ways: the Muslims by Mohammed, the Jews by the Law, and the Christians by Jesus.

First of all, that makes Jesus a liar because He said in John 14, [6]**I am the way, the truth, and the life. No one comes to the Father except through Me.**

Secondly, the Muslims, who worship Allah (who is not the God of Abraham but the moon god) and have as their prophet Mohammed, declare Jesus to be a prophet—though not as important a prophet as Mohammed—but not the Son of God come in the flesh. This again makes Jesus a liar. Apart from all else, John 8 tells us, [58]**Jesus said to them, "Most assuredly, I say to you, before Abraham was, I AM."** Muslims defend their acceptance of a liar as a prophet by averring that the Christian Bible is all wrong in that Jesus did not say the things attributed to Him.

Thirdly, the Jews worship the God of Abraham, but not one of them has been justified by the Law (Galatians 3:11). The Jews have to receive Jesus as Messiah, just like the rest of us. Apart from any other proof of this, if it were not so it would mean that Jesus wasted His entire ministry preaching to the only people on earth who did not need to hear Him.

Our role, as the body of Christ, is to pray for and minister to everyone—including but not limited to the Jew and the Muslim—in the attempt to bring him to Christ. The only unity is unity in the Spirit. There is not now, nor can there ever be, unity among denominations or religions.

> Ephesians 4
> **1 I, therefore, the prisoner of the Lord, beseech you to have a walk worthy of the calling with which you were called,**
> **2 with all lowliness and gentleness, with longsuffering, bearing with one another in love,**
> **3 endeavoring to keep the unity of the Spirit in the bond of peace.**
> **4 There is one body and one Spirit, just as you were called in one hope of your calling;**
> **5 one Lord, one faith, one baptism;**
> **6 one God and Father of all, who is above all, and through all, and in you all.**

We shall not win people to Christ by appeasing their false doctrines. Appeasement only perpetuates their separation from salvation in Christ Jesus. The only way by which any man can be saved is through the truth, the whole truth, and nothing but the truth, so help us God.

The Purity Of God's Truth

> Titus 2
> **11 For the grace of God that brings salvation has appeared to all men,**
> **12 teaching us that, denying ungodliness and worldly lusts, we**

> should live soberly, righteously, and godly in the present age,
> 13 looking for the blessed hope and glorious appearing of our great God and Savior Jesus Christ,
> 14 who gave Himself for us, that He might redeem us from every lawless deed and purify for Himself His own special people, zealous for good works.
> 15 Speak these things, exhort, and rebuke with all authority. Let no one despise you.

I have come to accept that many, who are blinded by the devil, have always, and will always, despise the truth. Therefore, the bearer of the truth will also be despised. The natural man is susceptible to every lie presented to him. If we are to stand upon the rock, stay on the narrow way, and qualify to rule and reign with Jesus, we must be prepared to be despised by men and love, and be loved by, God. Pleasing men cannot save us. Pleasing God, by faith in His Word, is the only thing that can and will save us. That is why Paul told us to keep our eyes on the prize and press on.

> Philippians 3
> 12 Not that I have already attained, or am already perfected; but I press on, that I may lay hold of that for which Christ Jesus has also laid hold of me.
> 13 Brethren, I do not count myself to have apprehended; but one thing I do, forgetting those things which are behind and reaching forward to those things which are ahead,
> 14 I press toward the goal for the prize of the upward call of God in Christ Jesus.
> 15 Therefore let us, as many as are mature, have this mind; and if in anything you think otherwise, God will reveal even this to you.
> 16 Nevertheless, to the degree that we have already attained, let us walk by the same rule, let us be of the same mind.

We must press on, through all opposition from the devil, men, and our own flesh, and overcome. We must hold fast to the truth as God has given it to us.

Revelation 3
5 He who overcomes shall be clothed in white garments, and I will not blot out his name from the Book of Life; but I will confess his name before My Father and before His angels.
11 Behold, I come quickly! Hold fast what you have, that no one may take your crown.

Chapter 15

Separating The Wheat From The Chaff

A field of wheat grows undisturbed until it is ready to be harvested. Harvest is a time of separation. When the crop is mature, and the time has come to gather it into the barns, the huge combines sweep through the ripe crop and separate the heads of grain from the husks and the stalks, the chaff. The whole purpose of growing a stand of wheat is for the grain heads to mature and be gathered. The chaff has little or no value. It is used, if at all, for bedding the stalls of animals. It is thrown out when it is soiled, fit only for the dung heap.

Harvest is a time of determining what is wheat and what is chaff. The closer we get to the time of the rapture, the farther we must be separated from the world. Jesus explains the process by which He will separate evil from righteousness at the harvest of the body of Christ—the rapture of the church—when He separates us unto Himself.

Matthew 13
**24 Another parable He put forth to them, saying: "The kingdom of heaven is like a man who sowed good seed in his field;
25 "but while men slept, his enemy came and sowed tares among the wheat and went his way.
26 "But when the grain had sprouted and produced a crop, then the tares also appeared."
27 So the servants of the owner came and said to him, "Sir, did**

you not sow good seed in your field? How then does it have tares?"

28 He said to them, "An enemy has done this." The servants said to him, "Do you want us then to go and gather them up?"

29 But he said, "No, lest while you gather up the tares you also uproot the wheat with them.

30 "Let both grow together until the harvest, and at the time of harvest I will say to the reapers, 'First gather together the tares and bind them in bundles to burn them, but gather the wheat into my barn.'"

The wheat (the body of Christ) and the tares (sons of the devil) have shared the earth from the beginning. God has patiently given all men time to see the truth of Christ Jesus and become part of His kingdom. At the time of the harvest, however, a division will take place.

Matthew 13

36 Then Jesus sent the multitude away and went into the house. And His disciples came to Him, saying, "Explain to us the parable of the tares of the field."

37 He answered and said to them: "He who sows the good seed is the Son of Man.

38 "The field is the world, the good seeds are the sons of the kingdom, but the tares are the sons of the wicked one.

39 "The enemy who sowed them is the devil, the harvest is the end of the age, and the reapers are the angels."

At the rapture, **the end of the age**, clouds of angels will take **the good seeds**, the body of Christ, out of the corrupted world and gather them into the Father's barn, New Jerusalem. The tares, **the sons of the wicked one**, will be left on earth.

Even now we can observe the wicked of the earth, **the tares**, gathering together into **bundles**, or groups of iniquity. People of like sin are becoming outspoken in their practices and forming organized groups, many in the political arena: pro-abortion (pro-choice) groups, homosexual rights groups, racist groups, gangs, terrorist groups, witches' covens, warlocks, occult practices, perverted religions and cults, satanists, the goth movement, and all like them. They are becoming more pervasive, more defined, and more aggressive. Wickedness is more brazen than ever as these groups prepare, unbeknownst to them, to be thrown into the lake of fire and burned.

Matthew 13
40 "Therefore as the tares are gathered and burned in the fire, so it will be at the end of this age.
41 "The Son of Man will send out His angels, and they will gather out of His kingdom all things that offend, and those who practice lawlessness,
42 "and will cast them into the furnace of fire. There will be wailing and gnashing of teeth.
43 "Then the righteous will shine forth as the sun in the kingdom of their Father. He who has ears to hear, let him hear!"

The **tares are gathered** at the beginning of and during the tribulation. Evil is identified by the mark of the beast and, at **the end** of the tribulation, all the forces of evil—the two hundred million man army of Antichrist, which includes all those bundled for burning—will be gathered and cast into the lake of fire, where there **will be wailing and gnashing of teeth**.

The righteous, the body of Christ, will, having been separated into the Father's kingdom, forever become part of the light of Jesus. Jesus is the Lord of the harvest. This is a critical time for the body of Christ. We must not be deceived by the world, or the desires of our own flesh, into participating in that which is outside the kingdom. There are many calling themselves Christians who rebel against this separation. They refuse to see why they cannot do whatever they feel like doing. They go, without hesitation, to movies containing occult plots and featuring characters with magical powers; they permit their children to see such movies and read books of similar content; they make excuses for immorality; they exalt the so-called wisdom of the world above God's wisdom; they are consistently in rebellion against the Word.

1 Samuel 15
23 For rebellion is as the sin of witchcraft, and stubbornness is as iniquity and idolatry.

Witchcraft in any guise is pure evil; it will destroy all who touch it. It does not matter whether it is participation in Halloween, satanic children's fare, Santa Claus, the Easter bunny, Ouija boards, satanic music, the psychic network, Tarot readings, or any false religion. It is all evil, it is all unclean, it debars anyone participating in it from being sons and daughters of almighty God. Participation in evil begets grave risk, risk of being among the bundles of tares to be burned.

A simple rule of thumb is this: anyone who claims or evidences supernatural powers and does not openly attribute such powers to the Lord Jesus Christ is operating in witchcraft and is evil. All things derive from one of two sources: God or Satan. If something is not of God, it is of Satan. There are no other options.

> Luke 12
> **54 Then He also said to the multitudes, "When you see a cloud rising out of the west, immediately you say, 'A shower is coming'; and so it is.**
> **55 "And when you see the south wind blow, you say, 'There will be hot weather'; and there is.**
> **56 "Hypocrites! You can discern the face of the sky and of the earth, but how is it you do not discern this time?"**

There is no room for error. Time is almost up. We have the instruction manual, the Bible, and are therefore without excuse.

> 2 Timothy 2
> **15 Be diligent to present yourself approved to God, a worker who does not need to be ashamed, rightly dividing the word of truth.**
> **16 But shun profane and vain babblings, for they will increase to more ungodliness.**
> **17 And their message will spread like cancer. Hymenaeus and Philetus are of this sort,**
> **18 who have strayed concerning the truth, saying that the resurrection is already past; and they overthrow the faith of some.**
> **19 Nevertheless the solid foundation of God stands, having this**

seal: "The Lord knows those who are His," and, "Let everyone who names the name of Christ depart from iniquity."

Harvest time is the time of division. We are either wheat or tares. We must make the choice; we must welcome separation unto God. One indication of our love for Jesus is our hatred of all evil.

Isaiah 60
1 Arise, shine; For your light has come! and the glory of the Lord is risen upon you.
2 For behold, the darkness shall cover the earth, and deep darkness the people; but the Lord will arise over you, and His glory will be seen upon you.
3 The Gentiles shall come to your light, and kings to the brightness of your rising.

Deception will increase as the world prepares for the rule of Antichrist. Remember, the antichrist spirit is against the anointing, the power of the Holy Spirit. As the body of Christ separates farther and farther from evil, the light of the glory will increase upon us. The greater the distance we are from all that is not of God's kingdom, the brighter the glory will shine in our lives and the more intensely God's blessings will overtake us and abound.

Psalm 119
137 Righteous are You, O Lord, And upright are Your judgments.
138 Your testimonies, which You have commanded, Are righteous and very faithful.
139 My zeal has consumed me, Because my enemies have forgotten Your words.
140 Your word is very pure; Therefore Your servant loves it.

The beginning of our separation unto Christ is the development of our love for His Word. It is not enough that we just accept it; we must adore and embrace it. The Word must be life and breath to us. We can have no opinions apart from the Word, no separate agendas, no "yeah, buts" or "what ifs." We must take the Word of God as our only truth and count it all joy, no matter what the natural circumstances tell us, no matter how hard it is on the flesh, no matter how foolish we look to others, no matter how we feel about it, no matter what our pasts contain.

1 John 2

28 And now, little children, abide in Him, that when He appears, we may have confidence and not be ashamed before Him at His coming.
29 If you know that He is righteous, you know that everyone who practices righteousness is born of Him.

One of the qualities of those who belong to Christ is that we bear good fruit. This is not possible unless we walk closely with Him.

John 15

1 I am the true vine, and My Father is the vinedresser.
2 Every branch in Me that does not bear fruit He takes away; and every branch that bears fruit He prunes, that it may bear more fruit.

Notice that the fruitless branches, despite their being members of the body of Christ, are removed if they fail to bear fruit.

John 15

4 Abide in Me, and I in you. As the branch cannot bear fruit of itself, unless it abides in the vine, neither can you, unless you abide in Me.
5 I am the vine, you are the branches. He who abides in Me, and I in him, bears much fruit; for without Me you can do nothing.
6 If anyone does not abide in Me, he is cast out as a branch and is withered; and they gather them and throw them into the fire, and they are burned.
7 If you abide in Me, and My words abide in you, you will ask what you desire, and it shall be done for you.
8 By this My Father is glorified, that you bear much fruit; so you will be My disciples.

Here again, Jesus tells us what it takes to be part of His body. We must be separated wholly unto Him. He says it is essential that His **words abide in** us. As we separate ourselves more and more from the world and unto Him, the world will see the power and blessing of God upon us and be drawn to Him. This is the Father's plan; we are obliged to walk in it.

Proverbs 10
5 He who gathers in summer is a wise son, but he who sleeps in harvest is a son who causes shame.

As sons and daughters of almighty God, we do not want to cause our Father shame. We want to be an honor, a praise and a joy unto Him.

Jeremiah 33
9 Then it shall be to Me a name of joy, a praise, and an honor before all nations of the earth, who shall hear all the good that I do to them; they shall fear and tremble for all the goodness and all the prosperity that I provide for it.

Jesus Came To Divide

Jesus said that He came to divide. He made no secret of this. He proclaimed that He came to divide His own from the unbelieving world, even if it meant dividing those of the same household.

This division within households may seem to be a contradiction of God's promise to save our whole household (Acts 16:31), but it is not. The salvation of a divided household is usually accomplished when the person who first receives the revelation of Christ Jesus separates himself from the others. The salvation of the whole family comes about as that born-again person stands in the gap, praying for the salvation of the rest of the family.

The principle at issue here is that we place Jesus Christ, and our relationship with Him, above all other relationships. We, like Abraham with Isaac, must place our families on the altar and take God at His

Word that He will restore them to us, as He did Isaac. Until we do this, God is not fully on the throne of our hearts.

> Luke 12
>
> **49 I came to send fire on the earth, and how I wish it were already kindled!**
> **50 But I have a baptism to be baptized with, and how distressed I am till it is accomplished!**
> **51 Do you suppose that I came to give peace on earth? I tell you, not at all, but rather division.**
> **52 For from now on five in one house will be divided: three against two, and two against three.**
> **53 Father will be divided against son and son against father, mother against daughter and daughter against mother, mother-in-law against her daughter-in-law and daughter-in-law against her mother-in-law.**

We can observe from verses 49 and 50 that Jesus does not take any pleasure in the process of division. If He had His way, every man, woman and child would be saved. However, the Father has given us free will and only we can make the decisions that determine our future. Jesus makes clear that He will be relieved when this is over and He no longer has to watch those who make the wrong choices walk into the fires of destruction.

Jesus came to give us supernatural peace while we are in the world, but peace in Him, not peace in or of the world. Only when we are separated completely unto Him, and have no part in the world's philosophies and methods, will we have peace. Only if we are new creatures in Christ will we be pure and holy and be gathered into His barn.

> 2 Corinthians 6
>
> **15 And what accord has Christ with Belial? Or what part has a believer with an unbeliever?**
> **16 And what agreement has the temple of God with idols? For you are the temple of the living God. As God has said: "I will**

dwell in them and walk among them. I will be their God, and they shall be My people."
17 Therefore "Come out from among them and be separate, says the Lord. Do not touch what is unclean, and I will receive you.
18 "I will be a Father to you, and you shall be My sons and daughters, says the Lord Almighty."

Chapter 16

The Judgment Seat Of Christ

The judgment seat of Christ and the great white throne judgment are unrelated events separated by 1007 years plus the little season during which Satan is released from the pit to tempt the nations; it occurs at the rapture. It is the place of reward where those who have been caught up and glorified will receive their crowns.

The great white throne judgment—which will be fully explained in Chapter 26—takes place at the end of the millennial reign of Christ. We, the body of Christ, shall not be the judged but the judges. We shall sit with Jesus and judge the angels and the nations. Immediately thereafter, God will make His new heaven and His new earth.

The judgment seat of Christ is a place that every believer should anticipate with eagerness and excitement. God is a just God. Everything we do on earth counts. Everything we do which is of faith unto righteousness is on the plus side of our ledger. All the useless, fruitless things count for nothing. Our reward—our heavenly rank or position—will be based on the good fruit of our lives. Our own opinion of our accomplishments will be irrelevant. God will determine our reward based solely on His evaluation of how well we kept His Word and did His will.

2 Timothy 4
7 I have fought the good fight, I have finished the race, I have kept the faith.

8 Finally, there is laid up for me the crown of righteousness, which the Lord, the righteous Judge, will give to me on that Day, and not to me only but also to all who have loved His appearing.

To **have loved His appearing** means to have been eagerly and joyfully expecting the pre-tribulation rapture of the church. The **crown of righteousness** to be given each member of the body of Christ is the symbol of his reward; **that Day** is the judgment seat of Christ.

1 Peter 5
4 and when the Chief Shepherd appears, you will receive the crown of glory that does not fade away.

Colossians 1:27 says that Christ in us is the hope of that **glory**. Our crowns are not of gold or silver but of the most precious substance of all: glory.

1 Corinthians 3
5 Who then is Paul, and who is Apollos, but ministers through whom you believed, as the Lord gave to each one?
6 I planted, Apollos watered, but God gave the increase.
7 So then neither he who plants is anything, nor he who waters, but God who gives the increase.
8 Now he who plants and he who waters are one, and each one will receive his own reward according to his own labor.

Our salvation is only through the blood of Jesus and the Spirit. Good works do not qualify us for eternity with Christ. Yes, we know from James 2, [20]**that faith without works is dead**, but there is a difference between the works of the flesh and the works of faith.

Ephesians 2
8 For by grace you have been saved through faith, and that not of yourselves; it is the gift of God,
9 not of works, lest anyone should boast.
10 For we are His workmanship, created in Christ Jesus for

good works, which God prepared beforehand that we should walk in them.

Jesus' requirement that we walk in good works and bear good fruit is mentioned in many places in many ways. He describes our relationship as He being the vine and we the branches.

John 15
**1 I am the true vine, and My Father is the vinedresser.
2 Every branch in Me that does not bear fruit He takes away; and every branch that bears fruit He prunes, that it may bear more fruit.
3 You are already clean because of the word which I have spoken to you.
4 Abide in Me, and I in you. As the branch cannot bear fruit of itself, unless it abides in the vine, neither can you, unless you abide in Me.
5 I am the vine, you are the branches. He who abides in Me, and I in him, bears much fruit; for without Me you can do nothing.
6 If anyone does not abide in Me, he is cast out as a branch and is withered; and they gather them and throw them into the fire, and they are burned.
7 If you abide in Me, and My words abide in you, you will ask what you desire, and it shall be done for you.
8 By this My Father is glorified, that you bear much fruit; so you will be My disciples.**

Even members of the body of Christ, those whom Jesus calls **branches in Me**, will be **cast out as a branch** if they bear no fruit. This is one of many reasons that the doctrine of "once saved, always saved" is untenable.

When we abide in Christ and are in the process of sanctification, or pruning, we bear the fruit of obedience and faith. It is not possible to accomplish anything of value apart from Christ. In Christ we can do all things (Philippians 4:13) and will, if we keep His word, bear much fruit, but Jesus says, **without Me you can do nothing**.

We cannot be saved by works but, once we are saved, we are expected to be ambassadors for Christ (2 Corinthians 5:20), representing Him in power and love. This is the only way the unsaved world can see Jesus in us and be drawn to Him. Anyone claiming to be born-again, but evidencing no outward change, will bear no fruit and be **cast out as a branch**.

Once we have been raptured, and are standing at the judgment seat of Christ, the issue of salvation to the glory has been settled. We would not even be standing there if we were not glorified members of the eternal body of Christ. The only unsettled issue at that point is the matter of rewards.

1 Corinthians 3
**9 For we are God's fellow workers; you are God's field, you are God's building.
10 According to the grace of God which was given to me, as a wise master builder I have laid the foundation, and another builds on it. But let each one take heed how he builds on it.
11 For no other foundation can anyone lay than that which is laid, which is Jesus Christ.
12 Now if anyone builds on this foundation with gold, silver, precious stones, wood, hay, straw,
13 each one's work will become manifest; for the Day will declare it, because it will be revealed by fire; and the fire will test each one's work, of what sort it is.
14 If anyone's work which he has built on it endures, he will receive a reward.
15 If anyone's work is burned, he will suffer loss; but he himself will be saved, yet so as through fire.**

The foundation is, and always will be, Christ. We are told to **take heed how** we build upon that foundation that we may receive a good reward. The building blocks are faith, obedience, and development of the fruits of the Spirit. The fruits of the Spirit are love, joy, peace, longsuffering, kindness, goodness, faithfulness, gentleness, and self control (Galatians 5:22-23). We must not only live in the Spirit but walk in Him as well (Galatians 5:25).

The **Day**, in this context, is the judgment seat of Christ, where **the**

fire will test each one's work, of what sort it is. The point is again made that, even if someone is not entitled to any reward, just by making it to the judgment seat of Christ **he himself will be saved**. This is not said to cause complacency in believers, but to inspire and exhort us to develop a large reward.

Romans 14
10 But why do you judge your brother? Or why do you show contempt for your brother? For we shall all stand before the judgment seat of Christ.

Notice who the **all** refers to. It refers exclusively to the brethren, the body of Christ. Only those who are members in good standing will stand before the judgment seat.

Matthew 16
27 For the Son of Man will come in the glory of His Father with His angels, and then He will reward each according to his works.

The **reward** that is **according to** our **works** is received at the judgment seat, when Christ **will come in the glory of His Father**, which is the rapture of the church.

Hebrews 9
27 And as it is appointed for men to die once, but after this the judgment,
28 so Christ was offered once to bear the sins of many. To those who eagerly wait for Him He will appear a second time, apart from sin, for salvation.

As you can see, sin is not judged when Christ appears **a second time**. There is no doubt that this is the rapture of the church; it is not His return, but His appearing. Christ's return is at the end of the tribulation when He rides back from New Jerusalem with the armies of heaven, us, to set up His millennial reign. When Jesus appears in the clouds it is the rapture. His appearing to gather His body is **apart from sin**; that was dealt with at the cross of Calvary and is under His blood. The

salvation mentioned here is the glorification of the church, the ultimate salvation from corruption. The Greek word is *soteria* which means to be "rescued, delivered from the wrath to come."

> 1 Corinthians 15
> **50 Now this I say, brethren, that flesh and blood cannot inherit the kingdom of God; nor does corruption inherit incorruption.**
> **51 Behold, I tell you a mystery: We shall not all sleep, but we shall all be changed**
> **52 in a moment, in the twinkling of an eye, at the last trumpet. For the trumpet will sound, and the dead will be raised incorruptible, and we shall be changed.**
> **53 For this corruptible must put on incorruption, and this mortal must put on immortality.**
> **54 So when this corruptible has put on incorruption, and this mortal has put on immortality, then shall be brought to pass the saying that is written: "Death is swallowed up in victory."**

Do not be concerned that those of us who go in the rapture will not have physically died before we stand at the judgment seat. God thought of everything, down to the tiniest of details.

> Colossians 3
> **3 For you died, and your life is hidden with Christ in God.**
> **4 When Christ who is our life appears, then you also will appear with Him in glory.**

The old man has died and our eternal **life is hidden with Christ in God.**

> John 5
> **24 Most assuredly, I say to you, he who hears My word and believes in Him who sent Me has everlasting life, and shall not come into judgment, but has passed from death into life.**

In this statement Jesus gives His absolute assurance, to all who continue in Him, that they are no longer subject to condemnation. In the new birth we have already passed **from death into life.**

1 John 2

28 And now, little children, abide in Him, that when He appears, we may have confidence and not be ashamed before Him at His coming.
29 If you know that He is righteous, you know that everyone who practices righteousness is born of Him.

1 John 3

1 Behold what manner of love the Father has bestowed on us, that we should be called children of God! Therefore the world does not know us, because it did not know Him.
2 Beloved, now we are children of God; and it has not yet been revealed what we shall be, but we know that when He is revealed, we shall be like Him, for we shall see Him as He is.
3 And everyone who has this hope in Him purifies himself, just as He is pure.

The process of purification in Christ began the day we were born again. Hebrews 12:29 tells us that our God is a consuming fire. If we yield to the fire of the Holy Spirit in us, and allow Him to burn up all the useless things in our flesh, we shall not suffer loss at the judgment seat, only gain.

1 Corinthians 11

31 For if we would judge ourselves, we would not be judged.
32 But when we are judged, we are chastened by the Lord, that we may not be condemned with the world.

We are told to **judge ourselves** that **we would not be judged** so that we suffer as little loss as possible when we stand before Christ. That is why we are taught to crucify the flesh daily, with all its worldly desires, and walk this earth like our Lord Jesus walked. The fire of the Holy Spirit in us has the capacity to burn up all our chaff, but this is only possible if we are determined to lay aside our own concepts and adopt God's. That is why, when we are baptized in the Holy Ghost, there is fire. Many who are baptized in the Holy Ghost never appropriate the fire. The fire of the Spirit is the power to consume the chaff of our lives, the power to release the authority we have been given in Christ.

Luke 3

16 John answered, saying to them all, "I indeed baptize you with water; but One mightier than I is coming, whose sandal strap I am not worthy to loose. He will baptize you with the Holy Spirit and with fire.
17 "His winnowing fan is in His hand, and He will thoroughly purge His threshing floor, and gather the wheat into His barn; but the chaff He will burn with unquenchable fire."

John prophesied about the separation of the wheat from the tares at the time of harvest—the rapture of the church—and the judgment seat of Christ to follow.

James 1

12 Blessed is the man who endures temptation; for when he has been proved, he will receive the crown of life which the Lord has promised to those who love Him.

To be overcomers, we must endure in the faith and be obedient. We must keep our eyes on the prize. We must keep our perspective. We must know what this life is all about and where we are bound. We must understand what is at risk if we decide not to continue the good fight of faith. We must also be aware that accepting false doctrine, doctrine that opposes Christ, will cost whoever does so his crown.

2 Corinthians 5

9 Therefore we make it our aim, whether present or absent, to be well pleasing to Him.
10 For we must all appear before the judgment seat of Christ, that each one may receive the things done in the body, according to what he has done, whether good or bad.

The forces of darkness, today, surround every believer, pressing in and attempting to overwhelm. We must not permit them to prevail. We have the upper hand, whether or not we feel like it at any given moment. The power of the blood, the power of the Name of Jesus, the power of the Word of God, and the fire of the Holy Spirit, are ever present in us to defeat the enemy and keep us on course. Failure is not an option. We are the army of God and we must win.

Revelation 3
11 Behold, I come quickly! Hold fast what you have, that no one may take your crown.

Chapter 17

A Few Good Men

Matthew 7
**13 Enter by the narrow gate; for wide is the gate and broad is the way that leads to destruction, and there are many who go in by it.
14 Because narrow is the gate and difficult is the way which leads to life, and there are few who find it.**

When Jesus describes the **narrow gate**, the one that **leads to life,** He tells us the way is **difficult** and **there are few who find it.** You can define **few** any way you like but, whatever you come up with, the number is definitely less than the **many** who go by the **wide gate** that leads to **destruction**. Destruction is the opposite of salvation.

The **wide gate** is the one that is irresistible to the liberal agenda, where one can create a designer god who is and does what one deems to be correct, where all roads lead to God and there is no responsibility to know and keep God's Word and His Word alone. The way to which the wide gate opens is riddled with false doctrine, false prophecy, and deceits of all kinds. There is no faith there and it is filled with darkness.

The deceits will become more aggressive as the end draws nigh. Only by knowing the truth will one recognize the lies and maintain holiness. Holiness is complete separation unto God, purified by the blood and the Word. Being a hearer and a doer of the Word is the only way to be in Christ as part of His body.

1 John 4

17 Love has been perfected among us in this: that we may have boldness in the day of judgment; because as He is, so are we in this world.
18 There is no fear in love; but perfect love casts out fear, because fear involves torment. But he who fears has not been made perfect in love.

There is no fear in love. Fear and faith cannot dwell together. Fear cancels faith and without faith it is impossible to please God (Hebrews 11:6). Faith works through love (Galatians 5:6). As a matter of fact, if we fear anything we bow our knee to fear and thereby to Satan. Shocking but true. Fear means we believe Satan but not God. If we do not trust God we do not believe Him, and we thereby classify Jesus as a liar.

1 John 2

5 But whoever keeps His word, truly the love of God is perfected in him. By this we know that we are in Him.

While it is true that God desires that none should perish (2 Peter 3:9), meaning go to the lake of fire, I do not believe that God is the least concerned about the number of people who qualify as the body of Christ. I believe His interest is in quality, the purity and obedience of those who do qualify. Yes, Jesus came because God loves the whole world, but that does not mean the whole world loves Him. Think about that. Only he who **keeps His Word** has **the love of God perfected in him**. In order to **have boldness in the day of judgment**—the judgment seat of Christ—**love** must be **perfected in us**.

Jesus declares in John 14, **[23]If anyone loves Me, he will keep My word; and My Father will love him, and We shall come to him and make Our home with him. [24]He who does not love Me does not keep My words; and the word which you hear is not Mine but the Father's who sent Me**. Much of the world that calls itself Christian does not qualify as loving Jesus.

Jesus says in Matthew 12, **[25]Every kingdom divided against itself is brought to desolation, and every city or house divided against**

itself will not stand. We know that God's kingdom will stand forever and cannot be shaken (Hebrews 12:28). Therefore, there will be no one in the body of Christ in whom the love of God has not been perfected by obedience to the Word.

Hebrews 10
**38 Now the just shall live by faith; but if anyone draws back, my soul has no pleasure in him.
39 But we are not of those who draw back to perdition, but of those who believe to the saving of the soul.**

To be part of Christ, justified by His blood, we must **live by faith**. Anyone who **draws back** from **faith** draws **back to perdition**, which is destruction. Faithlessness destroys one's relationship with God. In other words, either one lives by faith or dies by unbelief. There will be no one in the eternal body of Christ who did not live by faith.

Luke 18
**7 And shall God not avenge His own elect who cry out day and night to Him, though He bears long with them?
8 I tell you that He will avenge them speedily. Nevertheless, when the Son of Man comes, will He really find faith on the earth?**

I believe there will be many in the nations, but relatively few in the body of Christ. To be joined eternally with the Son of God, the King of kings and Lord of lords, is an awesome thing. I assure you that God does not take it lightly.

Jude
**14 Now Enoch, the seventh from Adam, prophesied about these men also, saying, "Behold, the Lord comes with ten thousands of His saints,
15 "to execute judgment on all, to convict all who are ungodly among them of all their ungodly deeds which they have committed in an ungodly way, and of all the harsh things which ungodly sinners have spoken against Him."**

The **ten thousands of His saints** are the whole body of Christ riding back from New Jerusalem with Jesus at the second advent. That is not very many compared to the number of people who, throughout history, have claimed to be Christians. It is not even many compared to the number of people alive in the world right now who claim to be Christians. That is why Jesus warned that the gate to eternal life is narrow and the way difficult. A price attaches to being part of the body of Christ: total obedience to Him.

> Luke 13
> **22 And He went through the cities and villages, teaching, and journeying toward Jerusalem.**
> **23 Then one said to Him, "Lord, are there few who are saved?" And He said to them,**
> **24 "Strive to enter through the narrow gate, for many, I say to you, will seek to enter and will not be able.**
> **25 "When once the Master of the house has risen up and shut the door, and you begin to stand outside and knock at the door, saying, 'Lord, Lord, open for us,' and He will answer and say to you, 'I do not know you, where you are from,'**
> **26 "then you will begin to say, 'We ate and drank in Your presence, and You taught in our streets.'**
> **27 "But He will say, 'I tell you I do not know you, where you are from. Depart from Me, all you workers of iniquity.'**
> **28 "There will be weeping and gnashing of teeth, when you see Abraham and Isaac and Jacob and all the prophets in the kingdom of God, and yourselves thrust out."**

The **many** who **will seek to enter and will not be able** will, regrettably, be in the majority. They will include: those who create their own image of God and think He will conform to it; those who are defiled by false doctrine; those drawn back under the Law; and all others who rebel against God's truth and stray from the narrow path.

Because I am a Word person and will not believe, or even entertain, any thought that does not line up with the whole of God's Word, many call me narrow minded. I choose to take that as a compliment—though the critics do not intend it so—and tell them they are right, that My

The Rapture, The Tribulation, And Beyond

mind is exactly the width of a Bible. One Christian even warned me against turning God's Word into an idol. There is an interesting thought! God's Word is God; God magnified it above His Name (Psalm 138:2). How do you make and idol out of God?

God's truth is my truth, God's wisdom is my wisdom, and so it must be with anyone counting himself a member of the body of Christ. Jesus is the Head of the body and there is no room for contradiction.

People tend to judge everything by statistics, but God does not think that way. Remember, God was satisfied with the fellowship of Adam alone. It was only because Adam needed a mate that God took Eve out of him. God was satisfied with the fellowship of one good man.

When the whole world was in sin and corrupted with the seed of Satan's fallen angels, God had no problem wiping them all from the face of the earth with a mighty flood, saving only Noah, his wife, three sons and their wives; a total of eight. Eight out of the whole world!

Genesis 6
5 Then the Lord saw that the wickedness of man was great in the earth, and that every intent of the thoughts of his heart was only evil continually.
6 And the Lord was sorry that He had made man on the earth, and He was grieved in His heart.
7 So the Lord said, "I will destroy man whom I have created from the face of the earth, both man and beast, creeping thing and birds of the air, for I am sorry that I have made them."
8 But Noah found grace in the eyes of the Lord.
9 This is the genealogy of Noah. Noah was a just man, perfect in his generations. Noah walked with God.
12 So God looked upon the earth, and indeed it was corrupt; for all flesh had corrupted their way on the earth.
13 And God said to Noah, "The end of all flesh has come before Me, for the earth is filled with violence through them; and behold, I will destroy them with the earth.
14 "Make yourself an ark of gopherwood; make rooms in the ark, and cover it inside and outside with pitch."

Noah is a type for the salvation and rapture of the body of Christ.

Those of us preparing for the rapture must also make ourselves an ark. Our ark, however, is not of gopherwood, but of faith and obedience to the Word. Where Noah was **a just man,** we are justified by faith. Where Noah was **perfect in his generations**, we are perfected by Christ, whose seed we are. Where Noah **walked with God**, so do we if we keep His Word.

God chose to withhold His wrath for these last two thousand years (Isaiah 54:9-10), but He hates evil and disobedience just as much as He ever did. James 1 tells us that in the Father, [17]**there is no variation or shadow of turning**. Father God has made the new covenant one of kindness and mercy, but that does not mean He has ceased despising evil. Keep in mind that unbelief is evil (Hebrews 3:12). The children of Israel, Hebrews 3 tells us, [19]**could not enter in because of unbelief**. How much more does this apply to new covenant people who have a better covenant established on better promises (Hebrews 8:6)? Born-again people will not qualify for the rapture apart from faith.

Romans 10
12 For there is no distinction between Jew and Greek, for the same Lord over all is rich to all who call upon Him.
13 For "whoever calls upon the name of the Lord shall be saved."
14 How then shall they call on Him in whom they have not believed? And how shall they believe in Him of whom they have not heard? And how shall they hear without a preacher?
15 And how shall they preach unless they are sent? As it is written: "How beautiful are the feet of those who preach the gospel of peace, who bring glad tidings of good things!"
16 But they have not all obeyed the gospel. For Isaiah says, "Lord, who has believed our report?"

Will Jesus find faith on the earth when He comes? Yes, and again I say yes! In how many? That is the question. Even though God sufficiently loved the whole world that He sent Jesus, He knew that only a few would reciprocate that love. Jesus did not even pray for the whole world, but only for those who **kept** God's **Word**.

John 17

**9 I pray for them. I do not pray for the world but for those whom You have given Me, for they are Yours.
10 And all Mine are Yours, and Yours are Mine, and I am glorified in them.**

This does not mean that Jesus prayed only for those who believed and loved Him while He was on earth.

John 17

20 I do not pray for these alone, but also for those who will believe in Me through their word;

Those who call upon Jesus without faith, without believing, are not heard. When Isaiah said, **Lord, who has believed our report?** it was the cry of his heart. He was in despair regarding how few really believed anything of God.

In Hosea 4 God says, [6]**My people are destroyed for lack of knowledge**. It is not that they do not hear, but that they reject the truth when it is spoken. They thereby destroy their relationship with God, who goes on to say that He will "reject" them and "forget" their children. Many are they who go by the broad way leading to destruction. They make up their own rules and jeopardize even their salvation. God is interested in quality, not quantity. The few who take the narrow path that leads to life will be the body of Christ. All have the same opportunity to walk that narrow path, but few will choose to do so.

That is what is meant in Matthew 20, [16]**For many are called, but few chosen**. When one plights one's troth, one becomes betrothed; when one makes a choice, one becomes chosen. When we choose God we become chosen of God. In the old covenant God chose the Jews and they became His chosen people, but in the new covenant we know from Galatians 3, [28]**There is neither Jew nor Greek, there is neither slave nor free, there is neither male nor female; for you are all one in Christ Jesus**. Jesus has become equally available to all; when we choose Him and walk in His righteousness, we become chosen of Him.

1 Peter 2
9 But you are a chosen generation, a royal priesthood, a holy nation, His own special people, that you may proclaim the praises of Him who called you out of darkness into His marvelous light;
10 who once were not a people but are now the people of God, who had not obtained mercy but now have obtained mercy.

Few understand what it is to love God. Few go by the narrow way. Few are chosen.

Hebrews 12
5 And you have forgotten the exhortation which speaks to you as to sons: "My son, do not despise the chastening of the Lord, nor be discouraged when you are rebuked by Him;
6 For whom the Lord loves He chastens, and scourges every son whom He receives."
7 If you endure chastening, God deals with you as with sons; for what son is there whom a father does not chasten?
8 But if you are without chastening, of which all have become partakers, then you are illegitimate and not sons.

The broad way—whose adherents say that anything goes and all roads lead to God—destroys relationship and makes even those who call themselves Christians **illegitimate and not sons**.

Romans 11
17 And if some of the branches were broken off, and you, being a wild olive tree, were grafted in among them, and with them became a partaker of the root and fatness of the olive tree,
18 do not boast against the branches. But if you boast, remember that you do not support the root, but the root supports you.
19 You will say then, "Branches were broken off that I might be grafted in."
20 Well said. Because of unbelief they were broken off, and you stand by faith. Do not be haughty, but fear.

**21 For if God did not spare the natural branches, He may not spare you either.
22 Therefore consider the goodness and severity of God: on those who fell, severity; but toward you, goodness, if you continue in His goodness. Otherwise you also will be cut off.**

Jesus is the vine and we are the branches. The original branches were the Jews. Some **of the branches were broken off, and you, being a wild olive tree, were grafted in among them**, which is the breaking off of the Jews who rejected Christ and the grafting in of the Gentiles who accepted Him. In the same way the Jews were broken off—removed from the family of God and no longer sons—so can we be if we do not continue in faith and obedience.

I do not write these things to discourage you, but to exhort you to greater faith in Christ. This faith walk of ours is neither a game nor a religious exercise. This is life or death, blessing or cursing. If you embrace God's wisdom and knowledge and act on it, you will have eternity with Christ; if you don't, you won't. You cannot afford to be lazy or complacent in your walk with the Lord. Satan is insidious, pernicious, and unrelenting in his attempts to deceive the body of Christ. He cannot take your salvation by force, but he will talk you out of it if he can. It is your obligation to heed Hebrews 10 and, [23]**hold fast the confession of our hope without wavering, for He who promised is faithful**.

1 Peter 4
**17 For the time has come for judgment to begin at the house of God; and if it begins with us first, what will be the end of those who do not obey the gospel of God?
18 Now "If the righteous one is scarcely saved, where will the ungodly and the sinner appear?"
19 Therefore let those who suffer according to the will of God commit their souls to Him in doing good, as to a faithful Creator.**

The desire of every true believer is to please God—otherwise he is not a true believer—and the only way to please God is to love Him. No true believer wants to go his own way, let alone contend with the Spirit. Anyone who argues against the truth has a god who is not God.

2 Peter 3
9 The Lord is not slack concerning His promise, as some count slackness, but is longsuffering toward us, not willing that any should perish but that all should come to repentance.

There is no excuse for ignorance or lack of understanding of the Word. We have the Holy Spirit, the Spirit of revelation and truth, to lead us into all truth.

1 Corinthians 2
**6 However, we speak wisdom among those who are mature, yet not the wisdom of this age, nor of the rulers of this age, who are coming to nothing.
7 But we speak the wisdom of God in a mystery, the hidden wisdom which God ordained before the ages for our glory,
8 which none of the rulers of this age knew; for had they known, they would not have crucified the Lord of glory.
9 But as it is written: "Eye has not seen, nor ear heard, nor have entered into the heart of man the things which God has prepared for those who love Him."
10 But God has revealed them to us through His Spirit. For the Spirit searches all things, yes, the deep things of God.
11 For what man knows the things of a man except the spirit of the man which is in him? Even so no one knows the things of God except the Spirit of God.**

Notice that **God has prepared** an extraordinary future **for those who love Him**. God loves everyone—He has declared it—however, His inheritance is **for those who love Him**. It is the privilege of the body of Christ, **those who are mature**, to know, **through His Spirit,** all the **deep things of God**.

It is impossible to know God apart from the ministry of the Holy Spirit within us.

1 John 2
4 He who says, "I know Him," and does not keep His commandments, is a liar, and the truth is not in him.
5 But whoever keeps His word, truly the love of God is perfected in him. By this we know that we are in Him.

We can only be confident of our position in Christ if we **keep His Word**. That is God's measure. Keep in mind what Jesus says in Matthew 7, [21]**Not everyone who says to Me, 'Lord, Lord,' shall enter the kingdom of heaven, but he who does the will of My Father in heaven**. Our place in the body of Christ does not depend upon us knowing Jesus, but upon Him knowing us (Matthew 7:22-23).

The glorious church for which Jesus is coming is a special, elect fellowship, a fellowship of believers. Father God, just like the Marine Corps, is looking for a few good men, men who have the will and determination to survive the training. Our life on earth is spiritual boot camp; only the strong survive it and move on. Our motto should be: Stop whining and start winning.

Revelation 2
25 But hold fast what you have till I come.
26 And he who overcomes, and keeps My works until the end, to him I will give power over the nations
27 He shall rule them with a rod of iron; as the potter's vessels shall be broken to pieces as I also have received from My Father;
28 and I will give him the morning star.

The glorified body of Christ, after the judgment seat, will be kingdom government with **power over the nations**. As you can see, however, the requirement to overcome is mentioned yet again. We must overcome doubt, unbelief, fear, false doctrine, and all the physical, emotional, financial and spiritual attacks of the enemy.

Revelation 3
5 He who overcomes shall be clothed in white garments, and I will not blot out his name from the Book of Life; but I will

confess his name before My Father and before His angels.
10 Because you have kept My command to persevere, I also will keep you from the hour of trial which shall come upon the whole world, to test those who dwell on the earth.
11 Behold, I come quickly! Hold fast what you have, that no one may take your crown.
12 He who overcomes, I will make him a pillar in the temple of My God, and he shall go out no more. And I will write on him the name of My God and the name of the city of My God, the New Jerusalem, which comes down out of heaven from My God. And I will write on him My new name.
13 He who has an ear, let him hear what the Spirit says to the churches.
19 As many as I love, I rebuke and chasten. Therefore be zealous and repent.
20 Behold, I stand at the door and knock. If anyone hears My voice and opens the door, I will come in to him and dine with him, and he with Me.
21 To him who overcomes I will grant to sit with Me on My throne, as I also overcame and sat down with My Father on His throne.
22 He who has an ear, let him hear what the Spirit says to the churches.

Christ's body is spiritually fit. We are in a marathon, not a sprint. Endurance and mental toughness are required if we are to cross the finish line and receive the prize.

1 Corinthians 9 (KJV)
24 Know ye not that they which run in a race run all, but one receiveth the prize? So run, that ye may obtain.
25 And every man that striveth for the mastery is temperate in all things. Now they do it to obtain a corruptible crown; but we an incorruptible.

Choose to be one of the few good men. God gave you free will. He placed your future in your hands. He wants everyone to make the right choices, though He is fully aware that few will do so.

If you choose to be blood-bought, Spirit-filled, know who you are in Christ (the body and not the bride), walk in righteousness, and are eagerly anticipating the pre-tribulation rapture of the church, you are one of the few good men.

You can do it. In Christ all things are possible. Do not fall for the lie that you are incapable of overcoming. Do not buy into the deceit that, "We'll all find out when the time comes." Those who do will indeed find out; they will find they missed it. You have been made to be the righteousness of God in Christ Jesus. You can do whatever you decide to do. Your future awaits you.

So run, that ye may obtain.

Chapter 18

Ruling And Reigning

We, as the body of Christ, will sit with Jesus on His throne and rule the nations for eternity.

Revelation 2
**25 But hold fast what you have till I come.
26 And he who overcomes, and keeps My works until the end, to him I will give power over the nations
27 'He shall rule them with a rod of iron...'**

Revelation 3
21 To him who overcomes I will grant to sit with Me on My throne, as I also overcame and sat down with My Father on His throne.

Even now we are being prepared to rule and reign with Christ. While it is true that we are not yet glorified, our lives are a process of sanctification and qualification for the rest of eternity. The process began when we were born again.

Ephesians 1
**5 having predestined us to adoption as sons by Jesus Christ to Himself, according to the good pleasure of His will,
6 to the praise of the glory of His grace, by which He has made us accepted in the Beloved.**

Ephesians 2
6 and raised us up together, and made us sit together in the heavenly places in Christ Jesus,

Religion has made a confused mess of **predestined us to adoption as sons**. Once we choose to be born again, the process of our transformation into the image and glory of Christ begins. Therefore, once we are born again we become predestined by God to adoption as sons.

2 Corinthians 5
17 Therefore, if anyone is in Christ, he is a new creation; old things have passed away; behold, all things have become new. 18 Now all things are of God, who has reconciled us to Himself through Jesus Christ, and has given us the ministry of reconciliation,

God has entrusted us with responsibilities. We must learn how to think and act with the mind of Christ, how to deal with, and dominate, the satanic forces over which we have authority.

Most believers think that it does not matter how well they learn the lessons of authority and holiness, that all they have to do is "hang in there." This is a dangerous attitude, one with which the devil is delighted. Those who embrace it are no threat to him. They are not willing to roll up their sleeves, lay down every preconceived notion, and quench every fiery dart of the devil by faith. If they are not willing to rule over him whom Jesus put under their feet, what makes them think they will qualify for a place in the throne of Jesus for eternity? It is their sovereign responsibility to wage spiritual war and wage it successfully.

Jesus defeated all principalities and powers, mights and dominions, the darkness of this present age, and hosts of spiritual wickedness in the heavenly places. All we have to do is enforce their defeat. Ruling and reigning means having leadership qualities. We must accept being unpopular, even hated. Jesus says that when we are reviled for His sake we are blessed. How? When we do whatever it takes to succeed, whatever it takes to glorify Him, the blessings of God abound to us.

Leading does not mean finding out where everybody is going so we can lead them there. It means standing up for the truth, walking the walk of faith, and not concerning ourselves with how many follow us. Those are the qualities that we, as the body of Christ, must develop of our own free will. It is a test that we must pass. We are not graded on the curve, but by the high standards of Christ Jesus, our Head.

We cannot have sideline mentality. We must be in the middle of the river of the Spirit, determined to go on with God. The sidelines of the river are where the quicksand lies, waiting for the unwary. Some think that even if they elect to be spiritual wimps during their lives, God will overlook it and glorify them anyway. He will not. Developing our leadership qualities in Christ, now, proves that we have what it takes to rule and reign.

The **ministry of reconciliation** requires close attention. Since we were separated from God by sin, prior to being born again, our soul, the natural man, needs to be in constant training if it is to reconcile our flesh with the Spirit. Reconciliation means bringing back to friendship after estrangement. We must make the choice, out of our love for the Lord, and acknowledgement of His love for us, to measure up, to be justified by faith, to fulfill our destiny in Christ.

Dominion

God told Adam to take dominion over the earth and subdue it. Six thousand years will have passed by the time we sit with Christ on His throne.

> Genesis 1
> **27 So God created man in His own image; in the image of God He created him; male and female He created them.**
> **28 Then God blessed them, and God said to them, "Be fruitful and multiply; fill the earth and subdue it; have dominion over the fish of the sea, over the birds of the air, and over every living thing that moves on the earth."**

To take dominion we must overcome our traditional ways of thinking and patterns of behavior. People come to me for counsel. I tell them what it will take to overcome. Some get it, some do not. Many rebuke me, claiming that what God requires is unreasonable, that they just cannot do it. What they really mean, of course, is they are unwilling to do it. When I tell them the choice is theirs, to win or lose, they tell me that obeying God's Word will take all their time and, after all, they "have a life."

We are now at the crux of the matter. We, apart from God, have no real lives. Our lives, as members of the body of Christ, are hidden with God in Christ Jesus. Anyone choosing to hang onto his life, apart from Christ, will lose it. Thinking we have our own lives precludes us from moving on with God. It certainly eliminates our ability to have dominion. Those who rule and reign with Christ will be given dominion over all God's creation, probably beyond the boundaries we now comprehend. Our lives are entirely in God. To think otherwise is to step aside from God's plans and purposes.

We and God are one in Christ Jesus (John 17:20-26). We are made perfect in the glory that God gave Jesus and which He offers us. Anyone who decides to have a life of his own will have it, however, he will not have a life in Christ. It is all or nothing.

To achieve dominion, as God has charged us, we must first take dominion over the flesh and walk by faith in the Spirit. Romans 8 tells us, **[14] For as many as are led by the Spirit of God, these are sons of God**. We must learn how to dominate the satanic kingdom. Colossians 2 says that we, the body of Christ, the true sons and daughters of God, **[10] are complete in Him, who is the head of all principality and power**. To refuse to put on our armor, hold up our shield of faith, take up the sword of the Spirit, and dominate the enemy, is to rebel against God's purposes for us.

This is spiritual boot camp. We are in training for glorification. We must complete our assignments if we are to walk in the dominion to which we have been called.

Isaiah 9
6 For unto us a Child is born, unto us a Son is given; and the government will be upon His shoulder. And His name will be called Wonderful, Counselor, Mighty God, Everlasting Father, Prince of Peace.

The Rapture, The Tribulation, And Beyond

7 Of the increase of His government and peace there will be no end, upon the throne of David and over His kingdom, to order it and establish it with judgment and justice from that time forward, even forever. The zeal of the Lord of hosts will perform this.

The **government** is the body of Christ. Jesus will always be the Head, but the body begins at the **shoulder**. That is where the government of the kingdom of God sits.

Judging

Jesus tells us in Matthew 7, [1]**Judge not, that you be not judged**, but we must understand the form of judging to which He refers, to wit, not judging another's relationship with Him. The brethren must judge all things but never each other. Only Jesus knows who belongs to Him, now, and who will belong to Him in the future. We are not to go about condemning people, but doing our very best to draw them to Jesus. When a village of Samaritans rejected Jesus, James and John wanted to deal with them on the spot.

> Luke 9
> **54 And when His disciples James and John saw this, they said, "Lord, do You want us to command fire to come down from heaven and consume them, just as Elijah did?"**
> **55 But He turned and rebuked them, and said, "You do not know what manner of spirit you are of.**
> **56 "For the Son of Man did not come to destroy men's lives but to save them." And they went to another village.**

We judge all things (1 Corinthians 2:15), we judge fruit and we judge spirits. If a brother is walking in a disorderly manner, practicing things that are not of God, we judge the spirits that he is of, not him. If he continues to have fellowship with foul spirits, we must, repeat must, separate ourselves from those spirits and, therefore—and mark this well—from him. So long as we continue to have fellowship with him, we continue to have fellowship with foul spirits. The expression, "hate the sin but love the sinner," is often interpreted to mean quite the opposite.

There are many examples of this in the epistles. When Paul was faced with gross immorality in the church, he said in 1 Corinthians 5, **⁵deliver such a one to Satan for the destruction of the flesh, that his spirit may be saved in the day of the Lord Jesus**. Paul warned Timothy about Hymenaeus and Philetus in 2 Timothy 2, **¹⁷And their message will spread like cancer. Hymenaeus and Philetus are of this sort, ¹⁸who have strayed concerning the truth, saying that the resurrection is already past; and they overthrow the faith of some**. Paul was not judging the individuals but the spirits they were of. We are to do the same.

2 Timothy 2
24 And a servant of the Lord must not quarrel but be gentle to all, able to teach, patient,
25 in humility correcting those who are in opposition, if God perhaps will grant them repentance, so that they may know the truth,
26 and that they may come to their senses and escape the snare of the devil, having been taken captive by him to do his will.

We must always stop short of judging salvation or potential salvation, and we must never judge other members of the body. However, since we are being prepared to judge the angels (1 Corinthians 6:3), judge the twelve tribes of Israel (Luke 22:30), and judge the whole world (1 Corinthians 6:2), we are required to start learning what this means and how to walk in it.

1 Corinthians 2
14 But the natural man does not receive the things of the Spirit of God, for they are foolishness to him; nor can he know them, because they are spiritually discerned.
15 But he who is spiritual judges all things, yet he himself is rightly judged by no one.
16 For "Who has known the mind of the Lord that he may instruct Him?" But we have the mind of Christ.

This is a sweeping statement: **he who is spiritual judges all things**. This is not simply an instruction for now, but a preparation for our role as the eternal body of Christ. It is why we are admonished to settle matters between ourselves, not go to the world for its unsatisfactory answers and failed solutions. We are learning to judge the world, not allow, let alone seek, the world's judgment of us.

1 Corinthians 6
1 Dare any of you, having a matter against another, go to law before the unrighteous, and not before the saints?
2 Do you not know that the saints will judge the world? And if the world will be judged by you, are you unworthy to judge the smallest matters?
3 Do you not know that we shall judge angels? How much more, things that pertain to this life?

It is imperative that we learn to think with the mind of Christ instead of our carnal intellect. If we anticipate the glory to come, in which Jesus will qualify us to share His throne, how can we not strive, with every fiber of our being, to justify the Father's elevation of us to such exalted position?

Romans 12
2 And do not be conformed to this world, but be transformed by the renewing of your mind, that you may prove what is that good and acceptable and perfect will of God.

How can we be transformed into the image of Christ, which is our preparation for ruling and reigning in glory, if we are still conformed to this world? Our training requires that we make judgments based on the Word of God. We must make the right choices, be confident, and set our faces like flint.

James and John, the sons of Zebedee, who obviously set themselves apart from the world and distinguished themselves in Jesus' service, were named by Jesus the "Sons of Thunder" (Mark 3:17). One infers from this title that they made a great impact wherever they went on behalf of the gospel and were pleasing to Jesus. Their mother was so proud of them that she took them before Jesus and asked special favor for them.

Matthew 20
21 And He said to her, "What do you wish?" She said to Him, "Grant that these two sons of mine may sit, one on Your right hand and the other on the left, in Your kingdom."
22 But Jesus answered and said, "You do not know what you ask. Are you able to drink the cup that I am about to drink, and be baptized with the baptism that I am baptized with?" They said to Him, "We are able."
23 So He said to them, "You will indeed drink My cup, and be baptized with the baptism that I am baptized with; but to sit on My right hand and on My left is not Mine to give, but it is for those for whom it is prepared by My Father."

Trust a mother to want the best for her sons and be fearless in trying to get it. Jesus did not specifically rebuke her; rather, He explained the impossibility of what she was asking. She obviously did not understand that God was no longer a respecter of persons and that Jesus loved all His followers equally.

I want you to understand the difference between the position of these two disciples, before the cross, and ours now, after the cross. Jesus had not yet been crucified, He had not yet defeated the devil in hell itself, He had not yet been resurrected, and He had not yet sent the Holy Spirit to make us legitimate sons and daughters of God. All this was yet to be done, and only the sinless Lamb of God was qualified to accomplish it. No man could partake of the cup of Christ before the finished work of the cross. The cup of the Lord and the baptism of the Holy Spirit were only available at the appointed time, after the cross of Christ.

If the mother of James and John had been able to understand what Jesus was saying, she would have known that it would not be they alone who would sit beside Him in glory, that the place with Him in His throne (Revelation 3:21) was reserved for the whole glorified body of Christ, **for those for whom it is prepared by My Father.**

1 Peter 5
5 Likewise you younger people, submit yourselves to your elders. Yes, all of you be submissive to one another, and be clothed with humility, for "God resists the proud, but gives grace to the humble."
6 Therefore humble yourselves under the mighty hand of God, that He may exalt you in due time,

God, and God alone, knows when we are ready to handle all He has prepared for us. Confidence in Christ is not pride. Confidence in the flesh and exalting the flesh above the Spirit is pride.

His Glory Will Be Seen Upon You

Isaiah 60
1 Arise, shine; For your light has come! and the glory of the Lord is risen upon you.
2 For behold, the darkness shall cover the earth, and deep darkness the people; but the Lord will arise over you, and His glory will be seen upon you.
3 The Gentiles shall come to your light, and kings to the brightness of your rising.
11 Therefore your gates shall be open continually; they shall not be shut day or night, that men may bring to you the wealth of the Gentiles, and their kings in procession.
12 For the nation and kingdom which will not serve you shall perish, and those nations shall be utterly ruined.

This is for the body of Christ. The **Gentiles** are the unsaved world. This transference of wealth and influence will become fully manifest before the rapture of the church. God is shaking all things and only the things of the kingdom will stand (Hebrews 12:26-29). The great endtime revival will be the result of the **glory of the Lord** upon His church. This is the position for which the Lord has been training us. We have been called for such a time as this. We have been in training that we might handle this power and position to the glory of God.

Haggai 2

6 For thus says the Lord of hosts: "Once more (it is a little while) I will shake heaven and earth, the sea and dry land;
7 "and I will shake all nations, and they shall come to the Desire of All Nations, and I will fill this temple with glory," says the Lord of hosts.
8 "The silver is Mine, and the gold is Mine," says the Lord of hosts.
9 "The glory of this latter temple shall be greater than the former," says the Lord of hosts. "And in this place I will give peace," says the Lord of hosts.

We are the temple of the Holy Spirit (1 Corinthians 3:16). When God says, **I will fill this temple with glory**, He is talking about us. And to make sure we understand that His glory contains unlimited wealth, he immediately says, **The silver is mine and the gold is mine**, all of it. To be in the position of influence for which we are destined, we must possess the wealth of the world. Money is the only thing the world respects. The **Desire of All Nations** is wealth and possessions. If we are to have credibility, the world must see us as "having it all."

Ecclesiastes 9

16 Then I said: "Wisdom is better than strength. Nevertheless the poor man's wisdom is despised, and his words are not heard."

Satan is fully aware of this. It is why he has worked so hard to keep the church poor. Satan, who was a liar from the beginning and the father of lies, spawned the religious doctrine that poverty is a requirement of holiness. He knew that few would listen to us if we were poor and weak. When Solomon asked for wisdom, God gave him not only wisdom but excessive wealth. Have you ever wondered why?

God knew that it would do no good to give Solomon wisdom without wealth. Without wealth, as evidence of God's goodness and glory, the world would not have taken Solomon seriously, no matter how much wisdom he had. **The poor man's wisdom is despised and his words are not heard.** Excessive wealth was required for the world to receive the wisdom God gave Solomon. God also wants our words of witness to be heard, respected and received.

When God said in Haggai 2 that, **⁹The glory of the latter temple shall be greater than the former**, He declared that those of this generation would have more wealth than Abraham, Lot, Isaac, David, and even Solomon! God requires that we become sanctified, able to handle excessive wealth now, to prepare us to rule and reign with Christ. If we cannot handle a simple thing like money, how can we rule and reign with Christ over everything?

Jeremiah 33
9 Then it shall be to Me a name of joy, a praise, and an honor before all nations of the earth, who shall hear all the good that I do to them; they shall fear and tremble for all the goodness and all the prosperity that I provide for it.

The world will not **fear and tremble** because of us as individuals, but because of the greatness of our God. The power of our witness will be that people around whom everything is failing will want our lives. In order to come to us for solutions (wisdom), they will have to find us credible and want our blessed lifestyle. They will have to see our prosperity—financial, physical, social, and spiritual—to be convinced that they need Jesus. If they do not want our lives, why would they want our Jesus? How can they see the glory upon us, talked about in Isaiah 60, if that glory is not evident in our prosperity? The world can only see natural things. It has no ability to discern supernatural things.

God said to Abraham, whose descendants we are in Christ Jesus (Galatians 3:16), that through him and his descendants all the needs of the families of the earth would be met (Genesis 12:3). Wealth will be the greatest witnessing tool there has ever been. Wealth will allow the church to demonstrate to a hurting world God's love for it. A poor church, or one just getting by, cannot possibly accomplish this. God equips us to accomplish that to which He calls us.

Isaiah 45
3 I will give you the treasures of darkness and hidden riches of secret places,

Isaiah 46
11 ...Indeed I have spoken it; I will also bring it to pass. I have purposed it; I will also do it.

An important step in accepting your position in the end-time church is getting rid of the devil's ways of expressing wealth. Eliminate expressions such as "stinking rich," "filthy lucre," and other such links between money and that which is unclean. Repent of your worldly view of wealth; embrace God's plans and purposes for the wealth He desires to give you. Do not insult God by fearing the corruption of wealth.

The misuse of wealth by others in the kingdom has nothing to do with you. There will always be people who fail. Have you stopped driving a car because others drive theirs into trees? No. You drive yours correctly and keep it on the road. The same principle applies to wealth.

As I said before, fear is of the devil, and anyone who bows his knee to fear bows his knee to the devil. Satan wants the body of Christ to fear wealth; that leaves it all to worldly people, his people, who will do with it want he wants and it will stay under his control. Fear of being corrupted by the wealth God wants to turn over to you is lack of trust in God. It declares your inability, or unwillingness, to have the mind of Christ. It is impossible to imagine Christ Jesus being corrupted by anything, let alone money. Therefore, you either have His mind or you do not. You either walk by faith or you do not. Without faith it is impossible to please God.

The parable of the talents, spoken by Jesus, was about preparation for, and the handling of, money. It exemplifies our responsibility to use to maximum effect all that God gives us. In the parable, a lord is travelling to a far country and gives the care of his goods to his servants. He gives to three servants one talent, two talents, and five talents respectively. It is not certain whether these were talents of silver or talents of gold but, either way, a talent had the equivalent, in today's dollars, of many thousands if silver, or tens of thousands if gold. Those who accomplished the most with what they were given were pleasing to their lord. Obviously, the lord of the servants in the parable was a type for Jesus Himself and, therefore, the good and faithful servants were pleasing to God Himself.

Matthew 25

20 So he who had received five talents came and brought five other talents, saying, "Lord, you delivered to me five talents; look, I have gained five more talents besides them.

21 His lord said to him, "Well done, good and faithful servant; you were faithful over a few things, I will make you ruler over many things. Enter into the joy of your lord."

22 He also who had received two talents came and said, "Lord, you delivered to me two talents; look, I have gained two more talents besides them."

23 His lord said to him, "Well done, good and faithful servant; you have been faithful over a few things, I will make you ruler over many things. Enter into the joy of your lord."

24 Then he who had received the one talent came and said, "Lord, I knew you to be a hard man, reaping where you have not sown, and gathering where you have not scattered seed.

25 "And I was afraid, and went and hid your talent in the ground. Look, there you have what is yours."

26 But his lord answered and said to him, "You wicked and lazy servant, you knew that I reap where I have not sown, and gather where I have not scattered seed.

27 "Therefore you ought to have deposited my money with the bankers, and at my coming I would have received back my own with interest.

28 "Therefore take the talent from him, and give it to him who has ten talents.

29 "For to everyone who has, more will be given, and he will have abundance; but from him who does not have, even what he has will be taken away.

30 "And cast the unprofitable servant into the outer darkness. There will be weeping and gnashing of teeth."

Becoming the **ruler over many things** refers to the time we shall sit with Jesus in His throne and rule and reign with Him. If we are not faithful with the resources God gives us now, how can we expect to handle all for which we shall be responsible later? The servant who received the single talent **was afraid, and went and hid** his lord's

talent in the ground. He refused all responsibility and was deemed a **wicked and lazy servant**. The **outer darkness** where there **will be weeping and gnashing of teeth**, into which his lord instructed that he be cast, can only refer to the lake of fire.

This, at first, seems too harsh to be possible, but look again at verse 24. God inhabits the praises of His people, so what do you suppose insulting and wrongly accusing God accomplishes? The **unprofitable servant** said to his lord—God—that he was afraid of Him because, **I knew you to be a hard man, reaping where you have not sown, and gathering where you have not scattered seed**.

Who are we to question God's methods? By what right could any of us say that God is a hard man, or that He has reaped where He has not sown? God was always fair in that He always explained cause and effect, always gave mankind a choice between blessing and cursing, life and death. And as far as sowing is concerned, He sowed His only begotten son for our salvation. No wonder this servant is described as **wicked**, **lazy** and **unprofitable**. He accused his lord of cruelty, dishonesty and dishonor.

Within this context, I urge you to consider all the "saved" people who declare that God causes sickness, disease, calamity, and disaster and blame Him for their personal failures. All such risk the lake of fire. They risk it out of ignorance, unbelief, or both. Don't be one of them. Be one of those to whom God says, **Well done, good and faithful servant**.

Chapter 19

Preparing The Way Of The Lord— The Spirit Of Elijah

The world is just as lost in a wilderness of pride and rebellion today as it was in the days of John the Baptist. It is the voice of the body of Christ today that is as one crying in the wilderness to prepare the way of the Lord and make His paths straight (Luke 3:4). John the Baptist was sent, in the Spirit and power of Elijah, to prepare the way for the ministry of Jesus; we have been sent to prepare the way, in the same Spirit, for His glorious appearing.

The angel Gabriel, before John the Baptist was born, spoke to John's father, Zacharias, and prophesied that he was coming in the Spirit and power of Elijah to make ready a people prepared for the Lord (Luke 1:17). That same anointing is available to this final generation, as indeed it has to be, for the people of today are no different than those with whom Elijah dealt in his day. We, of this generation, must rise up with the same boldness and confidence that Elijah demonstrated, in the same power of the anointing, with the same intolerance for false doctrine and double-mindedness, and the same willingness to stand alone before the whole world, if necessary, proclaiming the glory of our Lord and Savior Jesus Christ, knowing that God is with us and for us.

The Mark Of Elijah

Elijah lived under Ahab, a totally corrupt and evil king who considered

Elijah to be a thorn in his side. He called Elijah the "troubler of Israel" because he would never compromise the Word of God, nor bow to Ahab's gods. When Elijah could no longer tolerate the people going back and forth between God and Satan, he prepared a demonstration to settle the question of where the power lay.

King Ahab gathered all Israel, as well as four hundred and fifty prophets of Baal and four hundred prophets of Asherah (all satanic priests), to witness the event. The test with which Elijah challenged the prophets of the devil was that: he and they each prepare an altar; place wood beneath and pieces of a bull atop; then, without any natural fire to burn up the sacrifice, they would call upon their gods, and he would call upon his God, to send down fire to consume the offering.

The prophets of Baal went first while all watched.

1 Kings 18
26 So they took the bull which was given them, and they prepared it, and called on the name of Baal from morning even till noon, saying, "O Baal, hear us!" But there was no voice; no one answered. And they leaped about the altar which they had made.
27 And so it was, at noon, that Elijah mocked them and said, "Cry aloud, for he is a god; either he is meditating, or he is busy, or he is on a journey, or perhaps he is sleeping and must be awakened."
28 So they cried aloud, and cut themselves, as was their custom, with knives and lances, until the blood gushed out on them.
29 And it was so, when midday was past, that they prophesied until the time of the offering of the evening sacrifice. But there was no voice; no one answered, no one paid attention.

With the failure of the prophets of Baal complete, Elijah built his altar and placed the wood beneath and the bull upon it. In addition to that, he had an enormous trench dug around his altar and ordered that twelve huge water pots be filled and poured over his offering. Everyone knows that wet things do not burn and Elijah wanted to leave no doubt in people's minds that what they were about to witness was a supernatural act, an act which only the one true God could perform.

1 Kings 18
35 So the water ran all around the altar; and he also filled the trench with water.
36 And it came to pass, at the time of the offering of the evening sacrifice, that Elijah the prophet came near and said, "Lord God of Abraham, Isaac, and Israel, let it be known this day that You are God in Israel, and that I am Your servant, and that I have done all these things at Your word.
37 "Hear me, O Lord, hear me, that this people may know that You are the Lord God, and that You have turned their hearts back to You again."
38 Then the fire of the Lord fell and consumed the burnt sacrifice, and the wood and the stones and the dust, and it licked up the water that was in the trench.
39 Now when all the people saw it, they fell on their faces; and they said, "The Lord, He is God! The Lord, He is God!"

We no longer sacrifice animals to God—Jesus was the final sacrifice and His divine blood has redeemed us once for all—however, we have no less a powerful witness, no less ability to stand confidently before the world to proclaim and demonstrate the power, glory and faithfulness of our God.

There are many ways in which we can show the world the power of God in our lives: refusing to accept sickness or disease, proclaiming that by the stripes of Jesus we are already healed; being faithful tithers, depending on God to supply our every need; never succumbing to fear, even when all about us are consumed by it; in fact, living by faith. Whenever we refuse to be shaken by negative circumstances, trust God, maintain our peace and joy, and proclaim our confidence in the deliverance of the Lord, we demonstrate the power of God.

Elijah had a life of doing mighty exploits by faith. His life was marked by his close fellowship with God, his ability and willingness to hear, obey and trust. At God's command he proclaimed a drought for three years and it came to pass. At God's command he went to the brook Cherith, where God had the ravens bring him food each day. When the brook dried up, Elijah was neither disturbed nor fearful, but waited for God's next instruction.

This is where so many of God's people miss it. They have, by faith, been healed and delivered—they have received God's provision many times—but when the next attack comes, they panic. "Oh, no!" they wail, "What are we going to do now?"

Ephesians 6
10 Finally, my brethren, be strong in the Lord and in the power of His might.
11 Put on the whole armor of God, that you may be able to stand against the wiles of the devil.
12 For we do not wrestle against flesh and blood, but against principalities, against powers, against the rulers of the darkness of this age, against spiritual hosts of wickedness in the heavenly places.
13 Therefore take up the whole armor of God, that you may be able to withstand in the evil day, and having done all, to stand.
14 Stand therefore...

We must learn not to panic. We must learn to trust God immediately, not turn to Him later when all else has failed. God has called us to be friends as well as sons and daughters. He created us for fellowship. He requires that we walk with Him in order to fulfill our role as His friends. Friends need to trust each other, depend on each other. Elijah lived in confidence and friendship with God. Abraham was a friend of God (James 2:23). Jesus calls us His friends.

John 15
13 Greater love has no one than this, than to lay down one's life for his friends.
14 You are My friends if you do whatever I command you.
15 No longer do I call you servants, for a servant does not know what his master is doing; but I have called you friends, for all things that I heard from My Father I have made known to you.

Jesus says, **You are My friends if you do whatever I command you.** That includes His commands to love and trust Him. We cannot be His friends if we panic every time the devil growls and tries to intimidate us. Living by unshakable faith is how we please God and walk together as friends.

Elijah followed God's leading when the brook dried up, going to the widow and her son in Zarephath. He knew that God had already spoken to the widow about Him. With starvation but one meal away, the widow obediently shared the last of her food with the man of God. The miracle of increase promptly ensued, saving her and her son, and also providing for Elijah.

Then disaster struck the widow's son and he died. The widow turned against Elijah, even though he was the source of her blessings from God, and said in 1 Kings 17, **[18]What have I to do with you, O man of God? Have you come to me to bring my sin to remembrance, and to kill my son?** Elijah, however, knew just what to do.

1 Kings 17
19 And he said to her, "Give me your son." So he took him out of her arms and carried him to the upper room where he was staying, and laid him on his own bed.
20 Then he cried out to the Lord and said, "O Lord my God, have You also brought tragedy on the widow with whom I lodge, by killing her son?"
21 And he stretched himself out on the child three times, and cried out to the Lord and said, "O Lord my God, I pray, let this child's soul come back to him."
22 Then the Lord heard the voice of Elijah; and the soul of the child came back to him, and he revived.
23 And Elijah took the child and brought him down from the upper room into the house, and gave him to his mother. And Elijah said, "See, your son lives!"

Do you see the pattern? The anointing upon Elijah enabled him to stand firm in a position of faith, even while others, who had also experienced the supernatural power of God, were shaken and panicked. The widow could have said, "Elijah, the Lord has blessed me greatly through you, and I know He hears you. My son has died; please entreat the Lord your God, who has shown me mercy before, to restore him to me." Instead, she blamed Elijah for her son's death. The more things change in the realm of the flesh, the more they stay the same. However, despite the widow's lack of faith, Elijah's faith prevailed on behalf of the dead son and he lived.

Our faith, too, must prevail if we are to demonstrate the power and mercy of God to a hurting world. It is how we prepare the way for the coming of the Lord.

John The Baptist

When John the Baptist cried in the wilderness to prepare the way for the Lord's ministry, he also spoke of the baptism of the Holy Spirit and the fire of judgment that was to come.

> Matthew 3
> **11 I indeed baptize you with water unto repentance, but He who is coming after me is mightier than I, whose sandals I am not worthy to carry. He will baptize you with the Holy Spirit and fire.**
> **12 His winnowing fan is in His hand, and He will thoroughly purge His threshing floor, and gather His wheat into the barn; but He will burn up the chaff with unquenchable fire.**

It is our commission from the Lord, as ambassadors of Christ, to prepare the world for our soon coming King. The fire of the Holy Spirit is here; the fires of judgment to come upon the earth during the great tribulation are near. That is why Jesus wants us to understand that the anointing upon John the Baptist was the same as that upon Elijah and, further, that it is available to those of this final generation who are willing to receive it.

God has never failed anyone; He is not about to start now. He has promised never to leave us nor forsake us, even to the ends of the earth. God promises that we shall never be put to shame when we have faith in Him and trust His promises. It is for us to rise up in the Spirit and power of Elijah and John the Baptist, and prepare the way for the glorious appearing of Christ Jesus.

Chapter 20

The Great Tribulation

The tribulation begins immediately upon the rapture of the church. Even though the antichrist spirit is already at work in the world, Antichrist the man cannot rise to power until the body of Christ is taken out of the way.

> 2 Thessalonians 2
> **6 And now you know what is restraining, that he may be revealed in his own time.**
> **7 For the mystery of lawlessness is already at work; only he who now restrains will do so until he is taken out of the way.**

The body of Christ is **he who now restrains**. We are those who occupy until the Lord Jesus comes to take us out (Luke 19:13), those who have dominion over the satanic forces at work in the world. Satan is limited while we continue to oppose him. It may seem, judging by the condition of the world, that he has free reign, but the disease, destruction, terrorism, immorality, crime, violence, and wars we see about us are as nothing compared to what he would like to do, not to mention what he will do, when **he who now restrains...is taken out of the way**. Antichrist will explain our disappearance by announcing, "The wicked have been removed from the earth."

We do not know, nor is it important that we know, who Antichrist is, but we do know that he will be a man of international stature and credibility who will be embraced by all nations. Some will refer to him as the great peacemaker, during the first half of the tribulation, because he will, based on his one-world-order, bring an end to war through effective negotiation among nations.

The one-world-religion and the framework for the one-world-order are, at the very time of this writing, being drafted under the auspices of the United Nations by twelve prominent religious leaders. They began meeting in September of 2000 in Brussels, Belgium. Time is short. The world, unbeknownst to it, is in final preparation for the rule of Antichrist. Once the church is gone all hell, literally, will be free to break loose.

Antichrist Comes To Power

At the start of the tribulation there will be great confusion and fear.

> Luke 21
> **25 And there will be signs in the sun, in the moon, and in the stars; and on the earth distress of nations, with perplexity, the sea and the waves roaring;**
> **26 men's hearts failing them from fear and the expectation of those things which are coming on the earth, for the powers of heaven will be shaken.**

The failure of the world system will be evident in all areas of society. People will be in total panic. With the church gone and everything in chaos, Antichrist will arise and seem to have the solution to all the world's problems. He will make a peace treaty, a covenant, with all those who submit to his one-world-order but, naturally, he will soon reveal his true colors.

> Daniel 9
> **27 Then he shall confirm a covenant with many for one week; but in the middle of the week he shall bring an end to sacrifice**

and offering. **And on the wing of abominations shall be one who makes desolate, even until the consummation, which is determined, is poured out on the desolate.**

Antichrist will **confirm a covenant with many for one week**. This is Daniel's week of years (Daniel 9:24-26), the seven years of the tribulation. Antichrist will break the covenant **in the middle of the week** and will **bring an end to sacrifice and offering**.

When he breaks his covenant with Israel, Antichrist will prohibit the Jews from conducting their normal worship which, under the Law, involves the sacrifice of animals. Several years ago there was a great commotion in Israel, reported world-wide, about the birth of a red heifer. The rabbis declared this to be a prophetic event, announcing that they would soon be able to resume sacrifice and offering on the temple mount. This red heifer has been guarded fiercely because the Jews believe that the Arabs will try to kill it in order to prevent fulfillment of the prophecy.

A great bone of contention in the Middle East is control of Jerusalem, particularly the temple mount where The Dome of the Rock, a muslim mosque, now stands. Israel will not agree to any peace treaty that does not give it the temple mount, so Antichrist will give it to them and, since all peace treaties will hinge on peace with Israel, peace will disintegrate when Antichrist betrays Israel and takes back the temple mount for himself at mid-tribulation (2 Thessalonians 2:4).

Antichrist will become the **one who makes desolate** when he reneges on his covenants, ejects the Jews from the temple, and himself sits in the temple of God claiming to be God. The first half of the tribulation will have been a time of judgment, horror, and satanic oppression but, after Antichrist shows his true colors, his reign of terror will become unspeakable for the second half.

The Mark Of The Beast

It is probable that, as part of the one-world-order, all currency will be cancelled and units of credit in a central computer will be issued.

Everyone will be required to take the mark of the beast, probably an implanted computer chip without which they will not be able to buy, sell, or do any kind of business. The technology for this is already in use for various purposes of so-called safety, such as the identification of valuable animals, like thoroughbred racehorses, the location of kidnapped children, and for medical support.

Revelation 13
15 He was granted power to give breath to the image of the beast, that the image of the beast should both speak and cause as many as would not worship the image of the beast to be killed.
16 And he causes all, both small and great, rich and poor, free and slave, to receive a mark on their right hand or on their foreheads,
17 and that no one may buy or sell except one who has the mark or the name of the beast, or the number of his name.

Most of the world will accept the mark of the beast without demur. Many Christians who did not qualify for the rapture will also do so in the mistaken belief that, "God knows my heart. He knows that I don't really mean it." It makes no difference whether they mean it or not; the mark of the beast is eternal damnation from which there is no repentance.

Revelation 14
9 Then a third angel followed them, saying with a loud voice, "If anyone worships the beast and his image, and receives his mark on his forehead or on his hand,
10 "he himself shall also drink of the wine of the wrath of God, which is poured out full strength into the cup of His indignation. And he shall be tormented with fire and brimstone in the presence of the holy angels and in the presence of the Lamb.
11 "And the smoke of their torment ascends forever and ever; and they have no rest day or night, who worship the beast and his image, and whoever receives the mark of his name."

The False Prophet

Satan's perverted version of the Holy Trinity consists of Antichrist (the dragon), the beast, and the false prophet.

> Revelation 16
> **13 And I saw three unclean spirits like frogs coming out of the mouth of the dragon, out of the mouth of the beast, and out of the mouth of the false prophet.**

The **dragon** is anti-God.
The **beast** is anti-Christ.
The **false prophet** is anti-Holy Spirit.

> Revelation 13
> **11 Then I saw another beast coming up out of the earth, and he had two horns like a lamb and spoke like a dragon.**

This second satanic beast is the false prophet. The **two horns** represent testimony, in his case false testimony, whereas the ten horns of the first beast signify dominion. He speaks **like a dragon**, with a forked tongue, cunningly, craftily, deceitfully, working with the beast to deceive those in the tribulation.

Jesus, speaking of the tribulation, warned against false prophets and false christs and the power to deceive they would possess.

> Matthew 24
> **24 For false christs and false prophets will arise and show great signs and wonders, so as to deceive, if possible, even the elect.**

The spirit of false prophecy is embodied in the spirit of Jezebel (Revelation 2:20). It causes God's people to commit spiritual harlotry in the form of false doctrine, and is nowhere more evident than in churches.

Both the first beast and the second beast, the false prophet, are distinct individuals. No Scripture even suggests any other interpretation.

The false prophet will not literally have two horns but will undoubtedly appear to those in the tribulation as a man. He will be possessed of the foul spirit of Satan and will have his supernatural abilities. Those today who promote spiritism and the occult, who have their personal familiar spirits and spirit guides, are forerunners of the false prophet. They, too, are deceiving many and drawing them into satanic worship.

Revelation 13
12 And he exercises all the authority of the first beast in his presence, and causes the earth and those who dwell in it to worship the first beast, whose deadly wound was healed.

The dragon gives power and authority to the beast (Revelation 13:4) and we see again that the false prophet and the beast work hand in hand in the system of the resurrected Roman Empire. The beast is political while the false prophet is religious. The beast represents the one-world-order; the false prophet promotes the one-world-religion. This new satanic order will be a blend of the world's knowledge, ways, technology and science, and abrogation of all personal responsibility. It will appeal to the basest aspects of man's fallen nature.

Revelation 13
**13 He performs great signs, so that he even makes fire come down from heaven on the earth in the sight of men.
14 And he deceives those who dwell on the earth by those signs which he was granted to do in the sight of the beast, telling those who dwell on the earth to make an image to the beast who was wounded by the sword and lived.**

Since the body of Christ, the restraining force, has been removed and no longer opposes Satan, Satan is free to work unhindered his evil **signs**, both himself and through his false prophet.

2 Thessalonians 2
7 For the mystery of lawlessness is already at work; only He who now restrains will do so until He is taken out of the way.

**9 The coming of the lawless one is according to the working of Satan, with all power, signs, and lying wonders,
10 and with all unrighteous deception among those who perish, because they did not receive the love of the truth, that they might be saved.**

Unless Christians develop an intense and abiding love for the truth of God's Word, to the exclusion of all else, and walk in it every waking moment, they risk satanic deception, false prophecy, and false doctrine. Those who live apart from God's Word, now, hardening their hearts to His truth, are walking on spiritual quicksand.

Revelation 13
**15 He was granted power to give breath to the image of the beast, that the image of the beast should both speak and cause as many as would not worship the image of the beast to be killed.
16 And he causes all, both small and great, rich and poor, free and slave, to receive a mark on their right hand or on their foreheads,**

The false prophet will administer the mark of the beast as well as organize and promote the satanic manifestation of the statue of the beast. We have types for this in weeping statues of Mary, bleeding rocks, and other such evil manifestations that are accepted by huge numbers of people who attribute to them supernatural power and flock to worship them.

Revelation 13
17 and that no one may buy or sell except one who has the mark or the name of the beast, or the number of his name.

The false prophet will have the authority during the tribulation to dictate every facet of the lives of those on earth. He will cause to be executed those who do not worship the beast or who fail to comply with his laws.

Two Ways Of Escape

For those trapped on earth during the tribulation there will only be two ways to escape the mark of the beast: flee to the hills and caves and hide for the whole seven years, or refuse the mark and be killed.

For Christians, being killed for their faith will be the better of these two undesirable choices. Those who choose this route will be resurrected and raptured at mid-tribulation and join the body of Christ in New Jerusalem.

> Revelation 6
> **9 When He opened the fifth seal, I saw under the altar the souls of those who had been slain for the word of God and for the testimony which they held.**
> **10 And they cried with a loud voice, saying, "How long, O Lord, holy and true, until You judge and avenge our blood on those who dwell on the earth?"**
> **11 And a white robe was given to each of them; and it was said to them that they should rest a little while longer, until both the number of their fellow servants and their brethren, who would be killed as they were, was completed.**

Those who hide in the rocks, the hills and the caves without detection, avoiding the mark of the beast for the whole seven years, will, just before the battle of Armageddon, be gathered in by Jesus to become part of the millennial nations. Their existence during the seven years, however, will be a grizzly ordeal at best.

> Matthew 24
> **15 Therefore when you see the "abomination of desolation," spoken of by Daniel the prophet, standing in the holy place (whoever reads, let him understand),**
> **16 then let those who are in Judea flee to the mountains.**
> **17 Let him who is on the housetop not come down to take anything out of his house.**
> **18 And let him who is in the field not go back to get his clothes.**

**19 But woe to those who are pregnant and to those with nursing babies in those days!
20 And pray that your flight may not be in winter or on the Sabbath.
21 For then there will be great tribulation, such as has not been since the beginning of the world until this time, no, nor ever shall be.**

Jesus warns those who are hiding not to be deceived by the deceptions and trickery of Antichrist into leaving the safety of their hiding places and coming out into the open.

Matthew 24
**23 Then if anyone says to you, "Look, here is the Christ!" or "There!" do not believe it.
24 For false christs and false prophets will arise and show great signs and wonders, so as to deceive, if possible, even the elect.
25 See, I have told you beforehand.
26 Therefore if they say to you, "Look, He is in the desert!" do not go out; or "Look, He is in the inner rooms!" do not believe it.**

The first three and a half years will be terrible, but the second three and a half years will be all but unbearable. Those hiding will not only experience the reign of terror of Antichrist and the pollution and devastation of the earth, but also the full weight of the wrath of God. This wrath is all that God has withheld during the 2000 year church age. Consider what mankind has been doing for the last two thousand years and you will barely approach understanding the depth of God's pent-up wrath.

Even those who survive will not attain to the stature of the body of Christ; their option on that will have passed. The wedding of the Lamb will already have taken place when they are gathered in. Becoming the nations on a purified and perfected earth is surely better than going to the lake of fire, but it is not the inheritance that God planned for His children.

The 144,000

God has provided that the gospel be preached during the full seven years of the tribulation. The group to fulfill this assignment during the first half will be the 144,000 male, virgin, Jewish evangelists (Revelation 14:4). As incredible as this may seem, these men are alive today and, the moment the church is removed, they will be raised up, born again, and sealed with the mark of God.

> Revelation 7
> **3 saying, "Do not harm the earth, the sea, or the trees till we have sealed the servants of our God on their foreheads."**
> **4 And I heard the number of those who were sealed. One hundred and forty-four thousand of all the tribes of the children of Israel were sealed:**

The 144,000 are the only people not at risk of taking the mark of the beast; they are protected by the seal of God on their foreheads. This seal will enable them to move about freely and witness to the world. God has chosen them for this assignment. Those in the church who think they will be witnesses during the tribulation are guilty of both disobedience to the Father's plan and of overwhelming self-deception.

God has provided for the evangelism of the earth during this time and His plan is flawless. Do not be so foolish as to imagine that you can improve upon it. The 144,000 have been specially prepared by the Father to be evangelists during this dangerous and treacherous time and only He knows who they are. No one, not even a male Jew who is a virgin, can sign up of his own choosing.

The ministry of the 144,000 is completed at mid-tribulation and they are raptured.

> Revelation 14
> **1 Then I looked, and behold, a Lamb standing on Mount Zion, and with Him one hundred and forty-four thousand, having His Father's name written on their foreheads.**
> **3 And they sang as it were a new song before the throne, before**

The Rapture, The Tribulation, And Beyond

the four living creatures, and the elders; and no one could learn that song except the hundred and forty-four thousand who were redeemed from the earth.
4 These are the ones who were not defiled with women, for they are virgins. These are the ones who follow the Lamb wherever He goes. These were redeemed from among men, being firstfruits to God and to the Lamb.
5 And in their mouth was found no guile, for they are without fault before the throne of God.

The Angels Are Released To Preach The Gospel

Immediately after the rapture of the 144,00 Jewish evangelists the angels of God are released to proclaim the gospel until the end of the tribulation.

Revelation 14
6 Then I saw another angel flying in the midst of heaven, having the everlasting gospel to preach to those who dwell on the earth to every nation, tribe, tongue, and people

This is the fulfillment of the statement Jesus made in Matthew 24, **[14] And this gospel of the kingdom will be preached in all the world as a witness to all the nations, and then the end will come.** The **end** is the end of the tribulation. The angels will fulfill this assignment as only they can: they can fly over the earth and see the tops of the mountains, the remotest uncharted islands, the most inaccessible jungles and hidden valleys, and reach **every nation, tribe, tongue and people**. They will be able to speak every language and their commission is to ensure that every last person on earth is given one last opportunity to choose Jesus.

Daniel 8
19 And he said, "Look, I am making known to you what shall happen in the latter time of the indignation; for at the appointed time the end shall be."

The **latter time of the indignation** is the tribulation period. Its **end** is for an **appointed time**. There are many who hold the absurd notion that Jesus will wait, to infinity I guess, until mankind, or some ministry or other, fulfills Matthew 24:14. Wrong! God has a specific timetable. Jesus is not waiting for man or some ministry. He is waiting for the divinely appointed moment when the Father says, "Go get them, Son. Bring the rest of My children home."

Jesus Looses The Seven Seals

Only Jesus, to whom all judgment has been committed by the Father (John 5:22-23), is qualified to open and loose the seven seals of the tribulation (Revelation 5:5). God's judgment begins at the start of the tribulation; His wrath is added at the mid-point.

The four horsemen of the apocalypse are the first four seals. They set the stage, define the progression of events, and establish the atmosphere of the tribulation.

The first seal: the conqueror rides a white horse.

> Revelation 6
> **2 And I looked, and behold, a white horse. And he who sat on it had a bow; and a crown was given to him, and he went out conquering and to conquer.**

This horseman, who has a bow but no crown and to whom a crown is given, is Antichrist himself. Some say he is Jesus, which is patently absurd because this clearly is not God. Jesus does not need to be given a crown; He is the King of kings and the Lord of lords. This rider is Antichrist, who tries to conquer all during the tribulation. Despite the fact that he is riding a white horse, as does Jesus, this is nothing more than another attempt by Satan to be like the most high God. Additionally, it is Jesus who opens the scroll and looses the seals; He would hardly have to loose Himself.

The second seal: the one who sits on the fiery red horse takes peace from the earth.

Revelation 6
4 And another horse, fiery red, went out. And it was granted to the one who sat on it to take peace from the earth, and that people should kill one another; and there was given to him a great sword.

Peace is removed from the earth with the departure of the church and all out war commences. The nations collapse, Antichrist negotiates peace treaties and then establishes his one-world-order.

<u>**The third seal:**</u> the black horse of famine.

Revelation 6
**5 When He opened the third seal, I heard the third living creature say, "Come and see." And I looked, and behold, a black horse, and he who sat on it had a pair of scales in his hand.
6 And I heard a voice in the midst of the four living creatures saying, "A quart of wheat for a denarius, and three quarts of barley for a denarius; and do not harm the oil and the wine."**

The black horse and his scale-bearing rider represent famine and economic chaos. A denarius represents a day's wage, and an entire day's wage is the price for one quart of wheat or three quarts of barley.

The reference to not harming **the oil and the wine** is extremely interesting. Most commentators ignore it completely; a few attribute it to not harming the sea and the vegetation, as mentioned in Revelation 7:3 and 9:4. The former is a cop-out, the latter a lack of revelation.

The black horse of famine in the third seal is a judgment of God. When God spoke a judgment of famine on the land in the old covenant it effected, as we see In Haggai 1, [11]**the grain and the new wine and the oil**. God's judgment during the tribulation will be different. In the new covenant, wine and oil are types for the new wine of the Holy Spirit and the oil of the anointing. Wine and oil are mentioned together in reference to the time of harvest in Joel 2, [24]**the vats shall overflow with new wine and oil**. This is a reference to the great end-time outpouring of the anointing.

Zechariah connects these symbols of the anointing to the two end-time witnesses.

Zechariah 4
**11 Then I answered and said to him, "What are these two olive trees, one at the right of the lampstand and the other at its left?"
12 And I further answered and said to him, "What are these two olive branches that drip into the receptacles of the two gold pipes from which the golden oil drains?"
13 Then he answered me and said, "Do you not know what these are?" And I said, "No, my lord."
14 So he said, "These are the two anointed ones, who stand beside the Lord of the whole earth."**

The **two anointed ones, who stand beside the Lord of the whole earth**, the two end-time witnesses, are assigned to represent God during the second half of the tribulation.

Revelation 11
**3 "And I will give power to my two witnesses, and they will prophesy one thousand two hundred and sixty days, clothed in sackcloth."
4 These are the two olive trees and the two lampstands standing before the God of the earth.**

The third seal is opened at mid-tribulation when God sends the two end-time witnesses to earth to begin their ministry. They are called the **anointed ones** because they are anointed with great power to torment Antichrist and his people. Therefore, we conclude that the instruction of Revelation 6, ⁶**do not harm the oil and the wine**, means that the rider of the black horse is debarred from harming the two end-time witnesses.

<u>**The fourth seal:**</u> death rides a pale horse.

Revelation 6
8 And I looked, and behold, a pale horse. And the name of him who sat on it was Death, and Hades followed with him. And power was given to them over a fourth of the earth, to kill with sword, with hunger, with death, and by the beasts of the earth.

This requires no elaboration.

The Rapture, The Tribulation, And Beyond

The fifth seal (Revelation 6:9-11) is opened upon the heels of the four horsemen. We see the martyrs and hear their cries. These are not the church, remember; the church was raptured before the start of the tribulation. The martyrs are people who did not hide but openly refused to bow to the beast or take his mark, who will be hideously executed by Antichrist. They are either Christians who failed to qualify for the rapture and were trapped on earth, or people born again after the rapture. They will be resurrected and raptured at mid-tribulation.

Not everyone born again through the witness of the 144,000 will be martyred. Some, when captured, will be overcome with fear and accept the mark of the beast; others will hide in the rocks and the caves until the end.

The sixth seal (Revelation 6:12-17) reveals the horror and desperation of the world as the great tribulation progresses toward the final moments. People are driven insane with agony and torment and beg for death, but death is not available (Revelation 9:6). Earthquakes abound, every mountain and island is moved out of its place, the sun is darkened, the moon becomes as blood, stars crash to earth. God's wrath is being poured out.

During the first half of the tribulation Antichrist establishes his one-world-order and pretends to be the great peacemaker, bringing everyone under his fist of oppression. As hideous as conditions will be, they will not be nearly as unbearable as during the last half of the tribulation when Antichrist declares himself God. That is when he breaks all his treaties and reveals the full brunt of his evil. He will dominate every facet of life with the purpose of killing everyone who will not worship the beast.

Antichrist will not, however, be able to destroy all the Jews because God has made provision to hide a remnant in the wilderness behind the wings of an eagle (Revelation 12:13-17). This remnant will, together with those who have avoided the mark of the beast and successfully hidden in the rocks and the caves, be gathered in by Jesus when He returns at the second advent. They will become the millennial nations.

The seventh seal (Revelation 8:1-6) reveals the seven trumpet judgments which contain the seven stages of God's wrath upon a world of unbelief, depravity and wickedness. When Joshua marched around the wicked city of Jericho for six days, with seven priests blowing seven trumpets, it was a type for the seven angels with seven trumpet judgments. Jericho fell on the seventh day, as will Antichrist and all who have taken the mark of the beast.

The half hour of silence that occurs when the seventh seal is opened is a mystery and I do not know of any scriptural explanation for it. I can only assume that all heaven holds it breath because of what is about to happen as the trumpet judgments unfold.

The first trumpet (Revelation 8:7) brings hail and fire mingled with blood spewing down upon the earth. One third of the trees will be burnt up along with all the green grass.

The second trumpet (Revelation 8:8-9) reveals something like a huge mountain burning with fire which is thrown into the sea, causing a third of the sea to become blood. One third of all the creatures in the sea die and one third of all the ships are destroyed.

The third trumpet sounds (Revelation 8:10-11) and a great star falls from heaven whose name is Wormwood, meaning poisonous bitterness. It lands on one third of all the waters, rivers, streams and springs, and causes them to become poisoned. Many die from these waters.

The fourth trumpet (Revelation 8:12-13) utterly destroys one third of the sun, one third of the moon, and one third of the stars; and an angel flies throughout the earth crying, "Woe, woe, woe to the inhabitants of the earth, because of the remaining blasts of the trumpet of the three angels who are about to sound!" In other words, if you think it is horrible now, you haven't seen anything yet!

The fifth trumpet (Revelation 9:1-12) begins with another star falling from heaven, and we see the angel who has the key to the bottomless pit. As the angel unlocks the pit, billows of putrid smoke arise, as from a fiery furnace, and darken the sun and the air. Out of this all-pervading, choking smoke locusts come upon the earth with the power of scorpions. They are commanded not to harm or damage any grass, tree or other vegetation, which plagues of locusts would normally do, but to exclusively focus on attacking and tormenting every person upon the earth except for those who have the seal of God on their foreheads. They have authority to torment, but not to kill, for five months. The wretched inhabitants of the earth, kicked, stung and bitten mercilessly by these creatures, will beg to die but death will flee from them.

These untold numbers of hideous locust-like beasts are demon spirits who look like horses prepared for battle, with breastplates of iron, faces of men, long hair like women, teeth like lions, and gold colored crowns on their heads. Their tails carry the sting of scorpions. The sound of their wings is like the sound of chariots pulled by many crazed, galloping horses charging into battle.

At the same time that this plague of demonic, locust-like beasts is loosed, Abaddon, the king of these monstrosities and the most horrible and abominable beast of all, comes out of the bottomless pit. He is the demon of the bottomless pit and is seen here for the first time. It seems that he is more horrible, more frightening, and more powerful than any other we have seen before.

The sixth trumpet (Revelation 9:13-21) commands the sixth angel to release the four angels who are bound to the river Euphrates, prepared for this hour, day, month, and year. They will kill one third of mankind. We then see the number of horsemen in Antichrist's army, two hundred million. The vision John has of them is that the riders have breastplates of fiery red, hyacinth blue, and sulphur yellow, and the horses have heads of lions breathing fire, smoke and brimstone. The horses' tails look like great serpents with heads. The similarity between the demon locusts from the pit and the horses of the two hundred million man army is inescapable. One should probably infer that once these creatures have finished tormenting the people, Satan has this second use for them.

Still, those who have survived to this point, faced with all these horrors beyond imagining, do not repent. They continue to worship demons, idols of gold, silver, brass, stone and wood; they continue in their witchcraft, their sexual debauchery, their stealing and murdering Revelation 9:20,21). They are beyond hope and time is up.

The seventh trumpet (Revelation 11:15-19) heralds the wrap-up of God's judgment and wrath. The seven years are at a close. Jesus is about to return, wipe out Antichrist and all his domain, take back the earth, and set up His millennial reign.

We get a glimpse of heaven where Christ and His body, the church, mounted on shining white horses, are preparing to ride out of New Jerusalem to conquer the two hundred million man army of Antichrist. The temple of God in heaven is opened and the ark of the covenant is revealed. Lightening, thunder, earthquake and great hail attend the awesome event of the second advent of Christ.

> Revelation 19
> **11 Then I saw heaven opened, and behold, a white horse. And He who sat on him was called Faithful and True, and in righteousness He judges and makes war.**
> **12 His eyes were like a flame of fire, and on His head were many crowns. He had a name written that no one knew except Himself.**
> **13 He was clothed with a robe dipped in blood, and His name is called The Word of God.**
> **14 And the armies in heaven, clothed in fine linen, white and clean, followed Him on white horses.**
> **15 Now out of His mouth goes a sharp sword, that with it He should strike the nations. And He Himself will rule them with a rod of iron. He Himself treads the winepress of the fierceness and wrath of Almighty God.**
> **16 And He has on His robe and on His thigh a name written: KING OF KINGS AND LORD OF LORDS.**

We have dealt with the seven seals and seven trumpets serially, but now we shall go back and fill in some gaps.

The Mortal Wound Of The Beast

> Revelation 13
> **1 Then I stood on the sand of the sea. And I saw a beast rising up out of the sea, having seven heads and ten horns, and on his**

horns ten crowns, and on his heads a blasphemous name.
2 Now the beast which I saw was like a leopard, his feet were like the feet of a bear, and his mouth like the mouth of a lion. And the dragon gave him his power, his throne, and great authority.
3 I saw one of his heads as if it had been mortally wounded, and his deadly wound was healed. And all the world marveled and followed the beast.
4 So they worshiped the dragon who gave authority to the beast; and they worshiped the beast, saying, "Who is like the beast? Who is able to make war with him?"

Many have interpreted, **one of his heads as if it had been mortally wounded, and his deadly wound was healed**, to mean that Antichrist is killed at mid-tribulation and then resurrected, but this is incorrect.

Satan does not have resurrection power, so Antichrist cannot die and be resurrected. Look at the precise wording, **I saw one of his heads *as if it had been* mortally wounded, and his deadly wound was healed**. This **deadly wound** is not inflicted upon Antichrist himself but upon his place of origin, the old Roman Empire. This empire died and was resurrected as the European Union. It has combined currencies, in the form of the Euro, as a preparation for the one-world-order. There is a computer that occupies a huge building in Brussels, Belgium, that will, if it does not already, contain information about every person on the face of the earth; it is referred to as "the beast."

Beginning with Revelation 13:1, the vision depicts the structure of world power during the second half of the tribulation. Daniel, in his vision, describes the beast of Revelation 13 as his fourth beast.

Daniel 7
23 Thus he said: "The fourth beast shall be a fourth kingdom on earth, which shall be different from all other kingdoms, and shall devour the whole earth, trample it and break it in pieces.
24 "The ten horns are ten kings who shall arise from this kingdom. And another shall rise after them; he shall be different from the first ones, and shall subdue three kings.
25 "**He shall speak pompous words against the Most High, shall**

persecute the saints of the Most High, and shall intend to change times and law. Then the saints shall be given into his hand for a time and times and half a time."

The **fourth beast** which **shall be a fourth kingdom** is the ancient Roman Empire. The lion, the bear and the leopard, spoken of in Daniel 7:4-6 and Revelation 13:2, symbolize the three empires that preceded the Roman Empire: the Babylonian, Persian, and Macedonian.

The beast who shall **speak pompous words against the Most High** and shall continue for **a time and times and half a time**—which is another way of expressing three and a half years—is the same beast whose deadly wound was healed in Revelation 13:3. The saints **given into his hand** are those Christians who failed to qualify for the rapture of the church.

Since we are again on the topic of the beast of Revelation 13:3, the resurrected Roman Empire, perhaps we should pause for a moment of the theoretical. I usually leave this sort of thing to others but, in this instance, it is too important to ignore. Since the resurrected Roman Empire is the European Union, the beast whose deadly wound was healed must surely come from within that Union. Some suggest the next pope, the successor to John Paul II, as the logical candidate, since popes, despite 2,000 years of the observable ills of the church they head, enjoy an unchallenged respect in the world. Not even Israel would resist accepting a pope as the great peacemaker and, if you read the description in Revelation 17 of, [5]**THE MOTHER OF HARLOTS AND OF THE ABOMINATIONS OF THE EARTH**, and the [9]**seven mountains on which the woman sits**, you can draw your own conclusions.

Daniel 7
7 After this I saw in the night visions, and behold, a fourth beast, dreadful and terrible, exceedingly strong. It had huge iron teeth; it was devouring, breaking in pieces, and trampling the residue with its feet. It was different from all the beasts that were before it, and it had ten horns.

Horns always denote authority and this is the fourth beast and his ten

The Rapture, The Tribulation, And Beyond 327

power bases. The ancient Roman Empire—symbolized by the beast's head and his death—has long passed away, however, its authority and influence have never been totally eliminated. Fragments of it have continued to exist as separate kingdoms. There has been an end, or death, to the imperial form of government, the one head with the mortal wound, but the Roman Empire has been resurrected in a different form.

Revelation 13:3 indicates that the ancient Roman Empire was destroyed but has been recreated as ten kingdoms. There is an emperor over this resurrected empire, the beast.

Revelation 13
**5 And he was given a mouth speaking great things and blasphemies, and he was given authority to continue for forty-two months.
6 Then he opened his mouth in blasphemy against God, to blaspheme His name, His tabernacle, and those who dwell in heaven.
7 And it was granted to him to make war with the saints and to overcome them. And authority was given him over every tribe, tongue, and nation.
8 And all who dwell on the earth will worship him, whose names have not been written in the Book of Life of the Lamb slain from the foundation of the world.**

The **forty and two months** are the same as the **time and times and half a time** of Daniel 7:25.

In Revelation 17 we again see this beast and are provided more associations between him and the Roman Empire.

Revelation 17
8 The beast that you saw was, and is not, and will ascend out of the bottomless pit and go to perdition. And those who dwell on the earth will marvel, whose names are not written in the Book of Life from the foundation of the world, when they see the beast that was, and is not, and yet is.

This beast **was, and was not.** He was killed and resurrected. He **will**

ascend out of the bottomless pit. I am convinced that this is Abaddon, introduced in the fifth trumpet judgment, who comes up out of the bottomless pit as king over the plague of demon locusts. Abaddon is the most ferocious and devastating of all the beasts. It would seem that Abaddon controls the resurrected Roman Empire. We shall see him again at the end of the tribulation.

> Revelation 17
> **9 Here is the mind which has wisdom: The seven heads are seven mountains on which the woman sits.**

Babylon is **the woman**. The **seven mountains on which the woman sits** represent the seven hills of Rome. Babylon represents both ungodly political world domination, and the one-world religious order of Antichrist, who is the abomination of desolation.

> Revelation 17
> **12 And the ten horns which you saw are ten kings who have received no kingdom as yet, but they receive authority for one hour as kings with the beast.**
> **13 These are of one mind, and they will give their power and authority to the beast.**

The ten horns, with the ten crowns of Revelation 13:1, depict the revival of a Roman Empire far greater than before. It will spread its demonic tentacles like a ten-armed octopus and become a world-wide power under the control of Antichrist and his beast, a recreated demonic kingdom.

The First Six Plagues Of God's Wrath

> Revelation 15
> **1 Then I saw another sign in heaven, great and marvelous: seven angels having the seven last plagues, for in them the wrath of God is complete.**

The Rapture, The Tribulation, And Beyond 329

At mid-tribulation God withholds no portion of His wrath but pours it all out. The seven last plagues of God's wrath are in addition to the seven seals and the seven trumpet judgments.

Revelation 16
1 Then I heard a loud voice from the temple saying to the seven angels, "Go and pour out the bowls of the wrath of God on the earth."

Only the raptured church will escape God's judgments and His wrath. We are told in 1 Thessalonians 1, [10]**to wait for His Son from heaven whom He raised from the dead, even Jesus who delivers us from the wrath to come**. Praise God that He also spoke to the body of Christ in Isaiah 54 saying, [9]**"so have I sworn that I would not be angry with you nor rebuke you.** [10]**For the mountains shall depart and the hills be removed, but my kindness shall not depart from you, nor shall My covenant of peace be removed," says the Lord who has mercy on you**. That means that all the way to God's creation of the new heavens and the new earth—following the great white throne judgment at the end of Christ's millennial reign—we have a covenant of kindness and peace. No one will find kindness, let alone peace, during the tribulation.

<u>**The first bowl:**</u> malignant sores.

Revelation 16
2 So the first went and poured out his bowl upon the earth, and a foul and loathsome sore came upon the men who had the mark of the beast and those who worshiped his image.

<u>**The second bowl:**</u> the sea turns to blood.

Revelation 16
3 Then the second angel poured out his bowl on the sea, and it became blood as of a dead man; and every living creature in the sea died.

The third bowl: the rivers turn to blood.

> Revelation 16
> 4 Then the third angel poured out his bowl on the rivers and springs of water, and they became blood.
> 5 And I heard the angel of the waters saying: "You are righteous, O Lord, the One who is and who was and who is to be, because You have judged these things.
> 6 For they have shed the blood of saints and prophets, and You have given them blood to drink. For it is their just due."

The fourth bowl: men are scorched with fire.

> Revelation 16
> 8 Then the fourth angel poured out his bowl on the sun, and power was given to him to scorch men with fire.
> 9 And men were scorched with great heat, and they blasphemed the name of God who has power over these plagues; and they did not repent and give Him glory.

The fifth bowl: darkness and pain.

> Revelation 16
> 10 Then the fifth angel poured out his bowl on the throne of the beast, and his kingdom became full of darkness; and they gnawed their tongues because of the pain.
> 11 And they blasphemed the God of heaven because of their pains and their sores, and did not repent of their deeds.

The sixth bowl: the river Euphrates is dried up.

> Revelation 16
> 12 Then the sixth angel poured out his bowl on the great river Euphrates, and its water was dried up, so that the way of the kings from the east might be prepared.
> 13 And I saw three unclean spirits like frogs coming out of the mouth of the dragon, out of the mouth of the beast, and out of the mouth of the false prophet.

The Rapture, The Tribulation, And Beyond

14 For they are spirits of demons, performing signs, which go out to the kings of the earth and of the whole world, to gather them to the battle of that great day of God Almighty.
15 "Behold, I am coming as a thief. Blessed is he who watches, and keeps his garments, lest he walk naked and they see his shame."
16 And they gathered them together to the place called in Hebrew, Armageddon.

The seven years are almost up and God gathers the **whole world** to one place. This includes those who have hidden in the rocks and the caves and the Jewish remnant who have been hidden in the desert. They are all gathered at Armageddon for **the battle of that great day of God Almighty**. Armageddon means the "mountain of Megiddo."

Jesus says in Matthew 24, [13]**But he who endures to the end will be saved**. When all the world is gathered at Armageddon Jesus sends the angels to pluck out the Jewish remnant and whoever else has not taken the mark of the beast. To protect them until after the battle He puts them behind the army of God.

Revelation 14
14 And I looked, and behold, a white cloud, and on the cloud sat One like the Son of Man, having on His head a golden crown, and in His hand a sharp sickle.
15 And another angel came out of the temple, crying with a loud voice to Him who sat on the cloud, "Thrust in Your sickle and reap, for the time has come for You to reap, for the harvest of the earth is ripe."
16 So He who sat on the cloud thrust in His sickle on the earth, and the earth was reaped.

Jesus reaps the harvest of souls who have endured to the end, and they are saved from destruction.

The Two End Time Witnesses

During the second half of the tribulation God sends His two end-time witnesses to accomplish their ministry. They are, beyond a shadow of a doubt, Enoch and Elijah. Hebrews 9:27 states that it is appointed only once for a man to die, therefore, since these two are the only men throughout all of history who have not died—they were raptured (Genesis 5:24, 2 Kings 2:11)—they, and they alone, qualify to be sent back from heaven to die and be resurrected.

Many have erroneously taught that Moses and Elijah, because they appeared with Jesus on the Mount of Transfiguration (Matthew 17:1-9), are the two end-time witnesses. As explained in Chapter 3, that vision was a type for the rapture of the church; it has nothing to do with the two end-time witnesses.

Revelation 11
3 "And I will give power to my two witnesses, and they will prophesy one thousand two hundred and sixty days, clothed in sackcloth."
4 These are the two olive trees and the two lampstands standing before the God of the earth.
5 And if anyone wants to harm them, fire proceeds from their mouth and devours their enemies. And if anyone wants to harm them, he must be killed in this manner.
6 These have power to shut heaven, so that no rain falls in the days of their prophecy; and they have power over waters to turn them to blood, and to strike the earth with all plagues, as often as they desire.

The two end-time witnesses follow Antichrist wherever he goes and get in his way at every available opportunity. They have power to add, to all the other miseries being poured out by God's wrath, both pollution of waters and as many plagues as they choose to send upon the earth. Antichrist cannot touch them, nor can the beast or any of His demons. They are inviolable.

Anyone who tries to harm the two witnesses will regret it, for **fire proceeds from their mouth and devours their enemies.** They are the nemesis of Antichrist. They can proclaim the gospel and bring people to salvation anywhere on earth, including the inner courts of Antichrist, and there is nothing he can do to stop them until the appointed time.

Revelation 11

7 Now when they finish their testimony, the beast that ascends out of the bottomless pit will make war against them, overcome them, and kill them.
8 And their dead bodies will lie in the street of the great city which spiritually is called Sodom and Egypt, where also our Lord was crucified.
9 Then those from the peoples, tribes, tongues, and nations will see their dead bodies three and a half days, and not allow their dead bodies to be put into graves.
10 And those who dwell on the earth will rejoice over them, make merry, and send gifts to one another, because these two prophets tormented those who dwell on the earth.

When they have completed their ministry—which is exactly 1,260 days, three and a half years, the second half of the tribulation—they are killed. It is the way God planned it.

It is interesting to note that, while Antichrist has dominion over Jerusalem its name **spiritually is called Sodom**, which means that the spirit of sodomy, or homosexuality, prevails there. Antichrist is a homosexual. The city, under his reign, takes on his character and moral tone. That is why homosexuality has become so prevalent in today's society.

I want to remind you that it is still available to everyone, through the blood of Jesus, to turn from sin, be delivered, saved, and born again. Homosexuals do not have to continue being homosexuals any more than thieves have to continue being thieves, murderers to be murderers, drug addicts to be drug addicts, or the sick to be sick. All these things and more were defeated on the cross of Calvary. Homosexual sin is no worse than any other sin from which all can be delivered by the blood of Jesus and the power of the Holy Spirit.

Those who choose to remain homosexuals, however, like all others who oppose Christ, will be part of the tribulation. Knowing that Antichrist is a homosexual does not condemn homosexuals, it merely points out that homosexuality is part of the satanic agenda.

When the two end-time witnesses are assassinated Antichrist is elated to be rid of their harassment. He wants the whole earth to see their dead bodies, left to rot in the middle of the street in Jerusalem.

Yet again Satan is stupid enough to think he has won.

The people of the earth are so relieved to be rid of these two tormentors, who appeared to be invincible, that they have a world-wide celebration. They even **send gifts to one another**. Heaven only knows where they find gifts in the chaos the world has become. I cannot get an image of a shopping mall after all that has ensued during the last seven years. However, they do get gifts from somewhere, so we shall move on.

The whole world can view the bodies of the two end-time witnesses, so Antichrist must have satellite-feed cameras set up all over Jerusalem, and following him wherever he goes, that will broadcast into every home and be seen on every street corner, world-wide.

Whether he will use satellite transmission, the internet, cable, something else, or all of the above, is unimportant. I believe that a system of two-way transmission, the disconnection of which will result in arrest and death, will be Antichrist's strangle-hold over the earth. Such systems are being worked on and set up even now—consider interactive television—and the world is being conditioned to accept them, not only for entertainment but "for the good of mankind." The fiction of "big brother is watching"—only in the tribulation it will be the beast police—will become fact. Praise God, none of it is for us!

The merriment of the people on the earth is short lived, however.

Revelation 11
11 Now after the three and a half days the breath of life from God entered them, and they stood on their feet, and great fear fell on those who saw them.
12 And they heard a loud voice from heaven saying to them, "Come up here." And they ascended to heaven in a cloud, and their enemies saw them.
13 In the same hour there was a great earthquake, and a tenth of the city fell. In the earthquake seven thousand men were killed, and the rest were afraid and gave glory to the God of heaven.

I can only imagine the intense fear that will grip the people—who have been partying and celebrating the death of the two witnesses, perhaps even dancing around their dead bodies in the city street—when they see them resurrected after only **three and a half days**. They may even recall that Jesus Himself was raised from the dead after three days.

The two witnesses then, with the whole world watching, **ascended to heaven in a cloud**, whereafter, **there was a great earthquake and a tenth of the city fell**. When **seven thousand men were killed, and the rest were afraid**, the people were finally so afraid that they **gave glory to the God of heaven.**

Too little, too late! Way too little and way too late. Their fate was sealed.

Chapter 21

Heaven During The Great Tribulation

Religion has promoted the absurd idea that heaven, the location of the throne of God almighty from which He rules the universe, is just bright blue sky with puffy little clouds on which we all float blissfully while angels play their harps. This bears no resemblance to New Jerusalem and the heavenlies. What awaits us is a whole new life.

In the twinkling of an eye, we who have overcome all the devil has thrown at us will, when Jesus appears in the sky, be lifted up by clouds of angels. We shall have fought the good fight of faith and won. We shall have finished our race and be ready to receive our prize. We shall have shaken the dust of the earth's corruption from our feet, never again to contend with Satan or our own frail, corrupted, fleshly natures. All that will be over; our real lives in Christ will have begun. The world's end is the beginning of all we have hoped and believed for, the fulfillment of God's promise.

The Dead In Christ

At the very moment we are raptured, the bodies of those whose spirits have gone on to heaven before us will be resurrected. We shall all meet in one, great, ecstatic reunion.

1 Corinthians 15
52 ...For the trumpet will sound, and the dead will be raised incorruptible...

The bodies of those whose spirits have preceded us into the Lord's presence will not only be resurrected but **raised incorruptible**, which means glorified, just as we shall be changed or glorified. We shall all have the same body that Jesus did after His resurrection (Philippians 3:21).

Hebrews 11
39 And all these, having obtained a good testimony through faith, did not receive the promise,
40 God having provided something better for us, that they should not be made perfect apart from us.

The saints of the old covenant who qualified **through faith** are **all these** who, even though their spirits are with the Lord, have not yet been able to **receive the promise**. They have had to wait until we, the last generation, are raptured. Thus, the whole body of Christ is glorified together in one shining moment.

In The Lord's Presence

As we enter the Lord's presence we shall be transformed into the supernatural condition in which Jesus lives. That is what glorified means. We shall have no more corruptible flesh and no more weaknesses. We shall have been made incorruptible and immortal, to live and reign with Christ forever.

As the now-glorified members of the body of Christ we immediately stand before the judgment seat of Christ, receive our rewards, and are assigned our positions of authority in heaven. This is based on our works of faith and obedience to the Word during our time on earth (1 Corinthians 3:13-15). Do not confuse works of faith with works of the flesh. Works of faith are those that overcome the devil's attacks of sickness, disease, poverty, lack, oppression, bondage, addiction, affliction, fear, grief, unforgiveness, bitterness, and false doctrine (Mark 16:15-18). The works of faith also appropriate God's vision for our lives. We do not please God and establish our faithfulness with works of the flesh. Community church programs are undoubtedly "good works" but they have nothing to do with the works of faith on which we shall be evaluated and rewarded at the judgment seat of Christ. That is why Paul talked about fighting the good fight of faith, and completing his assignment (finishing the race), so that he could hear the Lord say when he stood before Him, "Well done, My good and faithful servant."

Exercising faith once in a while is not the good fight of faith. It is also to be born in mind that a losing fight is a bad fight; only a winning fight is a good fight.

Government Training

We shall, following the judgment seat of Christ and bearing our crowns of glory that never fade away (1 Peter 5:4), begin our seven years of training to be God's kingdom government. Since we are to sit with Jesus in His throne, and rule and reign with Him over the whole universe unto eternity—and despite the fact that we shall be in an incorruptible, glorified state—there will be things we need to learn. God does everything decently and in order (1 Corinthians 14:40). When the millennial reign of Christ begins we shall all know precisely what to do, where to go, and our part in establishing and administering the government of God. It will be a smooth transition.

> Revelation 5
> **9 And they sang a new song, saying: "You are worthy to take the scroll, and to open its seals; for You were slain, and have redeemed us to God by Your blood out of every tribe and tongue and people and nation,**
> **10 and have made us kings and priests to our God; and we shall reign on the earth."**

I believe the **new song** we sing will be a new language, the language of heaven. Since we shall have been **redeemed** from **every tribe and tongue and people and nation** we shall need a common language.

1 Corinthians 13
8 Love never fails. But whether there are prophecies, they will fail; whether there are tongues, they will cease; whether there is knowledge, it will vanish away.

The Word says that where **there are tongues, they will cease**. The plurality of tongues will be replaced with one new tongue.

Sitting or Standing

There are more categories of people in the heavenlies than just the body of Christ and the angels. Two categories of people—the mid-tribulation martyrs and the 144,000 Jewish evangelists—join us in heaven at mid-tribulation. We, the body of Christ, will have a seven year course of study but they will only have a three and a half year course. God's plan is perfect in every detail, therefore, it must be that we need to learn more to fulfill our roles than they do to fulfill theirs. The distinction between us and them, revealed by Scripture, is our respective relationships with Jesus: sitting in His throne, or standing before His throne.

This difference of rank in heaven is the consequence of faithfulness and obedience during our lives on earth, or the lack thereof. The body of Christ—who will have overcome, been taken up in the fourth rapture and kept from the tribulation (Revelation 3:10), and received their crowns of glory—are told in Revelation 3 that they will, [21]**sit with Me on My throne**.

The mid-tribulation martyrs are those who lacked faithfulness and obedience on earth, failed to qualify for the fourth rapture, and failed to receive their crowns of glory, but thereafter refused the mark of the beast and were killed for their faith. They are resurrected and raptured at mid-tribulation. When they arrive in heaven they do not sit with Jesus, but stand before His throne.

Revelation 7
9 After these things I looked, and behold, a great multitude

The Rapture, The Tribulation, And Beyond 341

which no one could number, of all nations, tribes, peoples, and tongues, standing before the throne and before the Lamb, clothed with white robes, with palm branches in their hands,
10 and crying out with a loud voice, saying, "Salvation belongs to our God who sits on the throne, and to the Lamb!"

Those **clothed in white robes**, who are **standing before the throne and before the Lamb**, are the martyrs raptured at mid-tribulation.

Revelation 7
13 Then one of the elders answered, saying to me, "Who are these arrayed in white robes, and where did they come from?"
14 And I said to him, "Sir, you know." So he said to me, "These are the ones who come out of the great tribulation, and washed their robes and made them white in the blood of the Lamb.
15 "Therefore they are before the throne of God, and serve Him day and night in His temple. And He who sits on the throne will dwell among them."

The mid-tribulation martyrs **come out of the great tribulation** and are **before the throne of God, and serve Him day and night in His temple**. Jesus is even described as **He who sits on the throne**—where we sit with Him—Who **will dwell among them**.

The issue of sitting or standing does not end at mid-tribulation, but continues into the millennial reign of Christ where we see the martyrs and the body of Christ described as being in heaven with Him.

Revelation 20
4 And I saw thrones, and they who sat on them, and judgment was committed to them...

We, the body of Christ who overcame and were raptured prior to the tribulation, are the first group and are **they who sat on** the thrones. The second group in the throne room consists of the mid-tribulation martyrs.

Revelation 20
4...And I saw the souls of those who had been beheaded for their

witness to Jesus and for the word of God, who had not worshiped the beast or his image, and had not received his mark on their foreheads or on their hands. And they lived and reigned with Christ for a thousand years.**

This group, who will have joined heaven at mid-tribulation, will be in the throne room and will **reign with Christ for a thousand years**. They are not, however, enthroned, but are, as we see in Revelation 7, [9]**standing before the throne and before the Lamb, clothed with white robes, with palm branches in their hands**. They have no thrones, as we do, and their reign is limited to the length of the millennium, whereas we, as stated in Revelation 22, [5]**shall reign forever and ever**.

We are told in Revelation 20, [6]**Blessed and holy is he who has part in the first resurrection. Over such the second death has no power, but they shall be priests of God and of Christ, and shall reign with Him a thousand years**. Those in this group are blessed to be part of the first resurrection because they are thus exempt from judgment at the great white throne and the risk of being cast into the lake of fire. They are called priests of God and again their time of reign is stated as a thousand years. One concludes that the mid-tribulation martyrs will be part of kingdom government but fill a different, lesser role.

We, the body of Christ, are described many times in the authoritative position of sitting with Jesus in His throne.

Luke 22
**28 But you are those who have continued with Me in My trials.
29 And I bestow upon you a kingdom, just as My Father bestowed one upon Me,
30 that you may eat and drink at My table in My kingdom, and sit on thrones judging the twelve tribes of Israel.**

We are one with God and His Christ in His kingdom. We eat and drink with Him at His table and **sit on thrones judging the twelve tribes of Israel**. This corresponds to the statement at the beginning of Revelation 20:4.

We, the body of Christ, will have great and eternal authority committed to us, but much is required of us now. Now is when we establish our commitment to the Spirit and His leading, our faithfulness to, and love of, the Word, and our willingness to obey it. God had to know, beyond a shadow of doubt, whether He came first in Abraham's heart, even above Isaac, and He needs to know our hearts, too. We must put our lives on God's altar and say, as Jesus did in the garden of Gethsemane the night before He went to the cross, "Not my will, Father, but Yours be done."

The 144,000 Jewish evangelists did not accept Jesus in time, thus did not qualify for the fourth rapture and, like the martyrs, did not receive their crowns of glory.

Revelation 14
3 And they sang as it were a new song before the throne, before the four living creatures, and the elders; and no one could learn that song except the hundred and forty-four thousand who were redeemed from the earth.
4 These are the ones who were not defiled with women, for they are virgins. These are the ones who follow the Lamb wherever He goes. These were redeemed from among men, being firstfruits to God and to the Lamb.

The 144,000, like the tribulation martyrs, are **before the throne**. They **follow the Lamb wherever He goes**.

The Two End-Time Witnesses

Enoch and Elijah were as close to God as any men of their respective times could be. They walked with God, were faithful, anointed and obedient in all things, such friends of God that they are the only two, apart from Jesus, who qualified to be raptured prior to the rapture of the church. They had faith for their raptures, just as we must. They were chosen by God to represent Him in the presence of Antichrist during the second half of the tribulation, with power second only to His own. These two men have more than distinguished themselves in faith and obedience.

Scripture does not at first appear to offer illumination as to where they are after they are raptured. When we make the right connection, however, their place in eternity becomes obvious. When God speaks to them immediately after their resurrection, in Revelation 11 in [12]**a loud voice from heaven saying to them, "Come up here"**, they ascend to heaven. These are exactly the same words that John hears when Jesus calls the church up to heaven to receive its crown of glory in Revelation 4, [1]**the first voice which I heard was like a trumpet speaking with me, saying, "Come up here."**

Enoch and Elijah will receive their crowns of glory, become part of the body of Christ, and be part of the bridegroom. This is why the wedding of the Lamb cannot take place until they are raptured. To imagine anything less for these two would be profoundly unacceptable. In fact, they will have the distinction of being the only two men to be raptured twice: once by faith while alive as we shall be, and once after physical death as the dead in Christ will be.

The Crown Of Glory

The crown of glory is received at the judgment seat of Christ, following the fourth rapture.

> 2 Timothy 4
> **7 I have fought the good fight, I have finished the race, I have kept the faith.**
> **8 Finally, there is laid up for me the crown of righteousness, which the Lord, the righteous Judge, will give to me on that Day, and not to me only but also to all who have loved His appearing.**

The crown of righteousness, or glory, will be given **to all those who have loved His appearing**, which includes Enoch and Elijah. Obviously those who are saved but remain for the tribulation, and those not saved until after the tribulation begins, have not **loved His appearing**.

1 Peter 5
4 and when the Chief Shepherd appears, you will receive the crown of glory that does not fade away.

The **crown of glory that does not fade away** is presented at the judgment seat of Christ. There is no mention of this eternal crown being presented to the martyrs or the 144,000.

The Wedding

It is impossible to comprehend the splendor and overflowing joy that will attend the wedding of the Lamb.

Revelation 19
7 Let us be glad and rejoice and give Him glory, for the marriage of the Lamb has come, and His wife has made herself ready.
8 And to her it was granted to be arrayed in fine linen, clean and bright, for the fine linen is the righteous acts of the saints.
9 Then he said to me, "Write: 'Blessed are those who are called to the marriage supper of the Lamb!'" And he said to me, "These are the true sayings of God."

Even now, New Jerusalem is being made ready to receive her bridegroom. We add to that readiness every time our **righteous acts** are added to her ornamentation. Our bride is being decorated with our faith. Faith is accounted to us as righteousness (Romans 4:20-22). Every act of faith by a saint of God is added to New Jerusalem to adorn her as a bride for her husband (Revelation 21:2).

Luke 20
34 And Jesus answered and said to them, "The sons of this age marry and are given in marriage.
35 "But those who are counted worthy to attain that age, and the resurrection from the dead, neither marry nor are given in marriage;"

After the wedding, as we dwell within the city in our robes of righteousness, our presence will further adorn her. The reason that there will be no marriage among the saints in heaven is that we already have a wife. We could not be married to New Jerusalem and be married to each other as well.

> Isaiah 62
>
> **1 For Zion's sake I will not hold My peace, and for Jerusalem's sake I will not rest, until her righteousness goes forth as brightness, and her salvation as a lamp that burns.**
>
> **4 You shall no longer be termed Forsaken, nor shall your land any more be termed Desolate; But you shall be called Hephzibah, and your land Beulah; for the Lord delights in you, and your land shall be married.**

The name **Beulah** literally means *married*. It appears nowhere else in the Bible. **Hephzibah** means *My delight is in her*. New Jerusalem will no longer be desolate and forsaken because she will no longer be waiting, empty and alone. Her bridegroom, the body of Christ with Jesus as its head, will have arrived.

> Isaiah 62
>
> **5 For as a young man marries a virgin, so shall your sons marry you; and as the bridegroom rejoices over the bride, so shall your God rejoice over you.**

Our Father will rejoice over us at His Son's wedding. All the angels will sing. We shall rejoice over our bride. The celebration will be explosive. Right now, the call is going forth from heaven, pulling on our hearts as we live in glorious expectation of the coming of Christ.

> Revelation 22
>
> **17 And the Spirit and the bride say, "Come!" And let him who hears say, "Come!" And let him who thirsts come. And whoever desires, let him take the water of life freely.**

We are he **who hears** and say **come** Lord Jesus. The wedding reception will be a triumphant ride back from heaven, with Jesus at our head, to wipe evil from the face of the earth.

The Horses Of Heaven

In addition to our training as kingdom government we shall have to learn to ride our white horses. The Lord has shown me many visions of New Jerusalem, including the heavenly stables. God spoke to me once and said, "No one can ride your horse but you, and you cannot ride anyone else's. Each horse is as unique as his rider."

I saw these magnificent white horses, with coats like creamy satin, manes and tails like transparent spun silk, with muscles rippling and hooves that resemble polished grey granite, standing in row upon row as the angels groomed them. I saw their large intelligent eyes, their ears flicking this way and that to catch every sound as their nostrils flared, and it was as though I could feel their warm, hay-scented breath. One in particular captured my attention. I thought he was the most beautiful, the most majestic of them all; I do not doubt that each of us will feel the same way about his own steed.

Then God again spoke to me and said, "He's yours."

"I want to ride him!" I exclaimed.

"Not yet, but soon," He responded.

I gazed in awe at this splendid spectacle, realizing that this indescribably gorgeous city was my bride, that of which I would be an integral part for all eternity. The Spirit showed me many other parts of New Jerusalem in that vision, but I always wanted to go back to the stables.

New Jerusalem is beyond description. Each jeweled mansion is one of a kind, suited to our individual tastes. Each garden is like no other, and the golden light of God's glory and love shines on every leaf and iridescent petal. The colors of the rainbow dance all around as the light of the Lamb streams through the emeralds, rubies, sapphires, diamonds and topaz of which the city is constructed. The fragrance of the Lord fills the air with delicious, delicate perfume that smelled to me like jasmine. Everything feels like early morning after a spring rain. This earth has nothing to compare with the splendor of New Jerusalem.

The Armies Of Heaven

We have already established that the body of Christ, together with the two end-time witnesses, are part of the armies of heaven who ride back with Jesus at the second advent to conquer the two hundred million man army of Antichrist at Armageddon. Scripture is elusive, however, as to whether or not the mid-tribulation martyrs and the 144,000 Jewish evangelists will join us in those armies. We do, however, have a clue with respect to the martyrs and it lies in the description of clothing: the armies are clothed in fine linen.

> Revelation 19
> **14 And the armies in heaven, clothed in fine linen, white and clean, followed Him on white horses.**

The body of Christ, the bridegroom, is also described as being clothed in fine linen but it takes two Scriptures to make the connection:

> Revelation 19
> **7 Let us be glad and rejoice and give Him glory, for the marriage of the Lamb has come, and His wife has made herself ready.**
> **8 And to her it was granted to be arrayed in fine linen, clean and bright, for the fine linen is the righteous acts of the saints.**

> Isaiah 61
> **10 I will greatly rejoice in the Lord, my soul shall be joyful in my God; for He has clothed me with the garments of salvation, He has covered me with the robe of righteousness, as a bridegroom decks himself with ornaments, and as a bride adorns herself with her jewels.**

The bride is **arrayed in fine linen, clean and bright**—we must assume that it is white—and the linen **is the righteous acts of the saints**.

In the same context of brides and bridegrooms we, the saints whose righteous acts adorn the bride, are described as covered **with the robe of righteousness**. It is not unreasonable, therefore, to infer that wearing a **robe of righteousness** is the same as being **arrayed in fine linen**. Hence the conclusion that we—the body of Christ, the bridegroom—are clad in robes of fine linen.

The fine linen with which the bridegroom is clothed may or may not be different from the white robes of the mid-tribulation martyrs. That is why the makeup of the armies remains uncertain.

Revelation 7
13 Then one of the elders answered, saying to me, "Who are these arrayed in white robes, and where did they come from?" 14 And I said to him, "Sir, you know." So he said to me, "These are the ones who come out of the great tribulation, and washed their robes and made them white in the blood of the Lamb."

Regarding the 144,000, we know nothing beyond the already established fact that they have the Father's Name written on their foreheads. Their clothing is not mentioned.

The only thing regarding the makeup of the armies of heaven as to which we can be absolutely certain, therefore, is that we, the body of Christ, are part of them. This gives new intensity to the exhortation from Jesus in Revelation 3, [11]**Behold, I come quickly! Hold fast what you have, that no one may take your crown**.

Chapter 22

Armageddon

Before Jesus speaks the word that begins the battle of Armageddon, He gathers in two groups who move on to the nations: those who have hidden in the rocks and the caves without taking the mark of the beast, and the remnant of the Jews who have been hidden from Antichrist in the desert (Revelation 12:13-17).

> Isaiah 11
> **11 It shall come to pass in that day that the Lord shall set His hand again the second time to recover the remnant of His people who are left, from Assyria and Egypt, from Pathros and Cush, from Elam and Shinar, from Hamath and the islands of the sea. 12 He will set up a banner for the nations, and will assemble the outcasts of Israel, and gather together the dispersed of Judah from the four corners of the earth.**

They will be picked up by the angels and carried to a safe place until the destruction is complete.

> Matthew 24
> **29 Immediately after the tribulation of those days the sun will be darkened, and the moon will not give its light; the stars will fall from heaven, and the powers of the heavens will be shaken.**

**30 Then the sign of the Son of Man will appear in heaven, and then all the tribes of the earth will mourn, and they will see the Son of Man coming on the clouds of heaven with power and great glory.
31 And He will send His angels with a great sound of a trumpet, and they will gather together His elect from the four winds, from one end of heaven to the other.**

This is not the departure of the church, as many have supposed. It is, as already stated, the gathering of those who will become the millennial nations. It occurs **after the tribulation**. Here we see **the tribes of the earth,** who are those people of the tribulation who **will see the Son of Man coming on the clouds of heaven with power and great glory.**

The people of the earth will not see Jesus when He comes to catch the church away. Only the body of Christ will see and be able to respond to that trumpet. Jesus warns those who are here for the tribulation that, when they see Him returning with His armies at the end of the seven years, they should run for their lives and not look back.

Luke 17
**30 Even so will it be in the day when the Son of Man is revealed.
31 In that day, he who is on the housetop, and his goods are in the house, let him not come down to take them away. And likewise the one who is in the field, let him not turn back.
32 Remember Lot's wife.**

Those who stay completely out of sight and literally hide in mountain caves, tunnels, and underground caverns, will not be the only ones to avoid the mark of the beast. There will also be those who successfully camouflage themselves, in the midst of tribulation society, who never take the mark.

We have as an example the Jews in Nazi Germany who managed to hide their identity. The few who succeeded in this convinced everyone, including the authorities, that they were Gentiles. There were also Gentile Germans who never became Nazis, who abhorred Hitler's policies. They managed to fool even their own Nazi wives and children that they were going along with the Nazi program while, in fact, they

The Rapture, The Tribulation, And Beyond 353

took no part in it, some even helping Jews to escape from Germany.

Jesus will gather in every person who has refused the mark of the beast, no matter where he is at the moment of the second advent.

Luke 17
33 "Whoever seeks to save his life will lose it, and whoever loses his life will preserve it.
34 "I tell you, in that night there will be two men in one bed: the one will be taken and the other will be left.
35 "Two women will be grinding together: the one will be taken and the other left.
36 "Two men will be in the field: the one will be taken and the other left."
37 And they answered and said to Him, "Where, Lord?" So He said to them, "Wherever the body is, there the eagles will be gathered together."

Jesus likens this moment to God's rescue of Lot from Sodom just before He rained down fire and brimstone from heaven and destroyed the city and everyone in it (Luke 17:29). In Revelation 11:8 God calls Jerusalem, during the rule of Antichrist, Sodom. The parallel is crystal clear. Jesus even reminds these people of the destruction of Lot's wife when she hesitated and looked back. The same thing will happen in this case if they do not heed Jesus' warning.

The angels, before the battle of Armageddon, gather out of the earth those who qualify for the nations. There can be no argument against this being the gathering in of the nations because Jesus Himself answers those who ask Him where this will happen when He says, **there the eagles will be gathered**. This is the same event as in Revelation 19:17-18 when the angel calls the vultures/eagles to consume the dead remains of the armies of Antichrist, in the valley of Megiddo, following the battle of Armageddon.

We are now at the moment toward which everything has been building.

Revelation 19
11 Then I saw heaven opened, and behold, a white horse. And

> He who sat on him was called Faithful and True, and in righteousness He judges and makes war.
> 12 His eyes were like a flame of fire, and on His head were many crowns. He had a name written that no one knew except Himself.
> 13 He was clothed with a robe dipped in blood, and His name is called The Word of God.
> 14 And the armies in heaven, clothed in fine linen, white and clean, followed Him on white horses.
> 15 Now out of His mouth goes a sharp sword, that with it He should strike the nations. And He Himself will rule them with a rod of iron. He Himself treads the winepress of the fierceness and wrath of Almighty God.
> 16 And He has on His robe and on His thigh a name written: KING OF KINGS AND LORD OF LORDS.

We can only imagine the splendor of our ride to earth with Jesus following the wedding of the Lamb. Every eye and every fiber of our glorified being will be fixed on the blood-red robe of our glorious King and the sculpted gold of the many crowns upon His head. To our right and to our left, before and behind us, stretch rank upon rank of the armies of God astride their white horses, with one heart and one purpose as we move down from heaven in a steady stream of light.

<u>**The seventh bowl:**</u> God's final cleansing.

> Revelation 16
> 17 Then the seventh angel poured out his bowl into the air, and a loud voice came out of the temple of heaven, from the throne, saying, "It is done!"
> 18 And there were noises and thunderings and lightnings; and there was a great earthquake, such a mighty and great earthquake as had not occurred since men were on the earth.
> 19 Now the great city was divided into three parts, and the cities of the nations fell. And great Babylon was remembered before God, to give her the cup of the wine of the fierceness of His wrath.

The Rapture, The Tribulation, And Beyond 355

20 Then every island fled away, and the mountains were not found.
21 And great hail from heaven fell upon men, every hailstone about the weight of a talent. And men blasphemed God because of the plague of the hail, since that plague was exceedingly great.

God's wrath is complete and Jesus wipes all evil from the face of His earth. Satan's lease has expired and he is no longer the god of this world. **It is done!**

Jesus does not return to earth gently or quietly. His return to destroy Antichrist and his kingdom is an event of epic proportions. The air is filled with **noises and thunderings and lightnings**. When He sets foot on the Mount of Olives the city, Jerusalem, splits into three parts in **a great earthquake as has not occurred since men were on the earth**. Next, all the cities of the earth are utterly demolished, the islands disappear into the seas, the mountains crumble to dust, and hailstones weighing 200 pounds each rain down; and this is only the overture to the battle of Armageddon.

We see an angel standing before the sun who cries in Revelation 19, [17]**with a loud voice, saying to all the birds that fly in the midst of heaven, "Come and gather together for the supper of the great God,** [18]**that you may eat the flesh of kings, the flesh of captains, the flesh of mighty men, the flesh of horses and of those who sit on them, and the flesh of all people, free and slave, both small and great."**

The sky will fill with huge vultures, circling hungrily with their hideous heads and sharp beaks looking downward in anticipation of their coming feast. The sight before us in the valley of Megiddo is the two hundred million man army of Antichrist (Revelation 9:16) above which the vultures are gathered.

Revelation 16
16 And they gathered them together to the place called in Hebrew, Armageddon.

Revelation 19
19 And I saw the beast, the kings of the earth, and their armies,

gathered together to make war against Him who sat on the horse and against His army.

When the dust settles and the earth stops shaking Jesus speaks the Word and the two-edged sword—the Word of God—that proceeds from His mouth smites the nations of Antichrist before Him. We watch all those who have opposed Christ, by taking the mark of the beast, as they are hideously and grotesquely killed, consumed by the carrion-eating birds of the air, and their remains melt like wax in the fervent heat of God's truth.

This moment is recounted in the Bible in many places. Here are a few to give you a more complete image:

Psalm 68
2 As smoke is driven away, So drive them away; As wax melts before the fire, So let the wicked perish at the presence of God.

Psalm 97
5 The mountains melt like wax at the presence of the Lord, At the presence of the Lord of the whole earth.
6 The heavens declare His righteousness, And all the peoples see His glory.

Micah 1
4 The mountains will melt under him, and the valleys will split like wax before the fire, like waters poured down a steep place.
5 All this is for the transgression of Jacob and for the sins of the house of Israel...

Nahum 1
5 The mountains quake before Him, the hills melt, and the earth heaves at His presence, yes, the world and all who dwell in it.
6 Who can stand before His indignation? and who can endure the fierceness of His anger? His fury is poured out like fire, and the rocks are thrown down by Him.

Zechariah 14
12 And this shall be the plague with which the Lord will strike

all the people who fought against Jerusalem: Their flesh shall dissolve while they stand on their feet, their eyes shall dissolve in their sockets, and their tongues shall dissolve in their mouths.

2 Thessalonians 2
8 And then the lawless one will be revealed, whom the Lord will consume with the breath of His mouth and destroy with the brightness of His coming.

2 Peter 3
**10 But the day of the Lord will come as a thief in the night, in which the heavens will pass away with a great noise, and the elements will melt with fervent heat; both the earth and the works that are in it will be burned up.
11 Therefore, since all these things will be dissolved, what manner of persons ought you to be in holy conduct and godliness,
12 looking for and hastening the coming of the day of God, because of which the heavens will be dissolved being on fire, and the elements will melt with fervent heat?**

Revelation 19
21 And the rest were killed with the sword which proceeded from the mouth of Him who sat on the horse. And all the birds were filled with their flesh.

The earth, and everything and everyone on it, will melt down and be purified with fire. Following the battle, and amid the smoke and ashes, Jesus will deal with the satanic trinity.

Revelation 19
20 Then the beast was captured, and with him the false prophet who worked signs in his presence, by which he deceived those who received the mark of the beast and those who worshiped his image. These two were cast alive into the lake of fire burning with brimstone.

Revelation 20
1 Then I saw an angel coming down from heaven, having the key to the bottomless pit and a great chain in his hand.
2 He laid hold of the dragon, that serpent of old, who is the Devil and Satan, and bound him for a thousand years;
3 and he cast him into the bottomless pit, and shut him up, and set a seal on him, so that he should deceive the nations no more till the thousand years were finished. But after these things he must be released for a little while.

Chapter 23

The Millennial Reign Of Christ

A deep hush will fall upon the earth. The battle will have left us dumbstruck. Satan's reign of terror is finally over. We shall have watched him thrown into the pit and sealed for a thousand years. We shall have watched the beast and the false prophet cast alive into the lake of fire for ever and ever.

The Earth Is Restored

Stretching out before us will be a polluted, burned, dried up, smoldering planet. Mountains will have been pulverized and flattened, islands will be no more, and the landscape will be unrecognizable. The work of God's restoration of the earth and all that is in it will now begin. The transformation from the blackness of death and destruction to lush green life and the original beauty of God's creation will be breathtaking.

> Acts 3
> **20 and that He may send Jesus Christ, who was preached to you before,**
> **21 whom heaven must receive until the times of restoration of all things, which God has spoken by the mouth of all His holy prophets since the world began.**

The Father spoke to Jesus about the time when He would restore the earth.

> Isaiah 49
> **8 Thus says the Lord: "In an acceptable time I have heard You, and in the day of salvation I have helped You; I will preserve You and give You as a covenant to the people, to restore the earth, to cause them to inherit the desolate heritages;"**

New Jerusalem Comes Down

> Revelation 21
> **2 Then I, John, saw the holy city, New Jerusalem, coming down out of heaven from God, prepared as a bride adorned for her husband.**
> **3 And I heard a loud voice from heaven saying, "Behold, the tabernacle of God is with men, and He will dwell with them, and they shall be His people, and God Himself will be with them and be their God."**

The holy city, our bride, will be brought down to sit above earthly Jerusalem. She will be close and available to the earth, even though still separate.

The Temple Rebuilt

As soon as the earth has been returned to its original condition, with the beauty of green fields and lush forests, waters again running pure and deep, and air that is clean and fresh, the work of rebuilding will begin. The first thing to be rebuilt will be the temple of the Lamb.

> Zechariah 6
> **12 Then speak to him, saying, "Thus says the Lord of hosts, saying: 'Behold, the Man whose name is the BRANCH! From His**

place He shall branch out, and He shall build the temple of the Lord;
13 'yes, He shall build the temple of the Lord. He shall bear the glory, and shall sit and rule on His throne; so He shall be a priest on His throne, and the counsel of peace shall be between them both.'"

Jesus Himself will build His own temple. It is inconceivable that the temple where Antichrist, the abomination of desolation, sat during his rule will remain standing in the midst of the rubble of the most devastating earthquake the world has ever experienced. It is unthinkable that Jesus would sit in the same throne as that occupied by Antichrist. As God said to Zechariah, He will not.

Therefore, it is irrelevant whether the Dome of the Rock, the muslim mosque currently on the temple mount, remains or is demolished and replaced by the Jews with a temple of their own making. Whatever building stands there will not be the temple of the Lord. Jesus, **the Man whose name is the BRANCH**, will build the temple of the Lord at the beginning of the new millennium and **shall sit and rule on His throne**.

Kingdom Government On Earth

Each member of the body of Christ will receive personal and specialized training during his seven years in heaven while the earth goes through the tribulation. This training, a course on kingdom government, will be tailored to his specific assignment.

When I address a group of young people I frequently take the time to tell them that their efforts to achieve an education and develop skills will not be wasted. I encourage them to realize that the rapture is not an end but a beginning. I am convinced that all the skills and abilities we have developed will be increased and used during the millennium, and beyond, in our capacity as kingdom government. The nations will be natural people with natural needs, and there is a great deal involved in running a whole world. Our training during those seven years will be extensive and specialized.

As glorified people, the capacity of our minds to absorb and maintain knowledge will be unlimited. No matter our struggles with academics in this life, we shall be unfettered as glorified beings. We shall have the desire and ability to learn all that is necessary to complete the required course in the time allowed. The mind of Christ, which we were given when we were baptized into the Holy Spirit (1 Corinthians 2:16) will no longer have our flesh and its limitations with which to contend.

Revelation 3
21 To him who overcomes I will grant to sit with Me on My throne, as I also overcame and sat down with My Father on His throne.
22 He who has an ear, let him hear what the Spirit says to the churches.

Revelation 2
25 But hold fast what you have till I come.
26 And he who overcomes, and keeps My works until the end, to him I will give power over the nations
27 He shall rule them with a rod of iron; as the potter's vessels shall be broken to pieces as I also have received from My Father;
28 and I will give him the morning star.
29 He who has an ear, let him hear what the Spirit says to the churches.

Our homes will, from the time of the rapture onward, be our mansions in New Jerusalem (John 14:2). We shall also, as kingdom government, have offices on the earth. We shall go back and forth to carry out our responsibilities and be a presence among the people of the nations as God's representatives. That is why we shall need physical bodies. Physical bodies are required for us to function on earth. Our Lord Jesus has had a glorified body since His resurrection but, during His ministry on earth, between his resurrection and His rapture, He had a physical body.

Isaiah 9
7 Of the increase of His government and peace there will be no end, upon the throne of David and over His kingdom, to order it and establish it with judgment and justice from that time forward, even forever. The zeal of the Lord of hosts will perform this.

Chapter 24

The Millennial Nations

Jesus will, upon His return for the battle of Armageddon, send His angels to gather the nations.

> Matthew 24
> **30 Then the sign of the Son of Man will appear in heaven, and then all the tribes of the earth will mourn, and they will see the Son of Man coming on the clouds of heaven with power and great glory.**
> **31 And He will send His angels with a great sound of a trumpet, and they will gather together His elect from the four winds, from one end of heaven to the other.**

The nations are comprised of three groups: all those, Christian or otherwise, who survive the tribulation without taking the mark of the beast; the Jewish remnant hidden in the desert during the tribulation; and those gathered **from one end of heaven to the other**.

The Survivors

> Matthew 24
> **13 But he who endures to the end shall be saved.**

The **end** is the end of the tribulation. Those who survive the tribulation without taking the mark of the beast will be saved. They will not be destroyed in the battle of Armageddon, and they will be saved from the lake of fire for a thousand years.

The Jewish Remnant

> Isaiah 11
> **11 It shall come to pass in that day that the Lord shall set His hand again the second time to recover the remnant of His people who are left, from Assyria and Egypt, from Pathros and Cush, from Elam and Shinar, from Hamath and the islands of the sea.**
> **12 He will set up a banner for the nations, and will assemble the outcasts of Israel, and gather together the dispersed of Judah from the four corners of the earth.**

When the new nation of Israel was formed in 1948, God gathered His scattered people. When He sets His hand **the second time to recover the remnant of His people who are left**, it is the creation of the millennial nations.

> Micah 2
> **12 I will surely assemble all of you, O Jacob, I will surely gather the remnant of Israel; I will put them together like sheep of the fold, like a flock in the midst of their pasture; they shall make a loud noise because of so many men.**
> **13 The one who breaks open will come up before them; they will break out, pass through the gate, and go out by it; their king will pass before them, with the Lord at their head.**

Jesus is not at the **head** of Israel until His second appearance to it at the second advent. Israel, at this point, is **the remnant** preserved by God in accordance with His promise to Elijah who, despairing of Israel, cried out to God:

> 1 Kings 19
> **14 ...I have been very zealous for the Lord God of hosts; because**

the children of Israel have forsaken Your covenant, torn down Your altars, and killed Your prophets with the sword. I alone am left; and they seek to take my life.

God responded to Elijah's tormented, heartfelt lament:

1 Kings 19
18 Yet I have reserved seven thousand in Israel, all whose knees have not bowed to Baal, and every mouth that has not kissed him.

The Jewish remnant consists of the descendants of the **seven thousand in Israel, all whose knees have not bowed to Baal.** Only God knows what that number is today. God spoke of them through Paul.

Romans 11
5 Even so then, at this present time there is a remnant according to the election of grace.
27 For this is My covenant with them, when I take away their sins.
28 Concerning the gospel they are enemies for your sake, but concerning the election they are beloved for the sake of the fathers.

The **election of grace** is for **the sake of the fathers**, and **the fathers** can only be the seven thousand of whom God spoke to Elijah. This remnant, of unknown number, is protected by God during the tribulation. However, God makes it clear that these same people, who will be preserved at the end, are now **enemies** of **the gospel**.

Romans 9 (The Amplified Bible)
27 And Isaiah calls out (solemnly cries aloud) over Israel: Though the number of the sons of Israel be like the sand of the sea, only the remnant (a small part of them) will be saved (from perdition, condemnation, judgment)!

Only the Father knows whom He will select—**the election of grace**—

of those descended from the seven thousand He promised to Elijah. Scripture makes it clear, however, that the Jewish remnant will be but a fraction of all the Jews.

Revelation 12
4 ...And the dragon stood before the woman who was ready to give birth, to devour her Child as soon as it was born.
5 And she bore a male Child who was to rule all nations with a rod of iron. And her Child was caught up to God and to His throne.

The nation of Israel, in these verses, is **the woman**. Her **male Child** is Jesus. He was destined **to rule all nations with a rod of iron**, both now and in the time to come.

Revelation 12
6 Then the woman fled into the wilderness, where she has a place prepared by God, that they should feed her there one thousand two hundred and sixty days.

The **one thousand two hundred and sixty days** is the first half of the tribulation, however, **the woman** in this verse, is not the whole nation of Israel but the remnant promised by God to Elijah.

Revelation 12
14 But the woman was given two wings of a great eagle, that she might fly into the wilderness to her place, where she is nourished for a time and times and half a time, from the presence of the serpent.

The remnant of the Jewish nation flees **into the wilderness** for the first half of the tribulation, **one thousand two hundred and sixty days**. During the second half, **a time and times and half a time**, when the situation on earth becomes even more treacherous, God supernaturally rescues the remnant with the **wings of a great eagle** to a safer hiding place in the desert where Antichrist cannot reach it (Revelation 12:15-17).

Jesus was brokenhearted when the people of Israel rejected Him. They were the Father's first love and, when they failed to receive Him as Messiah, He lamented.

Matthew 23
**37 O Jerusalem, Jerusalem, the one who kills the prophets and stones those who are sent to her! How often I wanted to gather your children together, as a hen gathers her chicks under her wings, but you were not willing!
38 See! Your house is left to you desolate;
39 for I say to you, you shall see Me no more till you say, "Blessed is He who comes in the name of the Lord!"**

Only the Jewish remnant will be left of Israel, and only some of them will accept the truth and say, **Blessed is He who comes in the name of the Lord.**

Zephaniah 3
20 "At that time I will bring you back, even at the time I gather you; for I will give you fame and praise among all the peoples of the earth, when I return your captives before your eyes," says the Lord.

The remnant of Israel who receive Jesus as Messiah will be a favored nation on the earth during the millennium and in the eternal nations as well. This is the fulfillment of God's promise that He would preserve a place of honor for the Jews. They cannot have a place in New Jerusalem—they did not accept Jesus as Messiah in time to qualify—but they will have **fame and praise among the peoples of the earth**. They will not be kingdom government—that place is reserved for the body of Christ—but they will be leaders among the people of the nations.

Those Gathered From Heaven

Matthew 24
31 And He will send His angels with a great sound of a trumpet,

and they will gather together His elect from the four winds, from one end of heaven to the other.

The **four winds** are the four corners of the earth, but **from one end of heaven to the other** poses a question no one ever seems to address.

There are in heaven, right now, two categories of people: the dead in Christ, and those saved from condemnation. The dead in Christ are those who received Jesus both as Lord and Savior. Those saved from condemnation are those who received Jesus as Savior but rejected the baptism of the Holy Spirit. They thus refused to make Jesus Lord as well as Savior. They escaped hell and went to heaven, but they will not be part of the body of Christ. They will be resurrected but not glorified; they will join the nations.

The Language Of The Nations

The nations will be made up of people from all over the world with different languages. All will receive a common language.

> Zephaniah 3
> **9 For then I will restore to the peoples a pure language, that they all may call on the name of the Lord, to serve Him with one accord.**

The Nations Rebuild The Cities Of The Earth

> Isaiah 58 (KJV)
> **12 And they that shall be of thee shall build the old waste places: thou shalt raise up the foundations of many generations; and thou shalt be called, The repairer of the breach, The restorer of paths to dwell in.**

God will be the master architect of the new cities of the earth and Jesus—**The repairer of the breach, The restorer of paths to dwell in**—will be the master builder, but the nations will do the actual building.

Identity Of, And Worship By, The Nations

God is specific about the requirements for worship by the nations who dwell upon the earth during the millennial reign of Christ.

> Isaiah 66
> **18 For I know their works and their thoughts. It shall be that I will gather all nations and tongues; and they shall come and see My glory.**
> **19 I will set a sign among them; and those among them who escape I will send to the nations: to Tarshish and Pul and Lud, who draw the bow, and Tubal and Javan, to the coastlands afar off who have not heard My fame nor seen My glory. And they shall declare My glory among the Gentiles.**

These Scriptures come at the end of Isaiah's prophecy, which completes God's picture of His plans for mankind. When God says here that He **will gather all nations and tongues**, He is talking about the nations of the millennium, for only they will be able to respond to, **come and see My glory**.

God names the countries within the millennial nations to which **those among them who escape** will be sent. Do not be concerned about the phrase, **who draw the bow**, since it merely describes the service of **Tarshish and Pul and Lud** as warriors for God during the tribulation. The **coastlands afar off** are remote areas and islands which came to salvation at the very last moment through the witness of the angels during the second half of the tribulation (Revelation 14:6). The saved millennial nations **shall declare** God's **glory among the Gentiles**. The **Gentiles**, who are unbelievers, are those who avoided the mark of the beast by hiding in the rocks and caves but who never made Jesus their Savior. They will be on the earth during the millennium and some will be saved.

> Isaiah 66
> **20 "Then they shall bring all your brethren for an offering to the Lord out of all nations, on horses and in chariots and in litters, on mules and on camels, to My holy mountain**

Jerusalem," says the Lord, "as the children of Israel bring an offering in a clean vessel into the house of the Lord."

God declares that the saved millennial nations will come to worship at His **holy mountain Jerusalem**, meaning New Jerusalem, not earthly Jerusalem. The **children of Israel** are the remnant of the Jews who have survived the tribulation and who will also come to New Jerusalem and worship if they have made Jesus their Savior. When they are saved they become **a clean vessel** and may enter **the house of the Lord**.

Isaiah 66
21 "And I will also take some of them for priests and Levites," says the Lord.
22 "For as the new heavens and the new earth which I will make shall remain before Me," says the Lord, "So shall your descendants and your name remain.
23 "And it shall come to pass that from one New Moon to another, and from one Sabbath to another, all flesh shall come to worship before Me," says the Lord.

God will **take some of** the saved Jewish remnant **for priests and Levites**, meaning He will put them in charge of the worship of God among the nations on the earth, but not in New Jerusalem where worship is led by Christ Jesus. The nation of Israel will always be part of both the millennial and the eternal nations and God declares this when He says to them, **So shall your descendants and your name remain**.

God will require **all flesh**, the nations, to go to His **holy mountain Jerusalem** to worship at prescribed days and times. Failure to comply will have dire consequences.

Zechariah 14
16 And it shall come to pass that everyone who is left of all the nations which came against Jerusalem shall go up from year to year to worship the King, the Lord of hosts, and to keep the Feast of Tabernacles.
17 And it shall be that whichever of the families of the earth do

not come up to Jerusalem to worship the King, the Lord of hosts, on them there will be no rain.
18 If the family of Egypt will not come up and enter in, they shall have no rain; they shall receive the plague with which the Lord strikes the nations who do not come up to keep the Feast of Tabernacles.
19 This shall be the punishment of Egypt and the punishment of all the nations that do not come up to keep the Feast of Tabernacles.

The religious festivals—the Feast of Tabernacles, the New Moon, and the Sabbath—are ordained by God to ensure that all flesh remain in submission. The festivals are not for the incorruptible, glorified body of Christ, but for the corruptible, unglorified flesh of the nations. They also serve the purpose of preserving the faith and religious unity of the nations, and as a constant reminder of how God supernaturally delivered them from the past. Unity among the nations is sustained by their coming together in worship, and the development of tribal attitudes is counteracted. The religious festivals not only maintain the discipline of worship among the nations, but bring them together at regular intervals for fellowship.

How Can There Be Unbelievers In The Nations?

This question has always been perplexing. We know that there are individuals and groups of people calling themselves survivalists. They have been preparing for a catastrophic collapse of the world system for decades, some of them even trying to help bring it to pass. They have dug tunnels and caves in mountain ranges all over the United States and probably in other countries as well. They have stocked these well hidden retreats with vast supplies of ordnance, water, food, and all the exigencies of life. We know about the existence and preparations of these anarchists because many of them brag to the media about their disdain for the world system and their preparations for its demise.

It is certain that some, if not all, of these people have failed to receive Jesus as Savior, let alone make Him Lord. Even with the evangelism that will take place during the tribulation they will undoubtedly continue in their unbelief. Nonetheless, they will be gathered in by Jesus at the end of the seven years. What will happen to them once the nations are established?

God, as with all things, has made preparation for this contingency. Such of these people as are not saved, but survive the tribulation without taking the mark of the beast, will be screened out of the mainstream.

> Revelation 21
> **23 And the city had no need of the sun or of the moon to shine in it, for the glory of God illuminated it, and the Lamb is its light.**
> **24 And the nations of those who are saved shall walk in its light, and the kings of the earth bring their glory and honor into it.**
> **25 Its gates shall not be shut at all by day (there shall be no night there).**
> **26 And they shall bring the glory and the honor of the nations into it.**
> **27 But there shall by no means enter it anything that defiles, or causes an abomination or a lie, but only those who are written in the Lamb's Book of Life.**

The nations who come to worship in New Jerusalem and **walk in its light** will be **those who are saved**. Notice that only those whose names are **written in the Lamb's Book of Life** will be able to enter. Those who have a rebellious heart, who are living **a lie**, causing **an abomination**, or **anything that defiles**, will not be able to enter the holy city. Therefore, those who are living **a lie**, those apart from Christ who are defiled with false doctrine, will be excluded from the holy city. These will be the anarchists who continue their rebellious ways as well as members of the Jewish remnant who continue to reject Christ and follow the Law.

There will certainly be such people—else, why make provision to exclude them from the city and severely punish them?—and they will be barred at the gate from entering the city. Since the punishment for failing to enter and worship God, which they will be unable to do, will be a drought on their land and a plague, they will surely suffer and some will perish. Healing is only available through the leaves of the tree of life in the middle of the street, and the only way to get to this tree is to enter the city.

> Revelation 22
> **14 Blessed are those who do His commandments, that they may have the right to the tree of life, and may enter through the gates into the city.**
> **15 But outside are dogs and sorcerers and sexually immoral and murderers and idolaters, and whoever loves and practices a lie.**

These **dogs and sorcerers and sexually immoral and murderers and idolaters and whoever loves and practices a lie** are not just those in the lake of fire—who will be visible through the transparent streets at the gates of the holy city for eternity (Isaiah 66:22-24)—but also those of the millennial nations who cannot enter New Jerusalem during the millennium.

A Time Of Peace

The millennial nations, even though they are flesh, will live in a time of total peace. The seventh millennium, like the Sabbath, is a time of rest. Peace will prevail upon the earth because the accuser of the saints, Satan, has been cast into the pit and sealed there (Revelation 20:1-3). Those who obediently come and worship in New Jerusalem will be blessed, having the right to be healed by the leaves of the tree of life and eat of its fruit.

> Revelation 22
> **2 In the middle of its street, and on either side of the river, was the tree of life, which bore twelve fruits, each tree yielding its fruit every month. And the leaves of the tree were for the healing of the nations.**

Chapter 25

Satan's Season Of Release

At the end of the tribulation Satan is bound in chains and imprisoned in the bottomless pit for a thousand years.

Revelation 20
**1 Then I saw an angel coming down from heaven, having the key to the bottomless pit and a great chain in his hand.
2 He laid hold of the dragon, that serpent of old, who is the Devil and Satan, and bound him for a thousand years
3 and he cast him into the bottomless pit, and shut him up, and set a seal on him, so that he should deceive the nations no more till the thousand years were finished...**

Once the pit is sealed, with the devil securely inside, Jesus restores the earth and reigns over the nations in absolute peace.

Isaiah 11
**6 The wolf also shall dwell with the lamb, the leopard shall lie down with the young goat, the calf and the young lion and the fatling together; and a little child shall lead them.
7 The cow and the bear shall graze; their young ones shall lie down together; and the lion shall eat straw like the ox.
8 The nursing child shall play by the cobra's hole, and the weaned child shall put his hand in the viper's den.**

9 They shall not hurt nor destroy in all My holy mountain, for the earth shall be full of the knowledge of the Lord as the waters cover the sea.

God's righteous system of government will dominate the nations during the millennium and all will be well. Nothing upon the earth will be dangerous or harmful and everyone who comes to worship will live in peace and safety. The people will worship the Lord in New Jerusalem without disturbing the atmosphere of heaven because everyone in the nations who enters the holy city **shall be full of the knowledge of the Lord**.

Many will be born during the millennium while the nations live in God's peace and blessings upon the earth. The nations are natural people. They will marry and have children, and their children will marry and have children. If they obey the ordinance of God, and worship in the holy city, they will have access to the fruit of the tree of life and the healing leaves of the tree. They will continue to live in prosperity and health and they will probably come to number in the billions by the time of Satan's release.

Those born during this time will never have had to make a choice between good and evil. They will only have known good. God insists that we all choose Him of our own free will, and that is why Satan is released at the end of the millennium. The nations will be confronted with evil, as have all those on earth before them, and each individual will have to choose.

Revelation 20
**3 ...But after these things he must be released for a little while.
7 Now when the thousand years have expired, Satan will be released from his prison
8 and will go out to deceive the nations which are in the four corners of the earth, Gog and Magog, to gather them together to battle, whose number is as the sand of the sea.**

Even though the nations will have been living blessed, peaceful lives, they will still be flesh with all the weaknesses of the flesh, including a tendency toward pride and rebellion, the origins of man's downfall.

The Rapture, The Tribulation, And Beyond 379

It is what Satan will be counting on when he is **released from his prison** in the bottomless pit.

We can only surmise, based on Satan's Biblical record, the tactics he will use to **deceive the nations**. He will have had a thousand years, chained in the abyss with his hatred seething, to plot their destruction. During the time of his release, referred to as a **little while**, he will tempt the nations and convince as many of them as possible to turn from Jesus and follow him. Since he is not capable of original thought, he will most likely use the same deception that he used with Eve in the Garden of Eden.

The fruit, itself, was not the issue. The fruit represented rebellion. Throughout the ages Satan has goaded people into rebellion against God by presenting them with one lie or another that appealed to the flesh. It has been working in various guises for six thousand years; why would he try something new?

Genesis 3
4 And the serpent said to the woman, "You will not surely die. 5 "For God knows that in the day you eat of it your eyes will be opened, and you will be like God, knowing good and evil."

Satan always asserts that God does not really mean what He says. He tells people they misunderstand the Word. Then, he appeals to their pride and the weakness of their flesh. During his season of release he will promise that he, and all who follow him, will overpower God and **be like God** themselves.

Can you hear that slimy, lying serpent? "You don't have to go up to the city and worship God," he will croon. "You are better than that. When God says, 'Jump,' you don't have to say, 'How high?' I make no such arrogant demands in my kingdom. You can do whatever you feel like."

The vile, seducing voice of Satan will say whatever the flesh wants to hear. If the nations choose to listen they will be drawn in and forget all about the goodness of God. Tragically, a number so large that it **is as the sand of the sea** will believe the lies of Satan and turn their backs on Jesus.

Gog And Magog

Revelation 20 tells us that Satan, [8]**will go out to deceive the nations which are in the four corners of the earth, Gog and Magog, to gather them together to battle, whose number is as the sand of the sea**. Surely the people who come faithfully to worship in the holy city are not the ones referred to as **Gog and Magog**. So, who are Gog and Magog?

The earth will still be a big place. Jesus will have rearranged it and purified it, but its size will not have diminished. That will not happen until the new heavens and the new earth are created. So, the four corners of the earth still cover all the far flung lands with which we are now familiar.

The unbelievers—you will remember that these consist of both the survivalists and those of the Jewish remnant who continued to reject Jesus—are still on the earth. They cannot enter the holy city, and so live with drought and plague, but they are out there. It stands to reason that they will get as far from Jerusalem and God's people as they can. *Smith's Bible Dictionary* describes Gog and Magog as a "generalized term for rude, ignorant, degraded. The name often included all the nomadic tribes, who dwelt mostly on the north of the Black and the Caspian sea, stretching thence indefinitely into inner Asia, and were regarded by the ancients as standing extremely low in point of intelligence and civilization." That probably gives a pretty good description of most of the outcast nations of the millennium who will, of necessity, be nomads living in remote places.

> Micah 4
> **1 Now it shall come to pass in the latter days that the mountain of the Lord's house shall be established on the top of the mountains, and shall be exalted above the hills; and peoples shall flow to it.**
> **2 Many nations shall come and say, "Come, and let us go up to the mountain of the Lord, to the house of the God of Jacob; He will teach us His ways, and we shall walk in His paths." For out of Zion the law shall go forth, and the word of the Lord from Jerusalem.**

The Rapture, The Tribulation, And Beyond 381

3 He shall judge between many peoples, and rebuke strong nations afar off; they shall beat their swords into plowshares, and their spears into pruning hooks; Nation shall not lift up sword against nation, neither shall they learn war any more.

This prophetic utterance clearly states that there will be two distinct groups of people in the millennial nations. There will be **many nations** who will **go up to the mountain of the Lord**, the holy city, and be faithful to Jesus; there are others whom God says He will **judge** and need to **rebuke...afar off**. The latter are those still in rebellion who cannot enter the holy city. However, because Jesus has total Lordship over the earth at this point, they are not allowed to wage war against anyone or cause harm. They will be forced to turn all their instruments of war into instruments for the peaceful working of the land. They will not be able to make war among the nations or disturb the peace in any way. Their children will not **learn war any more** but peace. These people are Gog and Magog.

There will be opportunity for unbelievers to receive salvation during the millennium. We have 2 Peter 3, [9]**The Lord is not slack concerning His promise, as some count slackness, but is longsuffering toward us, not willing that any should perish but that all should come to repentance**, and Hebrews 13, [8]**Jesus Christ is the same yesterday, today and forever**, upon which to base hope for these people.

Revelation 22
**14 Blessed are those who do His commandments, that they may have the right to the tree of life, and may enter through the gates into the city.
15 But outside are dogs and sorcerers and sexually immoral and murderers and idolaters, and whoever loves and practices a lie.**

Being **outside** could mean anywhere upon the earth. The **dogs** are male prostitutes, homosexuals; those who practice witchcraft, **sorcerers**; and people who are **sexually immoral, murderers and idolaters**, could easily describe the practices of huge colonies of anarchists who have established themselves in remote outposts of the planet. All such still have the weaknesses of the flesh.

The unsaved Jewish remnant will, at the very least, qualify as **whoever loves and practices a lie**. Those who exalt the Law above God also make an idol out of the Law. This brands them as **idolaters**.

Therefore, when Satan, during his season of release, goes to deceive the nations in the four corners of the earth, called Gog and Magog, we can safely infer that the anarchists and rebellious Jews will be among, if not a majority of, those **whose number is as the sand of the sea**, who follow Satan in the final attack upon the holy city. Hopefully, there will not be too many of God's people and their descendants who are stupid enough to succumb to Satan's final attempt at destruction.

The Consuming Fire Of God

The poor, foolish people who follow Satan in his last pathetic rebellion against God are doomed.

> Revelation 20
> **9 They went up on the breadth of the earth and surrounded the camp of the saints and the beloved city. And fire came down from God out of heaven and devoured them.**

These people are not ignorant of God or His power and His ways. They know how impenetrable a fortress is New Jerusalem. Some of them will have been travelling there to worship at regular intervals for a thousand years. Those who have will have beheld the glory of Father God and the Lamb. They will have partaken of the fruit of the tree of life and been blessed by it. They will have partaken of the leaves of healing and been kept healthy and vibrant (Revelation 22:2). They will have tasted of the goodness of God and chosen to rebel in spite of it.

What could Satan possibly offer them to compare with, let alone improve upon, the life that God has provided them for a thousand years? They go like sheep to the slaughter, these countless fools, undoubtedly drunk with some fraudulent concept of power and freedom, just as Eve and Adam were in the garden. There they will be, a sea of tragic rabble, rushing the massive, inviolable walls of the holy city. God does not even hesitate. He reacts instantly to this last demonstration of pride and rebellion: **And fire came down from God out of heaven and devoured them**. They all go to the lake of fire.

Satan Sealed Forever In The Lake Of Fire

Revelation 20
10 And the devil, who deceived them, was cast into the lake of fire and brimstone where the beast and the false prophet are. And they will be tormented day and night forever and ever.

Never again will Satan be able to deceive, rob or harm God's people. Never again will he know anything but torment, agony, and defeat. Never again will he have any illusions about being God. Satan's reign of terror and destruction is finally and forever ended.

Satan will forever be as a corpse trodden underfoot (Isaiah 14:19) in the incessant scorching flames and smoking stench of brimstone in the lake of fire. God's final declaration to him in Ezekiel 28 is, [19]**you have become a horror, and shall be no more forever.**

Chapter 26

The Great White Throne Judgment

When Satan is cast into the lake of fire, to join forever the false prophet and the beast (Revelation 20:10), the stage is set for the great white throne judgment.

Those of the millennial nations who did not rebel and follow Satan during his time of release, together with those who have been imprisoned in hell, will be brought up into the heavenlies to stand before God's great white throne of judgment.

God will then cast hell itself, and death which is the last enemy, into the lake of fire and destroy all of the existing heaven and earth. All that will remain is New Jerusalem where we, the body of Christ, with Jesus and the Father, will sit in thrones judging the world (1 Corinthians 6:2), the angels (1 Corinthians 6:3), and Israel.

Matthew 19
28 So Jesus said to them, "Assuredly I say to you, that in the regeneration, when the Son of Man sits on the throne of His glory, you who have followed Me will also sit on twelve thrones, judging the twelve tribes of Israel."

What an awesome sight it will be when we, the glorified body of Christ, seated on thrones with the Father and the Lamb, with the Holy Spirit in attendance, look out upon this scene. A sea of people and angels will stretch as far as the eye can see as they come, one at a time, before the throne of God. We cannot conceive how long this process will take but, when it is over, all iniquity will have been removed from God's kingdom.

Revelation 20
**11 Then I saw a great white throne and Him who sat on it, from whose face the earth and the heaven fled away. And there was found no place for them.
12 And I saw the dead, small and great, standing before God, and books were opened. And another book was opened, which is the Book of Life. And the dead were judged according to their works, by the things which were written in the books.
13 The sea gave up the dead who were in it, and Death and Hades delivered up the dead who were in them. And they were judged, each one according to his works.
14 Then Death and Hades were cast into the lake of fire. This is the second death.
15 And anyone not found written in the Book of Life was cast into the lake of fire.**

Those who are **judged, each one according to his works**, have but two destinations: the eternal nations, or the lake of fire.

Daniel 12
**1 At that time Michael shall stand up, the great prince who stands watch over the sons of your people; And there shall be a time of trouble, such as never was since there was a nation, even to that time. And at that time your people shall be delivered, every one who is found written in the book.
2 And many of those who sleep in the dust of the earth shall awake, some to everlasting life, some to shame and everlasting contempt.**

The great white throne judgment is not a place of reward. It is a place of survival. The blood of Jesus for the remission of sins is no longer available. Those being judged are spiritually **dead**, some having rejected Christ and His salvation, and others having placed themselves apart from the body of Christ by, for instance, embracing church-as-bride doctrine. They are those who went to hell, those of the millennial nations who did not follow Satan during his season of release, and the Jewish remnant. They will stand or fall based on the works of their flesh. Those who have embraced or practiced willful evil will not pass. Those who have been good, kind, loving people will pass. The fallen angels who have been chained in hell since Noah's flood will also be judged at this time.

The Books That Are Opened

Two sets of books are opened upon which judgment is based at the great white throne. And **the books were opened. And another book was opened, which is the Book of Life**. The records of all those standing before the throne have been kept in one set of books. And **the dead were judged according to their works by the things which were written in the books**. These records determine the future of each individual. All they have done is documented there. It is read when this first set of books is opened.

In addition to **the books** of works, the **Book of Life** is opened. The names listed in the Book of Life are not final until after the great white throne judgment. Until then, Jesus states, names can be added or blotted out. This is the final judgment. This is when God metes out eternal punishment upon the wicked.

Psalm 9
5 You have rebuked the nations, You have destroyed the wicked; You have blotted out their name forever and ever.

Revelation 3
5 He who overcomes shall be clothed in white garments, and I will not blot out his name from the Book of Life; but I will confess his name before My Father and before His angels.

Those who have qualified for the body of Christ over the ages will have had their names added to **the Book of Life**. Once the wedding of the Lamb takes place, the bridegroom, the body of Christ, is established forever and those names are permanent.

Philippians 4
3 And I urge you also, true companion, help these women who labored with me in the gospel, with Clement also, and the rest of my fellow workers, whose names are in the Book of Life.

Revelation 22
19 and if anyone takes away from the words of the book of this prophecy, God shall take away his part from the Book of Life, from the holy city, and from the things which are written in this book.

We must take seriously, and set ourselves in agreement with, every jot and tittle in the Bible, and that includes every word in the book of Revelation. Anyone—regardless of men's opinion of him, his stature in the kingdom, or the impressive size of his ministry—who ignores or disbelieves God's Word, qualifies as taking **away from the words of** God's book. God will erase his name and **take away his part from the Book of Life**.

Exodus 32
33 And the Lord said to Moses, "Whoever has sinned against Me, I will blot him out of My book."

God says that even those whose names are in the Book of Life can have their names removed. Once saved always saved is an insupportable doctrine. Jesus will not blot out the names of those who qualify, but He will indeed blot out the names of those who do not.

The Sheep And The Goats

The parable of the sheep and the goats refers to the great white throne judgment. It has nothing to do with judgment of the body of Christ; the body of Christ will be sitting with Jesus in His throne as the judges.

The Rapture, The Tribulation, And Beyond

Matthew 25
31 When the Son of Man comes in His glory, and all the holy angels with Him, then He will sit on the throne of His glory.
32 All the nations will be gathered before Him, and He will separate them one from another, as a shepherd divides his sheep from the goats.
33 And He will set the sheep on His right hand, but the goats on the left.
34 Then the King will say to those on His right hand, "Come, you blessed of My Father, inherit the kingdom prepared for you from the foundation of the world:
35 "for I was hungry and you gave Me food; I was thirsty and you gave Me drink; I was a stranger and you took Me in;
36 "I was naked and you clothed Me; I was sick and you visited Me; I was in prison and you came to Me."

There are those who preach that the sheep and the goats are Christians being judged now, in this time, and/or at the judgment seat of Christ. This is patent nonsense; we are under grace now, and the judgment seat of Christ is the place of our reward. No one at the judgment seat of Christ is cast into everlasting punishment; that only happens at the great white throne judgment. The above Scriptures refer to the great white throne and can refer to nothing else; no other time and no other event. The **sheep on His right hand** are those whose works are approved by Jesus.

Matthew 25
41 Then He will also say to those on the left hand, "Depart from Me, you cursed, into the everlasting fire prepared for the devil and his angels:
42 "for I was hungry and you gave Me no food; I was thirsty and you gave Me no drink;
43 "I was a stranger and you did not take Me in, naked and you did not clothe Me, sick and in prison and you did not visit Me."
46 And these will go away into everlasting punishment, but the righteous into eternal life.

The **goats on the left** are those whose works are not approved by Jesus. They are people in whom there was found no kindness or concern for others. They are **cursed** and thrown **into the everlasting fire prepared for the devil and his angels**.

Romans 14
**11 For it is written: "As I live, says the Lord, every knee shall bow to Me, and every tongue shall confess to God."
12 So then each of us shall give account of himself to God.**

The **righteous** who enter **into eternal life** in the nations are those whose works stand the test and who willingly bow their knee to Jesus, confessing Him as Lord and Savior. The great white throne judgment marks the end of all evil in God's kingdom, including the sin of unbelief.

Chapter 27

The Eternal Nations

It helps to remember, when trying to understand the difference between the millennial nations and the eternal nations, that the former precede the great white throne judgment while the latter follow it. The eternal nations, thus, are only established after all evil has been cast into the lake of fire.

God spoke His intentions regarding the Jews through the prophet Amos, explaining which of them would survive the outpouring of His wrath during the tribulation and move on to the millennial nations. He also made clear that there would be further sifting during the millennium. Only those who survive every sifting and finally accept Jesus as Messiah will move on to the eternal nations.

Amos 9
8 "Behold, the eyes of the Lord God are on the sinful kingdom, and I will destroy it from the face of the earth; yet I will not utterly destroy the house of Jacob," says the Lord.

The **sinful kingdom** is Israel, which rebelled against God and which He will cut off and destroy from the face of the earth (Jeremiah 44:27-28). However, God, ever mindful of His promise to Elijah to preserve a remnant of this people, says, **yet I will not utterly destroy the house of Jacob.**

Amos 9

**9 For surely I will command, and will sift the house of Israel among all nations, as grain is sifted in a sieve; yet not the smallest grain shall fall to the ground.
10 All the sinners of My people shall die by the sword, who say, "The calamity shall not overtake us nor confront us."**

God sifting **the house of Israel among all nations** is the millennium sifting. Those of the Jews who think themselves exempt from God's wrath because their biological ancestry can be traced to Abraham—and who are foolish and arrogant enough to suppose that they are still God's chosen people no matter what they say, think or do—are in for a great shock. Those who reject Christ **shall die by the sword**.

Amos 9

11 On that day I will raise up The tabernacle of David, which has fallen down, and repair its damages; I will raise up its ruins, and rebuild it as in the days of old;

God's creation of the new heavens and the new earth is **that day**, the day when He raises up **the tabernacle of David**, the temple, and restores its position on the earth as it was when He first built it. It is then that the Jews who have qualified for the eternal nations will occupy their rightful place. Bear in mind that, although unbelieving Jews are found in the millennial nations, not one will qualify for the eternal nations without first bowing his knee to Jesus (Isaiah 45:23).

Amos 9

12 "that they may possess the remnant of Edom, and all the Gentiles who are called by My name," says the Lord who does this thing.

In this context **possess** means dominate; **they** are the Jews of the eternal nations; **the remnant of Edom, and all the Gentiles who are called by My name** are the Gentile nations who have qualified for the eternal nations. The eternal Gentile nations will be subject to the authority of the eternal Jewish nation.

The Rapture, The Tribulation, And Beyond

Amos 9
14 "I will bring back the captives of My people Israel; they shall build the waste cities and inhabit them; they shall plant vineyards and drink wine from them; They shall also make gardens and eat fruit from them.
15 "I will plant them in their land, and no longer shall they be pulled up from the land I have given them," says the Lord your God.

Only when they are part of the eternal nations will the Jews be fully restored and **build cities, plant vineyards, make gardens,** and live in security and safety forever in the land that God has given them.

Zechariah 2
10 "Sing and rejoice, O daughter of Zion! For behold, I am coming and I will dwell in your midst," says the Lord.
11 "Many nations shall be joined to the Lord in that day, and they shall become My people. And I will dwell in your midst. Then you will know that the Lord of hosts has sent Me to you.
12 "And the Lord will take possession of Judah as His inheritance in the Holy Land, and will again choose Jerusalem."

The **daughter of Zion** is the Jewish remnant, **many nations** are everybody else, and together they are those from the millennial nations who remained faithful to Jesus during the time of Satan's release and whose works were found worthy at the white throne judgment. They are joined by those brought up out of hell whose works were likewise found worthy.

God **will again choose Jerusalem**. This is not New Jerusalem—the holy city wherein we have dwelt for a thousand years and to whom we are married—this is earthly Jerusalem, the seat of the Jews who have fulfilled Jesus' condition of Matthew 23 and said, [39]**Blessed is He who comes in the name of the Lord!** Earthly Jerusalem was partially restored at the beginning of the millennium (Isaiah 58:12), but God does not **take possession of Judah as His inheritance in the Holy Land** until He creates the new heavens and the new earth for the eternal nations.

Zechariah 9

10...He shall speak peace to the nations; His dominion shall be "from sea to sea, and from the river to the ends of the earth." 16 The Lord their God will save them in that day, as the flock of His people. For they shall be like the jewels of a crown, lifted like a banner over His land.

Those of the Jewish remnant who received Jesus will have authority in the millennial nations and will continue to do so in the eternal nations. They will never have authority over the church, the glorified body of Christ.

This has long been an area of confusion, in New Testament teaching, that derives from not separating the three categories of New Testament people: the Jews, the Gentiles (unbelievers), and the church (1 Corinthians 10:32). We must never confuse these categories, nor blur the lines between them. Doing so creates a quagmire of false doctrine.

As we have earlier established, it is for the remnant of the Jews who are saved and join the nations that God has provided a special place. That special place is not for the former Jews who have, along with the rest of the qualified church, become part of the body of Christ. There is no distinction between Jew and Greek in the body of Christ (Romans 10:12); distinction between the Jew and everybody else only occurs in the nations. I hear people on Christian television and radio, as well as in print and in person, perverting this issue with unfailing regularity.

The Lord will save them in that day refers to the day He creates the new heavens and the new earth. The Jewish people of the eternal nations will have position and authority, likened to **the jewels of a crown, lifted like a banner over His land**, but such position and authority will be over the nations, not the church. The church will be sitting with Jesus in His throne, ruling and reigning over the universe. (Author's note: Before you head for the telephone or the typewriter to accuse me of anti-semitism, please bear in mind that I have been married to a former Jew, now a born-again Christian, since 1963.)

Zechariah 8

6 Thus says the Lord of hosts: "If it is marvelous in the eyes of

The Rapture, The Tribulation, And Beyond 395

the remnant of this people in these days, will it also be marvelous in My eyes?" says the Lord of hosts.
7 Thus says the Lord of hosts: "Behold, I will save My people from the land of the east and from the land of the west;
8 "I will bring them back, and they shall dwell in the midst of Jerusalem. They shall be My people and I will be their God, in truth and righteousness."

God is clear about the position of the restored Jewish remnant. **They shall dwell in the midst of Jerusalem,** earthly Jerusalem, **in truth and righteousness.** They will have arrived at a place where God can again say they are His people because they will have finally received **truth and righteousness.** Truth and righteousness are only found in Christ Jesus, and they will have accepted Him at the white throne judgment.

Zechariah 8
11 "But now I will not treat the remnant of this people as in the former days," says the Lord of hosts.
12 "For the seed shall be prosperous, the vine shall give its fruit, the ground shall give her increase, and the heavens shall give their dew. I will cause the remnant of this people to possess all these things.
13 "And it shall come to pass that just as you were a curse among the nations, O house of Judah and house of Israel, so I will save you, and you shall be a blessing. Do not fear, let your hands be strong."
14 For thus says the Lord of hosts: "Just as I determined to punish you when your fathers provoked Me to wrath," says the Lord of hosts, "And I would not relent,
15 "so again in these days I am determined to do good to Jerusalem and to the house of Judah. Do not fear."

God poured out all, repeat all, of His wrath during the tribulation. He now says **you were a curse among the nations, O house of Judah and house of Israel,** but your punishment is complete and **again in these days I am determined to do good to Jerusalem and to the house of Judah.** God reestablishes His good will toward **the remnant of this people,** Israel, in the eternal nations.

God's Eternal Reminder Of Evil

Even in the eternal nations, when all evil has been sealed forever in the lake of fire, God has provided an ugly, perpetual view of evil and its consequences.

> Isaiah 66
> **22 "For as the new heavens and the new earth which I will make shall remain before Me," says the Lord, "So shall your descendants and your name remain.**
> **23 "And it shall come to pass that from one New Moon to another, and from one Sabbath to another, all flesh shall come to worship before Me," says the Lord.**
> **24 "And they shall go forth and look upon the corpses of the men who have transgressed against Me. For their worm does not die, and their fire is not quenched. They shall be an abhorrence to all flesh."**

Everyone, **all flesh**, in **the new heavens and the new earth**, will regularly come to New Jerusalem **to worship** the Lord. Revelation 21 reveals that the streets of the city are, [21]**pure gold, like transparent glass**. That means that all who enter will be able to see what lies beneath.

> Revelation 22
> **14 Blessed are those who do His commandments, that they may have the right to the tree of life, and may enter through the gates into the city.**
> **15 But outside are dogs and sorcerers and sexually immoral and murderers and idolaters, and whoever loves and practices a lie.**

The **dogs and sorcerers and sexually immoral and murderers and idolaters, and whoever loves and practices a lie** are no longer inhabitants of the earth, as they were during the millennium. They are, however, viewable where they reside for the rest of eternity, in the lake of fire. The nations will, every time they come to worship, look down and see them through the transparent streets outside the gates of the holy city. Jesus gave us a type for this with Lazarus and the wicked rich man.

Luke 16
23 And being in torments in Hades, he lifted up his eyes and saw Abraham afar off, and Lazarus in his bosom.
24 Then he cried and said, "Father Abraham, have mercy on me, and send Lazarus that he may dip the tip of his finger in water and cool my tongue; for I am tormented in this flame."
25 But Abraham said, "Son, remember that in your lifetime you received your good things, and likewise Lazarus evil things; but now he is comforted and you are tormented.
26 "And besides all this, between us and you there is a great gulf fixed, so that those who want to pass from here to you cannot, nor can those from there pass to us."

In the new heavens and the new earth the **great gulf** that is **fixed** is between the lake of fire and New Jerusalem. The eternal nations, who will remain at peace with God, will be reminded of what they escaped when they look down into the lake of fire and see the hideous torment of all those who transgressed against God and His Lamb.

****

Psalm 22
27 All the ends of the world shall remember and turn to the Lord, And all the families of the nations shall worship before You.
28 For the kingdom is the Lord's, And He rules over the nations.

Chapter 28

The New Heavens And The New Earth—A Return To The Garden Of Eden

God created Adam and gave him the Garden of Eden as his home. It was not a garden as we think of it—a few acres of estate landscaping—it was the size of a continent. Four huge rivers were in it: Pishon, Gihon, Tigris, and Euphrates. Each was in its own country; it was a lush, green beautiful place, with food, sunshine, flowers, and trees for shade (Genesis 2:9). There was even gold in the land of Havilah, which God said was good, and deposits of onyx stone and Bdellium (Genesis 2:11-12).

God's original plan was that we live in the beauty of His creation, eternally in peace and joy. We were charged to tend and keep the garden (Genesis 2:15). When Adam committed high treason against God by choosing to bow to the evil enticements of the serpent, he brought a curse into the earth. This curse was upon himself, the woman, the ground, and the serpent. It also introduced death into the earth (Genesis 3:14-24). The dominion God gave Adam went forfeit to the devil when Adam chose to follow him. Thenceforth, Adam had a fallen nature, one drawn to sin, which separated him from fellowship with God.

Romans 5
12 Therefore, just as through one man sin entered the world,

and death through sin, and thus death spread to all men, because all sinned.

The curse has been in the earth for six millennia. At the end of the first four millennia, God sent Christ Jesus as redemption from sin and death for all who would receive Him, but the earth was still under the authority of Satan and sin still reigned. At the end of the last two millennia, the seven year tribulation will come and virtually the whole earth will be polluted and scorched, and those apart from Christ will suffer the outpouring of God's wrath. Then will come the thousand years of Christ's reign, the seventh millennium, when Jesus will purify and restore the earth for the millennial nations.

Genesis 2
1 Thus the heavens and the earth, and all the host of them, were finished.
2 And on the seventh day God ended His work which He had done, and He rested on the seventh day from all His work which He had done.
3 Then God blessed the seventh day and sanctified it, because in it He rested from all His work which God had created and made.
4 This is the history of the heavens and the earth when they were created, in the day that the Lord God made the earth and the heavens,

The **history of the heavens and the earth** depicts not only the six days of creation and seventh day of rest, but presents an account of the seven thousand years of earth's history through the millennial reign of Christ.

The Eighth Day

At the end of the millennial reign of Christ—the end of the seventh "day" (1 Peter 3:8)—God's work of redemption will be complete in the earth. The great white throne judgment will take place and the old heavens and old earth will vanish and be no more.

The Rapture, The Tribulation, And Beyond

Revelation 20
11 Then I saw a great white throne and Him who sat on it, from whose face the earth and the heaven fled away. And there was found no place for them.

At the conclusion of the great white throne judgment, those whose works have not stood, those who have turned down their last chance to bow their knee to Jesus, Satan, the false prophet, the beast, the satanic angels, the demons, hell itself, and death, will be cast into the lake of fire and sealed forever in eternal condemnation and torment. The old will be finished and God will create a brand new home for the eternal nations, over whom Jesus and His body will rule.

2 Peter 3
11 Therefore, since all these things will be dissolved, what manner of persons ought you to be in holy conduct and godliness,
12 looking for and hastening the coming of the day of God, because of which the heavens will be dissolved being on fire, and the elements will melt with fervent heat?
13 Nevertheless we, according to His promise, look for new heavens and a new earth in which righteousness dwells.
14 Therefore, beloved, looking forward to these things, be diligent to be found by Him in peace, without spot and blameless;

The new heavens and the new earth will be God's new and everlasting creation. God's **righteousness** will be established among the people forever. Iniquity will have been purged and will never again be.

Daniel 7
14 Then to Him was given dominion and glory and a kingdom, that all peoples, nations, and languages should serve Him. His dominion is an everlasting dominion, which shall not pass away, and His kingdom the one which shall not be destroyed.

I believe that our Father is going to create our new earth as the Garden of Eden was, in all its lush beauty, crisscrossed with deep, clean rivers, and filled with all His goodness.

Isaiah 51

3 For the Lord will comfort Zion, He will comfort all her waste places; He will make her wilderness like Eden, and her desert like the garden of the Lord; joy and gladness will be found in it, thanksgiving and the voice of melody.

This creation will not be a duplicate, however, because it will be new. The new heavens and new earth will no longer be apart from each other but be as one. God will dwell upon the earth in New Jerusalem.

Revelation 21

**1 And I saw a new heaven and a new earth, for the first heaven and the first earth had passed away. Also there was no more sea.
2 Then I, John, saw the holy city, New Jerusalem, coming down out of heaven from God, prepared as a bride adorned for her husband.
3 And I heard a loud voice from heaven saying, "Behold, the tabernacle of God is with men, and He will dwell with them, and they shall be His people, and God Himself will be with them and be their God.
4 "And God will wipe away every tear from their eyes; there shall be no more death, nor sorrow, nor crying; and there shall be no more pain, for the former things have passed away."
5 Then He who sat on the throne said, "Behold, I make all things new." And He said to me, "Write, for these words are true and faithful."
6 And He said to me, "It is done! I am the Alpha and the Omega, the Beginning and the End. I will give of the fountain of the water of life freely to him who thirsts."**

Christ and His glorified body, together with His bride—**New Jerusalem...a bride adorned for her husband**—will descend from heaven to become part of the new earth. An angelic voice will proclaim, **the tabernacle of God is with men** and **He will dwell with** them, and heaven and earth will be one when God makes **all things new**. In the eternal nations of the new heaven and earth there will **be no more death**, for death, which came into the earth with the curse, will have been cast into the lake of fire forever. The nations will never again experience **sorrow, nor crying; and there shall be no more pain, for the former things have passed away**.

The Tree Of Life

Everyone in the eternal nations will have access to the tree of life located in the main street of New Jerusalem. This is the same tree from which Adam and Eve were separated when they sinned in the Garden of Eden. They had to be separated from it, otherwise they would never have died and sin itself would have become eternal.

> Genesis 2
> **9 And out of the ground the Lord God made every tree grow that is pleasant to the sight and good for food. The tree of life was also in the midst of the garden.**

> Genesis 3
> **22 Then the Lord God said, "Behold, the man has become like one of Us, to know good and evil. And now, lest he put out his hand and take also of the tree of life, and eat, and live forever:"**
> **23 therefore the Lord God sent him out of the garden of Eden to till the ground from which he was taken.**
> **24 So He drove out the man; and He placed cherubim at the east of the garden of Eden, and a flaming sword which turned every way, to guard the way to the tree of life.**

The **tree of life** had to be guarded until God removed Satan and his iniquity from the earth.

He Is God And He Changes Not

No matter how dramatically the heavens and the earth may change, God will not, and neither will the written Word He has given us.

Malachi 3
6 For I am the Lord, I do not change...

Matthew 24
35 Heaven and earth will pass away, but My words will by no means pass away.

It is awesome to realize how powerful the Word of God is. Even though the heavens and the earth will be destroyed, His Word will remain forever.

Perfect Peace

God tells us in Isaiah 65:17-25 that, when He creates the new heavens and the new earth, we shall not even recall the old. The pain and heartache of this world will be no more. Children will remain children for at least a hundred years. No one will grow old or die.

The labor of the eternal nations will produce much fruit and their children will be a blessing. The new earth will be a place of peace and joy, even among the animals that no longer need to kill each other for food, but eat grass and other vegetation. No person or animal will kill, or even hurt, another living creature. God, in His extraordinary and intricate plan, will have created His new Garden of Eden where He will dwell with and among His people in joyous fellowship.

The Rule Of Christ Over The New Eden

1 Corinthians 15
22 For as in Adam all die, even so in Christ all shall be made alive.
23 But each one in his own order: Christ the firstfruits, afterward those who are Christ's at His coming.
24 Then comes the end, when He delivers the kingdom to God the Father, when He puts an end to all rule and all authority and power.

In the magnificent new heavens and new earth all the forces that opposed God will have been eternally condemned to the lake of fire. God's perfection will never again be disrupted. Christ and His body, the glorious church, will be those who rule and reign over this majestic, incorruptible universe. Jesus paid the price in His divine blood to purchase for us eternity with Him. This is the prize we must seek to attain, the prize for which we must be willing to nail all we are to the cross. There is nothing this world can offer that can compare to our place in God's new Eden.

Romans 8 tells us that we are, **[29]to be conformed to the image of His Son, that He might be the firstborn among many brethren**. That was the joy that was set before Jesus, His prize if you will, for which He bore the degradation and horror of the cross of Calvary.

Hebrews 12
2 looking unto Jesus, the author and finisher of our faith, who for the joy that was set before Him endured the cross, despising the shame, and has sat down at the right hand of the throne of God.

Imagine the Father's joy and the delight of Jesus as they look upon this final Garden of Eden. They know what it cost, but the fruit is good. Surrounding Them and before Them will be those who have met all the requirements and passed all the siftings, finally at one with the Godhead in peace and harmony. The Father will love and be loved. He will never again have to endure rejection and sin.

Only one desire should burn in our hearts: to do whatever it takes to qualify for the body of Christ, to become one with Him, partaking of the divine nature, blessing Him for the rest of eternity. That is how we love the Lord our God with all our heart, all our soul and all our mind, which is the first and greatest commandment.

Never before has there been a generation like ours. Never again will there be the opportunities and responsibilities that have been given only to us. By the Holy Spirit we are capable of answering the call to overcome, to rise to this awesome occasion. We must be the ambassadors of Christ who usher in His appearing and join Him in the sky.

I would remind you of Chapter 17, and exhort you to make the right choice, the choice that only you can make. God does not do the choosing, you do.

You have to choose salvation from condemnation through the blood; you have to choose salvation to the glory through the Spirit; you have to expect and eagerly await the rapture of the church; you have to know who you are in Christ, the body and not the bride; and you have to do all in your power, all day every day, to be a person whom Jesus knows. This is not a complicated issue, but it is a profound one. I would also remind you that only those who truly seek the truth will find the truth. Think about that and then: Choose to be one of the few good men.

Revelation 3
21 To him who overcomes I will grant to sit with Me on My throne, as I also overcame and sat down with My Father on His throne.
22 He who has an ear, let him hear what the Spirit says to the churches.

Epilogue

This book was at the printer, the final corrections made and the presses ready to roll, when I suddenly received the full revelation of something that had been nagging at my subconscious for some time. I had caught glimpses of it in Scripture, but suddenly the glimpses became sharp images that were confirmed by the Holy Spirit and the Word. We stopped the presses so that this amazing revelation could be included. I pray you receive it with the same joy and excitement that I did.

AT THE LAST TRUMP GOD WILL STOP TIME FOR FORTY DAYS. THE BODY OF CHRIST WILL BE GLORIFIED AND THEN MINISTER FOR FORTY DAYS ON EARTH.

Keep an open mind and let the Spirit be a witness to you as you walk with me through the Word to test this revelation.

We shall start with Isaiah, from whom we learn that God spoke the end from the beginning and that He will do all His pleasure as He purposed it in His heart.

> Isaiah 46
> **9 Remember the former things of old, for I am God, and there is no other; I am God, and there is none like Me,**
> **10 Declaring the end from the beginning, and from ancient times things that are not yet done, saying, "My counsel shall stand and I will do all My pleasure,"**
> **11 ...Indeed I have spoken it; I will also bring it to pass. I have purposed it; I will also do it.**

This is reaffirmed in Ephesians, where God adds that He has revealed the mystery of His will for the dispensation of the fullness of times.

Ephesians 1
**9 having made known to us the mystery of His will, according to His good pleasure which He purposed in Himself,
10 that in the dispensation of the fullness of the times He might gather together in one all things in Christ, both which are in heaven and which are on earth in Him,**

God has, by His Spirit, made available to us the revelation of all mysteries, but our reception of revelation comes in layers, everything according to its season. One might say that the Holy Spirit reveals things on a need-to-know basis.

The body of Christ is going to move into a time of unprecedented power and glory prior to the rapture. All the power that abides in Christ Jesus **in heaven**, combined with the anointing upon all of us **which are on earth in Him**, will become manifest in us before we are raptured. As you have read earlier, we of this final generation have the spirit of Elijah upon us—to prepare the way for the glorious appearing of the Lord— just as had John the Baptist to prepare the way for His earthly ministry.

Isaiah 40
**3 The voice of one crying in the wilderness: "Prepare the way of the Lord; make straight in the desert a highway for our God.
5 "the glory of the Lord shall be revealed, and all flesh shall see it together; for the mouth of the Lord has spoken."**

God says, **the glory of the Lord shall be revealed, and all flesh shall see it together**, but the world will not see the glory of Jesus when He comes to rapture the church; only the body of Christ will. How can this be when God said, **all flesh shall see it together**? Simple. The body of Christ will no longer be flesh; it will already have been glorified. The glory that the world will see will be **the glory of the Lord** in us. That glory will **be revealed** in all members of the body of Christ during their final forty days on earth.

Why forty days? God said that everything that happens has happened before.

Ecclesiastes 1
9 That which has been is what will be, that which is done is what will be done, and there is nothing new under the sun.

It is perfectly logical, therefore, to use the past to gain knowledge of the future. To this end, recognize that **under the sun** is a type for "under the Son." Confirmation is found in Malachi 4 which says, ²**But to you who fear My name the Sun of Righteousness shall arise with healing in His wings;** note the spelling of **Sun of Righteousness**.

Jesus was the original body of Christ. He was the container of the anointing on earth. After His crucifixion, and for the forty days prior to His rapture, He had a resurrected, glorified body. At Pentecost, those who received the baptism of the Holy Spirit became the body of Christ and containers of the anointing. Since **that which has been is what will be**, and **that which is done is what will be done**, it follows that the members of the body of Christ will also have incorruptible, glorified bodies for their last forty days on earth.

I had always assumed, and indeed have written in this book, that the glorification of the body of Christ would happen at the rapture as it arose to meet Jesus in the air, but the Lord has now revealed that the glorification of the body of Christ will occur forty days prior to the rapture and, once one knows what to look for, there is abundant confirmation of this in Scripture.

1 John 3
2 Beloved, now we are children of God; and it has not yet been revealed what we shall be, but we know that when He is revealed, we shall be like Him, for we shall see Him as He is.

One must look at this Scripture from a new perspective. It does not say that **we shall be like Him** only after the rapture has taken place; it says **when He is revealed, we shall be like Him**. When He is revealed, we shall already be like Him. We shall already be in the same glorified state that He was during His last forty days on earth.

Ephesians 4
13 till we all come to the unity of the faith and the knowledge of the Son of God, to a perfect man, to the measure of the stature of the fullness of Christ;

How can we ever achieve **the measure of the stature of the fullness of Christ**—let alone **unity of the faith**—unless we are delivered from this corruptible flesh and become glorified?

Ephesians 5
27 that He might present it to Himself a glorious church, not having spot or wrinkle or any such thing, but that it should be holy and without blemish.

We do not become the **glorious church** as we arise. We are already a glorious church at His appearing, and we are presented to Jesus as such.

2 Corinthians 3
18 But we all, with unveiled face, beholding as in a mirror the glory of the Lord, are being transformed into the same image from glory to glory, just as by the Spirit of the Lord.

We all know, or at least we should by now, that every member of the body of Christ is in the process of glorification. However, no one can possibly imagine that we, in this flesh, will look in the mirror and behold ourselves as **transformed into the same image** as the glorified Christ. That can only happen if we are still on the earth but no longer in this flesh; the forty days.

1 Corinthians 15 tells us, [51]**Behold, I tell you a mystery: We shall not all sleep, but we shall all be changed** [52]**in a moment, in the twinkling of an eye, at the last trumpet**, and so we shall. Yes, absolutely. However, the instant change does not occur at the time of the rapture but when the trump sounds at the end of the lease, at the beginning of the forty days. At the exact moment the 6,000 year lease ends, **in the twinkling of an eye**, the last trump will sound and the change will take place. How will we know? If looking in the mirror is not sufficient, walking through doors and walls, as Jesus did (John

The Rapture, The Tribulation, And Beyond 411

20:19), will probably give us a clue that the forty days has begun.

This means that we will be able to testify to all that, "Jesus is coming in forty days and then the tribulation will begin." When the world is skeptical we can say, "Watch this!" and walk through a wall. We will be able to move about this earth without limit, anywhere we want, and, on top of that, no one will be able to stop or harm us.

1 Corinthians 15
49 And as we have borne the image of the man of dust, we shall also bear the image of the heavenly Man.
50 Now this I say, brethren, that flesh and blood cannot inherit the kingdom of God; nor does corruption inherit incorruption.
51 Behold, I tell you a mystery: We shall not all sleep, but we shall all be changed
52 in a moment, in the twinkling of an eye, at the last trumpet. For the trumpet will sound, and the dead will be raised incorruptible, and we shall be changed.
53 For this corruptible must put on incorruption, and this mortal must put on immortality.
54 So when this corruptible has put on incorruption, and this mortal has put on immortality, then shall be brought to pass the saying that is written: "Death is swallowed up in victory."

The **man of dust** is Adam and the **heavenly man** is Jesus, whose image we will bear before the rapture when **this corruptible must put on incorruption and this mortal must put on immortality**. This is what will happen **in the twinkling of an eye**. It certainly took longer than the twinkling of an eye for the people of earth to watch Jesus go up into heaven, Elisha to watch the chariots take Elijah into heaven, and someone to have watched Enoch go up in order to have reported it. We have always associated this Scripture with the rapture, but it actually describes the beginning of the forty days prior to the rapture.

There is no mention in 1 Corinthians 15 of the rapture, of going up. The statement **the dead will be raised incorruptible** refers to the righteous dead and defines their resurrection, not their rapture. The statement **we shall be changed** refers to the members of the body of Christ alive on the earth when the trump sounds, and does not relate to our rapture but our glorification. The resurrection of the righteous dead and the change, or glorification, of the body of Christ on earth mark the beginning of the forty days. In 1 Thessalonians 4:16-17 the actual rapture is described. These are two separate events and the event at the beginning of the forty days is the one that happens **in the twinkling of an eye**.

It has always been assumed that the events of 1 Corinthians 15:52 were the fourth rapture because of their occurrence at the **last trumpet**. Lacking revelation of the forty days, one could reach no other conclusion. These events do occur at the sound of the last trumpet, which sounds as the lease ends, however, a further forty days will elapse before we actually go up. As God did in Joshua's day, He will hold back time.

That which has been is what will be, that which is done is what will be done.

Joshua 10
**12 Then Joshua spoke to the Lord in the day when the Lord delivered up the Amorites before the children of Israel, and he said in the sight of Israel: "Sun, stand still over Gibeon; and Moon, in the Valley of Aijalon."
13 So the sun stood still, and the moon stopped, till the people had revenge upon their enemies. Is this not written in the Book of Jasher? So the sun stood still in the midst of heaven, and did not hasten to go down for about a whole day.**

God told the sun—which is a type for the Son at the rapture—to stand still, and so it did until the people of God had overcome their enemies. Our enemies are not people but satanic forces, and Jesus will wait while the great end-time revival takes place during our forty days of glory.

There is another instance of God stopping time, the occasion upon which He healed Hezekiah and extended his life.

Isaiah 38
**7 "And this is the sign to you from the Lord, that the Lord will do this thing which He has spoken:
8 "Behold, I will bring the shadow on the sundial, which has**

gone down with the sun on the sundial of Ahaz, ten degrees backward." So the sun returned ten degrees on the dial by which it had gone down.

It has long been accepted that all numbers in the Bible are significant and prophetic. Ten degrees equals one thirty-sixth of the circumference of the sundial (the compass). One thirty-sixth of a day is forty minutes. Forty minutes—forty days. This is not a coincidence. In Hezekiah's time the **sun returned ten degrees**, forty minutes, as a sign that God was healing Hezekiah and extending his life. When the last trump sounds the Son will wait forty days before catching up the body of Christ. It will have that much time to conduct the great end-time revival.

Matthew 13
43 Then the righteous will shine forth as the sun in the kingdom of their Father. He who has ears to hear, let him hear!

During the forty days we **will shine forth as the sun**. The sun is the Son and we will be like Him, shining in His glory. All mankind will have the opportunity to behold signs and wonders such as were performed by Jesus Himself during His earthly ministry, and even greater signs.

Matthew 27
50 Jesus, when He had cried out again with a loud voice, yielded up His spirit.
51 And behold, the veil of the temple was torn in two from top to bottom; and the earth quaked, and the rocks were split,
52 and the graves were opened; and many bodies of the saints who had fallen asleep were raised;
53 and coming out of the graves after His resurrection, they went into the holy city and appeared to many.

We see here the raising of the righteous dead at Jesus' resurrection and glorification, which is a type for the raising of the dead in Christ and the glorification of the body of Christ at the end of the age.

It is noteworthy that **many—not all—bodies of the saints who had fallen asleep were raised**. This is paralleled at the end of the age, as described in 1 Thessalonians 4, [16]**...And the dead in Christ will rise first**. Just as the dead saints of Jesus' time did not all qualify for resurrection, not all of those considering themselves Christians who have died since the time of Jesus will qualify at the end of the age, only the dead **in Christ**.

When the forty days of glory begins, therefore, there will be a world-wide resurrection of the righteous dead and, just as happened 2,000 years ago, they will walk the earth as witnesses.

When the religious people of His time asked Jesus for a sign, He declared that this exact thing would happen again at the end of the age. His response specifically declared the forty days of glory.

Matthew 12

38 Then some of the scribes and Pharisees answered, saying, "Teacher, we want to see a sign from You."
39 But He answered and said to them, "An evil and adulterous generation seeks after a sign, and no sign will be given to it except the sign of the prophet Jonah.
40 "For as Jonah was three days and three nights in the belly of the great fish, so will the Son of Man be three days and three nights in the heart of the earth.
41 "The men of Nineveh will rise in the judgment with this generation and condemn it, because they repented at the preaching of Jonah; and indeed a greater than Jonah is here."

When God stopped time for forty minutes, as reported in Isaiah 38:7-8, He said it was a sign. The sign that Jesus spoke to the Pharisees, **an evil and adulterous generation**—and who dare say that this generation is not as bad or worse than that one?—was **the sign of the prophet Jonah**. What was the sign of the prophet Jonah? Certainly more than just the preaching of repentance, as we have always assumed it to be. The sign of the prophet Jonah is an amazing confirmation of the forty days of glory.

The Rapture, The Tribulation, And Beyond

Jonah 3

**3 So Jonah arose and went to Nineveh, according to the word of the Lord. Now Nineveh was an exceedingly great city, a three-day journey in extent.
4 And Jonah began to enter the city on the first day's walk. Then he cried out and said, "Yet forty days, and Nineveh shall be overthrown!"**

Jonah is the sign given us by Jesus Himself, but not until now have we known the full impact of it. When the resurrection of the righteous dead occurs at the end of the age, the **men of Nineveh will rise in the judgment with this generation and condemn it, because they repented at the preaching of Jonah; and indeed a greater than Jonah is here.**

Jonah was three days in the belly of the fish before He went into Nineveh to preach repentance for forty days. Jesus was three days in hell before His resurrection and forty days of ministry.

We, now in this time, are in our equivalent of Jesus' three hour period referred to in Matthew 27:45 as the sixth to ninth hour. For the people of Jesus' time, these three hours were a time of darkness and destruction preceding Jesus' cry from the cross, "It is finished," His resurrection, the resurrection of the saints, and His forty day ministry in a glorified state. We are in a similar period of darkness and destruction preceding Jesus' sounding of the last trump, the resurrection of the righteous dead, and our forty day ministry in a glorified state.

As Jonah cried out, **Yet forty days, and Nineveh shall be overthrown**, we shall cry out, "Yet forty days, and the tribulation will begin!"

So, we have a picture here of the last trumpet sounding as the lease is up, God sovereignly telling Jesus to wait as He holds back time for forty days, the body of Christ **in the twinkling of an eye** being glorified and made immortal and incorruptible, and the righteous dead rising out of graves and walking about in their resurrected bodies. Death is swallowed up in victory (1 Corinthians 15:54); no one will be able to kill or even harm us and we will dominate the earth as immortals, proclaiming with accuracy that they have 40 days, 39 days, 38 days etc., to repent and prepare for the tribulation.

Do not be talked out of this by Acts 1, [7]**And He said to them, "It is not for you to know times or seasons which the Father has put in His own authority."** Remember Matthew 16, [3]**...Hypocrites! You know how to discern the face of the sky, but you cannot discern the signs of the times**. Jesus told the men of that day that it was not for them to **know the times and the seasons**. They had no need to know but, as I have said many times in this book, we do. Jesus did not say that no one would ever know; He said that the knowledge was in the Father's power and authority. He then went on to say that they would receive power when the Holy Spirit came upon them.

The information would be available in the Spirit from that time on, but Jesus knew it would not be revealed until our generation. The Father has now told us about the forty days—the season—but the timing is still known only to Him.

Not everyone will believe, of course, any more than they did when Jesus Himself preached to them. Even after His resurrection and glorification, when He told 500 to go to the upper room and wait, only 120 showed up. A 76% no-show rate seems discouraging, but 24% of the world's population is about a billion and a half people, so even such a disappointing percentage undeniably qualifies as a world-wide revival.

Matthew 13
30 Let both grow together until the harvest, and at the time of harvest I will say to the reapers, "First gather together the tares and bind them in bundles to burn them, but gather the wheat into my barn."

During the forty days of glory, with the 6,000 year lease expired, the satanic forces are bound until the body of Christ is removed from the earth and the tribulation begins. This is what the parable of the wheat and the tares illustrates.

Another illustration is Jesus casting Legion out of the man in the tombs who had the unclean spirit which no one could bind.

Mark 5
6 But when he saw Jesus from afar, he ran and worshiped Him.

The Rapture, The Tribulation, And Beyond 417

> 7 And he cried out with a loud voice and said, "What have I to do with You, Jesus, Son of the Most High God? I implore You by God that You do not torment me."
> 8 For He said to him, "Come out of the man, unclean spirit!"
> 9 Then He asked him, "What is your name?" And he answered, saying, "My name is Legion; for we are many."
> 10 And he begged Him earnestly that He would not send them out of the country.
> 11 Now a large herd of swine was feeding there near the mountains.
> 12 And all the demons begged Him, saying, "Send us to the swine, that we may enter them."
> 13 And at once Jesus gave them permission. Then the unclean spirits went out and entered the swine (there were about two thousand); and the herd ran violently down the steep place into the sea, and drowned in the sea.
> 14 Now those who fed the swine fled, and they told it in the city and in the country. And they went out to see what it was that had happened.
> 15 Then they came to Jesus, and saw the one who had been demon-possessed and had the legion, sitting and clothed and in his right mind. And they were afraid.

A Roman legion numbered 6,000, so Legion represents the 6,000 year lease. It is important to note that Jesus, in this instance and no other in the Bible, asked the demon to identify himself. People have puzzled over this for years, but now we know the answer: it was to reveal the prophetic significance of the event.

During the forty days the demons will be bound, unable to reassert Satan's authority until the tribulation begins; they will no longer be able to inhabit people, but animals only. The swine numbered 2,000 to indicate that at the end of the 2,000 year church age they will lose all their authority. When the unbelievers saw the formerly demon-possessed man **clothed and in his right mind...they were afraid**.

Those who witnessed this event **went and told it in the city and in the country**. Those to whom they told it **went out to see what it was that had happened**. Imagine the effect upon the world when all the poor souls who have been insane, drug addicted, and tormented with demons are suddenly in their right minds. Mental hospitals will be emptied and prisons will house sane, non-violent people. Everyone on earth will be free to receive, without satanic opposition, a witness of our soon-coming King.

We, in our glorified state, will finally be able to fulfill Jesus' prophecy regarding greater works than His.

John 14
12 Most assuredly, I say to you, he who believes in Me, the works that I do he will do also; and greater works than these he will do, because I go to My Father.

I close in gratitude to our heavenly Father that I was born for such a time as this. The forty days of glory is the icing on the cake of our inheritance.

Topical Index

A

Abaddon: 323, 328

Abraham: 15, 34, 40, 49, 80, 104, 106, 112, 133, 137, 172, 182, 219, 234-36, 239-40, 248, 259, 276, 297, 303-04, 343, 392, 397

Abraham's bosom: 49

Adam: 11, 26, 29, 38-40, 44, 67, 78-79, 95, 106, 132-33, 139, 153, 168, 277, 289, 382, 399, 403-04

age (timing of): 4-5, 7, 11, 13, 25, 33, 37-38, 41-44, 46, 49, 52, 55, 59, 61, 83, 91, 98, 103, 106, 108, 154, 203, 205, 211-13, 254-55, 315, 414-15

angel of light (satanic angels): 78, 94, 100, 224, 401

angels: 12, 40, 47-49, 51-53, 56, 58-59, 79, 93-102, 115, 118-19, 125-26, 132, 144, 155, 160-61, 179, 187, 207, 213, 236, 251, 254-55, 263, 267, 277, 284, 292-93, 310, 317, 322-23, 328-29, 331, 337, 340, 346-47, 351-53, 365, 370-71, 385, 387, 389-90, 401

anointing: 8, 14, 26, 51, 66, 85, 168, 174, 185, 192, 197-98, 201, 228, 232, 239, 242, 248, 257, 301, 305-06, 319, 408-09

Antichrist: 47, 51, 62, 64, 83, 87-88, 90, 92, 108, 115, 118, 120-21, 146-47, 149, 153-54, 163-64, 214, 229, 255, 257, 307-09, 311, 315, 318-25, 328, 332-34, 343, 348, 351, 353, 355-56, 361, 368

antichrist spirit: 82-83, 86-87, 137, 196, 198, 219, 224, 257, 307

apocalypse (four horsemen of): 318

apostasia: 148-49, 211

ark: 15-16, 33, 38, 129-32, 139, 155, 277-78

ark of the covenant: 50, 324

Armageddon: 18, 117-18, 121, 214-15, 314, 331, 348, 351, 353, 355, 365-66

armies of heaven: 159, 165, 168, 267, 324, 348-49, 352, 354

army of Antichrist: 121, 214, 255, 323-24, 348, 355-56

army of Christ: 109

army of God: 50, 121, 271, 331

B

beast: 47, 73, 97-98, 115-16, 118, 120-21, 123, 160-61, 213, 310-13, 321, 324-26, 328, 330, 332, 342, 355, 357, 359, 383, 385, 401

black horse: 319-20

blessed hope: 109, 152-54, 168, 250

Topical Index

Bible codes: 141
Book of Life: 124, 179, 189-90, 251, 283, 327, 374, 386-88
born again: 8, 61, 70, 77, 88, 105, 111, 117, 151, 160, 193, 239, 269, 287, 288-89, 316, 321, 333
born-again: 14, 75, 87, 94-95, 105, 108, 124, 185, 234, 259, 266, 278, 394
bottomless pit: 87, 120-23, 163, 214, 322-23, 327-28, 333, 358, 377, 379
bowl(s) (of wrath): 118-19, 187, 216, 329-30, 354
bride: 20, 48, 61, 113, 131, 177, 181-95, 197-98, 285, 345, 347-48, 360, 387, 402, 406
bridechamber (children of): 190-91, 195
bridegroom: 20, 41, 113, 122, 131, 164, 181, 188-191, 195-98, 344-46, 348-49, 388

C

command to overcome: 18, 20, 198, 204
crown(s) of glory: 19, 49, 107, 110, 112-13, 158, 189, 251, 263-64, 270-71, 284, 339-40, 343-45, 349

D

Daniel's seventieth week (week of years): 54, 309
dead in Christ: 57-58, 100, 108, 157, 337, 344, 370, 413-14
death: 4, 13-14, 26, 45, 55-56, 65-66, 89, 91, 104, 111-12, 114, 117, 124, 126, 143-44, 151, 153-54, 160, 164, 168, 170, 224, 229, 236, 239-40, 245, 268, 281, 300, 305, 320-21, 323, 327, 334, 342, 344, 359, 385-86, 399-403, 411, 415
defiled: 81, 118, 161, 179, 185-86, 189, 198, 243, 276, 317, 343, 374
demon(s)(ic): 65, 67, 71, 73, 76-79, 82-85, 89-91, 94, 96, 135, 174, 192, 199, 243-44, 323, 328, 331-32, 401, 417-18
denomination(s): 78, 80, 84, 145, 229, 249
discern the times: 61, 416
dispensation: 27, 173, 408
doctrine (of Christ): 3, 86-87, 192, 227, 234, 243
dominion: 26, 38-39, 67, 153, 204, 289-90, 307, 333, 399, 401
dragon: 121, 311-12, 325, 330, 358, 368, 377

E

ears (to hear): 1-5, 12, 25, 30-31, 33, 41-42, 56, 59, 134, 139, 151, 195-96, 217, 255

earth is restored: 359
earthquake(s): 25, 119, 164, 205, 214-16, 321, 324, 334-35, 354-55, 361
Easter: 90, 256
eastern mysticism: 80, 82
Elijah: 56-58, 81-82, 119-20, 143-44, 152, 155-57, 162-63, 167-73, 179, 291, 301-06, 332, 343-44, 366-68, 391, 408, 411
end (the): 7, 18, 25, 35, 37, 40, 45, 50-51, 54, 98, 109-10, 113, 117-19, 121, 134, 142, 149-50, 154, 159, 161, 162, 182, 200, 212-14, 216, 255, 267, 317, 321, 328, 331, 352, 366, 374, 377, 407, 410, 412-13
end of the age: 5, 7, 11, 13, 25, 33, 46, 83, 98, 106, 108, 154, 212, 254-55, 410, 412, 414-15, 417
Enoch: 119-20, 142-43, 152, 157, 162-63, 167-69, 179, 275, 332, 343-44, 411
Esau: 185-86
eternal nations: 124, 126-27, 369, 372, 386, 391-97, 401, 403-04
Eve: 38-40, 79, 277, 379, 382, 403
every nation, tribe, tongue, and people: 97, 119, 212, 317

F

false doctrine(s): 32-33, 35, 135-36, 154, 227-29, 234-35, 247-49, 270, 273, 276, 283, 301, 311, 313, 339, 374, 394
false prophecy(ies): 103, 209-10, 219-21, 223, 226, 273, 311, 313
false prophet (the): 47, 115, 121, 123, 229, 311-13, 330, 357, 359, 383, 385, 401
false prophet(s): 33, 209-11, 226, 229, 311, 315
few good men: 273, 283-85, 406
forty days: 39, 51-52, 144, 199, 407-18
forty minutes: 413-14
fourth beast (Daniel's): 87, 163, 325-28, 333

G

Gabriel: 35, 37, 99-100, 301
Garden of Eden: 11, 38, 126, 379, 399, 401, 403-05
Gentiles (unbelieving, unbelievers): 19, 23, 34-35, 62-63, 105, 133, 137, 150, 157, 163, 176, 189, 213, 216, 225, 235, 243, 257, 259-60, 281, 295, 352, 371, 373, 380-81, 392, 394
glorification: 56, 225, 268, 290, 409-10, 412-14, 416

glorified: 1, 3, 9, 48, 107-10, 113, 122-23, 144, 158, 233, 263, 266, 283, 287, 294, 338-39, 354, 362, 370, 373, 385, 394, 402, 407-10, 415, 418
glorious appearing: 106, 148, 155, 190, 202, 205, 217, 250, 301, 306, 408
glorious church: 4, 12, 19, 30, 86, 96, 108, 149, 224, 283, 405, 410
Godhead: 8-9, 67, 87, 178, 203-04, 230-33, 245
Gog and Magog: 123, 378, 380-82
grave(s): 57-58, 120, 164, 333, 413, 415
Greek(s): 105, 181, 278-79, 394

H

Halloween: 77, 256
Harry Potter: 73-75
hell: 66, 99-100, 124, 126, 153, 207, 294, 370, 385, 387, 393, 401, 415
homosexual(s)(ity): 64, 87-89, 221, 254, 333, 381

I

Israel: 10-11, 15, 46-47, 49, 54, 86, 92, 101, 115, 160, 214, 241, 278, 292, 302, 309, 316, 326, 342, 351, 356, 366-69, 372, 385, 391-93, 395, 412
itching ears: 3, 33, 227

J

Jew(s): 55, 105, 117, 176, 181, 195, 213-14, 234, 238, 240-41, 248-49, 278-79, 281, 309, 316, 321, 352-53, 361, 368-69, 382, 391-94
John the Baptist: 301, 306, 408
Jonah: 414-15
Jubilee(s): 43-44, 46, 48-49, 52
judged: 51, 100, 111, 124-25, 165, 263, 267, 269, 293, 330, 386-87, 389
judgment (God's): 16-17, 25, 40, 43, 50, 54, 89, 97, 118, 120, 126, 129, 139, 146, 165, 168, 212, 223, 226, 257, 274, 281, 291, 306, 309, 314, 318-19, 321-22, 324, 328-30, 344, 354, 363, 367, 381
judgment seat (of Christ): 19, 49, 51, 110-13, 162, 213, 263-64, 266-70, 274-75, 283, 338-39, 344-45, 389
judgment (white throne): 19, 45, 51, 99, 124, 126, 160, 263, 329, 341-42, 385-91, 393, 395, 400-01
judges: 43, 50, 99, 134, 158, 168, 216, 242, 245, 263-64, 267, 269, 277, 291-93, 324, 341, 344, 388
judging: 91, 94, 99, 116, 291-93, 341-42, 385

Topical Index

K
kingdom government: 122, 283, 339, 342, 347, 361-62, 369

L
lack of knowledge: 18, 61, 104, 130, 222, 238, 279
lake of fire: 45, 86, 100, 115, 121, 124, 126-27, 139, 177-78, 255, 274, 300, 315, 342, 357, 359, 366, 375, 383, 385-86, 391, 396-97, 401, 403, 405
language (Holy Ghost, tongues): 9, 80, 83-85, 131, 135, 174, 196, 221, 229, 340
language (new): 339-340, 370
last trump(et): 1, 3, 19, 33, 50, 57, 100, 108, 111, 139, 144-45, 157, 186, 211, 217, 268, 338, 344, 352, 407, 410-13, 415
Law (the): 25, 68, 173, 198, 221, 234-43, 245, 248-49, 276, 309, 374, 382
Legion: 416-17
locusts: 29, 114, 322-323, 328
Lord, Lord: 174, 191-92, 198-99, 276, 283
Lucifer: 75, 79, 99

M
manna: 10-12, 15, 27, 49, 202
mark of the beast: 46-47, 62, 73, 97-98, 115, 116-18, 139, 158-60, 213, 255, 309-10, 313-14, 316, 321-22, 329, 331, 340, 342, 351-53, 356-57, 365-66, 371, 374
Michael: 57-58, 99-100, 386
mount of transfiguration: 55, 162, 332
new heaven(s) and new earth: 126-27, 263, 329, 372, 380, 292-94, 396-97, 399, 401-02, 404-05
martyrs (mid-tribulation): 158, 321, 340-43, 345, 348-49
millennial nations: 63, 122, 124, 314, 321, 352, 365-66, 371-72, 375, 381, 385, 387, 391-94, 400
millennial reign of Christ: 12, 19, 38, 44, 51, 103, 113, 117, 121-23, 160, 202, 214-15, 263, 267, 324, 329, 339, 341, 359, 371, 400
Moses: 10-11, 49, 56-58, 162, 203, 236, 332, 388
mother of harlots: 326
mystery(ies): 8, 25, 27-28, 62, 111, 114, 147, 149, 192, 232, 268, 282, 307, 312, 408, 410-11

N

New Jerusalem: 19-20, 34, 44-45, 47-50, 107, 109, 111, 113, 121-22, 126, 145-46, 159, 187-89, 198, 254, 267, 276, 284, 314, 324, 337, 345-47, 360, 362, 369, 372, 374-75, 378, 382, 385, 393, 396-97, 402-03

Noah: 15-16, 27, 38, 41, 49, 104, 129, 130-133, 139, 146, 155, 277-278, 387

O

144,000 (Jewish evangelists): 117, 119, 159-61, 213, 316, 321, 340, 343, 345, 348-349

one-world-order: 62, 92, 308-09, 312, 319, 321, 325

one-world-religion: 308, 312

P

pale horse: 320

Pentecost: 7, 9, 51, 85, 173-74, 201

plagues: 114, 118, 120, 163, 187, 190, 323, 328-30, 332

Pokemon: 73, 75

prophecy: 42, 54, 91-92, 120, 141, 146, 163, 190, 209-13, 221, 225-26, 309, 332, 371, 388

Q

qualify(ication) for body of Christ: 12, 14, 53, 131, 185, 274, 387, 394, 405

qualify(ication) for glory: 4, 63, 250, 264, 287-88, 293, 388, 414

R

rapture (1st Enoch): 120, 142, 152, 157, 167-68, 332

rapture (2nd Elijah): 56, 58, 120, 143, 152, 155, 157, 167, 332

rapture (3rd Jesus): 45, 48-49, 144-45, 152, 157, 167, 409

rapture (4th, church): 1, 3-4, 7, 9, 13, 15-19, 21, 38, 40-41, 45, 47-49, 53, 55-59, 61, 63, 68, 96, 98, 100, 106, 108-10, 113, 116, 129-31, 133-34, 136, 139, 141, 144-47, 149, 151-54, 156, 158-59, 162, 164, 167, 173, 177, 186, 191, 197-98, 201, 207, 209, 211-13, 225, 253-54, 263-64, 266-68, 270, 277-78, 285, 295, 307, 310, 321, 326, 329, 332, 337-338, 340, 344, 361-62, 406, 408-412

rapture (5th martyrs): 116, 147, 158-9, 186, 314, 321, 340-41

rapture (6th 144,000): 117, 119, 147, 159-60, 213, 316-17

rapture (7th two witnesses): 121, 159, 161-62, 164, 332, 343-44
raptures (the seven): 18, 141
red horse: 318-19
religion(s): 4, 23, 76, 83, 112, 229, 238, 246, 249, 254, 256, 288, 337
remnant (Jewish): 117, 161, 321, 331, 351, 365-69, 372, 374, 380, 382, 387, 391, 393-95
restraining (force): 24, 62-63, 114, 147, 149, 307, 312
revival: 21, 24, 30-33, 36-37, 148, 209, 211, 295, 328
righteous dead: 56-58, 100, 162, 411-15
rule and reign: 4, 20, 44, 63, 113, 201, 250, 287, 289-90, 297, 299, 339, 405

S

Santa Claus: 90, 256
satanic trinity: 47, 115, 357
Satan's season of release: 121, 123-24, 263, 358, 377-79, 382, 385, 387, 393
seal(s): 116, 145, 158, 314, 318-22, 324, 329, 339
seasons: 15, 149, 154, 202, 214, 416
second advent: 17-18, 50, 109-10, 148-49, 151, 154, 212, 214, 217, 276, 321, 324, 348, 353, 366
sheep and the goats: 125-26, 388-89
six days: 38, 46, 50, 55, 322, 400
six thousand (year lease): 11, 29, 38-39, 44, 46, 50, 54-55, 106, 139, 202, 289, 379
6,000: 106, 202, 410, 416-17
Sodom: 15, 87-89, 120, 137-38, 164, 333, 353
Solomon: 33-34, 42-43, 45-46, 296-297
spiritual fornication: 184-86
sun: 56, 58, 62, 118, 139, 187, 202, 206, 255, 308, 321-22, 330, 351, 355, 374, 409, 412-13
Sun: 409

T

tares: 139, 253-57, 270, 416
temple (rebuilt): 121-22, 213-17, 360-61, 392
temple mount: 213, 217, 309, 361
ten virgins: 41, 190-91, 195-98

thousand years as one day: 11, 38
times (signs of): 4, 15, 61-62, 135, 149, 202, 214, 243, 408, 416
tongues: 9, 80, 83-85, 131, 135, 174, 196, 221, 229, 340
tree of life: 375, 378, 381-82, 396, 403
tribulation (great): 1-2, 11, 13, 15, 17-19, 24-25, 27, 37-38, 45-47, 50-51, 54, 62-64, 68, 73, 83, 88, 90, 92, 97-98, 103, 106, 108-10, 113-21, 126, 129-30, 145-47, 149-50, 153-54, 158-63, 182, 186, 206, 208, 212-14, 216, 255, 267, 306-09, 311-21, 325, 328-29, 331, 333-34, 337, 340-44, 348-49, 351-52, 361, 365-66, 368, 371-72, 374, 377, 391, 395, 400, 411, 415-17
Trinity: 229-30, 311
trumpet(s): 46, 48, 50, 165, 321-24, 328-29, 352, 365, 369
twinkling of an eye: 3, 19, 111, 144, 158, 268, 337, 410-12, 415
two thousand: 7, 19, 27, 40, 44-45, 49, 55, 151, 278, 315
2,000: 40-41, 106

U

unity: 41, 248-49, 373, 410
unveiled: 187, 410
unveiled face: 410
upper room: 305, 416

W

wealth of the wicked: 28, 32
wedding (of the Lamb): 20, 41, 50, 109, 113, 121-22, 159, 164, 175-77, 181-84, 186, 189, 191, 196-98, 214, 315, 344-47, 354, 387
white horse: 318, 324, 353
white horses: 165, 324, 347-48, 354
witchcraft: 64, 66, 68-74, 76-78, 89, 229, 237, 255-56, 323, 381
witnesses (end-time): 87, 119-20, 159, 161-64, 319-20, 331-35, 343, 348
wound (mortal, deadly): 312, 324-27
wrath (of God): 18, 27, 51, 53, 74, 97, 108-09, 115, 118-19, 146, 150, 158-59, 185, 203, 212, 216, 268, 278, 310, 315, 318, 321, 324, 328-29, 332, 354-55, 391-92, 395, 400

Y

Y2K: 210-11, 221

Other books by
B.D. Hyman

Oppressive Parents—
How to leave them and love them

The Church Is *Not* The Bride

For these books, teachings on audiocassette, or information about the B.D. Hyman Ministry

write
**The B.D. Hyman Ministry
P.O. Box 7107
Charlottesville, VA 22906**

or call
434-978-1513

or fax
434-978-7522

or go to
www.bdhyman.com

ABOUT THE AUTHOR

B.D. Hyman is a Spirit-filled Christian who heads her own non-denominational ministry, has her own television program, and pastors a church in Charlottesville, Virginia. She teaches a gospel of healing, deliverance, and prosperity.

She grew up in Hollywood as the daughter of film legend Bette Davis and is intimately familiar with what the world has to offer. She is, therefore, well aware of the deceits and emptiness of worldly success as opposed to kingdom prosperity. She has been married since 1963. She, her husband and two sons were born again in 1984. She has been in ministry since 1992 and her husband is her operations manager.

The specific commission the Lord spoke to her was, "Teach My starving lambs. Give life and remove the garbage!" Her God-given ability to make even the most complicated areas of the Bible understandable has enabled countless people to overcome lifetimes of frustration and failure. God impressed upon her the urgency for everyone of this final generation to grasp the truth of where they fit in today's events and what is coming, so her gift for the simplification of complex topics has now been extended to a book on end-time events.